Understanding Social Problems,
Policies, and Programs

Social Problems and Social Issues
Leon Ginsberg, Editor

Understanding Social Problems, Policies, and Programs

FOURTH EDITION

Leon Ginsberg and Julie Miller-Cribbs

University of South Carolina Press

Published in Columbia, South Carolina,
by the University of South Carolina Press

Manufactured in the United States of America

09 08 07 06 05   5 4 3 2 1

Library of Congress Cataloging-in-Publication Data
  Ginsberg, Leon H.
  Understanding social problems, policies, and programs / Leon Ginsberg, Julie
    Miller-Cribbs.—4th ed.
      p. cm.—(Social problems and social issues)
  Includes bibliographical references and index.
  ISBN 1-57003-581-4 (pbk. : alk. paper)
    1. Public welfare administration—United States. 2. United States—Social policy.
  3. Social problems—United States. I. Miller-Cribbs, Julie. II. Title. III. Series.
  HV95.G518 2005
  361.973—dc22

                                                                    2005003893

CONTENTS

PREFACE

Among the human services professions, social work is unique in the degree of its emphasis on social policy and services. Among the four traditional areas of the social work curriculum, social welfare policy and services, which this text shortens in name to "social policy," is unique because it is not shared with the curricula of related disciplines. Clinical services, which in social work fall under the curriculum area of social work practice, are central to several other professions such as counseling, clinical psychology, and school guidance. Human behavior and the social environment, a required area of study for social workers, is basically drawn from content developed by other disciplines such as biology, economics, psychology, and sociology. Social research, the final required area of social work study, is always a part of the curriculum for those who study in the social and behavioral sciences as well as other fields.

Although there are subdisciplines in some of the other human services fields that deal with social problems, policies, and services, in none of them is such content so central to the overall curriculum as it is in social work. Social work, which has a different sort of history than other fields that view their mission as that of helping people cope with or overcome personal or social problems, has historically focused on social policy and services.

The roots of social work are in social reform. References are made in ancient religious works to serving the needy and providing for the welfare of the aging, widows, people with disabilities, children, and other groups of people who cannot fully care for themselves. The provision of those services is a rudimentary form of social work. The religious injunctions requiring people to help the less fortunate are the earliest examples of social policies. The more formal, written history of the profession, which can be traced to early-seventeenth-century England, includes examples of the provision of assistance to the disadvantaged as well as the struggles of churches and governments to develop social policies that would achieve social welfare objectives without creating a dependent welfare class.

Although the current primary focus in educating social workers is on helping them learn how to serve communities, individuals, families, and groups, in a variety of circumstances and in a variety of ways, social policy precedes any social work practice. For that matter, it may be argued that all human services, including education, mental health, health services, and crime prevention and control, are based upon societal decisions that such services are needed and worthy of financial support. Without such policies there is an absence of legal and social mechanisms for the services to be provided (a process that social work calls "sanction") and no financing for those services. Large numbers of clinical psychologists provide their services within socially sanctioned and supported agencies such as schools, mental hospitals and centers, and clinics. Most physicians earn substantial portions of their incomes from programs that result from social policy, such as Medicaid and Medicare, but also from employer-provided health insurance. Hospitals have comparable sources of income.

Before one can speak about educating or employing teachers, policies must be established that provide for the financing of public education and the preparation of students. Before social welfare services are provided, the potential providers must begin with the creation and implementation of social policies that allow such provisions.

The historical reform nature of social work has long led to the recognition of the primacy of the development of policies. Not only are the professional social work organizations involved in the development and advocacy of such policies; the profession also considers it an obligation of each practitioner to engage in policy development and advocacy.

Throughout the history of organized social work the threads of social reform and policy development have been pervasive. For those viewing social work from the outside, however, the social policy orientation can be confusing. Nevertheless, it is of major importance because social work programs are involved with so many external analysts and controllers of their operations. Each agency—local, state, or federal, public or voluntary—is scrutinized and often governed by a board of directors, legislative committee, or executive branch structures that may have only a modest understanding of social workers and social programs Similarly, viewing the profession from the opposite direction, new students of social work often wonder why they are exposed to social policy courses when their reasons for enrolling have to do with "helping people," not studying the intricacies of problems, policies, and programs.

This book is designed to help two divergent audiences—the board, committee, and executive branch leaders of social work and the students who aspire to membership in the social work profession—understand the social policy dimensions of the discipline. A third audience is, of course, teachers of social policy, who are likely to be the ones who communicate those concepts to leaders and students.

There are already several books in print designed for those with interests in social work's approaches to social policy, many of them quite good. Most could be used in tandem with this guide to the overall concepts. This book is designed to help students of social policy understand the array of social policy concepts rather than specific elements of those policies. It is also designed to show how policies emerge from social problems and are translated into programs. It can be used as a stand-alone text for a beginning course, especially if it is supplemented with articles and reference books such as The Encyclopedia of Social Work as well as The Social Work Dictionary and The Social Work Almanac, all of which are published by the largest of the discipline's professional organizations, the National Association of Social Workers. This book, coupled with exploration of those references for detailed information on problems, programs, and policies, as well as the definitions, degrees, and levels of services, ought to help any student better understand the subject.

The original audience for these ideas consisted of doctoral students at the University of South Carolina, College of Social Work. The doctoral program at the college is designed to prepare social work teachers for baccalaureate and master's programs. For years before Ginsberg taught Theoretical Analysis of Social Policy, the one doctoral course in the subject, he had taught or supervised the teaching of social policy courses for bachelor of social work (BSW) and master of social work (MSW) students in the United States, Colombia, Korea, Mexico, and Romania. He had also served on accreditation site-visit teams to many schools in the United States and Canada; had been a member of the Commission on Accreditation of the Council on Social Work Education, which accredits social work programs; and had worked as a social policymaker and consultant in state and federal programs. Perhaps because of that extensive exposure and involvement in social policy theory from a number of perspectives, he realized that the task of educating social policy teachers, who might find themselves on faculties anywhere in the world, was more difficult than it seemed. That is because there is so little unanimity on what the fundamental course content ought to be. Each course, each text, and each of the thousands of social policy teachers seemed to have their own approach to or emphases of the subject matter. The accreditation guidelines are specific enough to help programs determine the content they must include in their teaching, yet they permit (as most educators would agree they should) wide latitude in the design and emphases of the courses.

Therefore, we found it necessary to help those potential social policy teachers understand the broad range of meanings and the variety of approaches used in the field to teach the subject matter. If we focused on historical, descriptive, and social problems approaches to the subject, which are the emphases of the College of Social Work's introductory MSW course, it would not well serve a student who might find employment as a faculty member in a program that emphasizes social policy analysis or the practice of social policy development and implementation. Or if we spent the semester teaching how to convey social policy ideas by tracing and coping with a specific social problem, as some instructors in some colleges and universities do, students would be baffled when they were required to teach a didactic course that focused heavily on social program descriptions.

Ginsberg resolved the problem by recognizing and categorizing the hundreds of social policy teaching examples to which he had been exposed. All of the social policy courses he had encountered were organized around one or a combination of several of six components: history, social problems and social issues, public policy, description, analysis, and policy practice. So the framework for teaching rested on these six components, with lectures, readings, book reports, class preparations, and term papers all organized around them. The students needed to understand all six if the course was to be useful to them.

We have taught the course many times, and, so far as we can determine, the six components effectively encompass the current understandings of social policy, the books, and the courses we encounter in accreditation consultations and reviews. Several doctoral graduates have assumed positions as teachers of social policy. All we lacked was access in book form to the model of social policy curriculum that is the basis for the kind of course described.

This is the book. For the spring semester of 1993 the University of South Carolina granted Ginsberg sabbatical leave to put his ideas into a more formal version than notes and course syllabi. Although this book is not designed to parallel the many fine social policy texts already in print, it should help students and instructors better understand one or more of those texts. As mentioned, the content is also sufficiently complete to make it useful as a stand-alone text, especially for foundation level—baccalaureate or first-year MSW—courses on social welfare policy and services. With some additional material from classroom lectures, additional readings, research papers, or the use of key reference works, the book could serve as a worthwhile and complete introduction to the subject. It is designed to meet the accreditation requirements of the Commission on Accreditation for the content area and to provide students with sufficient foundation knowledge to understand advanced courses in social policy as well as the social policy underpinnings of other content areas. Readers of the book, whether they are students or board members or other kinds of supervisors of social work programs, should capture a fundamental understanding of the nature and various perceptions of social policy as they are presently taught in social work and social work education.

The book, which is in its fourth edition, does not present any special ideological points of view. That is, it is not especially oriented to incremental, radical, conservative, or liberal ideologies—although social policy, by its nature, implies some belief that government ought to be involved in serving the needs of citizens.

The book also avoids specific religious orientations, which are important components for many of the social work education programs that are associated with religious denominations. Communicating the social policy components of those religious mandates is an important function for such programs, and this text does not interfere with the capacity of a program to add such orientations to the mix of information provided in social policy courses.

There are ideological differences among existing social policy texts as well as varying degrees of commitment to one or more of the orientations discussed here. Some texts are more historical than others, some are almost exclusively analytical, others focus on social issues and problems, and still others are largely descriptive. Most texts combine two or more of the components offered here, which is also true of most social policy courses. The only specific point of view advocated here is that there are several orientations for understanding and teaching about social policy. This book implies that all those orientations are legitimate and, in many cases, essential to a sound understanding of the subject matter. The book leaves the addition of ideology and specific values to the courses and instructors for whom it is intended. It should be noted here that the term "social policy" is often used in this volume as a shorthand designation for the total subject matter of this book—social problems, policies, and programs.

The first three editions, which this volume updates, filled a gap in the social problems, policies, and programs literature, according to professors and students. People liked the idea of a brief, accessible, but inclusive text that covered the key bases. They also appreciated the low cost of a paperback in the increasingly costly textbook business. Some have found the book useful for introduction to social welfare courses.

To date no reader has insisted that the book missed a seventh or eighth approach to the subject. The six that are included seem capable of encompassing the elements that most students of the subject would include. Therefore, this edition retains the structure of the first. It updates information on some of the literature, makes the historical chapter current, adds additional material on policy analysis, and changes a few examples. In some ways, social welfare has changed significantly since the first edition was published. President Bill Clinton, whose service was beginning when the manuscript for the first edition was completed, was finishing his second term when the third was prepared. The Republican Party had gained control of both houses of the U.S. Congress for the first time in more than forty years and established a clear agenda to make major policy changes, many of which had direct impact on social welfare. They made major changes in social welfare with the president's concurrence, which are described in this book.

This edition also discusses the results and some of the implications of the 1998 congressional elections, in which the Democratic Party exceeded most historical expectations by adding members to its minority in the House of Representatives and maintaining the same Democratic numbers in the Senate. A Republican move to impeach the president was credited, in part, for the Democratic successes. However, the 1998 results were not generally viewed as a repudiation of the social welfare changes made in 1996 under the Republican Contract with America. More likely, voters who had supported Republicans in larger numbers in 1994 because of their desire to change social welfare policies saw less need to do so in 1998 because their concerns had been resolved.

Other events too had at least an indirect impact on human provisions. Violence again became an inescapable part of the social problems agenda with the bombing of a federal facility in Oklahoma City; the murder trial of football hero and media personality O. J. Simpson, who was accused and acquitted of killing his former wife and her friend; as well as youth gang violence, the murder of employees of health facilities where abortions were performed, and increasing numbers of firearms deaths. Of course, the attacks of September 11, 2001, were the most significant reminder of violence in modern times. But change is the nature of the subject matter and should not surprise anyone familiar with the history of U.S. social welfare, which dates from the 1930s New Deal.

LEON GINSBERG
JULIE MILLER-CRIBBS

ACKNOWLEDGMENTS

My thanks go to several of my MSW and PhD students in social policy courses who helped me formulate the ideas that are presented here, as well as to my colleagues at the University of South Carolina and my former colleagues at West Virginia University and the University of Oklahoma. I also learned a good deal about teaching social policy from the faculty and students of two universities in Colombia, South America, at the Escuela de Trabajo Social at the Universidad Nacional Autónoma de México, and at social work schools in Romania, where social work had been outlawed under the former regime —as it had been in many Soviet Union nations, perhaps because of its inclusion of social policy—and restored during the 1990s. The 1992 University of South Carolina doctoral students in social policy—Dorothy Callahan, Liz Cramer, Steve Hardin, Debora Rice, and Jean Sullivan—were especially helpful with suggestions when they learned I was working on the first edition of this book. Some of their ideas were cited in the first edition.

At the time this edition was prepared, I was serving as dean of the College of Social Work. I realized that a new generation of social work scholars ought to be represented in the text. Therefore, this fourth edition was coauthored by Dr. Julie Miller-Cribbs of the University of South Carolina College of Social Work faculty. She teaches master's level social welfare policy and services courses and also teaches doctoral students the course described in this introduction. She's a graduate of the doctoral program in social work at Washington University in St. Louis, Missouri, and is an accomplished researcher and writer. She is also younger than some of my children, which I think demonstrates that the book is the product of both seasoned and emerging writers about social policy. I'm very pleased to have Dr. Miller-Cribbs's insights and excellent explanations of the complex world of social welfare policy and services.

Special thanks to Barry Blose, acquisitions editor for the University of South Carolina Press, for his guidance of and support for this project. Thanks also to Barbara Kohn and Joyce Shaw of the University of South Carolina College of Social Work for their help in manuscript preparation and Kelly Fetter and Mary Ellen Chafin for their research assistance.

Finally, I want to acknowledge the help and support of my wife, Connie Ginsberg, as well as the five children and six grandchildren we share, through the many months of effort that went into this book. And my thanks, also, to Julie Miller-Cribbs for participating in the project and for so markedly improving this fourth edition.

LEON GINSBERG

I would like to thank my coauthor, Dr. Leon Ginsberg, for providing me with an opportunity to work with him on this book. His insights and feedback throughout the book-writing process were invaluable to me.

Many of my colleagues at the College of Social Work listened to my ideas, read drafts, commented on tables, or just provided a listening ear. I appreciate their patience and support along the way.

I would also like to acknowledge my parents, Jim and Judy Miller, who have supported me throughout my life and have provided me with many opportunities. They continue to provide me with love and support for which I am grateful.

None of my work on this book would be possible without the support of my husband, Harry, and my two children, Carly and Cole, who had dinner without me a few nights while I was working on this book. At the end of a long day, I can always count on them to make me smile.

JULIE MILLER-CRIBBS

Understanding Social Problems,
Policies, and Programs

ONE

Social Policy in Social Work and the Other Human Services Professions

This book is about social welfare policy and services, which is one of the required curriculum areas for people who study social work and other human services fields in colleges and universities. The other areas of study in the human services are usually professional practice, which defines what social workers and others in the human services do in their efforts to help people; human behavior and the social environment, which teaches about the ways in which families, individuals, groups, communities, and societies develop and behave; and research, which covers the methods that are used to better understand and evaluate human services and social welfare programs.

Social welfare is, of course, the total system of programs, services, and policies that provides for human well-being. Social Security retirement benefits for older adults, medical care for people with disabilities, and protection against abuse or neglect for children are examples of social welfare, which some call "social services." Social work is the largest profession that works within the social welfare system. The creation of the social work profession a century ago, its growth over the years, and its occasional declines are all products of social policy. So are all the developments of the other human services professions such as gerontology, nursing, rehabilitation counseling, and other specialized disciplines that deal with the problems and needs of people. Policies are the sources of all social welfare. Services develop only when there are social policies that create, finance, and provide for administering them. Therefore, all human services workers are educated, employed, and paid because of social policies. Without social policy there would be no workers to carry out those policies.

The curriculum areas described earlier—social work practice, social research, human behavior and the social environment, and social welfare policy and services—are all part of the education of the helping professions. Psychology, counseling, nursing, medicine, education, physical therapy, speech therapy, physical education, and virtually all of the other professions that

1

help people overcome their personal, physical, or social problems or needs include those areas in their curricula. Social work, however, is somewhat different because it requires more extensive education about social policy than some other human fields. That is because social workers have always believed that human problems are not simply individual problems, but can often best be solved through social policies. Conversely, social workers have found that many human problems result from the lack of social policies that could prevent those problems. In other cases, social workers believe that some social policies *cause* human problems. Increasingly, all of the human services fields are adopting that point of view and are finding, in the practice of their work, that attention to social policy is crucial to the effective resolution of human problems.

How Social Policy Affects Life

The worst social policy and the starkest example of how influential social policies are have to do with the socioeconomic system of slavery. Slavery was an American social policy prior to the Civil War that allowed some people to own other people. White slave owners could buy and sell black people. They could punish them in any way they wanted. They could kill them if they chose to do so. They could keep them from learning to read or write. During and after the Civil War, President Abraham Lincoln, Congress, and the northern states implemented two new social policies—freeing the slaves; making them citizens; guaranteeing all people, including former slaves, equal rights; and providing the former slaves the right to vote. Those new policies were contained in presidential proclamations, federal laws, and amendments to the Constitution. The treatment of human beings as property and the changes in that treatment—redefining black people as American citizens—were both consequences of social policies.

Although not as brutal as slavery, the segregation in the South that began decades after the end of the Civil War is hard to imagine in today's environment. From the late 1800s through the middle 1950s, there was strict, legal segregation of African Americans from white people in schools, restaurants, hospitals, public transportation, movie theaters, and virtually every other kind of situation in which people might mingle. This was legal, or de jure, segregation by color.

Still, there are examples of de facto segregation in which, in fact, white and black people are separated from each other—often by choice and even more often by economics that make it difficult for many African American families to participate in the same activities as many white families. Legal segregation is gone, but realistically, actual segregation continues in many elements of American life.

2

Until 1920, when the Nineteenth Amendment to the U.S. Constitution was passed, most American women were not permitted to vote, a fact that is unthinkable today. Both the denial of the vote to women and the extension of suffrage to them were social policies.

In the 1930s and 1940s, it was the official policy of the Nazi regimes in Germany and its allied European nations to seize, relocate, and kill Jews, Gypsies, homosexuals, people with mental disabilities, and other groups. Another example of social policy is the "ethnic cleansing" in the former nation of Yugoslavia in the 1990s, in which many Muslims were arrested, raped, and murdered.

Almost everything that affects people is a social policy. Social policies determine, in part at least, the ways we marry and divorce, the ways parents may treat their children, the ways we work, the rules under which we employ others in jobs, and our educations. Social policies define what is and is not a crime, how we receive medical care, and the kinds of help we receive when we are unemployed, disabled, or too old to work. Almost anything that influences our lives can be found in social policies.

Social Work and Social Policy

Social work's counseling or casework services are somewhat similar to those we find in many of the other helping professions. Our understandings of the ways in which people behave are actually taken from other helping professions and social sciences. Our social research is often indistinguishable from that employed in other helping professions and the social and behavior sciences. In fact, the methods we use were often developed by and are now borrowed by social work from other fields, especially psychology and sociology. Our *Code of Ethics,* when it deals with the ways we treat clients, is, in most respects, similar to those of the other helping disciplines.

It is our extensive involvement with social policy that actually distinguishes social work as a profession. It is what makes it different from related approaches to helping people.

A Definition

Social policy textbooks define *social policy* in various ways, some (DiNitto and Cummins, 2005) emphasizing policies that are developed through government—public policies—and others extending the definition to include policies made by professional organizations such as the National Association of Social Workers and voluntary agencies such as United Way and Family Service Societies. For us the best definition is taken from the *Social Work Dictionary;* according to this widely used and comprehensive source, *social policy* is the activities and principles of a society that guide the way it intervenes in and regulates relationships between individuals, groups, communities, and social institutions. These principles and activities are the result of the society's values and customs and largely determine the distribution of resources and level of well-being of its people. Thus, social policy includes plans and programs in education, health care, crime and corrections, economic security, and social welfare made by government, voluntary organizations, and the people in general. It also includes social perspectives that result in society's rewards and constraints (Barker, 2003, 485).

Dear (1995, 2226) defines policy as "just about anything a government does." He says that policies are "principles, plans, procedures, and courses of action—established in statute, interpreted in administrative code, spelled out in agency regulation, and supported by judicial decree." By Dear's definition, anything that is formally spelled out, whether by a governmental or non-governmental agency, about their operations is a policy.

The examples of slavery, segregation, and the Holocaust have to do with the well-being of people. The issue of suffrage deals with society's rewards and constraints. Rules about work and family life are concerned with the ways society regulates relations among people. Clearly, almost anything that has an impact on our lives is a product of a social policy or a group of social policies.

Social Work Ethics and Social Policy
Social work's long-standing professional interest in social policy has been underscored in a number of ways other than, most obviously, the ways it educates its new practitioners. Today social workers are obligated *to do something* about social policy. The 1996 National Association of Social Workers Code of Ethics says that social workers have ethical responsibilities to the broader society. According to the statement, "Social workers should promote the general welfare of society, from local to global levels, and the development of people, their communities, and their environments. Social workers should advocate for living conditions conducive to the fulfillment of basic human needs and should promote social, economic, political, and cultural values and institutions that are compatible with the realization of social justice."

The code goes on to say that social workers should

1. Facilitate informed public participation in shaping public policies and institutions.

2. Engage in social and political action geared toward gaining equal access to opportunities that help all persons meet their basic needs and develop fully in areas such as employment.

3. Advocate for legislative and policy changes to improve social conditions and promote social justice.

4. Act to expand the choices people have, with special attention to vulnerable, oppressed, exploited, and disadvantaged groups.

5. Promote conditions that will in turn promote respect for cultural and social diversity in the United States and the rest of the world.

6. Work to eliminate discrimination on bases such as ethnicity, sex, race, sexual orientation, religion, age, marital status, political beliefs, and physical or mental disabilities (see Fig. 4, p. 289).

The statement makes it clear that social workers need to learn about social policies not only when they are students; we are also obligated to practice— to do something about—social policy throughout our careers.

Of course, social workers have different routes to being involved in social policies. Some of us are administrators or have other policy jobs in voluntary and government agencies and can propose, implement, or even develop and promulgate social policies that affect the well-being of people. Other social workers carry out their social policy mandates by involving themselves in social action organizations and political campaigns. Others contribute to social policy by writing and speaking to legislators and administrators to influence them to support policies to improve people's lives. Still others of us support social policies by being active in our professional organizations or by simply carrying out policies that make a difference in the lives of people.

No matter what our specific roles, social workers have always known that helping people involves much more than talking to clients or meeting with groups or even providing assistance and other services to those who need them. Helping people requires helpful policies. In the long run a social policy can make much more difference in the lives of those we serve than all of the counseling, economic, or protective services we might provide them. Social policies can change the bases of their lives, prevent future problems, and continue to help them cope with their problems long after they have received the services of a human services agency or professional.

An agency may help a client find a job; a social policy may guarantee that person employment for as long as he or she can work. A human services worker may help a client find ways to pay medical bills; a social policy may guarantee the client medical care. An agency may provide a family with a Christmas basket, but a social policy may provide that family with enough money to support itself and buy its own holiday baskets in the future.

Social Policy and the Practice of Social Work

In addition to knowing about and working toward improvements in social policy as a professional, ethical obligation, social workers also *use* social policy in their professional work. At times social work students believe that practicing, or "doing," social work is, for most social workers, a process of talking to people about their personal or family problems. Others believe social work practice involves meeting with groups of clients and helping them solve one another's difficulties or helping a community identify and take steps to resolve its social needs. While these examples are clearly parts of the roles of most social workers, many also perform their duties by understanding, explaining, and applying social policies.

For example, parents who visit with a human services worker to help them cope with a troubled child need and receive casework or counseling services of some kind from that worker. The counseling is designed to help them cope with their feelings about the troubled child, develop some strategies for dealing with the child, or even obtain additional help such as group treatment, recreational involvement, or tutoring for the child. The worker, however, would also call upon a fund of knowledge about social policies that might assist the family. If, for example, the child has handicaps or limitations, he or she might be eligible for a program of financial assistance called Supplemental Security Income (SSI) or special health care through the Crippled Children's Program; or transportation to special education classes; or a court action that could "emancipate" a minor child, which in effect helps a child who cannot be kept under control at home to become a legal adult, despite his or her young age. In many cases the contribution of the worker is based upon knowing about and helping clients use social policies that provide necessary services.

Social programs are the real source of help for clients. In the example above, the worker and the client would never have come together had it not been for a social policy that provided a program in which parents with such problems have access to human services workers who can help them. It was social policy that made the whole interchange possible. Little happens in the human services unless there is social policy to authorize, sanction, and pay for it. So, as was suggested earlier, the practice of the human services professions is a product of social policy, and social policy is fundamental to everything else that goes on in human services work.

Religion

Religion has traditionally been an important source of social policy. The original mandates to help the needy and the ethical bases for providing social services are found in sacred books such as the Bible as well as in the oral traditions and holy documents and teachings of various religions.

A development in the 2000s, principally with the election of President George W. Bush in 2000, was the redeveloped emphasis on religion in government. Although much of American history, the U.S. Constitution, and many Supreme Court decisions are based on the separation of church and state, President Bush placed a special emphasis on the importance of religion in American policy. The president has developed a stronger connection with religion, especially evangelical Christianity, than he had as a younger person, when he was an adult who was troubled with the excessive use of alcohol. He gave up alcohol and became, as some evangelical Christians describe it, "born again."

According to Fineman (2003) religion dominated many presidential policies and presidential positions. Speeches that the president gave often contained classic Christian religious references. The president's insistence, during an early State of the Union message, that certain nations, especially Iraq, Iran, and North Korea, were part of an axis of evil, suggested the classic Christian conflict between good and evil or Satan and Christ. He also proposed government support of "faith-based" social services and hoped to deliver services for persons encountering unwanted pregnancies, alcohol and drug problems, and other personal and social concerns through religiously organized services or through religious institutions.

Some observers suggested that Bush felt a special kinship with God in taking positions on such matters as war and peace, biological developments, and such medical concerns as abortion. There is nothing new in social work about religious organizations playing roles in the provision of human services. However, the blending of government with faith-based or religiously oriented services is an approach that was presumed to be in violation of the U.S. Constitution. However, so long as there is no religious discrimination against service recipients, it is likely that there is no reason why religious organizations cannot contract with government and deliver some of its services.

Some thought, however, that a federal administration that is decidedly supportive of religion and that also bases its policies on religious concepts seemed to be more akin to governments in predominantly Roman Catholic and Islamic nations.

The emphasis on religion in the Bush administration had significance consequences in the development and delivery of human services programs.

Government itself has also been influential in defining jobs of some social workers to actually *practice* social policy—to develop, write, and promulgate policies.

Other Disciplines and Social Policy

None of what has been suggested so far means that social work is the only human services discipline that deals with social policy. All human services workers need to understand and use social policy, and all are, to an extent, products of the implementation of social policy. Professional ethics are also taught to students, sometimes with greater emphasis than social work devotes to the subject. In the other disciplines, however, there is usually less attention to and a less central role for social policy in educational programs. In some cases social policy is an elective subject rather than a required part of the curriculum, as it is in social work at both the baccalaureate (BSW) and master's (MSW) levels.

Some fields are even more emphatic about the importance of social policy. For example, students of political science, especially those who study in the related field of public administration, may be required to take a number of social policy courses. Some colleges and universities have whole programs, with undergraduate majors and graduate degrees, in policy or public policy, which, of course, include social policy. Political science and public administration are not, however, primarily human services fields, although many students of both often have careers in the human services. Therefore, social work, among the human services professions, is the field that most directly includes and emphasizes social policy in its curriculum.

The Components of Social Policy

Even with the knowledge that social policy is central to social work teaching and practice and even with the clear definition provided by Barker (2003), it is still true that social policy is often a confusing subject for some social workers. Chances are good that they had never heard of social policy before entering a social work major or an MSW program. It is a term not normally discussed in high school or in other undergraduate courses. In fact, it is a term that is not usually heard in the normal course of conversations or even featured in newspapers and magazines. Social policy discussions, unless they are concrete and personal, are not what people pursue at home, at parties, or in classrooms. Many people may have an opinion, say, on the marital relations of the president and his wife, but few will have more than the broadest attitudes about presidential policies. Remarks such as "Get those bums off welfare" are often as close as we get to real policy discussions. Therefore, objective, well-informed analyses of policy issues, books and films about policy, and term paper assignments on social policies may be relatively new or uncommon experiences for students.

Even seasoned human services workers may not know very much or think very much about social policies. A distinguished hospital social work director many years ago told a story that illustrates this. He had recently interviewed a job applicant and asked what the applicant would like to emphasize if employed at the hospital. The applicant expressed a strong interest in policy. Policy, the applicant hoped, would be the emphasis of her professional career. The social work director later complained to a colleague: "Policy! We don't need policies! We have bookshelves full of policies, and more of them is the last thing we need!" Of course, the applicant was not proposing the writing of more policies. But the hospital social work director's understanding of the term was quite different from the applicant's.

8

Neither, however, was wrong. *Social policy* has many meanings, and, in the absence of background in the subject, it is a confusing term for many students and practitioners. It is even a confusing term for many social work professors, a group for whom this book was originally designed. Part of the reason for the confusion about the meaning of *social policy* is that the term actually means many things. Educators and authors in the social policy field define the subject in different ways. The textbooks in the social policy field are also quite varied and emphasize different aspects of the term.

As a way of describing the field of social policy and the various approaches taken to it, it is worthwhile to analyze and define these approaches and what they seek to emphasize. Several years of study of the field, review of the textbooks and articles that have been written about it, and consideration of the ways that numerous baccalaureate and graduate social work programs teach the subject suggest that there are six components of social policy as it is studied and taught in the field of social work. These components are the organizing themes of this book.

Sources of the Components

The components of social policy teaching and scholarship come from a number of different sources. Primary among them are the curriculum requirements of the social work accrediting bodies. Accreditation has long been a critical part of social work education, and, historically, social work education programs have aspired to offer degrees that were accredited. According to Frumkin and Lloyd (1995), formal social work education began at the end of the nineteenth century and continued throughout the twentieth. In the 1930s professional standards were developed, and graduate social work education programs joined together in the American Association of Schools of Social Work (AASSW). For several reasons, the most important being that most people did not enter social work until they had finished their undergraduate studies, social work education was long considered a postgraduate field, despite the fact that undergraduate programs had been offered for many years and finally became eligible for accreditation some twenty years ago. There was even a competing organization to the American Association of Schools of Social Work, the National Association of Schools of Social Work (NASSW), which began in 1942. The conflict between the two organizations was over whether social work, at the graduate level, should be a one- or a two-year program, with the AASSW favoring two years and the NASSW one year. The conflict was resolved with the development of the Council on Social Work Education (CSWE) in 1952, which has continued since then to be the sole organization representing and accrediting social work education. It has accredited master's programs since it began, and in 1974 it began accrediting baccalaureate social work degrees, many of which had existed as long or longer than the master's programs (Lloyd, 1987). There are also more than

9

fifty doctoral education programs in social work in the United States (Ginsberg, 1995).

Throughout these procedures for setting standards for social work education, curriculum materials on social policy have always been required. They have been a necessary component since education for social work practice began. The ideas about social work curriculum were clarified and refined in the thirteen-volume *Social Work Curriculum Study* (1959), a project that was led by Werner Boehm and involved many of the leading social work educators of the time. Based upon that study, the Council on Social Work Education promulgated, in 1962, a curriculum policy statement (Frumkin and Lloyd, 1995). The statement has been updated every few years since then, most recently in 2003 with the Educational Policy and Accreditation Standards documents (Council on Social Work Education, 2003).

The curriculum statements on social policy have changed over the three decades since they began. In some statements, perhaps responding to the activism of the 1960s, it was expected that programs would prepare students to become active participants in social policy development. In later statements such commitments to action were dropped, but the learning content has remained similar. Students have been consistently required to learn about the history of social work, which often includes learning about some of the figures that have influenced its development, about the making of public policy and the political process, and how to analyze and evaluate social policies and programs.

In the 2000s, the Council on Social Work Education re-created and issued the standards for accreditation of bachelor's and master's programs. The revised standards are contained in a new publication of the *Handbook of Accreditation Standards and Procedures* (Council on Social Work Education, 2003).

The document covers the profession's Educational Policy and Accreditation Standards, in a form somewhat different from what had gone before. It also redefined the standards for educating social work students about social welfare policy and services. The standard says:

Programs provide content about the history of social work, the history and current structures of social welfare services, and the role of policy in service delivery, social work practice, and attainment of individual and social well-being. Course content provides students with knowledge and skills to understand major policies that form the foundation of social welfare; analyze organizational, local, state, national, and international issues in social welfare policy and social service delivery; analyze and apply the results of policy research relevant to social service delivery; understand and demonstrate policy practice skills in regard to economic, political, and organizational systems, and use them to influence, formulate, and advocate for policy consistent with social work values; and identify financial, organizational, administrative, and planning processes required to deliver social services. (Council on Social Work Education, 2003, 35)

One of the significant additions to the statement about social policy is the added influence about international social policy—a reliable indicator of how influenced local policies are by events in the rest of the world. Understanding the practice of social work in the modern era requires some knowledge of the rest of the world. For social workers, it is ideal to know something about the ways programs operate in other nations as well as knowing how social programs can operate internationally. International adoptions, emigration issues, and the increasing role of violence in world affairs all combine to make an international perspective crucial to the knowledge base of social workers.

But in many ways the standards for learning about social welfare policy and services are closely tied to and quite similar to the ideas that have persisted for the whole history of the profession.

Scholarship by social work writers and researchers as well as scholarship from other fields, such as public policy and political science, has also made a mark on social policy content. Several books written by social workers have been influential in defining the field of social policy and the knowledge that students are expected to acquire during their studies. Some of those scholars and researchers are oriented to understanding the history of the social work profession, others the systematic analysis of social programs and services, and still others have written about the practice of social policy, an orientation that has consistently involved large numbers of human services professionals, many of them social workers.

The Six Components of Social Policy

Systems theorists tell us that everything is made up of smaller and smaller building blocks, down to such tiny things as electrons, genes, and viruses. A social policy paradigm with ten thousand components would simply not provide a comfortable route for learning about the subject. Six components of social policy are highlighted here; they are interrelated rather than mutually exclusive. That is, each contains some elements of all the others. Each, in turn, could easily be subdivided into smaller parts; another observer could assert, for example, that there are really four or eighteen to twenty-six key components of social policy. After years of work defining the field of social policy, we find that these six components are distinct and broad enough to provide an effective range of study and teaching, as well as broad enough to offer students and teachers a useful model, or paradigm.

Historical. Social policy can be understood in terms of its historical roots and developments. As mentioned, all social work students are required to learn about the history of the organized profession. History is the branch of knowledge that records and/or analyzes past events. Chapter 2 discusses the historical component of social policy, the early development of social welfare services, and the modern era, from Social Security to the present.

Social Problems / Social Issues. Another way to study social policy is by studying social problems, or social issues, a subject that is well developed in sociology and, to an extent, in other social sciences. As has already been suggested, social policy is viewed by many as a consequence of social problems. When society determines that a problem is large enough to be considered a problem for large numbers of people, it becomes a social problem. For example, the personal misfortune of having nowhere to live became the social problem of homelessness; the personal misfortune of having a poor or unsafe family life became the social problem of child neglect or maltreatment; and the personal lack of income or resources became the social problem of poverty. Chapter 3 examines the social problems / social issues component of social policy.

Public Policy. One of the most critical of the six components in this model is public policy. Chapters 4 and 5 deal with public policy in detail. The component includes all of the policy decisions made by public, or governmental, bodies such as legislatures and courts; executives such as governors or the president; executive branch agencies such as state departments of social services of the U.S. Department of Health and Human Services; and independent agencies, which are not executive, legislative, or judicial bodies but do perform some of the same functions.

Descriptive. Part of learning about social policy is simply learning about the programs and services that constitute social welfare. Those programs and services are results of social policy. One classic way of discussing social policy is in the form of a triad: *problem, policy, provision.* In other words, many observers believe that social problems lead to the development of social policies, the ultimate outcomes of which are provisions of social services. Understanding the myriad provisions that arise from social policy—mental health services, financial assistance, job training, day care, and everything else that social agencies and social workers provide—is necessary for understanding social policy. And, of course, being able to help others means, among other things, knowing what services are available to people who face problems. The policy follows the problem and the program implements the policy.

Analytical. Understanding social policy requires much more than simply knowing what those policies entail. To be an effective professional in the human services one must also know what those policies consist of—who is helped by them most and who is helped by them least, how they are financed, and what alternatives may exist. Chapter 8 covers the analytical approach, the subject of many social policy textbooks.

Policy Practice. Some social workers and other human services profession-als practice social policy. That is, they promulgate social policies; write poli-cies for agencies; translate statutes passed by legislative bodies into regulations that agencies and their employees implement; interpret and consult about policies for those who deliver services to clients; and draft legislation for state legislatures and the U.S. Congress. Chapter 9 explains the practice compo-nent of social policy.

Conclusion

This chapter has offered definitions of social policy and explained why social policy is central to human services professions. It has examined the ways social policy affects people's lives and pointed out its special place in the field of social work as well as its roles in some of the other human services profes-sions. The chapter also introduces the six components of social policy that constitute the basic outline for this book and upon which the subsequent chapters are based.

Discussion Questions

1. Describe some of the ways in which social policy affects the lives of all people. Provide examples from social services programs you have studied, from your employment in social welfare, or from your field placement or internship.

2. This chapter suggests that social policy is more central to the study and practice of social work than to the other human services professions. Do you agree? If so, explain why you agree, or, if you disagree, explain that position.

3. Based upon your experience or other readings, do you agree with Barker's definition of social policy? If so, explain why you agree. If not, explain how you might want to change it.

4. Do you believe that social policy ought to have a greater or lesser role within the social work curriculum you have experienced? Explain your answer.

References

Barker, R. (2003). *The social work dictionary,* 5th ed. Washington, DC: NASW Press.

Boehm, W. M. (1959). *Social work curriculum study.* 13 vols. New York: Council on Social Work Education.

Council on Social Work Education, Commission on Accreditation (2003). *Handbook of accreditation standards and procedures,* 5th ed. Alexandria, VA: Author.

Dear, R. B. (1995). Social welfare policy. In R. L. Edwards et al. (Eds.), *Encyclopedia of social work,* 19th ed., 2226–2237. Washington, DC: NASW Press.

DiNitto, D. M., & Cummins, L. K. (2005). *Social welfare: Politics and public policy,* 6th ed. Boston: Allyn and Bacon.

Fineman, H. (March 10, 2003). Bush and God. *Newsweek,* 22–30.

Frumkin, M., & Lloyd, G. A. (1995). Social work education. In R. L. Edwards et al. (Eds.), *Encyclopedia of social work,* 19th ed., 2238–2247. Washington, DC: NASW Press.

Ginsberg, L. (1987). Economic, political, and social context. In A. Minahan et al. (Eds.), *Encyclopedia of social work,* 18th ed., xxxiii–xli. Silver Spring, MD: NASW Press.

Ginsberg, L. (1990). Introduction. In L. Ginsberg et al. (Eds.), *Encyclopedia of social work,* 18th ed., 1990 supp., 1–11. Silver Spring, MD: NASW Press.

Ginsberg, L. (1995). *Social work almanac,* 2nd ed. Washington, DC: NASW Press.

TWO

The Historical Component
Milestones in Social Policy

Although not as well known as other social institutions such as education and religion, social services have a long history. Historians who specialize in the study of social work history note that as long as there have been civilizations there have also been social welfare services to help people deal with their needs or problems. The earliest forms provided mutual help; that is, when a family was in need because, for example, its crops failed or because of illness or death, other families came to its assistance with food, shelter, and other resources. It is probably true that in modern society mutual help is still the most pervasive form of assistance. Often when parents are temporarily or permanently unable to care for children, neighbors and family members will pitch in to help. Families share food, pass around clothing, help one another with transportation, and make loans or provide cash assistance to those who cannot handle their own requirements.

Any study of social policy history demonstrates that the roots of all current programs and services, such as those discussed in chapters 6 and 7 and elsewhere in this book, can be found in the earliest recorded history. There is nothing really new about most of our social policies. Whatever they are, many have probably been attempted or proposed earlier in some form.

This chapter is not intended to comprehensively cover the total history of social welfare services or social policy. Instead, its purpose is to highlight the fundamental facts about the history of social welfare and social policy and to demonstrate some of the ways in which current as well as proposed social policies are rooted in the past. The goal is to help the reader place social policy in historical context—to learn about the sources of some of the fundamental programs and also how new programs might be better designed and administered with the knowledge available from earlier efforts.

Those who want to embark on a more serious study of social policy history or the histories of social welfare or social work should consult one of the many excellent social welfare histories, such as those by B. S. Jansson (2005),

P. J. Day (2003), and J. Axinn and H. Levin (2005). Each has a different emphasis, but each also outlines the fundamental concepts that are important for understanding how social policy had developed throughout history. Another excellent historical analysis of the threat of poverty is M. B. Katz's *The Undeserving Poor* (1989). Noble (1997) wrote a political history of the welfare state, which traces the American experience, in particular.

Persistent Themes in Social Policy

Studying the history of social policy is a reliable way to confirm the fundamental and persistent themes of social policy, according to this book's point of view. These themes are

1. Human societies have tended to provide those in need with resources that will help them physically survive.

2. Societies resist helping people more than they need to be helped in order to physically survive.

3. Those who receive society's help are expected to use no more help than they need.

4. Those who receive social help are ideally expected to contribute to the society if they are able to do so—through public service work or through training and rehabilitation activities that will reduce or eliminate their need for help.

5. In some way societies categorize those who seek aid, finding "worthy" and "unworthy" groups, although social workers and other human services professionals believe that this is a false dichotomy. The worthy are typically those who "cannot help themselves," and the unworthy are those for whom having unmet needs is considered to be "their own fault" (see Katz, 1989).

6. Assistance benefits should never be as great as or greater than the income of the community or society's lowest-paid workers.

7. The primary responsibility for assistance ought to belong to oneself and one's own efforts. Secondarily, it may fall to family members or neighbors or, if those sources cannot provide help, to an organized charity, church, or other nongovernmental institution. Beyond these sources, responsibility lies with the government.

In these discussions of social work history, as well as those in subsequent chapters, it should be possible to see these fundamental principles at work. Chapter 6 focuses on economic social policy for those whose primary problem is a lack of money, food, housing, and other necessities. Chapter 7 focuses on the services designed to help people with other kinds of needs such as those faced by maltreated children, the aging, and those with physical and mental disabilities.

The division of social programs into economic and noneconomic programs and services is relatively common in the modern social welfare field. In some situations separate agencies are responsible for the two kinds of help. Generally, there is different legislation covering the two kinds of help. The reality is, however, that many of those needing financial assistance and other concrete forms of help also face the kinds of problems addressed by personal, noneconomic social services, and vice versa. Although there is often a distinction made between financial assistance and personal social services, the problems that cause them to be needed are often interrelated.

Social Policy before Nations

Social policy predates the development of the nation-state. Before there were governments there were churches, communities, tribes, and feudal lords. Religious groups, in particular, have always provided some forms of social welfare; although they recognize different doctrines, all of them require their adherents to help the disadvantaged and have done so historically (Reid, 1995). Religious involvement in social welfare, which continues, has traditionally been central to the history of social welfare. Feudal lords, many of whom attributed their power to God, provided some forms of social assistance to those who were dependent upon them.

Day (2003) provides an excellent discussion of the ways in which social welfare developed in a variety of cultures and regions. She covers ancient as well as modern social welfare development and shows that China, Greece, and early Roman society, among others, developed social welfare policies. She also describes the Jewish and Christian contributions to such policies as well as later British programs, which are often emphasized in the study of social welfare history.

Among the early biblical injunctions to provide social assistance are those found in Deuteronomy 24:19–22. God orders his people to refrain from going over their fields, olive trees, and vineyards a second time after harvesting their produce because the second harvests should be given to aliens, orphans, and widows. He promises his blessings to those who follow the injunction. The order to help the disadvantaged is a reminder to the Jews that they were once slaves in Egypt and then had been in need themselves.

Religious groups have also governed other elements of family and community life, which have, in turn, affected the social welfare of people. Day (2003), for example, points out that Christianity, a religion that spread throughout the world, supported monogamy and viewed divorce negatively. That Christian social policy was important in securing and extending the well-being and rights of women by providing a social context in which women would not bear the sole responsibility of caring for and raising children. The

17

traditional Islamic law that men could have as many as four wives provided a clear structure to social relations at the family level in the face of an unbalanced population in which there were more women than men.

The Elizabethan Poor Law of 1601

The most important of the laws governing social policy in all of history, especially after the rise of the nation-state, was the English Elizabethan Poor Law of 1601. That law, which was officially called an Act for the Relief of the Poor, is reproduced completely and in its original form in Axinn and Levin (2005) and contains or implies the seven themes listed previously.

According to Leiby, the 1601 Poor Law

1. Defined the duty of the parish (which was the local government, comparable to today's counties) to provide relief to the poor.
2. Established overseers of the poor to relieve poverty. These were among the earliest social workers.
3. Gave the overseers the power to raise funds and use them in their poverty relief.
4. Affirmed that government relief was a last resort, after family and friends assisted the poor.
5. Defined helpless (or worthy) people, whose problems included illness, the feebleness of old age, being orphaned, and disability.
6. Established workhouses and other solutions, such as deporting to the colonies "sturdy beggars," often as indentured servants, who asked for help but who appeared capable of providing for themselves. (Leiby, 1987)

According to Leiby (1987), the Statute of Charitable Trusts and Uses, which was also enacted in 1601, made possible and established the rules for the creation of charitable trusts and benefits by the wealthy or groups of people with the desire to be helpful and the resources to provide the help.

The Elizabethan Poor Law, compared to earlier statutes, represented humanitarian reforms. Day describes, for example, the punitive 1536 "Act for Punishment of Sturdy Vagabonds and Beggars," which outlawed begging and giving to beggars and penalized violators with "branding, enslavement, and execution" (1987).

Today American and European social policy contains many of these same programs, principles, and services. Although the programs and services have, of course, changed substantially, the basic concepts have had an amazing constancy.

Laws were passed in England to uphold the principles of that country's social policy: the Workhouse Test Act, for example, which forced the unemployed to work for any relief they received (Alexander, 1995), was passed in 1697 by the English Parliament. There were some policies in England, and elsewhere, that have not persisted. For example, the Law of Settlement and

Removal of 1662 prevented those who needed help from moving from parish to parish to find that help (Alexander, 1995). That law and similar policies were designed to make certain that people received no more than they were entitled to receive by preventing them from collecting twice, in two different parishes. The law also helped maintain a labor pool in the parish so that employers could readily employ workers.

Although in our day assistance agencies try to follow careful procedures to prevent clients from collecting from more than one agency or receiving more than they are entitled to receive, aggressive efforts to prevent free movement from place to place have largely been abandoned. In fact, states are no longer permitted to impose residency requirements as conditions for receiving assistance.

Colonial Social Policy
Social policy in the American colonies was based, as might be expected, on the English laws, and during that time there was no central American government. Each colony passed and enforced its own laws. The first of the colonial poor laws was passed in Rhode Island in 1647 (Alexander, 1995).

In the colonies as well as in England a variety of methods was used to provide assistance to those in need who could not otherwise benefit from mutual assistance. Orphaned or abandoned children, for example, were often "farmed out" to the lowest bidder—sent to families where they could work for a very low fee: the receiving family would charge the parish for providing them with basic necessities. That practice is something of a forerunner of our system of foster care for children, although foster children cannot be required to work. In the 1536 act, idle children could be taken from their parents and indentured (Day, 2003). It is important to remember that these kinds of laws governing children were established before universal, compulsory education and, in fact, before children were viewed as special kinds of humans, with needs that were different from adults' needs, an attitude that persisted until late in the nineteenth century. The creation of child labor laws, for example, was a relatively late social policy development in the United States and elsewhere.

Workhouses and poorhouses, which were used to provide lodging and food to those who could not live on their own in return for productive work such as sewing military uniforms or farming surrounding property, were another form of social assistance during the colonial period.

An innovation that has continued to dominate public assistance was the provision of "outdoor" relief—that is, giving assistance directly to the person, or family, in need, within his or her own home, rather than in an institution. Assistance was also provided in two general forms—cash and kind—which have continued for the centuries during which social policy has been recorded. Cash is simply money, which the person or family can use as they choose in meeting their needs. Kind is assistance in the form of goods or services such as housing, food, clothing, and medical care. Cash and kind remain the methods of assistance in such diverse programs as financial aid, public or community housing, food stamps, and Medicaid, the medical welfare program of the United States.

Crises

One of the understandings of social policy that arises from the study of history is that human success or need often results not from the good or evil nature of the persons in need but is, instead, a consequence of social, economic, and natural forces, which change human circumstances, sometimes in astounding ways. For example, the bubonic plague, or Black Death, in the fourteenth century in Europe caused extensive suffering and need among large populations and created a social policy crisis. Similarly, the end of feudalism there, with its dislocation of the serfs, who had long relied on their feudal lords for support and been tied to them, and the Protestant Reformation, which ended the employment and support of many Roman Catholic people, created the need for help on a broad scale. In colonial America, Indian massacres and smallpox epidemics, among other crises, also caused otherwise self-sufficient people to become needy. More current phenomena, such as the Great Depression of the 1930s, as well as other economic dislocations, wars, droughts, famines, and epidemics such as AIDS are examples of the ways in which forces far beyond the control of individuals and families cause them to experience need.

There is still dispute in social policy debates, however, about the degree of responsibility individuals or families and larger social forces have for handling social problems and needs. How a society thinks about that issue is a significant factor in how that society will cope with its citizens' needs and how it will develop social policy.

Local Responsibility

It is critical to understanding social policy history in the United States to be aware that services were originally local rather than national. Local responsibility for services was reasonable in a time when life was local, economies were largely agricultural, and there were not yet such national innovations as stock exchanges and commodity markets or even provisions for the interchange of funds among localities. Communication and transportation of all kinds—mail, roads, vehicles—were limited. Larger units of government had limited responsibilities and powers, and matters had to be settled on a local level. A major phenomenon in the development of American social policy is the passing of primary social policy responsibility from local governments to increasingly higher levels of government. In the second half of the twentieth century the federal government became the unit with the largest influence over American social policy.

The Role of Voluntary Efforts

In early America, according to B. S. Jansson (2005), a strong tradition of private philanthropy developed rapidly before the American Revolution and continued after the nation was founded. He describes an early series of efforts to develop firefighting services, educational programs, and orphanages, sometimes with private funds and sometimes with partnerships between private donors and governments. Jansson (2005) emphasizes the importance of religious bodies in the development of American social welfare. Churches were among the few voluntary organizations that developed in early times. Protestant churches also incorporated ideas about the religious mandate to share one's blessings with the less fortunate.

Jane Addams and the Settlement Movement

Voluntary efforts were, of course, the essence of social welfare policies and programs in England as well as in the United States in its early days. Charity and other forms of aid through churches and voluntary efforts were the essential form of help in the early days of American social welfare. Actually, two nineteenth-century movements are often considered the primary antecedents of professional social work.

The first of these was the settlement house movement, which also operated in England, beginning with London's Toynbee Hall, which is still in operation. The primary figure in the American settlement movement was Jane Addams, who lived 1860–1935 and who founded Hull House, the first American settlement, in Chicago. She is remembered by a sculpture at Toynbee Hall, the institution that inspired her to begin Hull House (Quam, 1995).

At Hull House, Addams and many others who became top leaders in both public and voluntary social welfare provided educational and cultural activities for the disadvantaged people—often new immigrants to the United States—including citizenship and English language training. She also mobilized the people of her community to fight for their rights, often against entrenched elected officials in Chicago.

Settlements such as Hull House were the source of many important American social institutions such as community theater and community orchestras. They were also early providers of day care and child development programs. In some ways, religious and ethnic organizations such as the YMCAs and YWCAs as well as the Jewish Community Centers were based on the settlement movement.

The settlement movement spread to many other urban areas of the United States. Many still exist today and continue to provide services and opportunities to neighborhood residents. They were always located in low-income neighborhoods and worked to change those neighborhoods for the benefit of their residents. The residents of the neighborhoods change. The original settlements served groups such as immigrant Jews, Irish, and Italians, who are now often prosperous and well integrated into American life. Later groups such as persons from Africa and Asia as well as African Americans from rural areas and immigrants from Latin America became the members of settlements.

The community organization, social group work, and social planning movements and methods often trace their roots to settlement houses.

Mary Richmond and Charity Organizations

Mary Richmond (Longres, 1995) is considered one of the major founders of social work. In fact, she may be the most direct ancestor of the professional preparation of social workers because of her role in teaching in and conducting research in the New York School of Philanthropy, which was the forerunner of the first social work education program at Columbia University. Richmond called for the development of professional education for social work at the 1897 national Conference on Charities and Correction and began writing books on the processes of friendly visiting with the disadvantaged in 1899.

She was one of the earliest workers in the Charity Organization movement and worked for such organizations in Baltimore and Philadelphia. She was also involved in developing juvenile courts and services for deserted wives. Her most famous book is *Social Diagnosis*. In many ways, her efforts laid the basis for the professional practice of the profession. The Charity Organization societies were the original groups that led to the development of many current programs in the United States and around the world such as the family service societies and the community mental health movement.

Although she was an active social reformer as well as a direct services provider, she is often considered the founder of the social casework and related social work intervention methods.

In some ways, these early voluntary efforts were the ancestors of modern social work, which has two main forms of operation—direct practice with individuals to help them develop and change, and community work, to change larger systems for the benefit of individuals and families. These two approaches, although they may seem distinctive, are simply different routes for reaching the same objectives.

Residential Approaches

Throughout the history of social welfare in America, however, there has been a belief that disadvantaged people should not be coddled—that they should be helped only minimally lest they become dependent upon charity. The workhouse concept, the major form of "indoor relief," was a popular way of dealing with the needy. According to Jansson (2005), the Virginia Colony's legislative body decided in 1688 that every county should have a workhouse. New York also created a number of these facilities in the early and middle eighteenth century. Throughout the early years of U.S. history workhouses dotted the landscape. In later years the same facilities became "county farms," "poor farms," and other kinds of institutions for the poor, elderly, or disabled, which were in some ways forerunners of our current residential services for the aged. J. W. Landon (1985) says that these kinds of facilities were the primary means of dealing with poverty in early America. They were overcrowded, and the living conditions were poor. Of course, in a society that believed poverty resulted from the individual's character flaws (Colby, 1990), a punitive environment was a reasonable choice. Again, one of the significant developments throughout social welfare history has been the change from institutional care of the disadvantaged—including the poor, the disabled, the elderly, and children who could not live with their own families—to assistance to people in their own homes or to smaller, more homelike group facilities.

The Early Federal Role
Social assistance programs for the disadvantaged, as mentioned, began essentially as local services. The federal government, despite the clause in the preamble of the U.S. Constitution obliging it to "promote the general welfare," was not viewed as the level of government that ought to be involved directly or even indirectly in helping individual citizens. The role of the federal government was historically limited to matters such as international relations, operating the money system and the national banks, and resolving disputes between states.

That principle was most dramatically clarified by a presidential veto dealing with congressional legislation to provide help to persons with mental illness. A reformer of services to that group, Dorothea Dix, traveled the nation seeking financial support for decent housing and treatment and for the construction of state asylums. She and her supporters persuaded Congress to provide public land for the "insane," which Congress did, in the amount of ten million acres. Their legislation added care for the blind and deaf to services for mentally ill individuals (Axinn and Levin, 1997), yet President Franklin Pierce, one of the least-known American presidents, vetoed the legislation in 1854. In his veto message he acknowledged the responsibility of citizens to discharge a high and holy duty of providing for those who "are subject to want and disuse of body or mind." He concluded, however, that providing such help was not the job of the federal government: "I can not find any authority in the Constitution for making the Federal government the great almoner of public charity throughout the United States" (qtd. in Axinn and Levin, 1997, 47).

Both before and after the Pierce veto of the land grants pursued by Dix, charitable services were the province of private charities and state and local governments, not the U.S. government.

People with Mental Disabilities. Despite the Pierce veto of the Dix proposal, the federal government later became involved in helping the states with services for people with disabilities in a variety of ways. For example, in a pattern that has been used for many other kinds of efforts, including highways and law enforcement, the federal government gave grants to the states to help provide services to people with mental disabilities, including mental illness and mental retardation. As is discussed in chapter 7, in later years the government became active in providing funds to care for people with such disabilities in their homes, and in group facilities. Medicaid, the federal health assistance program for low-income people, also provides funding for care. So despite the fact that all of the land grant programs supported by Dix were vetoed and not attempted again, the principle of the federal government helping with the problems of disabled individuals has become and remains a part of federal responsibility and state action. The National Institute of Mental Health, founded in the 1950s, became a research, advocacy, and supportive organization for people with mental illness, under federal auspices and with federal financing.

War Veterans. From early in the nation's history there were federal programs for persons who were in need and who were clearly the responsibility of the federal government. After each war, beginning with the Revolutionary War, for example, financial assistance was provided to veterans and their widows and orphans (Axinn and Levin, 1997).

Native Americans. In one of the least humane examples of American social policy, the U.S. government also developed social policies regarding American Indians, who were on the continent before the European settlers. At the time the national government was created, and for many years thereafter, U.S. presidents, themselves white males, upheld the idea that white European Americans should control all of North America. When American Indians resisted and defended their territories, the national government responded with legislation, armed action, raids, and murders (Day, 2003). By the second half of the nineteenth century the American Indian population had been severely reduced, and those who remained were largely without power.

In 1824, the federal government established the Bureau of Indian Affairs, which was originally under the jurisdiction of the War Department but later moved to the Department of the Interior. The bureau has never been specifically a social welfare agency, but it has always carried out social policies regarding Indians. It is another example of the federal government's direct service relationships with some individuals. It was not until one hundred years after the establishment of the Bureau of Indian Affairs that Native Americans were made citizens of the United States, with passage of the Indian Citizenship Act in 1924 (Lewis, 1995).

Alaska Natives have a similar relationship with the federal government, although the issues they face and their cultural groupings are significantly different from those of American Indians. Of course, the relationship between the U.S. government and Alaska Natives began with the purchase of Alaska in 1871 and was modified when Alaska became a state in 1959 (Lally and Haynes, 1995).

The Civil War and Former Slaves. Federal policies were necessary after the Civil War to deal with the large number of freed slaves from the southern states whose state governments had been defeated by the federal government and were, therefore, unlikely to be of assistance. The United States established the Freedmen's Bureau, which existed from 1865 to 1872, to assist the former slaves economically, although, according to J. Leiby (1987), the policy itself was better than the execution of the policy. The federal bureau was quickly dissolved, and care of the former slaves was made a function of the local authorities within a few years.

With the exception of war veterans, Native Americans, immigrants upon their arrival to the nation, and former slaves, the U.S. government remained clear of direct helping relationships with individual citizens for most of its history, until the twentieth century. Social policy was the province of state and local governments and charities, which received their funds from contributions by private donors.

The Great Depression. A worldwide economic crisis was the impetus for the development of new national social policies and the greatest changes in the relationship of the U.S. government with its citizens. That crisis was the Great Depression, which began in 1929, under the presidency of Herbert Hoover, a Republican who was known for having organized a food relief program in Europe to help those who were unable to care for themselves at the end of World War I. There were several causes of the Great Depression, but the dramatic incident with which it began was the crash of the stock market. Its results were widespread unemployment, instant poverty for many who had been prospering, and very low prices—although few could purchase even low-priced goods (Jansson, 2005). By the time all the effects of the Depression were known, a large proportion of the American population was unable to provide for itself financially. It is difficult for middle- and upper-class Americans today to understand the atmosphere of that era, a time when many people suffered—or had close friends, neighbors, or relatives who suffered—from the crippling economic realities of poverty.

Simply put, the effects of the Depression were so pervasive that human need became a common, no longer an isolated, experience. The poor could no longer be blamed for their poverty; there were simply too many poor.

Even among the hardest-working, best-prepared people in the nation there were those who were unable to support themselves. Old means of providing assistance—such as charities, workhouses, and local relief programs financed primarily by donations—as well as the relative isolation of the federal government from its citizens, in terms of addressing social needs, became untenable. Nevertheless, President Hoover continued the policies of Pierce and agreed with the former president's ideology and interpretation of the Constitution on this matter—that social policy issues were the responsibility of local governments and private charities (Jansson, 2005).

Local governments, which relied upon local taxes, were, in fact, finding it difficult to survive. Those who were required to pay the taxes had few or no funds with which to pay. Many local governments could not support helping programs and certainly could not add thousands of impoverished citizens to their assistance rolls. Private charities, which relied upon funds from benefactors with sufficient means to make generous donations, could not sustain their services, in many cases, and certainly could not expand them to incorporate large numbers of newly disadvantaged people. The benefactors were as likely to have experienced financial reversals and unemployment as those they once supported.

In short, the entire social and economic structure of the United States was near collapse. The old rules could no longer prevail because new circumstances made them irrelevant.

Franklin Delano Roosevelt

In 1932 Franklin Delano Roosevelt of New York, often referred to as FDR, was elected president. He defeated Hoover under circumstances common to other elections in which an incumbent is not returned to office. When there are economic difficulties U.S voters tend to defeat incumbent presidents, a situation that Jimmy Carter, in 1980, and George Bush, in 1992, found to be true. In the 2004 election, in which President George W. Bush was reelected over John Kerry, the Democratic candidate, economic problems were of some concern to voters. Unemployment was relatively high, and some corporations and the jobs associated with them were "outsourced" to other nations during Bush's first term. However, a war in Iraq and concerns about terrorism (which is discussed later) appeared to be of greater concern. It may be that the less-than-severe economic problems (when compared to those of earlier economic crises) were outweighed in the minds of voters by concerns about safety and security.

Roosevelt was an exceptionally interesting president for those connected with human services. He was, for example, the only president who had a physical disability; as a consequence of polio, he could not walk and used a wheelchair to get around. He was also the only president to be elected more than twice. Others before FDR had voluntarily limited themselves to two terms. After Roosevelt the Constitution was amended so that no president would be allowed to run for more than two terms. But Roosevelt was elected three more times after his initial win in 1932—in 1936, 1940, and 1944. He died in office in 1945.

Franklin Roosevelt is remembered by social workers for more than those personal and political characteristics. He is best remembered for making major changes in the role and functions of the U.S. government.

The New Deal. Roosevelt called his legislative program the New Deal. Several of its elements were economic in emphasis and are, therefore, beyond the direct scope of this chapter. His major programs were directed toward the goals of restoring the U.S. economy, controlling the buying and selling of stocks and bonds, preventing future depressions, and providing the U.S. government with the authority to respond to economic crisis such as the Great Depression. His main tools followed the teachings of the economist John Maynard Keynes, whose ideas about economic policy are discussed in chapter 5. Several of his programs, however, had major social welfare connotations.

The New Deal Social Welfare Programs. Primary examples of the ways in which the New Deal established social welfare programs that dealt directly with individual citizens as means for reducing individual or family economic need were two programs, the Works Progress Administration (WPA) and the Civilian Conservation Corps (CCC). These had been preceded by other efforts such as the Federal Emergency Relief Administration (FERA), which also helped create jobs as well as providing other forms of assistance for promoting economic recovery. The FERA was headed by Roosevelt's top assistant in his social programs, Harry Hopkins, who is widely regarded as one of the most important figures in the historical development of social work.

The WPA was created by Roosevelt's executive order in 1935 and continued until 1943. It eventually provided jobs for eight million people. It provided for the creation of work in many fields, such as construction of public buildings and roads, as well as providing employment for artists and scholars who, for example, painted murals in public buildings and conducted research on social issues (Axinn and Levin, 1997). WPA workers received compensation that was greater than they would have received under relief programs. The WPA is the forerunner of many other work programs that followed it and that continue into the current era, such as the Manpower Development and Training Act of 1961, the Comprehensive Employment and Training Act (CETA) of 1973, the Job Training Partnership Act of 1982, and many others. The WPA marked the formal beginning of the federal government's interest and activity in job training, work experience, and employment for those who cannot obtain employment on their own (Jansson, 2005).

The Social Security Act of 1935. For human services workers, and perhaps for the domestic history of the United States, the most important of the New Deal innovations was the Social Security Act of 1935. It was and remains one of the most complex pieces of legislation ever passed in the nation. It established the fundamental social services policy of the United States and continued to govern most of human services provided to the nation's citizens. Although it preserved a major role for the states in the operation of some of its provisions, it established for all time that the U.S. government could have a direct, helping relationship with its citizens. B. S. Jansson (2005) calls the Social Security Act the Magna Carta of American welfare. He has good reason for his conclusion. The act touches or has the potential to touch the lives of all Americans.

The act was developed by many people who were early social workers and who became social workers, such as Eveline Burns (see chapter 8), Wilbur Cohen, and Ernest Witte. The days when the act was developed must have been exhilarating for those young social reformers. Their goal, and Roosevelt's, was not only to provide aid for people who were suffering from economic disadvantage but to prevent permanently such disadvantage in the future. The basic idea was to finance a system for the permanent security of the American people through an insurance program in which employed people would make contributions while they worked and receive benefits when they no longer worked. It was designed as a massive, low-cost insurance program that could end poverty once and for all. It also provided for those who were in temporary economic need and had provisions for the survivors of employed people who were covered by Social Security. An excellent source of information on the historical development of social policy in the United States is Berkowitz's *Mr. Social Security* (1995), a biography of Wilbur J. Cohen. Cohen was one of the main architects of all the programs in the Social Security Act, which include most of the programs that are associated with American social welfare policy.

Provisions of the Social Security Act. Financing of most of the Social Security Act insurance provisions comes from contributions paid by employees and their employers or by self-employed people alone. Virtually all working people in the United States are now covered, although there were many exceptions when the original act was passed. The amounts of the contributions have changed often over the years to reflect inflation and increased benefits.

The major provisions of the Social Security Act are

1. Old-Age and Survivors Insurance. This program provides for pensions for employees when they retire and payments to their surviving spouse and minor children should they die.

2. Disability Insurance. This program was added in the 1956 amendments and provides for payments to workers who are physically or mentally disabled and to eligible family members.

3. Medicare. This program was added in 1965 and provides health care insurance for people sixty-five years old and older as well as some younger people who have specific disabling health problems. A related component is Medicaid, another state and federally financed program that provides medical coverage for low-income people who are not old enough for Medicare as well as for Medicare recipients whose medical needs cost more than Medicare pays (Ozawa, 1987; Ginsberg, 1983).

4. Unemployment Compensation. This program provides cash benefits to people who have lost their jobs and is paid for by a tax on employers. It provides benefits for up to six months in amounts that vary from state to state. In time of great economic problems such as recessions, the period of time is often extended (Day, 1997).

5. Family Assistance. The Social Security Act included assistance for families whose members' work histories and contributions did not provide them enough social insurance benefits to take care of themselves if the wage earners grew old, died, or became disabled. Originally called Aid to Dependent Children, or ADC, the program later became Aid to Families with Dependent Children, or AFDC. It provided cash assistance from a combination of federal and state funds to poor families with children. The states determined the benefit levels, and the federal government provided matching funds proportionate to each state's per capita income. The lower the per capita income, the larger proportion the federal government contributed, even though the federal portion was always, even for the richest states, at least half the amount of the assistance checks. The Family Assistance Program, when it was ADC or AFDC, was carefully defined and restricted by the federal government. For example, the money provided had to be in cash—not in forms such as housing, food, or clothing. Until 1981 clients could not be required to work, although since then there has been a steady increase of client work requirements, which are discussed below. In 1996 the AFDC program was replaced by Temporary Assistance for Needy Families, or TANF, a radically different approach to assisting disadvantaged families. The new program is described in more detail in other sections of this book.

6. Supplementary Security Income (SSI). This is a program that, like TANF, is financed by general tax revenues, although in this case they are all federal funds, for low-income, elderly physically or mentally disabled, or blind people. Originally, the programs and services of SSI, which was created in 1972, were three federal-state programs for those now served by SSI, which were similar to the AFDC program. SSI placed the administration of

the programs with the federal government through the Social Security Administration, which also administers the social insurance program and sets national payment standards (Ginsberg, 1983).

7. The Maternal and Child Welfare Act was also part of Social Security. It established child welfare services in the states for dependent, neglected, homeless, and potentially delinquent children as well as vocational training and rehabilitation programs for physically and otherwise disabled children. It also provided funds for programs to promote the health of children and mothers through prenatal and birthing services for mothers (Day, 2000).

Clearly the Social Security Act became the primary source of social and economic assistance in the United States. It provides extensive services that go beyond those enumerated here, although for the most part it follows the persistent themes of social policy described in this chapter.

For example, those who receive services such as retirement benefits and Medicare are people who in all but a small number of cases contributed financially to the Social Security Trust Fund, in which the payments are deposited. The beneficiaries are expected to help themselves through a mechanism established by the government. The principle that those who receive assistance should generally be victims of forces that they cannot control is demonstrated by numerous provisions of many of the programs described here. For example, recipients of unemployment insurance must have been employed and must have lost their jobs through no fault of their own: those who voluntarily quit their jobs or who are fired for good cause are ineligible. Similarly, children are not expected to meet their own needs, and therefore TANF and the Maternal and Child Welfare Act provide for the young. Even though families are restricted by federal law to no more than five years of assistance (in some states as few as two years), cases in which children alone are served are exempt from those restrictions. In other words, a child who is living in a foster family or with relatives can continue to receive help. It is only the child living with his or her parent or parents who is restricted to five years of assistance from federal funds. The SSI services and the aid programs that were its forerunners are for older adults and persons with disabilities.

There are also features of the assistance provisions of the Social Security Act that require recipients to help themselves. The unemployed must be searching for work, for example, or must be involved in work training or experience programs. The 1996 change in the family assistance program, TANF, requires more work from clients. Most recipients of help have to be working or seeking work or involved in work experience or community service kinds of jobs. Work experience provides clients with a chance to work, often without pay, in public services, schools, and government programs. The clients receive their grants during the experience. The federal legislation sets specific requirements about the percentage of those receiving assistance who must be working if the state is not to be penalized by receiving fewer dollars. By 2002, for example, the state would have to demonstrate that half or more of those receiving assistance are employed in some way. The details of these work requirements and of other provisions of the law are provided in the appendix.

If recipients are working at jobs that are not subsidized or have not been created for assistance recipients, they must be paid the minimum wage at least, and they must be protected by the same kinds of labor and employment laws as other workers. Those who are in community service or work experience positions, however, can be paid less and do not have similar protections. Therefore, created jobs pay less than the lowest paid regular work, a principle that can be found in the 1601 Elizabethan Poor Law.

When Roosevelt died in 1945, Harry S. Truman, who had been vice president, succeeded him. Truman was also a significant figure for social welfare policy. As discussed in detail later in this book, he introduced legislation to guarantee full employment. He suggested national health insurance, which became a reality twenty years later with Medicaid and Medicare. By executive order, he also ended the segregation of black servicemen, and the military became the most integrated institution in the United States following Truman's bold executive action. He was re-elected in 1948, although he was not favored in the political polls at that time.

Rediscovering and Treating Poverty and the Civil Rights Movement—
the Kennedy and Johnson Presidencies
The most notable and active era for social policy development, after the New Deal, was in the 1960s, through programs and legislation introduced and supported by President John F. Kennedy and his successor, President Lyndon Johnson. President Kennedy called his program the New Frontier, and President Johnson called his the Great Society. The 1960s was a decade of major social ferment. Two separate but interrelated issues and phenomena marked the era, civil rights and affirmative action.

Civil Rights. Perhaps most significant in the development of the civil rights movement of the 1960s were events that occurred in the 1950s. Among these were the Supreme Court decision in a case called *Brown v. Board of Education,* in 1954, which brought an end to the South's long-standing policy of separating African American and white schoolchildren, an example of the ways in which courts actually make social policy. Until that decision, states were permitted to have "separate but equal" educational facilities for pupils. The effect of the *Brown v. Board of Education* decision was to decree that separate schools were inherently unequal schools. That decision was accompanied by many others requiring states to allow African Americans to enter formerly white-only colleges and universities and led to legislation guaranteeing such things as equal opportunity in employment and the end to discrimination in public places.

Another event of the 1950s that led to the civil rights changes of the 1960s was the Montgomery, Alabama, bus boycott in 1954, led by the Reverend Martin Luther King, Jr., who was assassinated in 1968 and whose birthday is now honored by a national holiday. King's boycott and the many other protests, demonstrations, and vigils that followed it were a major part of the impetus for the civil rights executive orders and legislation that followed.

It is difficult to explain the impact of the civil rights movement of the 1960s to those who did not live through the times that preceded it, especially in the South. That is because the changes are largely the elimination of certain acts rather than the development of new programs or structures. Until the 1960s, public facilities such as hotels, restaurants, theaters, and buses maintained strictly separate accommodations for African Americans and whites. Public parks had separate water fountains and bathrooms, one set marked White and another marked Colored. Likewise, buses posted statements that said the front was reserved for whites and the back for African Americans, then commonly called Colored or Negroes. Theaters had seats in the balcony for African Americans; main auditoriums were reserved for whites. In some places white and African American professionals were forbidden to hold meetings or have meals together, even in private facilities. White and African American athletes could not, of course, be on the same teams, and they were also forbidden to compete against one another in some sporting events. Some major southern colleges and universities, which now have large numbers of African American athletes, had none, and their sports teams were furthermore forbidden to play against teams that did. Housing was sold and rented in a discriminatory fashion. African Americans did not live in white neighborhoods, and African Americans and whites were not legally permitted to marry one another in many states.

African Americans protested, lobbied for legislation, sought relief in the courts, and, before the Kennedy-Johnson presidential era was over, had overturned virtually all of the legally sanctioned discriminatory practices that had been the pattern in the South and, in some ways, in the North as well for all of the twentieth century.

Leaders such as Thurgood Marshall, the National Association for the Advancement of Colored People (NAACP) attorney who designed the legal battles that led to the court decisions and, ultimately, much of the legislation that reduced discrimination against African Americans, prompted major social changes for the American population. He was appointed to the U.S. Supreme Court by President Lyndon Johnson and remained a justice until 1991.

The civil rights movement led to federal laws guaranteeing African Americans the right to vote and ending discrimination in education and employment and in "public accommodations" such as restaurants, theaters, and transportation. Of course, federal laws could not deal with all of the individual issues associated with the discriminatory practices in the United States. Many state and local governments passed laws, however, which applied the civil rights requirements of the federal laws to their own governments.

Among the many changes that resulted from the civil rights movement have been the election of large numbers of African Americans to public office, often in places where they might previously have had difficulty voting, and affirmative action policies that require employers with histories of discrimination to balance their work forces to include minority workers.

Affirmative Action. One of the social policy issues that has consistently been of interest to social workers is affirmative action. Affirmative action calls upon organizations to take steps that overcome prejudicial employment. For example, a company that has a history of an all-white, or predominately white-male work force might establish a plan to add to the company's diversity by recruiting and employing more qualified women and people of color.

Most of the recent issues dealing with affirmative action have to do with higher education admissions. Some state laws and Supreme Court cases suggest that affirmative action is not appropriate in the American constitutional system. However, the Supreme Court, in its most recent decisions, upheld the legality and constitutionality of affirmative action.

One source (*In Motion,* 2003) lists notable events in the more than forty-year history of affirmative action, which began with President Kennedy in 1961. The list, originally developed by an organization called Americans for a Fair Chance, follows below.

The History of Affirmative Action Policies
Americans for a Fair Chance Washington, D.C.
The following history of affirmative action policies is republished with the permission of Americans for Fair Chance and was updated as of August 7, 2003 by Shirley J. Wilcher, president, Wilcher Global LLC, and former executive director of Americans for a Fair Chance.

1961. President John F. Kennedy's Executive Order (E.O.) 10925 used affirmative action for the first time by instructing federal contractors to take "affirmative action to ensure that applicants are treated equally without regard to race, color, religion, sex, or national origin." Created the Committee on Equal Employment Opportunity.

1964. Civil Rights Act of 1964 was signed into law. This was landmark legislation prohibiting employment discrimination by large employers (over 15 employees), whether or not they have government contracts. Established the Equal Employment Opportunity Commission (EEOC).

1965. President Lyndon B. Johnson issued E.O. 11246, requiring all government contractors and subcontractors to take affirmative action to expand job opportunities for minorities. Established Office of Federal Contract Compliance (OFCC) in the Department of Labor to administer the order.

1967. President Johnson amended E.O. 11246 to include affirmative action for women. Federal contractors now required to make good-faith efforts to expand employment opportunities for women and minorities.

1970. The Labor Department, under President Richard M. Nixon, issued Order No. 4, authorizing flexible goals and timetables to correct "underutilization" of minorities by federal contractors.

1971. Order No. 4 was revised to include women.

1971. President Nixon issued E.O. 11625, directing federal agencies to develop comprehensive plans and specific program goals for a national Minority Business Enterprise (MBE) contracting program.

1973. The Nixon administration issued "Memorandum-Permissible Goals and Timetables in State and Local Government Employment Practices," distinguishing between proper goals and timetables and impermissible quotas.

1978. The U.S. Supreme Court in *Regents of the University of California v. Bakke,* 438 U.S. 912 (1978) upheld the use of race as one factor in choosing among qualified applicants for admission. At the same time, it also ruled unlawful the University Medical School's practice of reserving 18 seats in each entering class of 100 for disadvantaged minority students.

1979. President Jimmy Carter issued E.O. 12138, creating a National Women's Business Enterprise Policy and requiring each agency to take affirmative action to support women's business enterprises.

1979. The Supreme Court ruled in United Steel workers of America, *AFL-CIO v. Weber,* 444 U.S. 889 (1979) that race-conscious affirmative action efforts designed to eliminate a conspicuous racial imbalance in an employer's workforce resulting from past discrimination are permissible if they are temporary and do not violate the rights of white employees.

1983. President Ronald Reagan issued E.O. 12432, which directed each federal agency with substantial procurement or grant making authority to develop a Minority Business Enterprise (MBE) development plan.

1985. Efforts by some in the Reagan administration to repeal Executive Order 11246 were thwarted by defenders of affirmative action, including other Reagan administration officials, members of Congress from both parties, civil rights organizations and corporate leaders.

1986. The Supreme Court in *Local 128 of the Sheet Metal Workers' International Association v. EEOC,* 478 U.S. 421 (1986) upheld a judicially-ordered 29% minority "membership admission goal" for a union that had intentionally discriminated against minorities, confirming that courts may order race-conscious relief to correct and prevent future discrimination.

1987. The Supreme Court ruled in *Johnson v. Transportation Agency, Santa Clara County, California,* 480 U.S. 616 (1987) that a severe under-representation of women and minorities justified the use of race or sex as "one factor" in choosing among qualified candidates.

1989. The Supreme Court in *City of Richmond v. J. A. Croson Co.,* 488 U.S. 467 (1989) struck down Richmond's minority contracting program as unconstitutional, requiring that a state or local affirmative action program be supported by a "compelling interest" and be narrowly tailored to ensure that the program furthers that interest.

1994. In *Adarand Constructors, Inc. v. Pena,* 513 U.S. 1012 (1994) the Supreme Court held that a federal affirmative action program remains constitutional when narrowly tailored to accomplish a compelling government interest such as remedying discrimination.

1995. President Bill Clinton reviewed all affirmative action guidelines by federal agencies and declared his support for affirmative action programs by announcing the administration's policy of "Mend it, don't end it."

1995. Senator Robert Dole and Representative Charles Canady introduced the so-called Equal Opportunity Act in Congress. The act would prohibit race- or gender-based affirmative action in all federal programs.

1995. The Regents of the University of California voted to end affirmative action programs at all University of California campuses. Beginning in 1997 for graduate schools and 1998 for undergraduate admissions, officials at the University were no longer allowed to use race, gender, ethnicity or national origin as a factor in admissions decisions.

1995. The bipartisan *Glass Ceiling Commission* released a report on the endurance of barriers that deny women and minorities access to decision-making positions and issued a recommendation "that corporate America use affirmative action as a tool ensuring that all qualified individuals have equal access and opportunity to compete based on ability and merit."

1996. California's Proposition 209 passed by a narrow margin in the November election. Prop. 209 abolished all public-sector affirmative action programs in the state in employment, education and contracting. Clause (C) of Prop. 209 permits gender discrimination that is "reasonably necessary" to the "normal operation" of public education, employment and contracting.

1996. In *Texas v. Hopwood,* 518 U.S. 1033 (1996) the U.S. Court of Appeals for the Fifth Circuit ruled against the University of Texas, deciding that its law school's policy of considering race in the admissions process was a violation of the Constitution's equal-protection guarantee. The U.S. Supreme Court declined to hear an appeal of the ruling because the program at issue was no longer in use.

1997. Voters in Houston supported affirmative action programs in city contracting and hiring by rejecting an initiative that would banish such efforts. Houston proved that the wording on an initiative is a critical factor in influencing the voters' response. Instead of deceptively focusing attention on "preferential treatment," voters were asked directly if they wanted to "end affirmative action programs." They said no.

1997. The U.S. Supreme Court refused to hear a challenge to California's Prop. 209. By declining to review the case, the court did not decide the case on its merits but allowed Prop. 209 to go into effect.

1997. The U.S. House Judiciary Committee voted 17–9, on a bipartisan basis, to defeat legislation aimed at dismantling federal affirmative action programs for women and minorities. Representative George Gekas (R-Pa.), who moved to table the bill, said that the bill was "useless and counterproductive. I fear that forcing the issue at this time could jeopardize the daily progress being made in ensuring equality."

1997. Bill Lann Lee was appointed Acting Assistant Attorney General for Civil Rights after facing opposition to his confirmation because of his support for affirmative action when he worked for the NAACP Legal Defense and Educational Fund.

1997. Lawsuits were filed against the University of Michigan and the University of Washington, School of Law regarding their use of affirmative action policies in admissions standards.

1997. In response to Hopwood, the Texas legislature passed the Texas Ten Percent Plan, which ensures that the top ten percent of students at all high schools in Texas have guaranteed admission to the University of Texas and Texas A&M system, including the two flagships, UT—Austin and A&M College Station.

1998. Both the United States House of Representatives and the United States Senate thwarted attempts to eliminate specific affirmative action programs. Both houses rejected amendments to abolish the Disadvantaged Business Enterprise program funded through the Transportation Bill, and the House rejected an attempt to eliminate use of affirmative action in admissions in higher education programs funded through the Higher Education Act.

1998. Ban on use of affirmative action in admissions at the University of California went into effect. UC Berkeley had a 61% drop in admissions of African American, Latino/a and Native American students, and UCLA had a 36% decline.

1998. Voters in Washington passed Initiative 200 banning affirmative action in higher education, public contracting and hiring.

2000. Many Circuit Courts throughout the country heard cases regarding affirmative action in higher education, including the 5th Circuit in Texas

(Hopwood), the 6th Circuit in Michigan (Grutter and Gratz), the 9th Circuit in Washington (Smith), and the 11th Circuit in Georgia (Johnson). The same District Court in Michigan made two different rulings regarding affirmative action in Michigan, with one judge deciding that the undergraduate program was constitutional while another judge found the law school program unconstitutional.

2000. The Florida legislature passed "One Florida" Plan, banning affirmative action. The program also included the Talented 20% Plan that guarantees the top 20% admission to the University of Florida system.

2000. In an effort to promote equal pay, the US Department of Labor promulgated new affirmative action regulations including and Equal Opportunity Survey, which requires federal contractors to report hiring, termination, promotions and compensation data by minority status and gender. This is the first time in history that employers have been required to report information regarding compensation by gender and minority status to the federal equal employment agencies.

2000. The 10th Circuit issued an opinion in *Adarand Constructors v. Mineta,* 228 F.3d 1147 (10th Cir. 2000) and ruled that the Disadvantaged Business Enterprise as administered by the Department of Transportation was constitutional because it served a compelling government interest and was narrowly tailored to achieve that interest. The court also analyzed the constitutionality of the program in use when Adarand first filed suit in 1989 and determined that the previous program was unconstitutional. Adarand then petitioned the Supreme Court for a writ of certiorari.

2001. In *Adarand Constructors, Inc. v. Mineta,* 534 U.S. 103 (2001) the Supreme Court dismissed the case as "improvidently granted," thereby leaving undisturbed the 10th Circuit's decision, which upheld the government's revised federal contracting program.

2001. California enacted a new plan allowing the top 12.5% of high school student's admission to the UC system, either for all four years or after two years outside the system, and guaranteeing the top 4% of all high school seniors' admission into the UC system.

2002. The Sixth Circuit handed down its decision in *Grutter v. Bollinger,* 288 F.3d 732 (6th Cir. 2002) on May 14, 2002, and upheld as constitutional the use of race as one of many factors in making admissions decisions at the University of Michigan's Law School.

2003. The Supreme Court handed down its decisions in *Grutter v. Bollinger,* 539 U.S. (2003) and *Gratz v. Bollinger,* 539 U.S. 2003). In Grutter, the Court held that the University of Michigan's use of race among other factors in its law school admissions program was constitutional because the program furthered a compelling interest in obtaining "an educational benefit that flows from student body diversity." The Court also found that the law school's program was narrowly tailored; it was flexible, and provided for a "holistic" review of each applicant. In Gratz, the Court rejected the undergraduate admissions program at the College of Literature, Science and the Arts which granted points based on race and ethnicity and did not provide for a review of each applicant's entire file.

Other Affected Groups. Ultimately, the civil rights movement also led to changes in the treatment of other population groups including Latinos, Native Americans, gay men and lesbians, and people with disabilities.

A book about the civil rights movement, *Weary Feet, Rested Souls: A Guided History of the Civil Rights Movement* (Davis, 1998), provides names, photos, maps, and sites about the major figures and events involved in the civil rights movement.

The Antipoverty Movement. In 1960s Michael Harrington published his landmark book, *The Other America,* which influenced Presidents Kennedy and Johnson, legislators, social scientists, and social workers. Harrington documented what Kennedy had discovered during his 1960 campaign for the presidency—that, although the United States was thought to be a prosperous nation that had eliminated poverty with the Social Security Act, there were still large numbers of Americans who did not share that wealth. Kennedy was particularly moved by the poverty he saw in West Virginia, a state that was pivotal in his winning the Democratic presidential nomination. Kennedy made an issue of poverty in his campaign, along with other reform issues.

Early in Kennedy's presidency he established the Peace Corps, a program that has continued into the twenty-first century and that enrolls Americans in a two-year period of service in nations that seek Peace Corps help, mainly for development projects. Kennedy was also instrumental in arranging for the distribution of surplus food, purchased by the federal government as a means of maintaining farm prices, to low-income people. He also helped to establish the Appalachian Regional Commission, which was designed to provide economic development, education, and other services to help that historically disadvantaged region overcome its poverty.

Other kinds of social policy changes were made in the 1960s, many of them in areas that have long been of concern to social workers. For example, states were required to employ more professionally educated social workers to help people overcome the basic causes of their poverty rather than simply giving them assistance that, the Kennedy administration believed, would tend to perpetuate their dependence on government. Restrictive rules governing recipients of family assistance were liberalized so that families could work and retain a larger part of their earnings. Food stamps were introduced as an alternative to distributing surplus foods. Causes and cures for juvenile delinquency were studied, and some programs were attempted.

Poverty in the United States was not viewed as an ethnic minority problem. In fact, Harrington (1962) and others have continually reminded the nation that most of the American poor are white. However, minorities of color such as African Americans, Latinos, and Native Americans are disproportionately poorer than white Americans. That is, the percentage of minority populations who are poor is much greater than the percentage of whites who are. Therefore, it is assumed that real discrimination could not be overcome so long as minorities were denied social and economic justice or opportunity, even if their legal rights were protected. It was a time of great social unrest among minorities, especially African Americans, whose neighborhoods were the scenes of riots in many large American cities during the 1960s.

It was also a time of mass social action of other kinds, such as the development of the National Welfare Rights Organization, which protested against financial aid programs it considered to be punitive and lobbied for reforms. In general, following the demands for civil rights in the 1960s, there was great social concern and action about poverty and minority rights.

In that context Kennedy outlined, and Johnson worked with Congress to pass into law and implement, the Economic Opportunity Act of 1964, a comprehensive attack on poverty. The act established the Office of Economic Opportunity and put into place a variety of programs and services. Among them were Head Start, a program for preschool children; the Job Corps, a residential and job training program comparable in some ways to the Civilian Conservation Corps; work-study programs for students; and community action programs, which provide funds to local communities to make it possible for them to work on problems they identify themselves. Many of these programs continue to operate. In addition, there were accelerated efforts to place the unemployed and the underemployed in jobs, to develop training programs, and to create new aid programs for colleges and public schools. The federal government created Volunteers in Service to America (VISTA), which functions in impoverished areas of the United States in a manner similar to the Peace Corps overseas.

Many minorities were involved as participants in these programs and as staff members who helped operate them. While problems still remain, the combination of the civil rights and affirmative action reforms and the antipoverty efforts has made major changes in the socioeconomic status of minorities in the United States.

There were many other social policy changes associated with the Lyndon Johnson presidency, some of which were inspired by the Kennedy presidency. The Social Security Act was amended in 1965 to add Medicare for older adults and Medicaid for low-income families and individuals, two of the most costly and important social programs in American social policy.

From Nixon to Carter

From 1961 until 1981 social policy remained relatively constant. There were some additions to social services, including reforms in services to children. There were also some reductions in budgets and some efforts to reverse social policies that had been previously implemented. Although there were efforts at major social policy reform under President Richard Nixon, who was elected in 1968 and who introduced a sweeping welfare reform program called the Family Assistance Plan, and President Jimmy Carter, who introduced a similar plan called the Better Jobs and Incomes Program, through the presidencies of Nixon, Gerald Ford, who replaced Nixon when Nixon resigned, and Carter, elected in 1976, the nation did not substantially alter its social policies. Neither Nixon's nor Carter's plan was passed by Congress. Economic conditions that were less satisfactory than they had been in the 1960s led to some reductions in social programs. So did the lengthy, divisive, and expensive Vietnam War.

One of the reasons that the Nixon and Carter reforms failed to gain congressional approval was that they were projected to cost more than the existing programs. (Another was the opposition of the National Welfare Rights Organization, which thought the reform plans were not as generous as they should be.) Under President Nixon the federal government created the Supplemental Security Insurance program.

As discussed earlier, SSI combined the adult categories of assistance from the original Social Security Act. The development of SSI was a partial acceptance and implementation of the principles of Nixon's Family Assistance Plan. It placed responsibility for low-income older and disabled adults directly on the federal government and in the Social Security Administration.

The Reagan Years

In the 1980 presidential election Republican Ronald Reagan, former governor of California, defeated the incumbent, Jimmy Carter. Reagan had campaigned for, and ultimately implemented, policies that reduced social programs. His basic position was to remove the federal government from direct service relationships with citizens, which was the classic position of the Republican Party. Throughout the Reagan presidency, from 1981 through 1988, and, to a lesser extent under his vice president and successor, President George Bush, social programs were viewed largely as inappropriate for the federal government. The enunciated social policy was that the best solution to human problems was a strong economy—in which jobs would be plentiful and lucrative and in which investments would be profitable (Ginsberg, 1987, 1990). There were several reactions to and consequences of that policy. For one, Congress insisted on minimizing the reductions in social programs proposed by the presidents and, on its own initiative, added to them. Congress even passed, and President Reagan signed into law, a welfare reform plan, the

Family Support Act of 1988, which was somewhat similar to those plans proposed in the 1970s by Presidents Nixon and Carter.

The Family Support Act left assistance for families with the states, and the AFDC program remained a federal-state matching program. However, the Family Support Act required states to include families with two parents, an option under the law before 1988. It also increased the requirements of clients for training and work as conditions of receiving assistance.

Although political leaders such as Presidents Reagan and Bush might have preferred otherwise, the American commitment to social assistance programs has continued and grown since the major social policy developments of the New Deal. In 1992 the nation elected a new president, Bill Clinton. When he took office he undertook the establishment of youth services programs, health care reforms, and a number of other initiatives that resembled programs from John F. Kennedy's presidency. Among proponents of social policy and social provisions there was general enthusiasm for the new president.

The Clinton Presidency

The Clinton presidency embarked upon major changes in public welfare and the financing and structure of U.S. health care (which is discussed in greater detail in a later chapter). The former Arkansas governor took steps to eliminate some of the restrictions on abortions and to protect those who provided them. He enunciated policies to allow homosexuals to serve in the armed forces so long as they did not speak openly about their sexual orientation. Early in his term, laws were passed that provided additional funds to be used by local governments against crime and that set further restrictions on the sale of guns. Clinton's initiatives on health care reform, which involved task forces led by his wife, Hillary Rodham Clinton, and hundred of planners and commentators, did not pass Congress, largely because of opposition by elements of the health care industry, including health insurance companies and some providers. Citizens were reluctant to substitute a system with which they were often pleased for a new system that might not satisfy them.

In the midterm elections in 1994, the Clinton presidency was unsuccessful in its support of Democratic Party candidates, and the Republican Party won majorities in both houses of Congress for the first time since the Eisenhower era as well as the governorships of many states.

The next two years of the Clinton administration were dominated more by the actions of the U.S. Congress than by the initiatives of the president. With a Democratic executive branch and Republicans in control of the Congress, there were disputes between the branches about public policy, especially social policy. In some cases, compromises were reached. In others, President Clinton vetoed congressional actions. In yet others, bills were passed by the Congress over the president's vetoes. In 1995 and 1996 changes to the Medicaid

41

and Medicare programs were debated in an effort to hold down the increasing costs of health care—an effort similar in objectives but different in approach from President Clinton's failed proposals for health care financing reform, discussed earlier in this chapter. There was the related objective of reducing taxes as well, another popular idea, also discussed above and later in this chapter.

Some taxes, including taxes on the capital gains earned on property such as homes and stocks, were reduced. Many homeowners whose houses had increased in value and who had formerly been taxed on the increases when selling no longer had to pay those taxes. New Individual Retirement Accounts were developed that allowed many people to save money for retirement and pay no taxes on those savings.

For health care, new legislation was passed and signed by the president that extended government assistance for the health care of children. President Clinton also proposed that people younger than sixty-five be able to pay for and receive Medicare. For example, men in their fifties who had been laid off from their jobs would be able, under the president's proposal, to cover their health care needs through the Medicare program.

One of the most unusual and memorable events in recent U.S. political history was the preparation and implementation of the Contract with America, which was signed by 367 Republican candidates for Congress and became their platform during the 1994 election (Gillespie and Schellhas, 1994). The U.S. Senate, which was less deeply involved in the development of the Contract, was also less committed to its principles, although in 1995 it became the document on which much of the action in Congress was based.

In the 1994 election, as noted above, the Republican Party won majorities in the U.S. Senate and the House of Representatives for the first time in forty years and set about to enact its "contract." Much of the Contract with America had special significance for social welfare because, in many ways, it proposed an overhaul of the social welfare systems, a reduction in the size and influence of the federal government, and some major constitutional changes. The program led to efforts for a complete overhaul, as described earlier, of the AFDC program as well as changes in food stamps, Medicaid, and Medicare. One focus of the new Republican congressional majority and others was a reduction in the federal tax system, often at the higher income levels, in what is described in other parts of this book as a "trickle-up" approach to economic development.

Two of the key commitment proposals were a constitutional amendment that would require the United States to operate with a balanced budget and the provision of the line item veto for the president. Both of these failed to pass in 1995. However, the presidential line veto was passed by Congress in 1996, and President Clinton exercised the new power for the first time in 1997.

The line item veto allows the president to reject parts of bills sent by Congress, even though the balance of the bill becomes law. The president rejected some spending revisions, but his right to do so and the constitutionality of the presidential line item veto were challenged. The federal courts held that the line item veto was unconstitutional, and thus the new legislation and President Clinton's vetoes were invalidated.

The plan also called for a stronger national defense, a reduction in government regulations, and the creation of jobs, legal reforms, and limits on the terms of members of Congress, a proposition that was declared unconstitutional in the twenty-two states that had already enacted them by the U.S. Supreme Court in 1995 (*Time,* June 5, 1995).

The plan also called for stern action against violent criminals and steps to strengthen families and protect children. Among the proposals were financial assistance to families who would keep their elderly parents or grandparents at home, cash assistance for people who adopted children, and strong efforts to enforce child support orders and make absent parents pay. The authors of the Contract also proposed allowing senior citizens to keep more of their earnings and allowing tax deductions for those who purchase long-term-care insurance. There is an emphasis on reducing paperwork and federal regulations and on eliminating or reducing "unfunded mandates," requirements that the federal government places on states and localities but for which it provides no implementation funds. The Republicans in the House of Representatives worked long hours without breaks to pass and implement as much of their Contract as they could within the first hundred days of the congressional session.

The clear leader of the Contract with America, of the Republican successes in the 1994 congressional elections, and of the efforts to change the nation's social policies significantly was Georgia representative Newt Gingrich (Bruck, 1995; Gingrich, 1995). He had been the leader of the Republican minority in the House of Representatives when the Democrats were the majority. Now that the Republicans were the majority, he became the Speaker of the House, a position second in power, many believe, only to the presidency. He worked to help obtain funds for Republican congressional candidates, especially those running for the House. Many were grateful to him for their own elections and supported not only his candidacy for leadership but also his policy positions. According to Bruck, by 1995 Gingrich was able to ensure the passage of almost anything he wanted in the House of Representatives. He became one of the most interesting and frequently discussed political leaders in the nation. *Time* magazine named him the man of the year for 1995 (Gibbs and Tumulty, 1995–1996).

Despite or possibly because of his prominence and influence, Gingrich was investigated in 1996 and 1997 by the House of Representatives for using for political purposes money he had raised as educational funds. He was ordered to pay a fine of $300,000. In an interesting twist, the Republican presidential candidate defeated in 1996, Robert Dole, loaned Gingrich the money to pay the fine.

Several specific social welfare assistance programs were changed, as discussed in chapter 6. For example, the Aid to Families with Dependent Children program, which had been strongly controlled by the federal government since its inception in the New Deal, became more of a state-controlled program. States were permitted to impose limits on the length of time that assistance could be received, and federal funds were limited to five years of lifetime assistance to individuals. There was an attempt to eliminate assistance to women who bore children out of wedlock, but that provision was not finalized, in part because of the belief that it would increase the incidence of abortions.

As will be discussed in more detail in chapter 6, the provisions of the Contract with America dealing with public assistance were passed by Congress in 1996 as part of the Personal Responsibility and Work Opportunity Reconciliation Act of 1996. This act was implemented and began affecting low-income people in the United States in 1997. Complete descriptions of the former AFDC program and the new TANF, or Temporary Assistance for Needy Families, program that replaced it are provided in chapter 6 and the appendix. The details of the new program and its provisions are also discussed in Ginsberg's *Conservative Social Welfare Policy* (1998).

By 1998 the Personal Responsibility and Work Opportunity Reconciliation Act of 1996 appeared to be achieving some of its objectives, albeit during a time of economic strength. The South Carolina Department of Social Services, which was not very different from comparable departments in other states, studied 403 clients who had left the public assistance rolls in 1997 and found that two-thirds of them were working a year later (Stroud, 1998). Another 24 percent had worked but were not working at the time they were interviewed, and 14 percent had not worked at all since they left the assistance program (Stroud, 1998).

An important historical phenomenon tied closely to social welfare policy and services was public resistance to government itself. In the 1990s, many Americans again lost their positive feelings toward government because of what often appeared to be complicated and unreasonable administrative regulations. A best-selling book of 1994, *The Death of Common Sense* by Philip K. Howard, took the position that very little in administrative action is left to the wisdom of government officials. Instead, there are attempts to regulate everything with "self executing" regulations that are so cumbersome as to be almost unreadable. The book's examples of the cost of processing approvals for computer orders that could amount to the cost of the computers themselves;

of dozens of steps needed and hundreds of dollars required to change a lock in a public school; of environmental regulations that almost no one can understand but that almost anyone can inadvertently violate at the cost of losing one's business are all popular examples of the kinds of crises facing many people, according to the author. One story held that the tax return for the Chrysler Corporation was six feet tall, an example of wasteful use of resources that could be better spent improving products or lowering prices. The book hit a chord with governors, legislators, and even the president. Some began trying to eliminate regulations and replace them with the common-sense judgments of well-informed professionals.

Social welfare has traditionally been an area characterized by strict regulation. Reductions in regulations tend to have a major impact on social welfare programs and those who administer them.

Public Violence. Public violence was also an issue in the human welfare in the 1990s. For example, some two hundred people were killed in the bombing of the Murrah Federal Building in Oklahoma City. Blocks of public and private property were destroyed, and among the dead were several children who were being cared for in a day-care center in the facility. Timothy McVeigh was tried for the bombing, sentenced to death in 1997, and executed. An alleged accomplice, Terry Nichols, was tried for the crime later that year and found guilty of conspiracy and involuntary manslaughter and sentenced to life imprisonment.

Militia groups and others have strongly protested a 1993 incident in Waco, Texas, in which the headquarters of a religious organization called the Branch Davidians was destroyed in a battle with federal agents. One of the federal government's reasons for confronting the headquarters was the contention that there had been reports of child sexual abuse at the headquarters. Because the Murrah Federal Building was bombed exactly two years after the destruction of the Branch Davidian facility, some assumed that the explosion was an act of retaliation.

There is also hostility to the Internal Revenue Service and the income tax that it administers, as discussed earlier. Although it is not unusual for people to complain about taxes, hostility to the income tax has been profound, partly because of the level of taxation and partly because of the complexity of completing tax returns. Although it is probably the case that most Americans have no idea how much they pay each year in income taxes, they think it is a great deal—although the burden is less than it is in many other nations, especially industrialized nations in Europe and Asia. Speaker of the House of Representatives Newt Gingrich said that audiences invariably say yes when asked if they would spend an extra $10 or $200 a year in taxes if the tax system was less complicated and was perceived to be fairer.

Some proposed a "flat tax" instead of a graduated tax based upon income while others proposed that the idea of an income tax be abandoned completely and replaced with a value added tax, which is the most common form of taxation in much of the world. One of the leading proponents of the flat tax was Steve Forbes, a magazine editor who was a candidate for the Republican nomination for president in 1996 and 2000.

Concerns about taxation were also reflected in 1997 congressional hearings about the Internal Revenue Service, which administers the income tax. There were charges that taxation was unfair, discriminatory, and punitive. Based upon a convergence of various concerns and public policy positions, it seems possible that there will be major changes in the income tax system. Chapter 5 discusses public economic policy, including taxation and various alternative approaches to financing government.

The Contract with America also spoke of getting the federal government "off the backs" of Americans and devolving more and more programs, which had once been state programs, back to the states.

There are many other sources of discontent with government among Americans. Many custodial mothers were distressed that they were not receiving child support payments from their deserting, divorced, or otherwise absent husbands or partners. Strong federal and state government efforts were made, as described in chapter 6, to collect those payments and provide them to mothers and their children. Many fathers, however, equally resented being charged for child support when they felt they were unfairly kept from being with their children and felt that they might be equal or better parents than the custodial mothers.

In other words, there were strong and traditional reasons for many people to dislike the government, a pattern of American thinking that preceded the creation of the nation and the writing of the U.S. Constitution. Distrust and hostility toward government are traditional American attitudes in many ways (Dear, 1995).

The Future of Social Welfare

Dear (1995) says there are many reasons for optimism about social welfare developments in the next century, although he was writing before the major changes inspired by the Contract with America in 1995. His reasons are

1. Public expenditures for social welfare grew from almost nothing in the 1930s to the second largest government expenditure in the 1990s.

2. So many people are served by the social welfare system, which has become a part of everyday life, that it is not easy to reduce or eliminate any of the programs.

3. Programs for low-income people have continued to grow, despite some cutbacks and some support for totally eliminating them. Programs also cost

very little in the total scheme of government expenditures and, therefore, may not appear to be worth bothering to change.

4. Technological progress makes programs both more efficient and more necessary.

5. American society is becoming more tolerant of race and diversity of every kind, a phenomenon that seems to be associated with social welfare programs.

6. There was strong support of the then-current federal administration of President Bill Clinton and Vice President Al Gore for human services.

Dear was correct in many of his projections about social welfare. Clinton and Gore were reelected in 1996.

However, the programs for assistance to families became much more restrictive (as discussed earlier in this chapter, in chapter 6, and in the appendix, which outlines the new program of Temporary Assistance for Needy Families). Lifetime restrictions on receiving assistance and large reductions in the number of people receiving family welfare aid were experienced in the late 1990s. There was also a much stronger economy and much greater employment opportunity for more Americans, including low-income family members, and these conditions may have contributed to the reason for the reductions in assistance. However, the major changes in the family assistance program indicate a retreat from welfare assistance for low-income families even though overall efforts of the nation to help disadvantaged people may continue to increase.

Most of the criticism of social welfare programs has been about assistance to employment-age adults; there are few serious advocates of large-scale reductions in programs for children or for the elderly. In fact, most programs in some way are associated with providing help to older people and to children. Therefore, any reductions, if they were targeted to other groups, would have to be small because most services are associated with those two most vulnerable groups. There may be differences of opinion about how to care for them, but caring for them will probably remain a high priority.

Although Clinton and Gore were reelected by a large margin in 1996, they were also subjected to public criticism over issues of campaign financing and, in Clinton's case, allegations of harassment by Paula Jones, an employee of the state of Arkansas when Clinton was governor. Therefore, the leading figures in modern social welfare policy, Clinton, Gingrich, and Gore, were all three preoccupied with charges of misconduct in office.

Perhaps the most damaging charges were those against President Clinton, who, along with others in his administration, was investigated for years and at great public financial cost by a special federal prosecutor, Kenneth Starr. A series of investments and financial dealings in Arkansas under the Clinton governorship was called Whitewater, and although neither the president nor his wife was specifically charged, members of the administrations in both Arkansas and Washington were found guilty of crimes. Some were fined and served prison sentences.

In 1998 the president was charged with having sex with a presidential intern, Monica Lewinsky, in the White House, and with lying in courts about that relationship. He ultimately admitted, in some detail, to the relationship but denied having lied to courts about it, which would have constituted the crime of perjury.

The special prosecutor turned his information over to Congress and said that the president had engaged in acts that could lead to impeachment—a process for removing executive branch members, including presidents, from office. The House of Representatives impeached Clinton (sent him to the Senate for a decision on whether he should be removed from office) in 1998. In 1999 he became the first president since Andrew Johnson to be tried by the U.S. Senate for removal from office. A vote of two-thirds for removal ends the career of an executive branch official.

The House considered four charges against the president but only approved two: perjury, for not telling the truth in grand jury testimony, and obstruction of justice, for misleading his staff about his actions. After a lengthy trial in which the Republican members of the House of Representatives Judiciary Committee served as "managers," or prosecutors, the Senate found him not guilty of perjury and split the vote, fifty for guilty and fifty for not guilty, on the charge of obstruction of justice. The Democratic senators voted against removing the president from office while most of the Republican senators voted for his removal. The Republicans held a majority in the Senate but lacked the two-thirds majority needed to remove President Clinton. Therefore he retained the presidency.

The 1998 Election

Typically, in American "off-year elections," when there is no election for president, voter turnout is low, and the party that does not have the presidency gains seats in the House of Representatives and Senate. However, in the 1998 elections, in the midst of discussions of impeaching and removing Clinton from office, the Republican Party did not fare well. For the first time in recent history, the party that did not control the White House, the Republicans, lost seats in the House. For 1998 five more Democrats were elected than Republicans when, normally, the Republicans would have gained seats. The Senate balance between Democrats and Republicans stayed exactly the same as it had been before the election. Although the number of state governors remained the same for the Democrats, the Republicans ended the election with one less governor. An independent candidate, Jesse Ventura, a former professional wrestler, was elected governor of Minnesota over his Democratic and Republican opponents.

The failure of the Republicans to add seats in Congress disturbed many Republicans, and within days of the election it became clear that Speaker Newt Gingrich could not be reelected to head the House of Representatives. Some blamed him for pressing for the president's impeachment, which appeared to be unpopular with voters and a reason for the Democratic Party's 1998 successes. Others also said that he had authorized and encouraged the use of anti-Clinton television advertisements that had led people to vote against, rather than for, the Republicans. Gingrich now fell from power and even resigned his position as a member of Congress from Georgia, to which he had been reelected in 1998 by a large margin. Representative Bob Livingston, a Republican from Louisiana, was elected to replace Gingrich as Speaker.

However, Larry Flynt of *Hustler* magazine, who offered cash rewards for proof of sexual affairs with members of Congress, revealed that Livingston was identified as one such congressman. Livingston admitted that Flynt was correct and announced that he would later resign from Congress. Instead of Livingston, fellow Republican J. Dennis Hastert of Illinois became Speaker in 1999. Representative Henry Hyde of Illinois, the leader of the impeachment process, admitted that he had had a romantic liaison while both he and his partner were married in earlier years. Hyde served as chair of the House Judiciary Committee, which is responsible for issues such as impeachment, and as chief prosecutor of the case against President Clinton that was tried in the Senate.

It is possible that welfare was a decisive factor in the 1998 election—because it was no longer an issue. The Personal Responsibility and Work Opportunity Reconciliation Act of 1996, which is described in this chapter and others and detailed in the appendix, perhaps ended the kinds of concerns that earned support for Republican positions and candidates. Some criticized the Republicans for having no programs to promote in their election efforts.

Whatever all the reasons and issues, 1999 began with major changes in the Republican congressional leadership while President Clinton remained in office.

The George W. Bush Era

The major development of the year 2000, other than its signifying the beginning of the new millennium, was the resurgence in some ways of the Republican Party. George W. Bush, who was serving at the time of his election as governor of Texas, became president by defeating Al Gore, vice president under Clinton, in a very close election. In fact, the majority of the popular votes were for Gore rather than for Bush. The election was decided after a complicated and disputed process, in which the actual ballots in the state of

Florida appeared, to some, to be out of order. Voting machine problems made some ballots appear to be designated for candidates other than those for whom the voter intended to vote. The U.S. Supreme Court declared Bush the winner of the Florida electoral votes and, therefore, the 2000 election. The Florida electoral votes were all that were left to be determined to settle the election. The U.S. Supreme Court acted after the Florida Supreme Court had indicated that the vote should have gone for Gore because of some of the complicated issues of voting machine reliability and absentee ballots, including those of military personnel.

Social welfare issues were not a major point of discussion in the 2000 election. In some ways, the issue of welfare reform was settled with the 1996 legislation described earlier in this chapter.

The Republicans finished the election in control of the House of Representatives and with a fifty-fifty split in the Senate. However, one member of the Senate changed his party affiliation from Republican to independent, which gave the Democrats a one seat majority.

The September 11, 2001, Attacks and Their Aftermath

Perhaps the most alarming development of the early part of the new century, for Americans at least, was the destruction of the World Trade Center Towers in New York on September 11, 2001. This was a hostile act in which affiliates of Al Qaeda, a radical Muslim movement headed by Osama bin Laden, hijacked four American airplanes and flew two of them, including the passengers and the hijacker pilots, into the World Trade Center Towers. The Towers were destroyed by the action and the former site of the World Trade Center became known as Ground Zero. Another hijacked plane was flown into the Pentagon, killing and injuring hundreds of persons in that building in Washington, D.C., in addition to the passengers and hijackers on the plane.

A fourth hijacked plane was apparently crashed into the Pennsylvania countryside as a result of an offensive by some of the passengers to keep the plane from being used to destroy more American property and people. By the time the plane was in the air, the passengers knew what the Al Qaeda group was doing. All the passengers on that fourth plane, too, were killed when it crashed.

Americans were unaccustomed to such international violence and to attacks on the U.S. mainland.

The World Trade Center loss of life was some 3,000 people, although it took months to locate and identify the bodies, not all of which were found. A major social welfare issue was that of determining how to address the losses of family members of those who died in the attacks. Government and private donations were provided for those families and survivors of the casualties. Several social welfare issues emerged such as the ways in which to equitably distribute the available funds. In addition, there were issues about contributions made to the American Red Cross and the United Way of America. Both were criticized by some of the public and the press for their decisions about the allocation of funds, because of the delays in allocating the funds, and because of overhead costs that were charged for the distribution of the funds.

Of course, a disaster of that magnitude inevitably led to some of the most basic kinds of social welfare problems—the loss of breadwinners and the loss of one or in some cases both parents. Widows and widowers, orphans, persons without an employed family member, all emergend from what came to be called the attacks of 9/11.

The attacks led to more events, many of which had some social welfare implications, at least for the people and communities that were involved. For example, the United States embarked upon an attack on Afghanistan, the nation in which the Al Qaeda organization was headquartered with the Taliban, a radical Islamist party that controlled Afghanistan. The Taliban was defeated and Afghanistan had a new government after the actions of the United States and several of its allies.

In 2003, the United States invaded Iraq, a nation that had been the enemy in the Persian Gulf War in 1991. In that earlier war, Iraq had invaded and wanted to annex Kuwait. The United States and other nations intervened to stop that action. Although it was assumed by some that Iraq was involved in the World Trade Center actions and harbored weapons of mass destruction, there was no convincing evidence that was the case. The United States considered Iraq a threat to peace. Many other nations did not support the U.S. efforts in Iraq. Nonetheless, by 2004, the leader of Iraq, Saddam Hussein, had been deposed and captured and the U.S. and allied forces occupied the nation. However, guerrilla-type action in Iraq, perhaps connected with Al Qaeda, continued the violence, much of it directed toward American troops and others who were associated with the U.S. effort.

Violence carried out by radical groups of Islamists led to the destruction of life in places as different as Bali and Russia. Rebels from the province of Chechnya, in two separate incidences, kidnapped the patrons of a movie theater and took schoolchildren as hostages. Many died when the Russians used a chemical gas to overcome the movie theater hijackers. Many of the schoolchildren died as well.

The 2002 Elections: Thurmond and Lott
In the 2002 election, Americans voted largely for Republican candidates and both the Senate and the House came under Republican Party control.

One of the remarkable incidents of 2002 was the hundredth birthday of Senator Strom Thurmond of South Carolina, who had, in 1948, led the Democrats from several southern states out of the Democratic Party into a third party called the States Rights Party but more commonly called the Dixiecrats.

Thurmond, who had been a Democrat, as were most southern politicians, was a perennial electoral favorite in South Carolina. He had been governor and later became senator as a write-in candidate. He served longer in the Senate than anyone else in history. He later switched to the Republican Party. The South, which had been solidly Democratic, became just as solidly Republican beginning in the 1950s.

Thurmond, himself, however, continued, in some ways, in opposition to early civil rights legislation and was the major foe of that early legislation in the U.S. Congress. However, as decisions such as *Brown v. Board of Education,* which commanded the integration of the public schools, and other court decisions as well as legislative action just as the various civil rights bills became the law of the land, Thurmond changed with the times and rarely, if ever, spoke as a segregationist or a leader in the oppression of the African American population. At Thurmond's hundredth birthday party, the Republican majority leader of the Senate, Trent Lott of Mississippi, made comments suggesting that if the country had voted for Strom Thurmond for president in 1948, that the United States would not have had as many "problems" as it had faced in the succeeding years.

Everyone from President Bush to the least involved local officials condemned Lott's statements and called for apologies. By December 2002 Lott was so discredited that he resigned as majority leader in the Senate, although he retained his Senate seat.

In late 2003, Thurmond's survivors confirmed that he was the father of a seventy-eight-year-old retired California teacher, Essie Mae Washington-Williams. At age twenty-two, before he was married, he had fathered Mrs. Washington-Williams with a sixteen-year-old African American, the family maid. All parties kept the relationship secret.

Religion and Religious Issues
One of the issues in the days leading up to the Iraq war was the perception of the United States and its president as religious zealots. *Newsweek* quotes a French magazine editor as saying "how do you go around denouncing Muslim fundamentalism when in every one of Bush's speeches he talks about God?" (Hirsh et. al., 2003, 37). According to the *Newsweek* report, some Europeans were upset with the president's religiosity because they had, for centuries, fought religious wars in Europe to the detriment of the European nations' peoples. At one point, Bush had called the effort to deal with Muslim terrorists a crusade, something that concerned the Arab world because the Crusades had been holy wars conducted by Christians against Arabs—but the president apologized for his choice of metaphors.

President Bush, as mentioned earlier, supported faith-based initiatives and worked to bring religion and government closer, inappropriately, some believed, although he relied on the support of Jewish and Muslim leaders as well as Christians.

In the United States, there were growing religious differences as well as pluralism. Adherents to mainline Christian denominations such as the Methodists and Presbyterians sometimes found themselves at odds with the more fundamentalist "religious right" groups over issues such as the ordination of women ministers, marriage between people of the same gender, and the teaching of evolution as opposed to creationism, which some thought was the process described in the Bible. Increasingly, the United States was home to many religious persuasions—not only the traditional Catholic, Jewish, and Protestant groups, but many other traditions as well.

In some ways, the world seemed to be dividing into distinct religious groupings—Islamic religious groups, which in some nations were paired with governments and which followed Muslim religious rulings as the law; secular groups in much of the industrialized world, especially in some parts of Europe, Australia, and New Zealand; strong Roman Catholic societies in parts of Latin America; as well as strong Hindu and Buddhist devotion in much of Asia. Not all of these groups conflict with one another but, as the Europeans had come to believe, religious conflict is sometimes the most violent conflict.

Conclusion

The history of assistance programs for the socially and economically disadvantaged is lengthy. It can be traced to earliest times. That history shows that societies are generally unwilling to see their members go without adequate food, clothing, and shelter and that they typically take steps to prevent or otherwise address such problems.

Certain principles of assistance have long persisted among civilized societies. They provide that assistance ought to be adequate but no so generous that it discourages work; whenever possible, societies insist that those who receive help contribute something to the society through work or training for work. The abiding social policy principles also suggest that societies divide their needy persons into those who appear to be able to help themselves and those who appear to be unable to do so.

Discussion Questions

1. How fair is the concept that no one should receive assistance that is greater than the lowest-paid worker's earnings? Could family size or special conditions such as age or disability raise questions about the concept?

2. What are some of the primary similarities and differences between the social assistance programs of the New Deal and the programs of the Kennedy and Johnson presidencies?

3. Discuss the ways in which the civil rights movement and the movements for improved social programs were related.

4. Describe what you believe are the underlying differences in the concepts of social policy between Presidents Johnson and Reagan and between presidents George H. W. Bush and Clinton.

5. What indications of protest against government are currently being discussed in the media? Have they changed since that section of the book was written, or are the trends mentioned continuing to grow? Are there new protests?

6. Discuss some of the ways the Personal Responsibility and Work Opportunity Reconciliation Act of 1996 changed the family assistance program created by the Social Security Act.

References

Alexander, C. A. (1995). In R. L. Edwards et al. (Eds.), *Encyclopedia of social work,* 19th ed., 2631–2664. Washington, DC: NASW Press.

Axinn, J., & Levin, H. (1997). *Social welfare: A history of the American response to need,* 4th ed. New York: Longman.

Axinn, J., & Stern, M. J. (2005). *Social welfare: A history of the American response to need,* 6th ed. Boston: Allyn and Bacon.

Berkowitz, E. D. (1995). *Mr. Social Security.* Lawrence: University of Kansas Press.

Brown v. Board of Education of Topeka, Kansas. (1954). 74 SC 686.

Bruck, C. (October 9, 1995). Profile: The politics of perception. *New Yorker,* 50–76.

Colby, I. (1990). American social welfare: Miles to go before I sleep. . . . In D. Elliott, N. S. Mayadas, and T. D. Watts (Eds.), *The world of social welfare: Social welfare and services in an international context,* 13–34. Springfield, IL: Charles C. Thomas.

Davis, T. (1998). *Weary feet, rested souls: A guided history of the civil rights movement.* New York: W. W. Norton and Company.

Day, P. J. (1997). *A new history of social welfare,* 2nd ed. Englewood Cliffs, NJ: Prentice-Hall.

Day, P. J. (2003). *A new history of social welfare,* 4th ed. Boston: Allyn and Bacon.

Dickinson, N. S. (1995). Federal social legislation from 1961 to 1994. In R. L. Edwards et al. (Eds.), *Encyclopedia of social work,* 19th ed., 1005–1013. Washington, DC: NASW Press.

Gibbs, N., & Tumulty, K. (December 25, 1995–January 1, 1996). Man of the year. *Time,* 48–87.

Gillespie, E., & Shelhas, B. (1994). *Contract with America.* New York: Random House.

Gingrich, N. (1995). *To renew America.* New York: Harper Collins.

Ginsberg, L. (1983). *The practice of social work in public welfare.* New York: Free Press.

Ginsberg, L. (1987). Economic, political and social context. In A. Minahan et al. (Eds.), *Encyclopedia of social work,* 18th ed., xxxiii–xli. Silver Spring, MD: NASW Press.

Ginsberg, L. (1990). Introduction. In L. Ginsberg et al. (Eds.), *Supplement to the Encyclopedia of social work,* 18th ed., 1990 suppl., 1–11. Silver Spring, MD: NASW Press.

Ginsberg, L. (1995). *Social work almanac,* 2nd ed. Washington, DC: NASW Press.

Ginsberg, L. (1998). *Conservative social welfare policy: Description and analysis.* Chicago: Nelson-Hall.

Harrington, M. (1962). *The other America.* New York: Macmillan.

Hirsh, M., et al. (March 10, 2003). Blood, oil, and Iraq. *Newsweek,* 37–38.

Howard, P. K. (1994). *The death of common sense: How law is suffocating America.* New York: Random House.

Jansson, B. S. (2005). *The reluctant welfare state: A history of American social welfare policies,* 5th ed. Cambria, CA: Wadsworth.

Katz, M. B. (1989). *The undeserving poor: From the war on poverty to the war on welfare.* New York: Pantheon.

Lally, E. M., & Haynes, H. A. (1995). Alaska Natives. In R. L. Edwards et al. (Eds.), *Encyclopedia of social work,* 19th ed., 194–203. Washington, DC: NASW Press.

Landon, J. W. (1985). *The development of social welfare.* New York: Human Sciences.

Leiby, J. (1987). History of social welfare. In A. Minahan et al. (Eds.), *Encyclopedia of social work,* 18th ed., 755–777. Silver Spring, MD: NASW Press.

Lewis, R. G. (1995). American Indians. In R. L. Edwards et al. (Eds.), *Encyclopedia of social work,* 19th ed., 216–225. Washington, DC: NASW Press.

Longres, J. F. (1995). Mary Richmond. In R. L. Edwards et al. (Eds.), *Encyclopedia of social work,* 19th ed., 2605. Washington, DC: NASW Press.

Noble, C. (1997). *Welfare as we knew it: A political history of the American welfare state.* New York: Oxford University Press.

Quam, J. K. (1995). Jane Addams. In R. L. Edwards et al. (Eds.), *Encyclopedia of social work,* 19th ed., 2571–2572. Washington, DC: NASW Press.

Reid, P. N. (1995). Social welfare history. In R. L. Edwards et al. (Eds.), *Encyclopedia of social work,* 19th ed., 2206–2225. Washington, DC: NASW Press.

Stroud, J. S. (November 14, 1998). Off welfare, most finding jobs. *State* (Columbia, SC), B1–2.

Term limits: The fight dies hard (June 5, 1995). *Time,* 25.

Tracy, M. B., & Ozawa, M. N. (1995). Social security. In R. L. Edwards et al. (Eds.), *Encyclopedia of social work,* 19th ed., 2186–2195. Washington, DC: NASW Press.

THREE

The Social Problems and Social Issues Component

Social problems are the targets of social policies. It is impossible to talk about social policy history, analysis, or provisions without referring to the social problems those policies are designed to address. Throughout this book social problems are identified as the sources of social policy and programs. Were it not for the problems and the perception that those problems need to be resolved, there would be no interest in a society's developing these policies and programs.

Some of the scholarship and courses about social policy focus, in large measure, on social problems. In addition to social work courses on social welfare policy and services, courses on social problems are offered in many other fields, especially sociology. Like others of the components discussed in this book, the social problems field is, in some ways, a discipline unto itself with its own specialized scholarship and literature.

This chapter covers the social problems component of social policy. It suggests some conceptualizations of problems and provides methods for distinguishing social problems from more isolated, personal problems. It also includes examples of current social problems as well as analyses of how they came to be identified as such.

What Is a Social Problem?

Although the term has been used frequently in this book, as if the authors and the readers fully understood the term's meaning, there is actually a need to clarify just what is and what is not a social problem. Several authors have provided definitions of the term. R. W. Maris (1988, 6), a sociologist, says, "*Social problems* can be defined as general patterns of human behavior or social conditions that are perceived to be threats to society by significant numbers of the population, powerful groups, or charismatic individuals and that could be resolved or remedied." R. L. Barker (2003, 405) says that social problems involve "conditions between people leading to social responses

that violate some people's values and norms and cause emotional or economic suffering."

It is noteworthy that Barker's definition includes social responses, which is
another term for social policy, while Maris's definition does not. Barker, a
social worker whose *The Social Work Dictionary* was reviewed and, in some
cases, modified by many social workers before it was published, appears to
take the position that a problem is not really a social problem until society
decides to do something about it. Maris agrees, however, that social problems
ordinarily, at least potentially, have solutions. It would be difficult to say, for
example, that earthquakes and other natural forces are social problems; they
are not because they cannot be controlled or stopped. Aspects of the consequences of earthquakes, however, could be defined as social problems. Lack
of preparedness to deal with earthquakes in earthquake-prone areas could be
defined as a social problem. It meets Maris's and Barker's definitions, and
there are possible solutions. Similarly, when people continue to be allowed to
build residences along faults, that may also be defined as a social problem.

Among the most important theoreticians of social problems was the sociologist C. Wright Mills (1959), who helped make the distinction, implicit in
both Maris's and Barker's definitions, between the private troubles of the
individual and the social problems of the broader public and the society. Private troubles—those that impact relatively few people—may be tragic, yet they
constitute social problems only when they affect large numbers and when
society, as represented by government, sees the troubles as a threat to many
people or to the whole society. Threats may be perceived to exist when the
consequences of the problem are costly, when others fear they will be injured
because of the problem, or when people believe that they might be victims of
the problems. There are many humorous and ironic aphorisms that illustrate
the differences between private troubles and social problems. One is: "How
do you tell the difference between an economic recession and an economic
depression?" The answer, which has been attributed to President Harry Truman, is: "It's a recession when your neighbor loses his job; it's a depression
when you lose your own" (England & Anderson, 1992, 3–D4).

When AIDS, or acquired immunodeficiency syndrome, the disease affecting an alarming number of human beings worldwide, appeared to be a condition that affected small numbers of gay men and intravenous drug users, it
was thought of as a private trouble. When it became clear that AIDS affected
a wide range of people, including heterosexuals, and that it was quickly
spreading, governments and those they represent began to perceive it as a
social problem. According to the Centers for Disease Control, a federal agency,
there were an estimated 886,585 diagnosed cases of AIDS in the United
States by 2002. The overwhelming majority, 718,002, were among males and
the rest females. Of the overall total, 9,300 were children under 13. Of those

57

diagnosed, it was estimated that 501,669 had died of the illness by the end of 2002, 5,315 of whom were children. Not all AIDS cases are sexually transmitted. Some 240,000 of the total result from injection of drugs. And although the majority are products of male to male sexual contact, 135,628 cases were from heterosexual contact. New York, California, and Florida have the largest numbers of AIDS cases. Of course, the illness is not confined to the United States. Some 40 million people are living with AIDS around the world (National Center for HIV, STD, TB Prevention, 2003).

There are varying reactions to social problems. What appears to be a solution to a problem to one group of observers is viewed as yet another problem to others. For example, some social workers will say that the major social problem in the United States is poverty. They may cite the low payment levels and time limits for receiving Temporary Assistance for Needy Families. But the earlier AFDC program was eliminated and replaced by TANF because Charles Murray (1994) and others insisted that family welfare programs in themselves were the major cause of poverty. Congress was persuaded that assistance caused poverty rather than curing it and that the best solution to the problem of poverty was eliminating those programs. Ginsberg's 1998 book on conservative ideas about assistance describes some of the ways that programs to help eliminate poverty came to be perceived as the causes of the problems they purported to solve.

For some, a major social problem is the unwillingness of elected officials to use the death penalty for major crimes. For others the existence of the death penalty is the real social problem.

When President Bill Clinton, in 1993, proposed a social policy to deal with what he perceived as a problem—discrimination against gay men and lesbian women in the military—others said that the real problem was the possibility that the president would revise the discriminatory policies. As we will see, values affect perceptions of social problems. What does and does not constitute a social problem depends upon the values of the observer. Societies define issues as social problems when there is widespread concern about those problems among the citizenry. A classic community organization scholar, Murray G. Ross (1967), helped generations of social workers understand that communities have coalesced only around problems or needs that they themselves have considered significant, not necessarily problems that external experts have identified as social problems. It is the shared belief that the problem represents a serious threat to a community or the larger society that provides people with the will to do something about it.

An interesting means for studying social problems is used by the Fordham Institute for Innovation in Social Policy. Among its efforts is the publication each year of its "Index of Social Health," which translates sixteen social problems into one figure, based upon progress or decline in the statistics governing those problems. The 1995 index, for example, was 41, compared to an index of 75.3 in 1970 (Miringoff, 1995). The large decline represents a major decline in the nation's social health. The institute studies indicators such as infant mortality, poverty among the aging, unemployment, and child abuse, among others.

Kingdon (1984) developed a theory about the emergence of social problems onto the policy agenda of government. He notes that people develop concerns about social problems and generate proposals for changes in policies designed to reduce them. They engage in politics and lobbying to make their points. At times, he suggests, people pursue solutions and programs that may or may not be proven to be responsive to the problems they identify. That is, solutions are often sought even before problems are clearly defined.

Kingdon also notes that there are "windows," at which time policy changes are more possible than others. Examples of windows include when a program is about to reach the limits of its political authorization and will either be renewed or eliminated, when a new political administration comes into office (often with a desire to make its unique mark on public policy), and at other times of major political shifts. It is true that there are better and worse times for addressing social problems, and Kingdon's identification of "windows" is helpful in understanding those circumstances.

The Nature of Social Problems

Dear (1995) suggests four premises that underlie the making of social welfare policy. One might also define those premises as large social problems. The premises or problems he defines are:

Limited Resources. It is simply not possible to address in all ways every social problem or issue that arises. That is true of health care, education, and financial assistance. In the years when health care expenditures in the United States were expanding rapidly, some suggested that if the increases continued at their current rates, health care would eventually overtake the whole Gross National Product. Of course, that could not happen. People would still need to pay for housing, food, transportation, and other basics. Government would still need to provide law enforcement, education, roads, and national defense. So it was obvious that all of the limited resources of American society could not become devoted to only one government function.

When one of the authors served as the chief executive officer for a West Virginia higher education system in the 1980s, it was clear that every area of the state wanted its own college or university or at least a branch of one of the existing colleges or universities. Again, that was not possible. Some limits and some concentrations of effort had to take place. Many citizens also wanted to maintain the three medical schools that had been developed, because they found that health care was best in areas where medical schools operated. But

59

spending money on medical education meant spending less on other kinds of education—engineering, social work, and other fields. Limited resources always force policy choices that affect the extent to which social problems will be addressed. Dear says that resources are always going to be limited—an obvious fact that policy specialists as well as all citizens must comprehend.

Unmet Needs. Many social problems are addressed as unmet needs. But, as Dear suggests, there are always more needs or problems than there are resources to overcome them. Chambers (1993) and others suggest that the ranking of needs and decisions about which to address is a matter of society's values.

The problems considered worth addressing often are chosen because they seem to constitute a great evil or public concern or because they are a source of great fear. Some social scientists point out that society does not become nearly as upset about "white collar crimes" such as stock fraud or embezzlement as it does about violent crimes. However, most citizens would insist that violent crimes threaten their lives and that violent criminals are, therefore, worth more attention than those who steal money—even large amounts of money. One's personal security is viewed as a greater problem than one's financial security, which is a prioritization that is hard to view as incorrect.

Unfairness. Dear's third premise is that societies have persistent and built-in unfairness. Unequal incomes; unequal housing; unequal opportunity, education, health care, and so on are examples of constant and pervasive unfairness. Unfairness is a social problem that most societies attempt to address in one way or another—when there is agreement on the issues. Why should children suffer because of the behavior of their parents? Why should older adults, who have made contributions to the society, sometimes face deprivation in their later years? Why aren't people with mental illness protected from societal neglect and abuse? Or, on another side, why shouldn't productive workers and entrepreneurs be able to retain more of their earnings, since their contributions to the society are great? These issues of unfairness are constant subjects of discussion in the social welfare and public policy frameworks.

Lack of Consensus. Dear's fourth premise is perhaps the most significant. Societies as diverse as the United States do not always come to consensus on social welfare issues. There may be broad agreement that children and older adults should be provided with dignified and adequate lives, but there is even a lack of consensus on how to achieve that. What is a social problem and what is a social problem that should be addressed by society are complex issues that require a degree of consensus. There is increasing evidence that there are fewer and fewer social welfare policy issues on which there is a large consensus in American life, which means that there is conflict over the limited resources and the selection of unmet needs or unfair circumstances to become the targets of social welfare policy.

Public Opinion

Public opinion is what synthesizes the four concepts described above and is what M. G. Ross (1967) described. A social problem is what the society, which means the majority of the people or the opinion leaders who can sway a majority, believes is a social problem. Society's beliefs, norms, and values determine what is and is not a social problem, and these are all based in some way or another on public opinion. The opinion leaders may be political figures, the media, or businesses, any of which can mobilize public opinion to define an issue as a social problem. Maris (1988) suggests in his definition that charismatic individuals may also influence the perception that an issue is a legitimate social problem. Television personalities, leading members of the clergy, and leaders of mass organizations may influence what society believes is a social problem.

Segregation of African Americans in the South following slavery was one of the most profound social problems in American history. It may have taken the protests of a few charismatic individuals such as Rosa Parks, who refused to take a seat in the back of a bus in Montgomery, Alabama, in 1956; Martin Luther King, Jr., who mobilized the movement that arose from Ms. Parks's refusal; and Malcolm X (Branch, 1988) to solidify the discontent of African Americans and those whites who opposed segregation and to make it a widely acknowledged social problem that required resolution.

The Self-Fulfilling Prophecy

A special form of public opinion is the "self-fulfilling prophecy," a phenomenon in which people expect something from another individual or a group or a social phenomenon (Merton, 1957). When large numbers of people believe something is true, it will become true because they believe it. Of course, the prophecy cannot apply to purely physical phenomena; public opinion does not cause floods. If, however, people believe that the economy is failing, they might take actions because of that belief, such as removing their money from banks, ceasing to make purchases, or avoiding the expansion of their business, any of which weakens the economy and is a potential cause of economic failure. Stock market crashes happen in the same way. If people believe the market is going to decline, they sell their stocks, converting them to cash, and, in doing so, they cause a market decline. Believing that the market will rise has comparable consequences: people buy stocks so they will earn profits, and they attempt to do so before the prices rise too much. Their purchases, which constitute competition for stocks, cause an increase in the market. The self-fulfilling prophecy, here represented as an economic phenomenon, is a major factor in all things social, including the identification of social problems.

Identifications of Social Problems

R. W. Maris (1988, 7), in his definitions of social problems, suggests that cancer is considered a social problem because of its magnitude, severity, and primacy, in that cancer causes nearly a half-million deaths each year, while allergies, which are pervasive, cause only five to ten thousand deaths annually. The severity and magnitude of a problem help determine society's willingness to deal with it.

Values and, therefore, perceptions of social problems change over time. In the 1960s President John F. Kennedy suggested that a great social problem was the lack of meat in the diets of low-income Americans. By the 2000s too much meat (because of the fat and cholesterol) in the American diet was considered a social problem. Lack of exercise is also currently perceived as a social problem, but it was not widely considered a social problem during the 1960s.

For most Americans the most crucial problems are crime and violence or the fear of them. As Walinsky (1995, 44) says, "Our greatest fear is of violence from a nameless, faceless stranger." Public opinion polls and other efforts consistently identify this great concern. And although social scientists can demonstrate that crime rates are declining, they are still high and much higher than they had been decades ago. Similarly, scientific observers say that crimes are not committed by strangers but, most often, by relatives, friends, and neighbors of victims. But, Walinsky (1995) shows that observation applies to crimes that are solved, not, for example to the two of five murder cases that are never solved.

Public attention can lead to public definitions of social problems. For example, one of the most widely read news stories of 1997 was the death in an auto accident of Diana Spencer, the former wife of Prince Charles of the United Kingdom. Spencer, who held the title Princess of Wales, was killed while riding with a companion in Paris. Although that incident, which occurred a long way from the United States, had no direct bearing on the large number of auto accident deaths in the United States, the fact that the accident was somehow associated with photographers' pursuit of the princess for tabloid newspapers aroused interest in the United States for laws that would limit the activities and the access of photographers pursuing celebrities. Many celebrities in the United States spoke out against photographers who, they said, made their lives difficult through unwanted and aggressive efforts to photograph them. Efforts were mounted to boycott tabloid newspapers and publications that used photographs obtained to exploit public figures.

Methods for Studying Social Problems

Maris (1988, 99–104) also suggests a series of methods for studying social problems that stresses the study of actual data. He proposes four methodological approaches or sources:

1. Records, documents, and official statistics
2. Case studies and participation in small groups
3. Surveys
4. Experiments

Human services workers use all of these methods for identifying and assessing social problems, especially those who work in the social policy practice area. One of the most popular and widely used means is the "needs assessment," an approach that may involve any one or a combination of Maris's approaches. By conducting such assessments, community planners, administrators, and many other kinds of human services workers determine the course of action they or their agencies may most wisely take.

Prominent Social Problems

Human services workers deal with many problems, but these are among the most common:

Economic Disadvantage. The lack of sufficient income is the basis for most of the social policy expenditures and social programs in the United States. Social Security (or OASDI), food stamps, TANF, child support enforcement, unemployment compensation, worker's compensation, public hosing, school lunch programs, Head Start, and many others of the social provisions in this nation arise out of the economic problems of some people (in the case of means-tested programs) and the potential of economic disadvantage for others, in the case of some entitlements, especially those that are preventive in nature.

Addressing the problems of economic disadvantage is also fairly straightforward—to provide people with resources they need and lack. Although many critics of such programs assert that it does no good to "throw money at the problem," many recipients of aid would disagree. Providing money is the initial step in solving economic problems, followed by longer-range solutions.

One author, Mimi Abrmovitz (1995), shows that many other nations are much more effective than the United States in reducing the poverty of their citizens. She noted that the now-defunct AFDC reduced poverty by an average of 6.6 percent, while family assistance programs (excluding social insurance programs such as OASDI and Social Security) in Australia, Canada, Germany, Great Britain, and the Netherlands reduced poverty by an average of 16.5 percent. Children who lived in single-parent households in the United States, she found, had their poverty reduced by about 4 percent, while the programs in those other nations brought about a poverty reduction of 30 percent for such children. It seems likely that Abramovitz's conclusions would also apply to income assistance programs such as SSI and TANF.

Inequitable Distribution of Income. One slowly developing but potentially severe social problem is the change in the distribution of income in the United States. Americans for Democratic Action (2003) points out that the wealthiest people in society are gaining ground while the middle class is barely increasing its proportion of the national income. The poor are falling farther behind.

Statistics about income distribution are calculated by analyzing the earnings of the populations by quintiles, or dividing the population into fifths. According to ADA (Americans for Democratic Action, 2003), the top 20 percent of families receive 42 percent of the total American income while the bottom 20 percent receive only 4.3 percent. That means that the wealthiest earn eleven times as much as the poor. The top 5 percent of families earn 20.3 percent of the total American income, which is equal to the earnings of the bottom 20 percent (Americans for Democratic Action, 2003).

About 12 million children live in poverty, and the proportions of poor children among African American and Hispanic families are three times as great as for white child poverty (Americans for Democratic Action, 2003).

The wages of working people have actually declined in recent years. The average hourly wage for people who work for private organizations and who are in nonfarm and nonsupervisory jobs was $12.77 in 1998. However, in the late 1970s, the comparable wage was $14.23, as calculated in 1998 dollars (calculated to account for inflation) (Americans for Democratic Action, 2003).

Cassidy (1995) suggests that the income changes can be attributed to several factors: international trade (more products made by lower-wage workers overseas are being consumed in the United States); technological progress (workers who use computers and related technology trends to earn more than those who do not, and many workers whose incomes have declined are not prepared to work with computers or lack the opportunities to do so); the declining trade union movement (which had pursued higher wages for workers); and immigration of workers willing to work for lower wages. Cassidy points out that 75 percent of American men do not have college degrees, and generally, those with degrees have prospered more than those without.

Substance Abuse. One of the critical social problems facing the United States during the past several decades is the abuse of alcohol and drugs. There is a heavy focus on the use of illegal drugs such as cocaine, heroin, and marijuana. Created substances such as methamphetamine, LSD, and many others, have been the subject of extensive concern in the schools, law enforcement agencies, and human services programs.

New evidence suggests that the misuse of prescription drugs such as tranquilizers and painkillers may be an even more widespread and serious health and public order problem than the use of illegal drugs.

Chapter 7 discusses some of the ways in which abuse of substances is dealt with by social workers and other human services workers.

Physical Illness. Health problems are probably the second most serious social problem, although they too are often really problems of economic disadvantage. Treating illnesses is a technical, professional matter in the province of healing professionals such as practicing nurses and physicians. However, the social problem of physical illness relates to the delivery of and access to health care services and the financing of those services. Of course, some physical illnesses are also social problems because they are communicable and/or affect large numbers of people (such as cancer), resulting in economic hardships within families. Many human services workers are engaged in providing assistance to people who are affected by ill health.

AIDS has created new social problems associated with illness, as discussed earlier. By 1997 there were almost 600,000 people with AIDS in the United States, most of them young adult men. Their need for basic services such as food, shelter, and medical care and their frequent lack of eligibility for traditional programs are components of a new kind of social problem.

A fundamental issue related to physical illness is the cost of health care. In 1993 President Clinton proposed major changes in the organization and financing of health care designed to hold down costs. However, as is discussed in chapter 2, his proposal was not passed by Congress. In 1995 means for dealing with costs by cutting the amounts of money to be spent on Medicare and Medicaid were approved (see chapter 6).

Homelessness

One of the least well understood and most difficult of all American social problems is homelessness. It is a result, in some ways, of many other social problems and policies, although some who deal with the problem say there is no widespread, accurate information on why homelessness exists (Sittenfeld, 2003).

Mental health policies are part of the cause. As this text explains, mental hospitals have been depopulated and persons who might otherwise be in them are now supposed to receive services from community mental health centers—but live on the streets. Poverty and unemployment are other causes for people not having lodging. Another change has been the renewal of many areas of major cities, which once had many single room occupancy hotels or, as they are sometimes colloquially called, flop houses. Housing is now better and more costly but the lower cost alternatives have disappeared in many areas of the United States.

Rosanne Hagerty, founder and director of an organization called Common Ground Community, which is located in New York and focuses on non-profit housing and community development, thinks that the homelessness problem can be solved (Sittenfeld, 2003). She points out, based on her staff's interviews with homeless people, that there are many reasons for homelessness and there is a need for a variety of solutions to the problem—temporary housing for some while they overcome hardships, group housing and shelters for others, financial subsidies for still others. There isn't just a need for more housing, Hagerty says. There is a need for many different kinds of housing.

Clearly, homelessness is a problem that can be solved through appropriate social policies and programs.

Mental Illness. Mental illnesses have some of the same dimensions as physical illnesses in addition to threatening institutions or weakening the economic viability of the nation, as some special kinds of mental illness, such as alcohol or drug abuse, may do. Mental health programs are typically among the largest employers of social work professionals.

Crime and Delinquency. The social consequences of violence, theft, and other misbehavior are great. Social programs designed to deal with crime prevention, apprehension and treatment of offenders, and services in imprisonment, parole, and probation are among the most important tasks of human services workers.

Violence. Violence as a social problem, which had emerged and subsided throughout recent history, again became a high-profile issue in 1994 and 1995, largely because of two absorbing cases. The first was the murder of Nicole Simpson and her acquaintance Ron Goldman in Los Angeles on June 12, 1994. Nicole Simpson was the former wife of actor, TV personality, and former football hero O. J. Simpson. Simpson was accused of the murders, appeared to try to escape in an internationally televised police chase, surrendered, was imprisoned, and was tried, with national television coverage, for months and eventually acquitted.

The case, about which several books were written and which was covered in almost every issue of every newspaper, tabloid, and magazine for more than a year, raised issues of the extent of spousal abuse in the United States—acts of which Simpson was also accused during his marriage—the effectiveness of the justice system, and other issues, which are discussed in chapter 4. Some called it the crime of the century (Eliot, 1995). One writer who covered the Simpson trial for the media and who is also an attorney (Spence, 1997) thought that many Americans had learned about the judicial processes from following the Simpson trial. However, he thought the trial was a poor example of how justice is handled in the United States. He believed that a book authored by Jeffrey Toobin (1996) was the best of the books on the case. Although other crimes, such as the kidnapping of the child of aviation hero Charles Lindbergh and his wife, the author Anne Morrow-Lindbergh, have been designated the century's greatest, the murder of Nicole Simpson and Ron Goldman and O. J. Simpson's trial were clearly among the most absorbing events of the decade.

Other cases were the bombing of the federal building in Oklahoma City on April 12, 1995, and the New York City World Trade Center building in 1993, for which people of Middle Eastern, Islamic backgrounds were accused and eventually convicted. Of course, the attacks with hijacked airplanes in New York and Washington on September 11, 2001, is the most serious problem of violence in modern America.

Violence in the 2000s continues to be a special and perhaps growing problem. In part that is a result of the larger population. The incidence of aberrant persons such as mass murderers is quite small. However, the more people alive, the more mass murderers are at large. One of the more frightening cases of violence was a series of mysterious shootings in the Washington, D.C., area in the fall of 2002 that left ten people dead. Eventually, two men were arrested—John Allen Muhammad and a teenage companion, John Malvo. In separate trials, Muhammad was sentenced to death and Malvo was sentenced to life in prison without the possibility of parole. Malvo escaped the death penalty partly because of his youth and the belief that he was manipulated into committing the murders by Muhammad.

These kinds of cases continue to emerge—murderers who kill for reasons that are difficult to understand without resorting to mental illness diagnoses. Because they are so rare compared to the more mundane violence encountered in most large cities in most years, they constitute a relatively minor social problem. However, they create a climate of terror, which is a social problem itself. Even the natural environment such as the the tsunami of late 2004 that killed hundreds of thousands can lead to severe social problems of all kinds.

Maltreatment. The abuse and neglect of the aging population and of children are among the most severe and pervasive social problems in the United States. Large numbers of social and other human services workers are engaged in dealing with that abuse and neglect.

The Child and Aging Populations

Because so many social welfare problems are found among the youth and elderly populations, social welfare policy pays careful attention to these groups. Many social workers are directly employed in the services to children and youth and aging fields. In 2002, 25.5 percent of the population was under eighteen—72 million people—and 11.3 percent of the population, some 35 million people, were sixty-five or older (Encyclopedia Britannica, 2003).

Child Maltreatment

The well-being of children continues to be a preoccupation of social work, as it has been for most of the profession's history. According to the U.S. Department of Health and Human Services' National Clearinghouse on Child Abuse and Neglect Information, 275,000 children were removed from their homes in 2001 for reasons of neglect and abuse. In that same year, 1,300 children died from abuse or neglect, a rate of 1.81 children per 100,000. Although the birth rate is not increasing, the absolute numbers of children in the United States continue to grow, as do the numbers of cases of child abuse and neglect. Social workers, of course, are in the middle of these issues. Social workers have long been the primary profession involved in organizing and delivering child abuse and neglect services to American families and to the American community.

Lack of Services to Special Population Groups. Special help for the aging, children, adolescents, and other disadvantaged groups is the focus of many human services workers. It is beyond the scope of this text to discuss, in detail, the social problems associated with various groups such as those mentioned that are the focus of many social work agencies and social workers. There are detailed, high quality texts that cover these population groups. But it is important that social work employment and practice change with the changes in awareness of and definitions of social problems in a society. For example, modern public health and health care practices have extended the lives of large numbers of people throughout the world so that services for older adults, which were a minor consideration a century ago, are now the focus of many social policies and programs in the 2000s. The welfare of children, a major concern of social work for its whole history, continues to be a significant concern. Although the birth rate is lower than it had been earlier, the growth in the overall size of the population means that many more children, in absolute terms, are being born. So services for children and their families, such as those described in subsequent chapters, remain a large source of social work employment and social policy expenditures. Help for people with developmental disabilities and help for those with physical handicaps are among the major assignments of human services workers.

Lack of Resources for Programs. Human services workers raise funds to finance social programs. The lack of such funds may be viewed as a social problem.

Examples of the Emergence of Social Problems

Dramatic events that are brought to public attention by the media have been critical in a variety of cases in which so-called private troubles have become social problems. In December 1993, for example, an Illinois couple was charged with neglect and other crimes when they went to Mexico on vacation and left their children, aged nine and four, home alone. At nearly the same time, a ten-year-old child in New York was kidnapped and held in a tiny cell for several days, and in this case there were some indications of sexual abuse. These two cases received extensive coverage in the media and became subjects of public concern. Were they of sufficient concern to receive greater attention as social problems in the public mind? Perhaps not. It is likely that most of the many people who became aware of these cases viewed them as fairly singular dramatic events or examples, not as part of a widespread pattern, which they probably are.

In England in February 1993, a two-year-old child, James Bulger, was murdered by two ten-year-old children (Schmidt, February 1993). The story made news all over the world despite the fact that such incidents of children murdering other children occur frequently in many nations, including the United States. It is likely that the story was of special significance because of England's reputation for tranquility and its relatively small number of murders each year as well as because of the young ages of the victim and the perpetrators.

The two ten-year-olds, whose identities were made known to the public after they were convicted, were Jon Venables and Robert Thompson. The abduction and murder took place in Liverpool when Thompson and Venables found Bulger in a shopping mall, persuaded him to join them, and took him to a railroad track, where they murdered him with rocks and beatings.

When they were eleven years old the two boys were found guilty of the murder by a jury and were given indeterminate sentences. They would first serve in secure children's institutions and, when they became legally old enough, would be transferred to secure juvenile facilities (Schmidt, November 1993). They were released in 2001.

Child protective services workers are all able to describe cases of child sexual abuse, the restriction of children with chains and in locked rooms, and cases of children who are routinely left alone while their parents participate in recreation or work. Perhaps the cases that achieved such broad public recognition seemed different or striking because the families appeared to have middle-class socioeconomic status and thus the means to avoid neglecting or harming children. The parents who left the two children alone did so to vacation in an attractive Mexican resort. (They later relinquished the children for adoption.) Had they been lower socioeconomic status, parents who left their children alone while they spent their time in a local tavern, it is doubtful that the case would have achieved such notoriety. Such events, which occur every day, may reach public attention if, while the parents or guardians are away, there is a fire or other catastrophe in which the children die. There are, however, sufficient numbers of substantiated child neglect cases—518,000 in 1995.

Other prominently discussed social problems in recent U.S. history have been illiteracy, domestic violence (assaults against men, women, and children in the family system, by family members), and violence associated with illegal drugs.

Bioterrorism

The 2001 attacks on New York and Washington discussed in chapter 2 led to ongoing concern that the nation could be in danger again from biological agents released by terrorist groups. Agents such as smallpox, which had been eradicated in much of the world years earlier, could be used to infect large numbers of people, as a form of violence. Poisons could be released, it was feared, to harm citizens and intimidate those who were not harmed. In fact, in the early 2000s anthrax, an often deadly agent, was mailed to newspapers, TV networks, and congressional offices. Some illnesses and at least one death resulted from the inhalation of anthrax, although those who introduced the substance had not been caught by 2004 and it was not clear that the anthrax episodes were the products of terrorist efforts.

All sorts of policy changes resulted from the 2001 attacks and fears of future assaults. Airport security was increased significantly and a federal agency was created to screen passengers and work to insure security. Training on dealing with bioterrorism and other disasters was required for social workers and other health care personnel.

Immigration from other nations was tightened and visas to work in and visit the United States became more difficult to obtain.

Many functions of government were taken from the departments in which they existed and transferred to a new federal department, the Department of Homeland Security, designed to prevent, through a variety of means, future attacks on the United States.

Human Services Workers and Social Problems

One of the roles of human services workers is to identify and bring to public attention the social problems that they encounter in their daily work. In many ways human services workers are the "early warning system" for social problems. Social workers and their counterparts are among the first to see the development of widespread, disabling problems. This has been true for a number of widely accepted and publicly addressed social problems.

For example, physicians and nurses were among the first to identify the problem of physical child abuse. They began seeing children in emergency situations who were described by their parents as accident victims. In their diagnoses the medical personnel began identifying patterns of broken bones and contusions among large numbers of families. Out of their observations they identified the battered child syndrome, which was a forerunner of the more generally defined category of child physical abuse. Their observations helped child protective services workers and medical personnel learn to discern whether a child was the victim of an accident or actually a victim of abuse by his or her caregivers.

A more recent example is the elevation to the level of a social problem of a phenomenon called the Munchausen syndrome by proxy (Mercer & Perdue, 1993). That syndrome, which has been portrayed on television and in other popular media as well as in the professional literature, is one in which a parent causes severe health problems for a child, often through strangling or suffocation, takes the child for emergency health care, and credits him- or herself with heroic steps that saved the child's life. The typical reason for the child's illness is temporary cessation of breathing. Some children who are victims of the syndrome die. Physicians and others began noticing that the same parents were bringing their children to emergency care on a regular basis with difficult-to-diagnose, dramatic, and life-threatening conditions. Hidden camera observations were used to show that those parents were actually suffocating their children almost to the point of death. The issue—perhaps so small in its impact that it would be defined as the private trouble of children unfortunate enough to have parents who would harm them in that way—is increasingly being seen as a social problem, largely because the behavior is so deviant and the incidents are so dramatic. The social problem was identified as such by human services workers.

Many other problems—such as the introduction of new, dangerous, and illegal drugs; children sniffing glue and other substances, which can lead to brain damage and even death; increases in long-term unemployment; and family homelessness—were identified by professionals, who noticed that they encountered repeated examples of them.

Social Problems versus Private Troubles

In the human services it is crucial to identify real social problems rather than treat them as repeated examples of private troubles (Mills, 1959). Social problems cannot realistically be solved case by case. Dealing with a widespread, pervasive social problem requires policies and programs. Appropriate policies and programs can resolve the difficulties faced by individuals and, perhaps more important, prevent the problems from affecting others in the future. Giving money to a person who requests it on the street will often be followed by another request from someone else. Job training and placement programs, financial assistance, and mental health treatment programs are potential solutions to problems that can have long-lasting and pervasive results.

The Prevention Policy Equation

It is axiomatic in human services that policies, especially preventive policies, along with the programs or provisions that set those policies in motion, are the most efficient and least expensive means for dealing with human need. An example from the health and nutrition fields makes the point. Inadequate childhood nutrition can lead to delays or deficiencies in physical and mental development. Treating physical and mental deficiencies, which may be irreversible, can require hospitalization, institutionalization, and lifelong medical care, all of which may cost thousands of dollars per person per month. Yet a policy designed to prevent childhood nutrition deficiencies and programs such as food stamps or WIC (Women, Infants, and Children Program) provided during the early childhood years can, for a few hundred dollars, prevent the disabling conditions that later can be addressed only through expensive treatment.

Childhood immunizations against several severe illnesses are inexpensive. They are becoming even less expensive under the provisions of new federal policies that purchase serums directly from manufacturers and under programs of universal immunization of all children. Compared to the cost of treating conditions such as polio and the complications of measles, the cost of preventing those conditions through immunization is miniscule.

Preventing severe child abuse or neglect, which could lead to expensive foster or institutional care for many years, is potentially much more cost-effective than identifying and dealing with cases of abuse or neglect after they occur. Prevention in this case can take many forms, including public education, financial assistance to low-income families, and mental health counseling. Early identification by schools or health services can pinpoint the families in which prevention efforts should be pursued.

Clearly, there is an element of efficiency associated with identifying and defining social problems. Doing so can lead to the development of policies and programs that may prevent the problems from spreading.

Conclusion

This chapter has presented the social problems component of understanding social policy. To understand social policy and the programs designed to implement policies, one must also understand the phenomenon of social problems. It is from the identification of these problems that social policies are created.

Some of the ways in which private troubles or undiscovered phenomena become described as social problems are discussed in this chapter. The theories that classify social problems are also described, along with some of the means available for studying them. Public opinion and public attitudes about social problems as forces in bringing them to public consciousness and concerted action are also described. In addition, the chapter outlines some of the areas of social problems that are currently crucial to human services professionals and programs. The responsibility of human services workers to identify and deal with social problems is also covered.

Although the social problems component is only one part of the social policy process, it is a central component and one without which the others would have little reason for being realized. Problems—or, as some authors describe them, needs and discontents—are the source of the entire policy process.

Discussion Questions

1. What do you consider your community's most severe social problem? In your opinion, how did it come to be defined as a social problem rather than a private one?

2. Social policies may play a role in preventing the spread of social problems. Describe a social policy, other than one of those discussed in this chapter, that may have prevented the spread or increase in magnitude of a social problem.

3. Many of those who write about social problems think there may be some ways to use scientific means to gauge problems and agree about what are, in fact, social problems. Discuss the truth or falsity of that point of view. Why might those writers be correct, or why might they be mistaken, based upon what you have learned about the identification of social problems in the United States?

4. This chapter has proposed that social problems arise from public opinion, that the given problems are severe, that they represent need, and that they are sources of discontent. Do you agree with that position or do you believe that there may be more technical, or positive, ways to identify social problems? If you agree, explain why you do; if you disagree, explain that point of view.

References

Abramovitz, M. (1995). Aid to families with dependent children. In R. L. Edwards et al. (Eds.), *Encyclopedia of social work*, 19th ed., 185–187. Washington, DC: NASW Press.

Americans for Democratic Action. (2003). http://www.adaction.org/pub.LTmd (accessed December 30, 2003).

Barker, R. L. (2003). *The social work dictionary*, 5th ed. Washington, DC: NASW Press.

Branch, T. (1988). *Parting the waters: America in the King years, 1954–1963*. New York: Simon Schuster.

Brimhall-Vargas, M. (1993). *Poverty tables 1991*. Washington, DC: Center on Budget and Policy Priorities.

Cassidy, J. (October 16, 1995). Who killed the middle class? *New Yorker,* 113–124.

Centers for Disease Control and Prevention. (1997). *HIV/AIDS surveillance report: U.S. HIV/AIDS cases reported through June, 1997.* Atlanta, GA: Centers for Disease Control and Prevention.

Chambers, D. E. (1993). *Social policy and social programs: A method for the practical public policy analyst,* 2nd ed. New York: Macmillan.

Dear, R. B. (1995). Social welfare policy. In R. L. Edwards et al. (Eds.), *Encyclopedia of social work,* 19th ed., 2226–2247. Washington, DC: NASW Press.

Eliot, M. (1995). *Kato Kaelin: The whole truth: The real story of O.J., Nicole and Kato.* New York: Harper.

Encyclopedia Britannica. (2003). *Encyclopedia Britannica almanac, 2004.* Chicago: Encyclopedia Britannica.

England, L. C., & Anderson, S. W. (1992). *The great American bathroom book.* Salt Lake City, UT: Compact Classics.

Ginsberg, L. (1998). *Conservative social welfare policy: Description and analysis.* Chicago: Nelson-Hall.

Jary, D., & Jary, J. (1991). *The HarperCollins dictionary of sociology.* New York: HarperCollins.

Kingdon, J. W. (1984). *Agendas, alternatives, and public policies.* New York: HarperCollins.

Maris, R. W. (1988). *Social problems.* Belmont, CA: Wadsworth.

Mercer, S. O., & Perdue, J. D. (January 1993). Munchausen syndrome by proxy: Social work's role. *Social Work* 38 (1), 74–81.

Merton, R. K. (1957). *Social theory and social structure.* Glencoe, IL: Free Press.

Mills, C. W. (1959). *The sociological imagination.* New York: Oxford.

Miringoff, M. L. (1995). *1995 index of social health: Monitoring the social well-being of the nation.* Tarrytown, NY: Fordham Institute for Innovation in Social Policy.

Murray, C. (1994). *Losing ground: American social policy, 1950–1980,* 10th anniversary edition. New York: Basic Books.

National Center for HIV, STD, and TB Prevention, Divisions of HIV/AIDS Prevention. (December 3, 2003). *HIV/AIDS surveillance report.* http://www.cdc.gov (accessed January 5, 2004).

National Center on Child Abuse and Neglect. (1993). *National child abuse and neglect data system, working paper 2. 1991 summary data component.* Washington, DC: National Center on Child Abuse and Neglect.

Parents who left kids arrested aboard plane. (December 29, 1992). *Chicago Tribune,* 1.

Petit, M. R., & Curtis, P. A. (1997). *Child abuse and neglect: A look at the states: 1997 CWLA stat book.* Washington, DC: CWLA Press.

Ross, M. G., with Lappin, B. W. (1967). *Community organization, theory, principles, and practice.* 2nd ed. New York: Harper & Row.

Schmidt, W. E. (February 23, 1993). Two boys arraigned in Britain in killing of two-year-old. *New York Times,* A4.

Schmidt, W. E. (November 26, 1993). After murder, Britain asks why? Why? *New York Times,* A13.

Sittenfeld, C. (January 2003). What would it take to end homelessness? *Fast Company,* 42.

Spence, G. (1997). *O.J.: The last word.* New York: St. Martin's Press.

Toobin, J. (1996). *The run of his life: The people vs. O. J. Simpson.* New York: Random House.

U.S. Department of Health and Human Services, National Clearinghouse on Child Abuse and Neglect Information. http://nccanch.ACF.hhhs.gov (accessed December 30, 2003).

Walinsky, A. (July 1995). The crisis of public order. *Atlantic Monthly,* 39–54.

FOUR

Public Policy
How Governments Make
Decisions about Social Policy

Although not all American social policy is public, or governmental, most is. The evolution of social policy from the voluntary sector, especially from religious bodies, is traced in chapter 2. This chapter describes the ways in which public policy is made by government in the United States. Public policies have an impact not only on programs that governments operate but also on the nongovernmental services that are an important part of social policy. Many believe that public policy is the essential activity of government. J. M. Burns, J. W. Peltason, and T. E. Cronin (1995) call public policy the substance of what governments do.

How Government Policy Affects
the Voluntary Sector

Social services that are voluntary, such as the American National Red Cross, Boy Scouts and Girl Scouts, YMCAs and YWCAs, family service agencies, church-operated children's homes, and thousands of others in the United States, are directly related to government in several ways.

Taxation Policy
Perhaps the most important of the ways in which voluntary organizations are affected by public social policy is in taxation policy. In the United States most nongovernmental human services are exempt from taxes because they are usually delivered by nonprofit organizations. Their employees, of course, pay taxes on their incomes and sales taxes on their personal purchases. In some states, the organizations pay sales taxes. They do not pay income or business taxes, however, on the funds they raise.

Individuals and corporations who help support the voluntary organizations can make contributions and deduct the contributions from the income on which they pay state and federal taxes. Private foundations, which grant

76

funds from the contributions of individuals and organizations such as corporations, are also exempt from taxes on the earnings of their funds. They use their earnings to support nonprofit activities, many of them human services programs. These tax exemptions are, in most cases, the single most important way in which public policy affects nongovernmental organizations. One writer, Robert Hughes (1995, 65), suggests that the United States has always been a nation with an "extreme loathing of tax," a country built on the tax revolt at Boston Harbor in 1773. However, people in this nation tend to demand the kinds of services for which taxes pay. Decrying efforts to reduce federal funding for the arts and humanities, Hughes also notes that industrialized nations provide funds for the kinds of things that civilize societies.

Public Grant and Contracts

Many nongovernmental organizations today operate with government money through contracts and grants. For example, voluntary organizations seek and often receive government funds. Their policies are made by their own members, or boards, but their real operations may be primarily activities connected with government objectives and supported with government funds.

Perhaps the best example of government-voluntary partnership is in the child care field, which is described in more detail in later chapters. It is important to understand that group child care facilities, or homes, operated by churches or community boards receive much of their financing from government. State departments of human services, mental health, or youth corrections, which are responsible for child care or treatment, place children in those homes and pay a monthly fee for the children's room, board, and services. In some cases specialized programs of treatment for emotionally disturbed children are operated by such voluntary organizations.

Many children's homes are former orphanages. Today there are few orphans in the United States and many fewer than there were when those homes were created. There is still a need, however, for substitute care for children who cannot stay in their own homes for any number of social, economic, and psychological reasons. Therefore, the former orphanages have become today's children's centers, or children's homes, and they operate largely with government money.

There are thousands of other examples of agencies that operate with federal grants to support mental health activities, housing programs, services to the homeless, programs for people with disabilities (including mental retardation), and educational programs for parents and others who are responsible for children with disabilities.

Not all social welfare organizations are either governmental or nonprofit. An increasing number of profit-making organizations provide human services. These include some mental health facilities, alcohol and drug treatment programs, hospitals, organizations that provide information to state agencies on potential adoptive parents, programs for people with developmental disabilities, and youth offender treatment services. Such organizations pay the same kinds of business fees and taxes as any other business might. They are not eligible for and do not seek nonprofit, tax-exempt status.

Licensing and Regulation

Governments also directly control voluntary social services organizations through chartering and licensing them. Even though the organizations may receive little or no financing from government, public policy generally requires that organizations that operate on behalf of people be regulated in some ways by government. Even though they may not be licensed or otherwise sanctioned by government, every organization that seeks tax exemption must receive certification from the government and must make periodic financial reports to government proving that it deserves to continue being exempted from taxes.

A Primer of American Government

It is impossible to discuss any human services in the United States without discussing the public policies of which they are a part. Knowing how government in the United States makes social policy requires an understanding of the ways in which American government is organized and operated, although it is beyond the scope of this book to provide a complete description of American government. Textbooks on American government and critiques of it are widely available and cover the subject in depth. Readers who have backgrounds in government or political science or have had thorough introductory or advanced courses in those fields may find much of this chapter elementary and redundant and, therefore, unnecessary.

One central theme that may not be familiar even to students of the general subjects of political science or government is the blurring of the public and the voluntary, or private, sectors, a subject that is addressed in several different contexts in this book. Although there may have been a time in which there were sharp separations between public and voluntary human services, in the 2000s most human services are mixed and contain both public and private elements.

The Federal System

The United States operates under what is called the federal system, or federalism, which is somewhat different from the government structures found in most other nations. The federal system evolved from earliest American history, when the nation did not exist but several states, then called colonies, did. After the Revolutionary War and the adoption of the Constitution, the United States became a nation, and the federal government was organized.

Unlike the United States, many nations have parliamentary governments. The chief executives are prime ministers who are members of the parliament, which is comparable to our Congress. The U.S. government has strict separation of powers. The head of the executive branch, or president, is never a member of Congress when he is president, and no Congress member can serve simultaneously as president. We also use the jury system for trials, which is not the pattern in most of the nations of the world, which rely, instead, on the decisions of judges. Some nations have many of the same characteristics as the United States. In fact, much of what the United States does is based on the English government system, but the chief English executive is the king or queen, who is selected through inheritance rather than by election and who has no powers.

In the United States, however, even though there is a national government, it does not hold all of the powers of the nation. The Constitution specifies in the Eleventh Amendment that all of the powers not granted to the federal government in the Constitution are delegated to the states. Therefore, in most ways it is the state government that has always been highly significant in the social welfare of the citizens of the United States.

For the most part, social welfare programs are state programs, although the financial support of the federal government is often the basis for their financing and operation. Understanding the relationship between the state and federal governments is critical, and it is described in this chapter.

Although the federal government is supreme in cases in which there are conflicts, there are also specific powers reserved for each level; the federal government, for example, does not become involved in exercising those powers that belong to the states. A good illustration is law enforcement. With the exception of federal crimes, law enforcement is a state power. The states both make and enforce the laws on crimes as fundamental as homicide, robbery, and embezzlement. Unless federal law has been violated, the federal government is not involved in enforcing local laws.

Yet even that distinction is oversimplified. The federal government has, for example, provided financial assistance to state governments for law enforcement. That is an appropriate, constitutional use of federal power. In some cases a criminal act may violate both state and federal laws. Thus, a murder, which is a state crime, may also involve violation of the victim's civil rights, which is a federal crime. Understanding the details and complexities of state and federal relationships in all areas of government requires extensive study.

Party Politics

In the United States, one of the fundamentals of government is the two-party system. For virtually all of U.S. history, there have been two parties that have dominated government, despite the existence of many other special-interest and specialized parties. Although the political parties have no constitutional standing, they are the basis, as seen later in this chapter, of the organization of legislative bodies and of the executive branch. Party affiliation is also a test for the appointment of members of regulatory or independent agency governing boards.

Parties are strictly voluntary organizations in the sense that people join them and work within them as volunteers. Some federal financing has been provided to presidential candidates, but that is not limited to the two major parties—Republican and Democratic—but to those who garner sufficient numbers of registrants and voters in elections.

Although there are some general characteristics associated with each of the parties—large business has been traditionally Republican and organized labor traditionally Democratic, for example—there are no hard demarcations of party affiliation. Many wealthy business people are Democrats, and many labor union members are Republicans. The parties have general directions and beliefs, stated in the political platforms they adopt every four years, but parties in the United States are less ideological than parties are in other nations—especially those that have multiple rather than two-party systems and that have proportional representation in their legislative bodies based on the strengths of all the parties and the votes of citizens for candidates of those parties.

In the United States, parties other than the Democratic and Republican are called third parties, although there may be dozens of them at any time. Most receive few votes and elect no more than one or two members to legislative bodies. Some may, at times, garner enough votes to affect the election contests among the major party candidates. However, they are generally not direct and important influences in American politics. On the other hand, their positions often eventually become incorporated into the platforms of the major parties, and their influence is exercised in that way. From time to time, some members of Congress as well as some state legislators are "independents" and not members of any party. Many independents are former members of one party or another and have developed enough support so that they do not need party affiliation to be elected. They, like the third parties, are usually minor influences on government, although some individual independents may exercise significant influence in their legislative bodies. As noted in chapter 2, Minnesota once elected a governor who was neither a Democrat nor a Republican.

In some parts of the United States, especially the South, party politics have taken on the characteristics of racial politics. For most of U.S. history after the Civil War, the southern states were dominated by the Democratic Party. Most office holders were Democrats, and the southern states almost always voted for Democratic candidates for president. The region was called "the

Solid South." African American citizens joined the Republican Party, which was the party of President Abraham Lincoln, who ended slavery. During those years of racial segregation, in which African American and white people were forbidden by law to sit in the same sections on buses, to drink from the same water fountains, to stay in the same hotels, or to attend the same schools, the Democratic office holders maintained the segregated patterns and resisted any efforts to change them.

Perhaps one of the most profound influences on the membership of the two political parties was the Voting Rights Act of 1965, which ended the post–Civil War practice of denying many African Americans the right to vote. In some states that was accomplished with a poll tax, which required payment of a few dollars to vote. The burden fell disproportionately on African American voters because the African American population was traditionally economically disadvantaged. Many potential African American voters were excluded from voting by the tax on voting. Eventually the poll tax was declared unconstitutional by the Supreme Court, and the pool of African American voters sharply increased.

Some southern states also used other tactics to deny African Americans their right to vote. For example, voting officials in a few states required that people effectively be able to interpret the U.S. Constitution as a condition for registering to vote. White voters were given easy sections and more generous evaluations of their abilities, while African American applicants were given more difficult passages and were failed even when they knew what the passage meant.

The Voting Rights Act of 1965 was a product of Democratic Party presidents and a Democratic Congress, as were many of the other civil rights laws. The Voting Rights Act eliminated impediments to voting for minority group members. Federal monitors were sent to southern states where the offenses had occurred to supervise registration and voting procedures. It was that act that changed the voting patterns and the politics of the South.

For many years, since the New Deal of President Franklin Delano Roosevelt, the African American population had in large measure switched its support to the Democratic Party. When African Americans began voting in large number and also began holding local and state offices in large numbers, they typically did so through the Democratic Party and as Democratic candidates.

Before the 1965 Voting Rights Act, in the 1950s, there were challenges to the state Democratic Party delegations to national Democratic conventions, often led by African American groups. For a while they lost, but by the 1960s African American delegates were a large proportion of the Democratic national conventions and had strong roles in the Democratic Party. One of the consequences, particularly in the South, was a movement away from the Democratic Party by white people who did not want to yield power to African

Americans or to support color integration. The evolution in some southern states has been that of the Democratic Party becoming strongly influenced by African American voters and leaders and a departure from the Democratic Party for the Republican Party by some white political leaders at the state and national levels. As the century ended, southern states with large African American populations were becoming increasingly polarized, with large proportions of white office holders in the Republican Party and large proportions of African American office holders in the Democratic Party.

Separation of Powers
It is critical for understanding social policy in the United States to recognize that the U.S. government, at every level, operates under a philosophy called the "separation of powers." The three basic powers in American government are executive, legislative, and judicial. None of these is absolutely supreme: each requires the consent, cooperation, and support of the others; each is able, in one way or another, to affect the other two. Some observers call the separation of powers an arrangement of checks and balances, in which no one branch may dominate the others and, therefore, government and the nation. If citizens are unhappy with their state legislature or Congress, they may appeal to the governor or the president to battle for measures that will improve their circumstances. If they believe the legislative or executive branch has acted improperly, they may file suit in the courts. If they are displeased with the courts, they may ask the legislative branch to pass legislation that will negate or reverse court decisions. The separation of powers concept was destined to help avoid the development of a tyrannical government such as the one in England that the earliest English settlers came to America to escape.

The system of separation of powers is critical to policy making, and to making changes in policy, in the United States. Yet most of the nation's citizens are unclear about the separation of powers concept. Many are baffled by, or have misunderstandings about, the ways in which government decisions and policies are made.

The concept of separation of powers in the U.S. Constitution is based on three branches of government—the executive, the legislative, and the judicial. Each branch is generally independent of the others. The Constitution specifies the powers of each branch, incorporating a system of checks and balances that ensures that no branch exceeds its authority. This discussion illustrates the ways in which the three branches interact with and exercise checks and balances on one another.

The separation of powers concept applies to the federal government as well as to the states. In every state there are the same three branches—the executive, legislative, and judicial, as in the federal system. Although there are specific powers that apply in every state, the relationships among the three branches may vary from state to state. It is important for Americans interested in participating in government and social policy to understand how these things are done in their own states because the patterns may be quite different from those in other states.

The state and federal governments constitute the main governing bodies of the United States. While we are attentive to and concerned about cities and towns, they are basically recognized as creations of the states. The powers of the cities are granted to them by the states in which they are located and can be taken away by those same states. The structure of American government is based upon the U.S. Constitution, which is the document that covers the states and the federal government, where the basic powers lie. Counties also exercise significant influence in the United States because they are also convenient subunits and arms of state government. The counties were developed by the states to implement the laws and policies of a state government throughout its territory.

The discussions of social policy in this book focus primarily on the federal and state governments because they are the sources and implementers of U.S. social policy, as opposed to local governments, although there are exceptions. Some states use the county and city governments as the principal operators of social programs.

The Executive Branch

The executive branch of government, as the word implies, executes the nation's laws, or, to state it another way, enforces the laws. In the federal government the executive branch consists of the president and the executive agencies or departments of the government. The president's Cabinet consists of the heads of those executive branch departments such as the Department of State, the Department of Defense, and—more relevant to human services and social policy—the Department of Labor, the Department of Health and Human Services, the Department of Education, the Department of Agriculture, and the Department of the Interior.

Each of these departments at the federal level carries out the laws made by the legislative branch, the U.S. Congress, or orders of the courts, as discussed later in this chapter. It is important to mention here that the executive branch exercises enormous power by deciding how to implement legislative actions. Part of its basis for deciding how to do this is the intention of the legislature, which it studies and cites as it proposes policies and regulations.

Personnel. The people who operate the executive branch of government fall into two general classifications. In the U.S. government there are elected officials and their appointees and permanent "merit," or civil service, employees. The only elected federal officials in the U.S. government are the president and vice president. The president appoints many of the executive branch employees, especially the department heads or members of the Cabinet, as well as a number of other top officials of each of the government departments.

Presidents also appoint federal judges, and in this way the executive branch has influence over the judicial branch of the government. In addition, the President has appointment power for members of boards and commissions and regulator of bodies, as discussed later in this chapter.

The other broad classification of employees is civil service employees. These are people who are appointed to their jobs on the basis of examinations or an evaluation of their qualifications. They stay on the job so long as the job exists or until they voluntarily leave, retire, or are terminated for failure to perform their duties satisfactorily.

Some government scholars refer to those who are appointed by the president as political appointees and the civil service, or merit, staffs as nonpolitical employees. The overall system that governs the selection of nonpolitical personnel is called the civil service system. All but a few of the employees in government are civil service employees.

Many of those appointed by the president serve at the will and pleasure of the president. That is, the president may ask the secretary of Health and Human Services, for example, to leave at any time, and the appointee does so, as was the case in 1979 when President Jimmy Carter terminated the appointment of Joseph Califano, who had been in the position for two years. The same has been true for many other executive branch employees.

Federal judges who are appointed by presidents, on the other hand, serve for life and cannot be removed by the president. The members of regulatory bodies or boards and commissions appointed by the president generally serve for fixed terms—usually longer than the four-year term of the president and vice president.

The U.S. Senate must consent to the presidential appointments of executive and judicial branch officials. An example was the appointment of former senator John Tower to the position of secretary of defense by President George Bush in 1989. The Senate refused to confirm the appointment, and Tower did not serve. It is rarer for the Senate to refuse to confirm an executive appointment than a judicial one. Several nominees for the U.S. Supreme Court have been denied confirmation in recent years by the Senate; in 1992 the Senate came close to denying confirmation to current Supreme Court Justice Clarence Thomas, largely over a charge of sexual harassment by former University of Oklahoma law professor Anita Hill.

The States

In the states the separation of powers operates similarly, although the rules and structures change from state to state. It is important for human services workers to understand how their state governments operate. Essentially, the pattern is for the governor to be elected and to appoint most of the executive branch agency heads with state senate consent, much as the president appoints the Cabinet. In the states, however, there is usually more than one elected official. In many states there is a governor and lieutenant governor plus several other executive branch heads who are chosen by the voters rather than by the governor. Depending upon the state, these may include the state treasurer, state auditor, secretary of state, attorney general, superintendent of education, and secretary, or director, of agriculture. These individuals may not, of course, be removed by the governor. Their responsibility is to the electorate who chose them.

Election or Appointment—A Recurring Issue. A recurring issue in state government is the debate over the best method of selecting key state officials. Is appointing or electing them best for the programs and citizens of the state? Some political science theorists believe that a strong governor system is the best for efficient and effective administration. A strong governor can choose the people he or she wants, direct their work, and hold them accountable for the results of their efforts. If they are not satisfactory, they can be replaced. Electing officials, on the other hand, diffuses authority. They can ignore the governor's directions and may be inclined to take actions that will secure their own political bases and reelections rather than pursuing the best interests of the state. Some of those elected officials have relatively technical jobs, such as the secretaries of state, who issue corporate charters and perform other tasks that could, some argue, be directed by a relatively lower-paid appointed official. Those who favor a strong governor prefer that states elect only one or two officials, much as the U.S. government selects only a president and vice president and has the other officials appointed.

Those who prefer a larger number of elected officials believe that such arrangements provide citizens with more direct control over their officials. If they are unhappy, for example, with the educational program in a state that elects the superintendent of schools, they may replace that superintendent directly by election. Of course, those who prefer a smaller slate of elected officials argue that the same voters can simply turn out the governor at the next election. Nevertheless, the more elected officials there are, the more individuals a citizen can contact directly to pursue specific government objectives. The argument is really over the degree of direct control citizens have over their executive branch officials. Most of the elected positions are spelled out in state constitutions, which are difficult to change; this is why most states have more elected executive branch officials than the experts on public administration would recommend.

Permanent Employees. The states, like the federal government, have merit systems and civil service employment for most of their employees, and the rules are similar to those of the federal government. In fact, many states originally instituted merit systems as a condition for receiving federal funds for human services programs such as AFDC and others established by the Social Security Act, which require the use of merit principles in employing staff. Most states have expanded merit system coverage to a majority of state employees.

The executive branch functions differently in some states, although the trend is toward a powerful governor who performs in many ways as the president does at the national level, making appointments, designing the government's programs through a staff, and taking the lead in financial matters. In a few states the governor is merely part of an executive committee consisting of the governor and other elected executive branch officials, which makes decisions as a team rather than by the work of a single strong executive.

Budget. The basic power of the strong governor and, for that matter, the president, is power over the budget. The governor or president proposes a budget, spends the budget, and administers the finances of the government. Nothing happens in government without money; therefore, the way in which power is exercised is by the control over money.

Generally, in the states, the authorization of expenditures and the actual expenditure of money are functions shared by the governor with a state treasurer and perhaps an auditor. Their part, however, is merely to determine that the funds are available and that they are being spent legally. The decisions about how the funds are spent are made by the governor through the executive agencies, based upon the appropriations bills that are passed by the legislative branch.

Over the years the federal and state governments have developed large structures to deal with financial planning and forecasting, such as budget offices and, at the federal level, the Office of Management and Budget (OMB). Each executive agency also has a staff and special units that devote their time and energy to financial management.

How the Executive Branch
Influences the Legislative Branch

In the discussion of the federal system it was noted that the three branches have influence and power over one another. These are three separate, equal, and interrelated branches. The executive branch's influence over the legislative branch is important and not always thoroughly understood. There are several ways in which the executive branch exercises influence over the U.S. Congress in the case of the federal government and the state legislature in the case of state governments.

The most important way in which the executive branch influences the legislative branch is through the development and proposal of legislation. Most of the laws that the legislative branch considers come, in some way, from the executive branch agencies. In other words, when Congress deals with health and human services legislation, the legislation is likely to have originated within the Department of Health and Human Services. Even if the legislation has come directly from the thinking of a legislative committee or individual member of the legislative body, it is usually necessary for the executive branch agency to explain, through consultation with them or formal testimony before committees, how the legislative member or committee can achieve what they desire. Much of the advice given to legislative bodies about proposed legislation comes from the executive branch agencies, which often have to tell the legislative groups what can and cannot be done, how much the legislation will cost, and what impact it will have on citizens. The executive branch agencies prepare "fiscal notes" and other documents to assist the legislative body in making its decisions.

The executive branch also influences legislation by the ways in which it implements a statute or law. In many cases legislation is not as specific as it could be. The executive branch, in implementing legislation, may decide where a building is going to be constructed, how a highway is to be located, or which agencies will receive contracts to operate services. The way in which a piece of legislation is implemented is often as important and influential on the subject of that legislation as is the actual bill that is passed.

There have been examples throughout recent American history of the executive branch refusing to implement laws passed by the legislative branch. In some cases an executive branch has simply refused to spend the money appropriated or to implement the law, particularly when it applies to initiating or expanding programs. Both Presidents Richard Nixon and Lyndon Johnson, for example, permitted the withholding of appropriated funds from social programs. They referred to their actions as rescissions, "placing funds in reserve." During his presidency, Ronald Reagan appeared to define some legislation in ways that differed from the intent of Congress. For example, by executive order of the secretary of Health and Human Services, funds that might have been used for providing information on family planning were denied to organizations that provided or informed clients about abortion. In turn, when President Bill Clinton took office, one of his first acts was to reverse that executive action. The ability to do or fail to do what the legislative branch has passed is one of the most powerful influences of the executive branch over the legislative branch. The power of the executive branch in such matters has been tested in the courts and is not absolute. In many cases, however, it is legal.

The Role and Influence
of the Legislative Branch

The legislative branch of government is a crucial and central part of government operation. Some would suggest that it is the most important and most powerful of the branches, but, as has been suggested already, the three branches in fact influence one another and are essentially coequal. The legislative branches are different in each of the states and between the states and the U.S. Congress.

The U.S. Congress consists of 535 members, 100 in the U.S. Senate and 435 in the House of Representatives. Each of the fifty states has two senators, regardless of the size of its population. The House of Representatives members, however, are apportioned among the states based on population. Every ten years, after the census, which is required by the Constitution, some states lose members in the House of Representatives and others gain members.

In contrast, each state has a different kind of legislative structure. All have two houses, or chambers, except for Nebraska, which has a one-house, or unicameral, legislature. There is usually a senate, which is called the upper chamber, and a house of representatives, which is called the lower chamber. In many states the original structure was of a senate that represented each of the counties or a grouping of counties, much as the U.S. Senate represents the states. The lower houses represented the population.

The original theory behind these two houses was that there should be two kinds of influence operating in a state government and also in the U.S. government, a built-in form of checks and balances. Property, wisdom, and, perhaps, aristocracy would be the values of the upper chamber's members. The hope was that the members of the senate would not be influenced by the popular passions of the times. Instead, the upper chamber would deliberate carefully, maintain a sense of history, and not allow anything too radical to happen too quickly. In most of the upper chambers, including the U.S. Senate, the members are elected for longer terms than the members of the lower chambers, reflecting that tradition.

Originally, in the U.S. government, members of the Senate were not directly elected by the people of each of the states, but, instead, were selected by the state legislatures, which moved them even farther from the popular feelings and passions of the day. That system was changed, and now all senators are elected by the people.

Despite the original designs of the state legislatures, the courts have held that it is unconstitutional for state legislators to represent anything but people: members of the legislatures do not represent trees or cattle or land in a region but only people, the courts have said. Consequently, each state must now base the election of members of both its senate and its house on population alone. Therefore, many rural counties that once had their own representatives in the state senate have now been combined with many other counties for the sake of representation. Because they have small populations, they have less direct voice in the upper and lower chambers than larger metropolitan areas. These issues were decided in the U.S. Supreme Court cases of *Baker v. Carr,* 369 U.S. 186 (1962) and *Reynolds v. Sims,* 377 U.S. 533 (1964) (Plano & Greenberg, 1989).

In today's legislative bodies only the U.S. Senate represents something other than population—by representing states. Today every legislator, with the exception of U.S. senators, has to represent approximately the same number of people as other legislators in his or her state. That policy was decided by the courts, which is an example of how the judicial branch exercises profound influence upon the legislative branch.

Operations of Legislatures

Legislative bodies have a number of characteristics that are not well understood by many citizens but are important to comprehend when trying to analyze and influence legislative actions. One important consideration is that only a small portion of all the bills introduced in legislatures ever become law.

The Leadership. Every legislative body has a leadership structure, which is usually a small group of five to ten key members who are selected by their colleagues. That small group makes many of the decisions about the actions of the house or senate. The small groups are necessary because legislatures are bombarded with so much legislation that is highly technical and specialized that not all of the legislators can possibly understand and deal intelligently with everything. One bill may involve complicated issues of environmental pollution that are understood fully by only a few highly trained engineers. Another may deal with complex matters of health care. Still another may deal with the higher education system. Knowing about those systems requires extensive training and years of experience. Therefore, legislators know that they cannot be experts on all subjects. Consequently, they elect and defer to leadership groups.

The leadership usually consists of the top two officers of each house of the legislature. In the senate they are usually a president and a president pro tem. In the house they are typically a speaker and a majority leader. The other members of the leadership group often include chairs of some of the major committees, such as finance, judiciary, or ways and means, the chief financial committee in the house. The election of the leadership is obviously a pivotal issue in the operation of a legislative body. It is also where the political parties come into play. The political party that is dominant in the legislative body selects the leadership; the minority party has a lesser role. In fact, the minority often has no influence on the selection of the leadership. In a private meeting called a caucus, the majority party chooses whom it wants, and because they are the majority, they always win when the entire house or senate votes. Therefore, the chairs and most of the members of the committees are from the majority party. A minority of the members of each committee are from the minority party, which has a parallel structure to the leadership for its own purposes. There are a minority leader, a minority whip, and other leaders who represent the interests of the minority party in the legislative body.

Another factor in leadership selection is seniority. The longer a person has served in some legislative bodies, including the U.S. Congress, the greater his or her prerogatives in assuming committee membership and leadership. In some state legislatures seniority is more important than in others. Ordinarily, however, elected leadership positions such as those described in this section are not based upon seniority, although those who have served longest often build a great deal of support and credibility with their fellow members.

Committees and Their Chairs. Most of the work of the legislative bodies is done by committees. Once a committee approves a bill, unless it is terribly controversial or important to large numbers of citizens, the bill is likely to pass the entire house or senate. The discussions, debates, and controversy take place in committees. The small amount of debate on the floor of the body usually is not truly important to the bill's passage. The subject matter is, as has been suggested, so complicated that members not on the specific committee may not understand the issues well enough to usefully participate in the debates.

Many inexperienced visitors to the U.S. Congress are disappointed and surprised that so few members are actually on the floor engaging in debate. It is not unusual to observe the Senate with one person speaking and only a handful of other senators listening. The same can be seen in the House. The members pour into the chambers for votes but are not likely to be present for debates. Some observers assume, then, that legislators are shirking their duties. In fact, the members are likely to be engaged in committee meetings at the time the debates are going on. That is where the real, detailed work goes on. The committee chairs govern the agendas, in most cases, which gives them a great deal of power. Their appointments emanate from the leadership.

There is at least one important role played by floor debate, however, even when the bill is not controversial, and that is the building of a record about the intentions of the legislative body. Because the legislation does not spell out all the details, the executive branch determines how to implement much of the legislation. It has to justify its decisions, however, by citing the intentions of the legislative body. The floor debates provide a key source of information about what the legislative body intended the legislation to accomplish. Committee minutes are used in a similar way and have similar kinds of influence.

In some cases pieces of legislation have to clear more than one committee. For example, almost every piece of legislation has money attached to it, because it costs money to carry out almost any law that might be passed. Bills have to be taken before a subject matter committee, such as health, education, or human services, and also before a finance or ways and means committee, to make sure there will be money available to implement the law. The financially oriented committee may find that taxes will have to be raised to pay for carrying out the legislation or that the budget may have to be modified to include it.

Similarly, other bills may have impact on several different committees' responsibilities. A bill to license social workers, for example, may change the state laws regarding the practice of professions. Therefore, the bill might need consideration by the judiciary committee as well as the committee that deals with social services or health professions.

The Bill-Passing Process

There are several technical steps involved in turning a bill into a law. They vary among the states and between the states and the federal government. Each state provides information on its own procedures, often through pamphlets describing the flow of a bill from introduction to being signed into law. Such pamphlets can be obtained from the state libraries and from the legislative bodies themselves. The mechanics, however, are themselves only a technical outline and guide to some of the procedures that are followed, such as "reading" a bill three times before it is passed; that typically involves the clerk of the Senate or House reading the name of the bill, publishing it in the daily journal or record of the body, and then voting on it in final form. Rarely is the entire bill actually read aloud. Doing so would, in many cases, require hours. On some occasions members demand the actual reading of a bill, which is a form of filibuster, as a means of delaying action on it or otherwise preventing its passage. Unfortunately, the manuals or pamphlets that outline the bill passage process are not especially informative. They explain how things should happen, but they obviously cannot explain the negotiation, bartering, and conflict that constitute the reality of legislation in U.S. politics. Legislators do favors for one another, support or oppose issues largely on the basis of their own constituent interest without regard to the larger good, follow the lead of their party's governor or gubernatorial candidate, kill a bill by referring it to more committees than might be necessary, or boost or deny the chances of a bill by the way in which they schedule the vote on it—in ways like these the subtle and complex realities of the legislative process come to light. Understanding the dimensions of how a bill does or does not become law requires sophisticated analyses and knowledge of the legislative process such as that found in political science books.

A bill introduced in one house becomes law only after it is passed by the second house and signed by the president or the governor. The president or governor may veto the legislation, but even that is not a final step in the life of a particular bill. If the U.S. Congress chooses to do so, it may pass legislation over the veto of a president with a two-thirds majority, and likewise in the case of state legislatures and governors; most state legislatures, in fact, require a simple majority. If the bill is passed in such a fashion, whether or not it is signed by the governor or president, it becomes law.

Examples of the ways in which the two houses of Congress—the House of Representatives and the Senate—work together on legislation can be seen in the 1995 Contract with America efforts. In many cases, the House first passed legislation on such key items as tax reductions, ending AFDC, and making changes in Medicare and Medicaid. The Senate passed different versions of the same legislation, often with fewer or less dramatic changes in existing programs than the House had supported. In some cases, after the two houses compromised their differences in conference committees, the final legislation was signed by President Clinton, who had in some cases threatened to use his veto if the legislation was presented to him in the form passed by the House of Representatives.

Conflicting values are often a factor in the legislative process. For example, in 1995 some members of Congress wanted to deny states the power to refuse additional assistance to AFDC clients who had additional children while they were already receiving assistance. However, other members of Congress were concerned that such provisions would increase abortions, which they opposed.

Throughout the histories of most states, governors have had the right to exercise "line item vetoes." That is, they can veto parts of bills passed by their legislatures. However, American presidents have lacked that power. In 1996 Congress passed legislation giving the president veto power, and President Clinton exercised his new right in 1997. The legislation giving the president line item veto power was challenged in the courts. Some believe that granting the president the line item veto requires a constitutional amendment, not just a new federal law, a position with which the Supreme Court agreed, as discussed in chapter 2.

Line item vetoes increase the power of the executive branch significantly because they provide the chief executive with the power to reject programs he or she does not like while approving programs favored. When there is no line item veto, state legislatures and the U.S. Congress can extend their influence by combining legislation that they know the governor or the president wants to see passed with legislation they know that the chief executive wants to avoid. By their bill writing, legislators can attempt to force chief executives to sign bills that only half satisfy them. But the line item veto equals the relationship by letting the chief executive be more selective in what he or she signs. Of course, the legislature or the Congress can still pass the vetoed item over the governor or president's intentions, but success requires more than a majority vote, something that is often difficult to achieve.

Conference Committees. More commonly, there are disagreements between the two houses of the legislature. In those cases "conference committees" are appointed. These committees are representative of both houses. They deliberate and bring forth recommendations to modify the legislation without the objections voiced by either of the two houses. The conference committees meet and make reports, and the House and Senate must vote for the proposal put forward by the conference committee if the bill is to pass. They cannot amend the legislation or otherwise change it. If they do not agree, the bill goes back to the conference committee for another effort.

Most legislation of any consequence goes to conference committees so that even the smallest differences between the two houses can be worked out. A bill is not considered to have been passed and does not go to the president or governor until exactly the same bill is passed by both houses of the legislature.

It is noteworthy that the landmark public welfare legislation, the Personal Responsibility and Work Opportunity Reconciliation Act of 1996, is also called Conference Agreement for HR3734. That means the bill was finally drafted by a conference committee of Senate and House members who agreed on a modified version of a House bill. Both the Senate and House finally passed the bill, which the president signed and which therefore became law.

Legislative Staff

A development of more recent years has been the expansion of professional staff within legislative bodies. Both the federal and state legislatures employ large numbers of professionals to write legislation, conduct research, organize hearings, and otherwise administer the legislative process. Again, the complexity and amount of legislation are such that the individual members, on their own, cannot know enough or do enough to deal with it effectively.

State legislatures often centralize their professional staff in organizations called legislative councils or research services. These organizations have teams of professionals, many of them attorneys with expert knowledge in legislation. They are consulted by legislators who have ideas for new statutes. The organization staff converts the ideas into bills, which the legislators then introduce for action.

Professional staff members in Congress and in the state legislatures come from a variety of disciplines. Many, as mentioned, are attorneys with expert skills in legislation and the drafting of bills, which are specialized fields of law. Others have degrees in political science and public administration. In the human services areas many staff members are social workers, psychologists, counselors, or representatives of other human services disciplines. The roles of policy practitioners, including legislative staff members, are discussed in more detail in chapter 9. As the legislative process has become more complex, the numbers and responsibilities of legislative staff members have grown. Increasingly, those who want to have some impact on the legislative process in the federal or state legislatures must become acquainted with and work through staff members because they are often the most convenient and effective route to influencing the content of public policy.

It is worthwhile for those who want to understand the legislative process to also know something about the demands on members of Congress and state legislatures. Although the conventional definition of the job is that of studying problems and dealing with statutes about those problems, the reality of legislative work is that the first pressure on a member of Congress or a state legislature is constituent services. Constituent service means intervening with executive branch agencies on behalf of constituents, advising constituents on how to obtain services, often human services such as Social Security, and, on occasion, introducing legislation that will solve the problems of a constituent or group of constituents.

Members of legislative bodies are usually quite responsive to communications from constituents because their ultimate bosses are those constituent voters. Legislators also respond carefully to political party officials, to executive branch officials, particularly the governor or president, as well as to trusted members of their own staffs. That is why it is sometimes more effective for people who have human services legislative concerns to work with and through legislative staff members than with legislators themselves. Staff members have major influence on legislators; obtaining their support for a program or a position can help ensure the action one seeks from a legislative body.

Term Limits

There is apparently strong public support in the United States for limiting the terms of legislators. By 1995 twenty-two states had passed laws denying members of the U.S. Congress unlimited opportunities for reelection. However, in 1995, the U.S. Supreme Court ruled that the U.S. Constitution forbids term limits for elected federal officials such as members of the House of Representatives and the U.S. Senate. The states can, of course, set limits on the careers of their own state representatives and senators. Some state courts have held that voters need to be well informed as to what they are voting on. In some states the courts invalidated term limit laws that placed lifetime restrictions on government service, not because that in itself is unconstitutional but because voters were not informed about the details of the limits when they voted to impose them. The Court held that the Constitution sets specific requirements for members of Congress and that in drafting the Constitution, there had actually been a debate about term limits, with the result that there would be none. Therefore, in a 5–4 decision, the Court invalidated all of the state laws that placed limits on the terms of members of the U.S. Congress, as discussed in chapter 2. Although the voters may support term limits, it would be necessary for the Constitution to be amended if they are to apply to members of the U.S. Congress.

Lobbying and Lobbyists

One of the least-understood issues in the legislative process is lobbying and the roles of lobbyists. Lobbyists are simply people who represent various concerns or interests and who attempt to influence the course (at times the passage, at other times defeat) of legislation or the implementation of legislation through the executive branch. Lobbyists often perform useful services for legislators such as bringing special issues to their attention, conducting research that helps inform legislators, and even drafting bills to deal with special issues for members of legislative bodies. The public stereotype of the lobbyist who spends money on legislators to try to sway a vote or draw attention to a cause is often accurate. Many times lobbyists find that the best way to get the attention of a legislator is to take him or her to lunch or dinner, which may be the only opportunity to capture the legislator's full attention. Many states and the federal government, however, have limitations on the amount of money that can be spent for entertaining legislators. Even when the limits are stringent, lobbyists can influence legislators because they have vast knowledge in special areas and, in fact, represent groups of constituents, who are important to legislators.

Many human services organizations, such as the National Association of Social Workers, the Child Welfare League of America, and the American Public Human Services Association, have lobbyists. They advocate improvements in human services, at least improvements in the organizations that sponsor their efforts, and greater attention to issues of concern to the organization.

There is a variety of techniques used to lobby, aside from having lunch and dinner; others are letter-writing, telegram and telephone campaigns, all of which work best when the correspondence is highly individualized. When individual constituents write to members of legislatures about subjects of particular interest to them, they are more likely to be effective than if they had signed postcards all saying the same thing or sending obviously duplicated letters.

In any case, lobbying is a legitimate and effective practice in the process of influencing legislation. If it had not been for lobbying, there would not have been licensing laws for most of the human services professions, and programs for human services would have been much less generously financed or even maintained without lobbying.

In most state legislatures and in the federal government, those whose role is to try to influence legislation must be formally registered as lobbyists; they also must report on their activities and their expenditures. There is additional discussion of lobbying in chapter 9, which deals with human services workers who are involved in the practice of social policy.

The Judiciary

The judicial branch is the third of the coequal branches of government in the United States. Most people are familiar with the courts and their deliberation in criminal and civil matters, in resolving civil cases such as lawsuits, and in adjudicating domestic matters such as divorce and child custody. The courts also play a role, however, in developing social policy, largely through their decisions about cases that are brought before them.

J. Figueira-McDonough (1993) suggests that the courts are of special importance in shaping current social welfare policy. Many of the reforms of recent years have come through litigation in the courts, especially the federal courts. Litigation has become vital in social policy development, although, according to Figueira-McDonough, the human services literature has not given that route of social change the attention it deserves. Judicial decisions, along with other policy changes, have the capacity to help whole groups of people, not just individuals. Also, as Figueira-McDonough points out, the rights of the most vulnerable individuals can be pursued in the courts more readily than they might through the lobbying process. An individual who contacts a legislator may or may not be taken seriously, depending upon the group he or she represents and its influence. In the courts an individual is heard, and his or her concern must be addressed.

The principles of federalism apply to the courts just as they do to the other two branches of government. There are state and federal courts, each of which handles cases in its own areas of jurisdiction. In general, state courts hear cases about state matters and federal courts about federal matters. In certain situations a case deals with both federal and state laws and can sometimes be tried in both kinds of courts. Usually, however, cases are tried in only one jurisdiction. A federal court typically does not deal with matters of state law and vice versa.

There are different levels of courts. In the federal system there are three basic levels—district courts, circuit courts of appeal, and the U.S. Supreme Court. Similar levels exist in the states, although each state has its own unique arrangements. All but twenty states have no appeals court between the district, or "trial," courts and the supreme appellate courts, also called intermediate courts. Others have specialized appellate courts, and several have more than one supreme court—one for criminal and the other for civil cases, for example.

The lower courts are called trial courts because they are where the cases are actually tried. Trial courts decide issues of fact. Was the person guilty of the crime? Did one party injure another in a civil matter? Who is entitled to the property under dispute? Or how much financial compensation is the injured party entitled to receive? The appellate courts deal only with legal and procedural matters, such as whether or not the evidence used was properly introduced, the judge's instruction to the jury correct, and the indictment properly written. If an appellate court determines that a procedural or legal error was committed, it can order the lower court to try the case again. It cannot determine that a person found guilty by a jury is not guilty. It can, however, say that some element of the trial invalidated the guilty verdict and order that the whole matter be heard again. As a practical matter, many cases are dropped after they are reversed or the decisions invalidated by the appeals courts.

Appellate Courts and Judicial Review
Appellate courts are typically the sources of social policy because they have the power to determine whether a statute passed by a legislature is inappropriate or unconstitutional. They may also invalidate an act of the executive branch by finding that it is improper under the law. The courts may determine that a statute or an act is in conflict with the constitution of the state or the U.S. Constitution. Not all cases of executive acts or statutes being overturned by courts have been done on constitutional grounds. Instead, they may find that another law makes this law invalid or that the implementation of a given statute was improper and outside the intent of the legislation. In general, courts assume that legislative bodies acted properly and that statutes are valid, and they are reluctant to overturn decisions of those who were elected by the people unless the case for doing so is quite strong. The process of reviewing and deciding on the constitutionality of legislation is called judicial review.

Landmark Court Decisions
In making social policy, the courts always make decisions about specific issues in specific cases.

A useful listing of some of the most important cases involving human rights and social policy issues is the following, which was developed by the American Civil Liberties Union. It covers cases before the U.S. Supreme Court, the ultimate source of judicial policy, in which the ACLU was involved.

Many of the cases are about free speech, a particular concern of the ACLU, but others are about the right to travel, the rights of prisoners, segregation (*Brown v. Board of Education* in 1954), and other subjects of concern to human services agencies and workers.

The rights of minorities, both minorities of color and religious minorities, are carefully covered in many of these cases.

One historic Supreme Court decision that was issued in 2003 is not on the list of one hundred cases—but was an emphasis of the ACLU—the overruling of the 1986 U.S. Supreme Court decision in *Bowers v. Hardwick,* in which the Court held that it was legal for governments to prosecute homosexual people for having sexual contact with one another. Only seventeen years later, in a case styled as the *Lawrence v. Texas* case, the Court overruled its earlier decision when two men in Texas were arrested after their house was broken into for suspected homosexual contact. The Court, which rarely reverses itself so quickly, said that the 1986 decision was wrong then and wrong now. The 2003 decision invalidated laws against homosexual activity, defined as sodomy, that existed in twelve states.

In the list of "100 Greatest Hits" prepared by the American Civil Liberties Union and used here with permission, some of the later examples such as 1998's *Oncale v. Sundowner Offshore Services* begin dealing with matters of same-sex relations such as those involving sexual harassment. In recent years, the issues of the legal relationships between same-sex partners had become a public and judicial issue, as discussed above. The Massachusetts Supreme Court ruled that the state could not deny the legal status of marriage to persons of the same sex. Vermont permitted legal unions (although not the formal status of marriage) between two women or two men. And some in Congress endorsed the idea of a constitutional amendment specifying that marriage is reserved for two people of opposite sexes. President George W. Bush announced his belief that marriage should be reserved for heterosexual couples and said he supported a constitutional amendment to codify that opinion.

It is likely that the rights of same-sex couples and persons of minority sexual orientation such as homosexuals and bisexuals would be an issue for the coming years with the evidence being a movement toward a liberalization of laws dealing with such rights in the courts.

ACLU—100 Greatest Hits

1925
Gitlow v. New York
Gitlow's conviction for distributing a pamphlet calling for the overthrow of the government was upheld. But the ACLU's first Supreme Court landmark case established that the 14th Amendment "incorporates" the First Amendment's free speech clause and therefore applies to the states.

1927
Whitney v. California
Whitney's conviction for membership in a group advocating the overthrow of the state was upheld. But Justice Brandeis laid the groundwork for modern First Amendment law in a separate opinion, in which he argued that under a "clear and present danger" test, the strong presumption should be in favor of "more speech, not enforced silence."

1931
Stromberg v. California
A California law leading to the conviction of a communist who displayed a red flag was overturned on the grounds that the law was vague, in violation of the First Amendment.

1932
Powell v. Alabama
This appeal by the "Scottsboro Boys"—eight African Americans wrongfully accused of raping two white women—was the first time constitutional standards were applied to state criminal proceedings. The poor performance of their lawyers at the trial deprived them of their 6th Amendment right to effective counsel.

1935
Patterson v. Alabama
A second "Scottsboro Boys" decision held that excluding black people from the jury list denied defendants a fair trial.

1937
DeJonge v. Oregon
A conviction under a state criminal syndicalism statute for merely attending a peaceful Communist Party rally was deemed a violation of free speech rights.

1938
Lovell v. Griffin
In this case on behalf of Jehovah's Witnesses, a Georgia ordinance prohibiting the distribution of "literature of any kind" without a City Manager's permit, was deemed a violation of religious liberty.

1939
Hague v. CIO
Invalidating the repressive actions of Jersey City's anti-union Mayor, "Boss" Hague, the Supreme Court ruled that freedom of assembly applies to public forums, such as "streets and parks."

1941
Edwards v. California
An "anti-Okie" law that made it a crime to transport poor people into California was struck down as a violation of the right to interstate travel.

1943
West Virginia v. Barnette
Compelling Jehovah's Witness children to salute the American flag against their religious beliefs was unconstitutional.

1944

Smith v. Allwright

This early civil rights victory invalidated Texas' "white primary" as a violation of the right to vote under the 15th Amendment.

1946

Hannegan v. Esquire

In a blow against censorship, this decision limited the Postmaster General's power to withhold mailing privileges for magazines containing "offensive" material.

1947

Everson v. Board of Education

Justice Black's pronouncement that, "In the words of Jefferson, the Clause . . . was intended to erect a 'wall of separation' between church and State . . ." was the Court's first major utterance on the meaning of the Establishment Clause.

1948

Shelley v. Kraemer

This major civil rights victory invalidated restrictive covenants, or contractual agreements among white homeowners not to sell their houses to people of color.

1949

Terminiello v. Chicago

In this exoneration of a priest convicted of disorderly conduct for giving a racist, anti-Semitic speech, Justice William O. Douglas stated, "the function of free speech under our system of government is to invite dispute."

1951

Kunz v. New York

The Supreme Court ruled that a permit to speak in a public forum could not be denied because a person's speech had, on a former occasion, resulted in civil disorder.

1952

Rochin v. California

Reversing the conviction of a man whose stomach had been forcibly pumped for drugs by police, the Court ruled that the 14th Amendment's Due Process Clause outlaws "conduct that shocks the conscience."

Burstyn v. Wilson

Overturning its own 1915 decision, the Supreme Court decided New York State's refusal to license the film "The Miracle" because it was sacrilegious violated the First Amendment.

1954
Brown v. Board of Education
One of the century's most significant Court decisions declared racially segregated schools unconstitutional, wiping out the "separate but equal" doctrine announced in the infamous 1896 *Plessy v. Ferguson* decision.

1957
Watkins v. United States
The investigative powers of the House UnAmerican Activities Committee were curbed on First Amendment grounds when the Court reversed a labor leader's conviction for refusing to answer questions about membership in the Communist Party.

1958
Kent v. Dulles
The State Department overstepped its authority in denying a passport to artist Rockwell Kent, who refused to sign a "noncommunist affidavit," since the right to travel is protected by the Fifth Amendment's Due Process Clause.

Speiser v. Randall
ACLU lawyer Lawrence Speiser successfully argues his challenge to a California law requiring that veterans sign a loyalty oath to qualify for a property tax exemption.

Trop v. Dulles
Stripping an American of his citizenship for being a deserter in World War II was deemed cruel and unusual punishment, in violation of the Eighth Amendment.

1959
Smith v. California
A bookseller could not be found guilty of selling obscene material unless it was proven that he or she was familiar with the contents of the book.

1961
Mapp v. Ohio
The Fourth Amendment's Exclusionary Rule—barring the introduction of illegally seized evidence in a criminal trial—first applied to federal law enforcement officers in 1914, applied to state and local police as well.

Poe v. Ullman
This unsuccessful challenge to Connecticut's ban on the sale of trial contraceptives set the stage for the 1965 *Griswold* decision. Justice John Harlan argued in dissent that the law was "an intolerable invasion of privacy in the conduct of one of the most intimate concerns of an individual's private life."

1962
Engel v. Vitale
In striking down the New York State Regent's "nondenominational" school prayer, the Court declared "it is no part of the business of government to compose official prayers."

1963
Abingdon School District v. Schempp
Building on *Engel,* the Court struck down Pennsylvania's in-school Bible-reading law as a violation of the First Amendment.

Gideon v. Wainwright
An indigent drifter from Florida made history when, in a handwritten petition, he persuaded the Court that poor people charged with a felony had the right to a state-appointed lawyer.

1964
Escobedo v. Illinois
Invoking the Sixth Amendment right to counsel, the Court threw out the confession of a man whose repeated requests to see his lawyer, throughout many hours of police interrogation, were ignored.

New York Times v. Sullivan
Public officials cannot recover damages for defamation unless they prove a newspaper impugned them with "actual malice." A city commissioner in Montgomery, Alabama, sued over publication of a full-page ad paid for by civil rights activists.

Jacobellis v. Ohio
The Court overturned a theater owner's conviction for showing the film "The Lovers," by Louis Malle, and Justice Potter Stewart admitted that although he could not define "obscenity," he "knew it when he saw it."

Reynolds v. Sims
This historic civil rights decision, which applied the "one person, one vote" rule to state legislative districts, was regarded by Chief Justice Earl Warren as the most important decision of his tenure.

Baggett v. Bullitt
A Washington State loyalty oath required of state employees was held void for vagueness in violation of the First Amendment.

Carroll v. Princess Anne County
A county's decision to ban a rally without notifying the rally organizers of the injunction proceeding was invalidated on free speech grounds.

1965

U.S. v. Seeger

One of the first anti–Vietnam War decisions extended conscientious objection status to those who do not believe in a supreme being, but who oppose war based on sincere beliefs that are equivalent to religious objections.

Lamont v. Postmaster General

Struck down a Cold War–era law that required the Postmaster General to detain and destroy all unsealed mail from abroad deemed to be "communist political propaganda"—unless the addressee requested delivery in writing.

Griswold v. Connecticut

Invalidated a Connecticut law forbidding the use of contraceptives on the ground that a right of "marital privacy," though not specifically guaranteed in the Bill of Rights, is protected by "several fundamental constitutional guarantees."

1966

Miranda v. Arizona

The Court held that a suspect in police custody has a Sixth Amendment right to counsel and a Fifth Amendment right against self-incrimination, and established the "Miranda warnings" requirement that police inform suspects of their rights before interrogating them.

Bond v. Floyd

The Georgia state legislature was ordered to seat state senator-elect Julian Bond who had been denied his seat for publicly supporting Vietnam War draft resisters. Criticizing U.S. foreign policy, said the Court, does not violate a legislator's oath to uphold the Constitution.

1967

Keyishian v. Board of Regents

Struck down a Cold War–era law that required public school teaches to sign a loyalty oath. Public employment is not a "privilege" to which government can attach whatever conditions it pleases.

In re Gault

Established specific due process requirements for state delinquency proceedings and stated, for the first time, the broad principle that young persons have constitutional rights.

Loving v. Virginia

Invalidated the anti-miscegenation laws of Virginia and 15 other southern states. Criminal bans on interracial marriage violate the 14th Amendment's Equal Protection Clause and "the freedom to marry," which the Court called "one of the basic civil rights of man."

Whitus v. Georgia
Successful challenge to the systematic exclusion of African Americans from grand and petit juries. In the county in question, no black person had ever served on a jury in spite of the fact that 45% of the population was black.

1968

Epperson v. Arkansas
Arkansas' ban on teaching "that mankind ascended or descended from a lower order of animals" was a violation of the First Amendment, which forbids official religion.

Levy v. Louisiana
Invalidated a state law that denied an illegitimate child the right to recover damages for a parent's death. The ruling established the principle that the accidental circumstance of a child's birth does not justify discrimination.

King v. Smith
Invalidated the "man in the house" rule that denied welfare to children whose unmarried mothers lived with men. The decision benefited an estimated 500,000 poor children who had previously been excluded from aid.

Washington v. Lee
Alabama statutes requiring racial segregation in the state's prisons and jails were declared unconstitutional under the 14th Amendment.

1969

Brandenburg v. Ohio
The ACLU achieved victory in its 50–year struggle against laws punishing political advocacy. The Court agreed that the government could only penalize direct incitement to imminent lawless action, thus invalidating the Smith Act and all state sedition laws.

Tinker v. Des Moines
Suspending public school students for wearing black armbands to protest the Vietnam War was unconstitutional since students do not "shed their constitutional rights to freedom of speech or expression at the schoolhouse gate."

Gregory v. Chicago
The Court unanimously overturned a conviction of disorderly conduct against Dick Gregory and others who picketed Chicago's Mayor Daley. When disorder is created by a hostile audience, peaceful demonstrators cannot be arrested because of a "heckler's veto."

Street v. New York
A state law under which a man was convicted for burning the American flag to protest the assassination of civil rights leader Medgar Evers was unconstitutional.

Watts v. U.S.

Threats against the life of the President of the U.S., if they were no more than "political hyperbole," are protected by the First Amendment.

1970

Goldberg v. Kelly

Setting in motion what has been called the "procedural due process revolution," the Court ruled that welfare recipients were entitled to notice and a hearing before the state could terminate their benefits.

1971

Cohen v. California

Convicting an anti-war protester of disturbing the peace for wearing a jacket that bore the words, "Fuck the draft," was unconstitutional. The government cannot prohibit speech just because it is "offensive."

Organization for Better Austin v. Keefe

An injunction against the distribution of leaflets in an entire residential suburb was struck down on the grounds that the privacy interests of the residents did not justify such a sweeping restraint.

U.S. v. New York Times

Enjoining the press from publishing the Pentagon Papers, leaked by a former Defense Department official, was an unconstitutional prior restraint which was not justified by national security interests.

Reed v. Reed

Struck down a state law that gave automatic preference to men over women as administrators of decedents' estates. This was the Court's first ruling that sex-based classifications violated the Equal Protection Clause of the 14th Amendment.

U.S. v. Vuitch

Although the Court upheld a statute used to convict a doctor who had performed an illegal abortion, it expanded the "life and health of the woman" concept to include "psychological well-being," thereby allowing more women to obtain legal "therapeutic" abortions.

1972

Eisenstadt v. Baird

In an extension of the Court's evolving privacy doctrine, the conviction of a reproductive rights activist who had given an unmarried Massachusetts woman a contraceptive device was reversed.

Furman v. Georgia

This decision led to a four-year halt to executions nationwide when the Court ruled that existing state death penalty statutes were "arbitrary and capricious" in violation of the Eighth Amendment.

1973

Frontiero v. Richardson

Struck down a federal law that allowed a woman in the armed forces to claim her husband as a "dependent" only if he depended on her for more than half of his support, while a serviceman could claim "dependent" status for his wife regardless of actual dependency.

Holtzman v. Schlesinger

The ACLU took on Rep. Elizabeth Holtzman's lawsuit to halt the bombing of Cambodia as an unconstitutional Presidential usurpation of Congress' authority to declare war. Although a federal order to stop the bombing was eventually overturned, the bombing was halted for a few hours.

Roe v. Wade / Doe v. Bolton

Recognizing a woman's constitutional right to terminate a pregnancy, *Roe* erased all existing criminal abortion laws. Its companion case, *Doe*, established that it is the attending physician who determines, in light of all factors relevant to a woman's well-being, whether an abortion is "necessary."

1974

Communist Party of Indiana v. Whitcomb

Invalidated a state requirement that political parties swear that they do not advocate the violent overthrow of government as a condition of getting on the ballot.

Smith v. Goguen

A Massachusetts state law that made it a crime to treat the American flag "contemptuously" was found by the Court to be void for vagueness.

U.S. v. Nixon

In the only *amicus* brief filed in this critical case, the ACLU argues: "There is no proposition more dangerous to the health of a constitutional democracy than the notion that an elected head of state is above the law and beyond the reach of judicial review." The Court agreed, and ordered Nixon to hand over crucial Watergate tapes to the Special Prosecutor.

1975

Goss v. Lopez

Invalidated a state law authorizing a public school principal to suspend a student for up to ten days without a hearing. Students are entitled to notice and a hearing before a significant disciplinary action can be taken against them.

O'Connor v. Donaldson

In its first "right to treatment" decision, the Court ruled that mental illness alone did not justify "simple custodial confinement" on an indefinite basis in the case of a non-violent patient who had been involuntarily held in a mental institution for 15 years.

1976
Buckley v. Valeo
This challenge to the limits on campaign spending imposed by amendments to the Federal Elections Campaign Act represented a partial victory for free speech, as the Court struck down the Act's restrictions on spending "relative to a candidate."

1977
Wooley v. Maynard
A New Hampshire law that prohibited a Jehovah's Witness from covering up the license plate slogan "Live Free or Die" was invalidated by the Court as a denial of the "right not to speak."

1978
Smith v. Collin
A Nazi group wanted to march through a Chicago suburb, Stokie, where many Holocaust survivors lived. The ACLU's controversial challenge to the village's ban on the march was ultimately successful.

In re Primus
An ACLU cooperating attorney had been reprimanded for "improper solicitation" by the state supreme court for encouraging poor women to challenge the state's sterilization of welfare recipients. The Court distinguished between lawyers who solicit "for pecuniary gain" and those who do so to "further political and ideological goals through associational activity."

1980
Prune Yard Shopping Center v. Robins
Shopping mall owners appealed a California state court ruling that a shopping center allow distribution of political pamphlets on its premises. The Court rejected the owners' property rights claim, and ruled that a mall was comparable to streets and sidewalks.

1982
Board of Education, Island Trees School District v. Pico
Students successfully sued their school board on First Amendment grounds for removing certain "objectionable books" from the school library. While acknowledging a school's right to remove material that was "pervasively vulgar" or "educationally unsuitable," the Court held that in this case, the students' First Amendment "right to know" had been violated.

1983

Bob Jones University v. United States

Two fundamentalist Christian colleges that practiced racial discrimination lost their tax exempt status. The IRS can set rules enforcing a "settled public policy" against racial discrimination in education.

1985

Wallace v. Jaffree

Alabama's "moment of silence" law, which required public school children to take a moment "for meditation or voluntary prayer," violated the First Amendment's Establishment Clause.

1986

Edward v. Aguillard

In a case reminiscent of the 1925 Scopes "monkey" trial, the Court struck down a Louisiana law that required public school science teachers to give "equal time" to so-called creation science if they taught students about the theory of evolution.

1989

Texas v. Johnson

In invalidating the Texas flag desecration statute, the Court provoked President Bush to propose a federal ban on flag burning or mutilation. Congress swiftly obliged, but the Court struck down that law a year later in *United States v. Eichman*—in which the ACLU also filed a brief.

1990

Cruzan v. Director of the Missouri Department of Health

In the Court's first right-to-die case, the ACLU represented the family of a woman who had been in a persistent vegetative state for more than seven years. Although the Court did not go as far as the ACLU urged, it did recognize living wills as clear and convincing evidence of a patient's wishes.

1992

R.A.V. v. Wisconsin

A unanimous Court struck down as overly broad a local law banning the display, on public or private property, of any symbol "that arouses anger, alarm or resentment in others on the basis of race, color, creed, religion or gender."

Planned Parenthood v. Casey

Although the Court upheld parts of Pennsylvania's restrictive abortion law, it also reaffirmed the "central holding" of *Roe v. Wade* that abortions performed prior to viability cannot be prohibited by the state.

Lee v. Weisman

The inclusion of a prayer at the beginning of a public high school graduation ceremony violated the Establishment Clause.

Hudson v. McMillian

The beating of a shackled and handcuffed Louisiana prisoner was deemed a violation of the Eighth Amendment ban on cruel and unusual punishment. "Unnecessary and wanton infliction of pain" was recognized as an appropriate standard in the prison context.

1993

J.E.B. v. T.B.

A prosecutor could not use peremptory challenges to disqualify potential jurors based solely on their gender.

Church of the Lukumi Babalu Aye v. Hialeah

A city's ban on the ritual slaughter of animals as practiced by the Santeria religion was overturned as a violation of religious liberty since the city did permit such secular activities as hunting and fishing.

Wisconsin v. Mitchell

Wisconsin's "hate crime" statute providing for additional criminal penalties if a jury found that a defendant "intentionally selected" a victim based on "race, religion, color, disability, sexual orientation, national origin or ancestry," did not violate the First Amendment because the statute punished acts, not thoughts or speech.

1994

Ladue v. Gilleo

A Missouri town's ordinance that barred a homeowner from posting a sign in her bedroom window that said, "Say No to War in the Gulf—Call Congress Now!" was deemed to violate the First Amendment.

1995

Lebron v. Amtrak

An artist argued successfully that Amtrak had been wrong to reject his billboard display because of its political message. The Court extended the First Amendment to corporations created by, and under the control of, the government.

McIntyre v. Ohio Elections Commission

A state prohibition against the anonymous distribution of political campaign literature violated the right to anonymous free speech.

Capitol Square Review Board v. Pinette
Upheld the right of the KKK to put up a cross in an area in front of the Ohio State Capitol building that was a traditional public forum used by many other groups, rejecting Ohio's argument that allowing the display violated the separation of church and state.

Hurley v. Irish American Gay, Lesbian,
and Bisexual Group of Boston
Upheld the right of private groups to exclude participants from their parades who do not share the values and message the parade sponsors wish to communicate.

1996
Romer v. Evans
In this first gay rights victory, the Court invalidated a state constitutional amendment, passed by public referendum in Colorado, that prohibited the state and its municipalities from enacting gay rights laws.

Board of Commissioners v. Umbehr
Government contractors cannot be subjected to reprisals, such as the loss of a contract, for expressing their political views.

1997
Reno v. ACLU
The Court struck down Congress' Communications Decency Act, which was an attempt to censor the Internet by banning "indecent" speech, ruling that "the interest in encouraging freedom of expression in a democratic society outweighs any theoretical but unproven benefit of censorship."

Chandler v. Miller
Struck down a Georgia law requiring candidates for political office to take a urine drug test on the grounds that it violated the candidates' Fourth Amendment right to privacy.

1998
Bragdon v. Abbott
The anti-discrimination provisions of the Americans with Disabilities Act was interpreted to apply to persons in the early stages of HIV infection, even if they did not have any overt symptoms of AIDS.

Oncale v. Sundowner Offshore Services
Title VII of the Civil Rights Act, which prohibits sexual discrimination and harassment in the workplace, applies to same sex as well as opposite sex harassment.

1999

Chicago v. Morales

Struck down Chicago's anti-gang loitering law which disproportionately targeted African American and Latino youth who were not engaged in criminal activity, and resulted in the arrest of 45,000 innocent people.

Saenz v. Roe

Invalidated California's 12–month residence requirement for welfare applicants new to the state as a violation of the constitutional right to travel, and reaffirmed the principle that citizens select states; states do not select citizens.

Courts do not simply decide issues that interest them; they deal with cases that are brought to them. Appellate courts, however, can refuse to hear cases that are appealed to them. The U.S. Supreme Court, for example, hears only a small fraction of the cases that are presented to it each year; it must reject many others. When it agrees to hear a case it is usually on a write of certiorari, the term used when a higher court calls upon a lower court to send up the record of a case for review (Plano & Greenberg, 1989). Appellate courts cannot order an action, but they can stop a government from taking actions that are, in the court's decision, illegal. The case of *Roe v. Wade* (410 U.S. 113, 1973), which was decided by the U.S. Supreme Court in 1973, held that a state could not prevent a woman from having an abortion under some specific circumstances, among other things. The Court could not order states that did not permit abortions to do so, yet it invalidated the laws that forbid abortion, which had the same consequences.

The executive branch is legally obligated to carry out the decisions of the judicial branch. Generally, the courts cannot execute their decisions with their own resources. They do not have implementers in the executive branch. They certainly do not command armies or police forces, which are the ultimate enforcers of laws. There have been situations in which the courts have taken steps to ensure the implementation of their decisions. In several school desegregation cases courts appointed administrators to make sure their decisions were implemented because the executive branch agencies of the states in which the cases were heard were reluctant to desegregate the schools. Figueira-McDonough (1993) notes that in many cases judges have been asked to oversee the setting in place of the standards and changes they have ordered, although they have few resources of their own for implementing decisions. In general, it is the responsibility of the executive branch, which is the implementing branch of government and has the resources to enforce the law, to carry out the orders of courts.

In some cases state matters become matters for the federal courts to decide, if the parties think a federal issue is involved. This is true in death penalty cases, almost all of which begin in state trial courts but progress to federal appeals courts because constitutional issues are raised. In a famous 1992–1993 case, several Los Angeles police officers were charged in the beating of Rodney King, a private citizen, in Los Angeles. King had been arrested on traffic charges, and the police had difficulty subduing him. A videotape of King being beaten by the police was shown throughout the world. A California jury, however, found the police officers not guilty of improperly using force against King. The verdict caused widespread rioting in Los Angeles, and shortly after it was rendered, federal officials charged the same officers with a violation of King's civil rights. Ultimately, two of the officers were found guilty of the federal charge.

In addition to the state and federal courts described here, there are local courts that deal with more or less minor matters—small claims about financial issues, misdemeanor crimes, and other issues that, while important to the litigants, the accused, or the public, do not often lead to public policy changes.

Criminal versus Civil Cases

The key players in the judicial system depend upon the kinds of cases that are brought. There are two fundamental kinds of cases that come before the courts—civil cases and criminal cases. In some circumstances civil and criminal cases are handled by the same courts; in other cases there are separate courts for the two kinds of cases. Civil cases are those involving disputes between individuals over matters such as property, money, or relationships such as marriage and child custody. Criminal cases are between the government and individuals or groups of individuals who are charged with crimes. The courts resolve disputes, but they also specify actions, as the law requires, against those found guilty of crimes against the people of a state, when they exercise their criminal court functions.

The role of the courts in criminal matters has less importance in the policy-making process than does their role in civil cases. The criminal function is important, of course, in such special cases of human services policy as corrections and juvenile offenses. The nature of the crime, the penalties for it, and decisions about guilt and innocence are, however, typically determined by the legislation dealing with the crime, by juries, and by prosecutors. Although criminal cases occasionally have social policy implications, civil cases usually yield the most important social policy decisions because they deal so often with matters of interpersonal relationships, social programs, and human rights.

The key players in criminal cases are prosecuting attorneys, who are called solicitors or district attorneys in some states. These elected officials and their staffs determine which cases will be prosecuted. In some areas, for example, parents who are delinquent in their child support payments are rigorously prosecuted; in others they are not prosecuted at all. In some places laws against "sodomy" are prosecuted; in others those laws are ignored and still others have repealed them. In some jurisdictions mothers who give birth to children with drug addictions are prosecuted for child abuse; in others no such cases are tried.

Prosecutors, on their own, do not bring cases to trial. They must present a case to a grand jury, which may choose whether or not to indict a person for a crime. The indictment means that there is sufficient evidence to try the person who is, by constitutional right, presumed innocent unless proven guilty. In practical terms, however, the prosecutor exercises strong influence over the grand jury. If the prosecutor believes a case should be tried, the grand jury typically agrees. The process of sending a case to trial is usually called the process of issuing a "true bill" by a grand jury. If the prosecutor does not believe that the person should be tried, then the grand jury is unlikely to indict that person. There are exceptions, and some grand juries take actions opposite those recommended by the prosecutors. But in the large majority of cases the wishes of the prosecutor and the grand jury are the same.

Readers may remember that Hillary Rodham Clinton, the wife of President Bill Clinton, was called before a federal grand jury in 1996 (Mauro & Phillips, 1996). The federal prosecutor and the grand jury investigating a defaulted savings and loan in which Mr. and Mrs. Clinton had some involvement wanted to know about her association with the financial institution, for which she performed some legal work while she was in law practice in Little Rock, Arkansas. Grand jury deliberations are secret, and those who appear before them, including Mrs. Clinton, cannot have their lawyers present when they testify. The can be asked anything and must answer truthfully.

Not all those who are called before grand juries are "targets" of the investigations, as Mrs. Clinton was not. The purpose is to gather information in order to know whether or not it is appropriate to indict someone for a crime or, as is frequently the case, to find there is no basis for indicting anyone.

Perhaps the most important way in which courts influence policy is a result of the way in which law is really made in the United States. Some people believe that court decisions are based upon written laws, or statutes, passed by legislatures. That is true in some cases. Most of the content of the law, however, is based not upon statutes but, rather, upon earlier court decisions. In the American judicial system it is precedent—earlier decisions by courts—that counts. That approach to law is based upon the British judicial system. In fact, early British decisions are built into the law of the United States.

Common law is the name given to the American as well as the British system. In that kind of law each case is argued on the basis of earlier cases that were decided about the same or similar issues. Lawyers are educated by studying cases. They prepare for trials by identifying previous cases that held the position that they are pursuing on behalf of their client. Statutes, of course, take precedence when they are passed, but in many situations there are no statutes, only cases.

The opposite of common law is called Roman, or civil, law, which is used in many Latin American and most European nations. Louisiana law operates under the civil law approach. Under that system the laws are statutory and are modified by statute. Under civil law, judges often have a larger role in determining whether or not the law has been violated than they do under common law, partly because the statutes are more specific in the former case. In practice, however, many common law nations have statutes that define the law, and civil law nations may informally rely upon precedents in making legal decisions.

Selection of Judges

Federal judges are appointed by the president with the advice and consent of the U.S. Senate, which means that the Senate must approve the judges before they can take office. In the states, judges may be appointed by the governor, elected by the people for specified terms, or in some cases chosen by the legislature.

In the federal system, judges serve for life or until they choose to retire. They can be removed from office only by impeachment, which is one of the ways in which the Congress exercises power over the courts. In the states there are a number of different patterns, including lifetime appointments, long-term elections, reappointments after periodic evaluations, and a variety of other arrangements.

Social Policy and the Courts

Among the issues decided by the courts are many that deal directly with social policy. For example, the courts may remove children from their homes, finalize adoptions, and take other child welfare actions. They are also involved in the involuntary commitment of persons with mental disabilities to institutions. They deal with divorces, child support, and many other domestic matters that involve critical social policies. Of course, they are also directly involved in adjudicating juvenile misbehavior cases and in deciding the fates of persons accused of crimes.

The courts enter, at some point, into almost all of the issues of American social policy. In many cases when a court makes a decision it is also making a policy. For example, a child custody case that works its way through the judicial system to the U.S. Supreme Court can impact the ways in which other courts will decide child custody cases. If the Supreme Court were to decide, for example, that courts must presume that a child is best cared for by its mother except in unusual circumstances, that would have an impact on all other U.S. courts deciding similar cases. The Supreme Court would have made a policy. The rights of juveniles who are in conflict with the law, the rights of nonresidents of states who seek public assistance in those states, the rights of clients to hearings when they think they are being mistreated, and many other social policies have been determined by the courts.

Again, one of the most important social policy functions of the courts is judicial review. Recall the Dorothea Dix–inspired federal support for mental hospitals, discussed in chapter 2.

Some Practical Sources and Ideas

One of the most graphic and best illustrations of the ways in which courts actually operate can be found in the writings of John Grisham, an attorney and popular American novelist. In his book *The Client* (1993), there is an instructive discussion of the ways in which government attorneys attempt to compel a child to testify about the murder of a U.S. Senator. The eleven-year-old child is afraid to testify because he has been threatened with harm to himself or his family if he does so. The courts are capable, under some circumstances, of compelling citizens to testify.

In Grisham's novel the legal maneuvering between the government attorneys, who want the information so they can prosecute, and the defense attorneys, whom the boy has hired to help him, provides insight into the ways in which contending parties conflict in legal procedures. Perhaps the most instructive element is the commentary of the judge. This juvenile judge has to work with the child's defense attorney and with the government attorneys to determine whether or not the child must tell what he knows. If he does so, his life will be in danger. If he does not, he could be held in contempt of court and imprisoned in a juvenile facility. The judge rails at the prosecutors and advises the child's defense counsel. Most important, he scrupulously upholds the law, which says that the child has no right to refuse to provide the information that he has about the crime, even if he is in danger.

Judges are immensely powerful within their own purview. Individually, they have greater power than most other public officials in American government. There is very little that can be done to force a change in the mind or the behavior of a judge on a matter within his or her jurisdiction. Judges have great power over sentencing people who are convicted of crimes; in their instructions, they can tell a jury what the law is and is not, and the jury is bound to follow the judge's instructions about legal matters; and they do not tolerate misconduct or lack of respect toward themselves.

Despite comments from some observers such as Gerry Spence (1997), who is quoted below, judges are generally scrupulous about applying the law accurately and correctly. They rarely make decisions that they do not feel are justified by law. And, of course, the law is both the common law decisions that have been passed down over the generations as well as the statutes that are part of the code of laws that the judge applies. Judges resist taking actions that might be counter to the law because of their general desire to be competent, as do all other professionals, but they also dislike being reversed by appellate courts. A reversal of a decision may be considered a mark against the judge's wisdom and professional competence.

Spence, in a chapter analyzing Judge Lance Ito, who presided at the O. J. Simpson trial mentioned earlier, was clear in his assessments of and warnings about judges.

> Judges are untouchable. You are at their mercy, and many have none. Your case is at their mercy. Your client is at their mercy. The only protection you have from a bad judge is an appeal to other judges, who will likely be of the same political bent, who will probably not have read the record, and who may or may not play golf with the tyrant at whose iron hands and stony heart you have suffered. If the judge has committed heinous error, the appeals court is likely to find that it was error, but harmless. I tell you, judges, on the whole—laudable exceptions admitted—habitually abuse their power, most often to the detriment of the accused. (Spence, 1997, 171)

Spence proposes a lottery system in which practicing attorneys would be chosen to preside at trials, rather than using permanent judges.

Judges are able to have close personal relationships with lawyers from all sides and with clients but also are able to separate their personal sentiments from their professional actions. When coauthor Ginsberg served in state government, he had many personal experiences with lawyers and judges. One of the functions of state officials in appointed roles often is to be sued by people who think laws are being improperly applied. Therefore, many state officials have their names attached to important common-law cases, even though they were not directly involved in the cases and may not have even appeared in court when the cases were heard. There is a case dealing with child custody, in removal of children from their biological parents, called *Gibson v. Ginsberg* that had some notoriety, for example. In that case, Gibson and several other parents charged that the West Virginia Department of Human Services improperly removed children from their homes without guaranteeing families the services they needed to properly care for their children and without giving them opportunity to improve their child care before their children were taken from them. The case was settled after lengthy legal discussions. Changes were made in the child removal policies of the Department of Human Services, which the coauthor headed, because of the case. Ginsberg also testified in other cases, including some of the early Medicaid abortion cases.

One of the more frightening elements of relationships with courts Ginsberg experienced was when his Medicaid fraud investigative unit believed that a pharmacy in a small community was abusing the Medicaid program by substituting low-cost generic medicines for high-priced name-brand medicines and charging the state for the name brands. The agency, under Ginsberg's name, suspended the man from participation in the Medicaid pharmacy program. The accused employed an attorney, and Ginsberg personally conducted a hearing on his charges, which was very much like a trial, one of the obligations of the state commissioner. After the hearing, Ginsberg was persuaded that the man had committed the acts and, therefore, implemented his suspension. Within a few hours his lawyer appealed to a judge in their local community, and the judge overruled Ginsberg and restored the man to the Medicaid program. The agency's lawyers, in turn, went immediately to the State Supreme Court of Appeals, the only appellate court in West Virginia at that time, and it overturned the local judge in favor of the Department of Human Services and allowed the suspension of the man from the program.

Within a few days the judge who had been overruled demanded that Ginsberg appear in his court, which was some distance away from the state capital, on a routine food stamp abuse case—totally unrelated to the pharmacy case. The Department of Human Services staff around the state regularly brought charges against food stamp recipients and took them to court so that the stamps they took could be recouped. Never before had a commissioner with no special knowledge of the particular case been ordered to appear in court. The lawyers checked with the judge, however, and it was clear that he wanted Ginsberg there in person, on time, and ready to testify.

As commissioner, Ginsberg appeared in the court and listened to the case. Every lawyer in the county, it seemed, was also there to witness the judge chastise the department for its handling of the case. After disposing of the case, the judge called Ginsberg into his office, and they had a friendly conversation.

The concern was that the judge had the power to confine the commissioner in his county's jail for whatever reason. Ginsberg traveled to the court with a lawyer and two other staff members. He also took the precaution of notifying a friend in the state police that he might find himself in jail and that he hoped his friend would find some way to help him get out without spending the night there. Ginsberg had done nothing wrong, and he was confident that it would not be difficult for him to be released. Yet he had heard of the unsavory kinds of things that can happen to people in jails overnight, and this was not something that he anticipated with pleasure. The problem never occurred, and all he really had to do was show up on time in that court. Nevertheless, the situation was more than slightly intimidating.

Conversely, Ginsberg was friendly with a number of state Supreme Court of Appeals justices when he served as a state commissioner. He attended the wedding of one, socialized with others, and generally found close friendships with the membership. Yet he frequently lost cases in that same court. In one case the court ordered the Department of Human Services to provide care for homeless people under a statute that, the department contended, had not been written to deal with the homeless. It was a statute dealing with adult protective services, and the homeless did not, it seemed, fit the definitions of adults needing protection. Parenthetically, since that time—in reflecting on the case, the law, and the court's actions—he thinks they were quite correct. Homeless people are in need of protection and met many of the emotional and mental deficiency definitions that were considered in the statute. At the time, however, because of the immediate demands of the job, he was more concerned about maintaining a balanced budget than scrupulous about providing services to people who surely needed them. In any case, he lost. Similarly, he lost another case involving services for youthful offenders— expensive services in therapeutic environments. He never noticed the judges providing him with any special kindness based on friendship. They always sought to read the law the way the law was written; and, although Ginsberg disliked losing cases, he found their behavior reassuring in the long run.

For a variety of reasons the judicial branch is the least understood part of the federal system and, as Figueira-McDonough (1993) suggests, the least likely to be mentioned in the human services literature. In fact, this branch of government exercises great power and authority as a coequal with the executive and legislative branches.

Independent Agencies

In addition to the three branches of government, there are relatively new kinds of organizations in government called independent agencies. These are bodies that are appointed by presidents or governors and approved by senates and that typically regulate some highly specialized area of government. They are intentionally separated from the political branches so that they can operate independently and do what is technically most sound without fear of losing their employment or otherwise facing unpleasant consequences because of their decisions; in other words, their jobs are for specified terms. Organizations such as the Securities and Exchange Commission, the Federal Communications Commission, and the Interstate Commerce Commission are examples. They deal with such subject matter as stocks and bonds, the rates that transportation companies may charge, and the licensing of radio and television stations.

These groups are sometimes called quasi-executive, quasi-judicial, and quasi-legislative bodies because they perform the functions of all three branches of government. That is, they may make rules and regulations as if they were an executive branch agency or a legislative group; they administer programs and functions such as licensing, as executive branch agencies do; and they resolve disputes, as the judicial system might do. In some cases they assess penalties for those who violate their own regulations, which makes them comparable to judicial bodies.

These organizations are not very active in human services areas at the federal level, but in some states they are directly associated with programs such as social welfare, health services, licensing of human services facilities, and the like.

Conclusion

This primer of how government makes policy provides fundamental information on the social policy process that is crucial to a full understanding of that process. Subsequent chapters, as they discuss social policies and programs, all require an understanding of the executive, legislative, and judicial branches of the federal and state governments, which are the main actors in the making of public policy.

The next chapter talks about economic policy, which is a special case in the U.S. policy process, and it describes some of the ways in which social policy is impacted by the economic policies of the federal government.

Discussion Questions

1. Discuss some of ways in which executive policy making and legislative policy making differ.

2. Visit an attorney's office or a law library and read a human services case decided by the U.S. Supreme Court. There are cases in the areas of child welfare, adoption, mental health, and other fields that you will be able to find with the help of the attorney or a librarian. Try to determine what the issues in the case were and note what the Supreme Court decided. Was there any invalidation of existing department or federal law on constitutional grounds? Did the Court uphold or reverse a lower court decision?

3. What are some of the virtues, in your opinion, as well as some of the deficits of the federal system followed in the United States? Why do you think the United States has continued that historic arrangement, even though transportation, the size of the population, and communications have changed so much since the system was first developed over two hundred years ago?

4. Discuss the ways in which the three branches of government are co-equal. How does each exercise authority over each of the others?

References

American Civil Liberties Union. (Spring 2003). ACLU 100 greatest hits. *Civil Liberties*, 1–4.

Burns, J. M., Peltason, J. W., & Cronin, T. E. (1995). *Government by the people*, 16th ed. Englewood Cliffs, NJ: Prentice-Hall.

Figueira-McDonough, J. (March 1993). Policy-practice: The neglected side of social work intervention. *Social Work* 38 (2), 179–188.

Grisham, J. (1993). *The client.* New York: Doubleday.

Hughes, R. (August 7, 1995). Pulling the fuse on culture. *Time,* 61–68.

Mauro, T., & Phillips, L. (January 24, 1996). First lady to be "witness vs. world in there."
USA Today, 1–2.

Plano, J. C., & Greenberg, M. (1989). *The American political dictionary.* New York: Holt,
Rinehart, and Winston.

Roe v. Wade. (1973). 410 U.S. 113.

Spence, G. (1997). *O.J.: The last word.* New York: St. Martin's Press.

Much of the content in this chapter has come from the study of and personal experiences in politics by one of the coauthors. For a detailed review of information on the structure and function of American government, readers are encouraged to consult current introductory texts in the field of government or political science. One of the most widely consulted and comprehensive of these texts is J. M. Burns, J. W. Peltason, and T. E. Cronin (1995), *Government by the People,* 16th ed. Englewood Cliffs, NJ: Prentice-Hall. Earlier editions of this work contain basic information on the public policy process that is sufficiently current to explain some of the concepts discussed in this chapter.

FIVE

Public Economic Policy

The ways in which a national government operates its economy, the total of all the nation's goods, services, and wealth—is a complicated subject that ought to be studied in depth by anyone engaged in social policy analysis and development. The components of social policy can be understood only by grasping the fundamental ideas of American politics and economics.

Government economic policy has an impact on all social policy. Public economic policy in the American system is made primarily by the executive and legislative branches. It is also made by some of the independent agencies, especially the Federal Reserve Board, which runs the American banking system and which, in large measure, governs the U.S. economy.

Basic Economic Concepts

Classic Free-Enterprise Economic Theory

There are several economic theories underlying American government. Among the most important and pervasive are the classic economic theories of Adam Smith (1910). They include the belief in capitalism and free enterprise as fundamental to a viable economic system. Among Smith's classic theories is the belief that the government that governs best is the government that governs least. Smith's laissez-faire (the French term for "to leave it alone") economic theory, in particular, suggests that government should let the economy operate through the activities of individuals who are trying to maximize their own gains and avoid losses. The desire to maximize one's wealth is, according to this classic theory, the essence of economic development. It is the philosophy that has been followed for much of the history of the United States, from early American times through the Great Depression era of Presidents Herbert Hoover and Franklin D. Roosevelt. It was also the predominant theory held by Ronald Reagan and, to an extent, informed the presidencies of George H. W. Bush and George W. Bush. Although other theories have been added to fundamental American economic practices, the basic ideas remain those of Adam Smith's classic economics.

Many classic American economic practices and beliefs follow the nation's commitment to free enterprise. The requirement under American policy that businesses avoid collaborating and work, instead, to compete directly and aggressively with one another comes from the thinking and writings of Smith, as well as other economic thinkers who share his beliefs. These convictions about the wisdom of government staying out of the economy were the basis, during much of American history, for the nation's refusal to deal with problems such as poverty and national health care. It was only the crisis of the Great Depression that turned the nation in a new direction, toward undertaking to solve pressing social problems as a nation.

The capitalist tradition in the United States is so strong that it is almost taken for granted. One author, E. S. Greenberg (1989), has written a complete descriptive text on American government that asserts that the whole system—executive, legislative, and judicial—is set up to support and maintain the capitalist tradition in the nation. His text emphasizes the maldistribution of wealth in the nation; the use of government to keep workers in line and capitalists on top; and the clear, although often unstated, premise that American democracy and capitalism are inseparable.

A nation that totally believed in Smith's classic approach would make little room for social welfare programs that promote social justice through the redistribution of wealth. Instead, classically oriented policy makers believe, the economy ought to be left alone and allowed to flourish; when it does, everyone will be better off, and social and economic justice will prevail. The American commitment to avoiding involvement by the national government in the economy is also a product of the federal system. Under the Constitution, before it was amended, most government activities directly affecting individuals came from the states. The national government dealt only with major national concerns, such as the money system, international relations, and defense (Ginsberg, 1987). Direct contacts between the federal government and individual citizens were rare. Over the years, however, through amendments to the Constitution, there have been more and more direct connections built between the federal government and its citizens.

Again, the fundamental concept underlying our economic system is free enterprise capitalism, and with it comes dislocation, which may, for example, cause people to lose their jobs, require them to move, or otherwise force them to endure changes that they would prefer not to make. In the classic economic philosophy such disruptions are essential to a healthy economy: those within the labor force who are situated where they are not needed ought to relocate to places where they are needed. Unemployed people, if left alone, the theory states, will make rational decisions that provide for their economic well-being. It is that pursuit of economic advantage by all the actors in the economy that builds economic viability. Any interference drags the economy downward, the classic theory asserts.

Adam Smith was writing in the eighteenth century, at a time when small merchants, shopkeepers, and tradespeople dominated economic activity. The notions of unbridled free enterprise and competition made good sense in such times, before there was instantaneous international trade and communications and before giant conglomerates, the antithesis of classical theory, could dominate large segments of the market.

Competition could, Smith envisaged, benefit everyone. Shoemakers, for example, would sell their shoes at the best price they could get. They would also compete with other shoemakers for quality production. Customers would flock to those with the best products and prices, and, thus, consumers and producers alike would benefit. The producers would use their earnings to expand their businesses or embark on other economic ventures, which would employ still more consumers. The free market, if left alone to pursue its own activities and values, would make everyone prosperous.

Although P. R. Popple and L. Leighninger (1993), among others, call the adherence to the classic ideas of free market economics a "conservative" approach, it is probably the case that this model is central to the U.S. economic system. Most national economies, including that of the United States, are mixtures of several different economic theories; nevertheless, belief in the value of the free market guides and colors many elements of American economic policy. American policy generally supports such principles as the virtue of competition, the negative consequences of fixing prices, and the belief that businesses must earn profits or fail. Many Americans believe in these ideas, elements of a strong national tradition, although they may do so without thinking of themselves as advocates of the philosophy of Adam Smith.

Marxism and Social Control of the Economy

A second approach is the planned, or socialist, economy, in which government controls and attempts to manage all economic activity. The theories behind these concepts are many, but most of them emanate from the concepts of Karl Marx and Friedrich Engels (Hirsch, 1993). Marx was born in Germany. His father was a lawyer and a Jew who converted to Christianity. Marx also spent much of his adult life in England and studied economic works such as those of Adam Smith in the British Museum almost daily for years. Marx's ideas laid the basis for the political system of communism as well as the economic system of socialism. Other philosophers, such as Claude Henri de Saint Simon (Bullock & Stallybrass, 1977) contributed to theories supporting an economic system based on socialist, or cooperative, ideals.

Under socialist economies, governments own the basic tools of production such as manufacturing, transportation, and utilities of various kinds. The former communist nations of Europe and parts of Asia have followed this philosophy, which is often attractive because it emphasizes the fair distribution of resources and wealth, fairness in the economy, the desire that no one suffer, universally adequate housing, and so forth. Most of these economic concepts have been rejected by the former communist governments, many of which are trying to develop free market, or capitalist, economies along the lines of that in the United States.

Of course, Marx's theories are more complex than what has been stated here. He and Friedrich Engels, his close associate for many years, believed that market economic systems exploited workers for the advantage of capitalists, who in fact "stole" the labor of their workers; profits, in this view, actually belonged to the workers. When a product is produced the owner might provide the tools and the materials, but the real value is the labor that goes into making the materials into something worthwhile. Workers are never paid the full value of their work, according to this theory, and the difference between what they earn and the price of the product goes to the owner in the form of profits; therefore, labor was exploited by capitalists, who enriched themselves through the work of others. Marx envisioned an ideal society in which all of the people owned all of the tools of production; in which people received what they were entitled to, based on their needs; and in which everyone worked as well as he or she could, because society belonged to everyone. A classless society without needs and a people with plenty was the Marxist ideal (Hirsch, 1993).

Popple and Leighninger (1993, 15) call those who support these Marxist approaches "radicals" who "would prefer an economic system where workers have control over the conditions of their work; where goods are produced for genuine need and not to satisfy whims created by advertising; where money is not the measure of worth; and where basic rights, such as medical care and housing, are not reduced to commodity status and sold in the marketplace to the highest bidder." They add that some such radicals want a government that organizes and delivers medical care, housing, and social welfare benefits for all citizens. Of course, it is not just these so-called radicals who seek such changes. So do many liberals and conservatives and others who support what is termed by some the pursuit of social justice.

Current Critiques of Nonmarket Economies. Socialist, or planned, economies, in theory, appear to have the advantage of distributing resources satisfactorily, providing essential services, and making sure there are no absolute poor. On the other hand, critics of planned, or nonmarket-based, economies demonstrate that in truth in such economies everyone is relatively disadvantaged, people tend to lose incentive and entrepreneurial spirit, and, generally, everyone has subsistence earnings and resources but not much more than that.

In Ginsberg's experience in communist countries, there does appear to be a sort of shared misery rather than a shared prosperity. When he visited Cuba in 1990 he was astonished at how poor virtually everyone was. That was, as likely as not, a consequence of the U.S. boycott of Cuba as much as of the communist system under Fidel Castro. When he visited Romania in 1992 and 1993 he saw the remnants of communist government; here again there were certain basic advantages of the system that were quite humane. People were well educated, medical services were readily available, and there was plenty of food, although the variety and quality were poor. Prices were low; people had places to live, although they were often unattractive dwellings in large apartment houses, which some of the people said they did not enjoy. But, of course, there are variations among Marxist nations. In Cuba, for example, which has remained communist at a time when many such countries have rejected communism, citizens are permitted to own their own homes, which was not always so for those living in the former Soviet Union.

Other critics insist that capital is necessary for the operation of a national economy, and they believe that without the profit incentive there will not be sufficient investment in capital. Capitalists make a vital contribution, they say, by investing their wealth in new or expanding enterprises.

Of course, a society that has no economic problems, which is the Marxist ideal, probably would have no other problems to be addressed by human services workers. Generally, Marxists believe that most social ills are economic and that, if the economy is just, there will be a just society. In many of the former communist countries, therefore, psychology, social work, and some other human services professions were eliminated. By the 1990s many of those countries, such as Romania, had no social work and psychology schools nor professors and practitioners. Ginsberg was pleased to be part of the efforts to help Romania reestablish its human services professions.

Some point to the Western European socialist nations, which seem to combine some of the more humane elements of socialism with some of the virtues of free enterprise economics so that life is relatively good for most people—in, for example, the Netherlands, Scandinavia, and Germany—as worthy models. Although few are terribly rich, taxes are high, and the population is not fully satisfied with every aspect of its economic life, basic needs are met.

At the same time, the nations with a fundamentally free enterprise system also seem to be doing well. Many are in Asia. For example, *Newsweek* reported on what it called the "Saigon Virus" (Moreau, 1993), which is the name being used for the strong, free-enterprise economy of the former capital of what was South Vietnam. Saigon, which has been called Ho Chi Minh City since the Vietnam War, is a city of four million inhabitants, which is only 7 percent of the Vietnamese population; they account, however, for one-third of the country's industrial production, much of it based on small, family-run businesses that would have fit the definitions of a proper economy developed by Adam Smith. Much of Southeast Asia follows similar patterns. Hong Kong, Japan, Singapore, and Taiwan are among the most prosperous economies in the world, yet in some of these nations the people work long hours and lack the wage and hour protection and other labor law advantages that those in more mixed economies have. There is little doubt that strong capitalist, free-enterprise operations helped Asian nations become economically powerful.

A good bit has to do with those nations' resources. Wealthy nations with abundant natural resources, well-educated people, and capital appear to function well under free enterprise economics. Overpopulated, impoverished nations of the world, on the other hand, have sometimes pursued socialist, central planning as a means of preventing great economic need.

However, the Asian economic strength and some of Marx's critiques of capitalism came to mind in the late 1990s, when several Asian economies neared collapse. Indonesia, Japan, Korea, and Thailand, among others, were suddenly in economic decline. Some thought that the inherent desire of capitalist economies to grow had led to excessive growth—production of more goods than could be sold. In order to prevent a worldwide economic catastrophe (many non-Asian nations had invested in Asian economies and were likely to lose those investments), an organization called the International Monetary Fund loaned large amounts of money to several Asian nations. Those nations, in turn, laid off employees and otherwise cut back their economic activity such as production of goods. Perhaps the Asian experience illustrated, when Asia was growing miraculously, the truth of Adam Smith's theories. But the Marxist critiques also came into play when that miracle turned to economic disaster for many Asians.

Some modern economists are reassessing the contributions and theories of Marx. Although major discussions of his influence have been about the communist systems that were attributed to him and by and large failed, others such as Cassidy (1997) view Marx as an effective and cogent student of capitalism. Marx's basic theory is that history can best be understood by studying economics, which is all pervasive. Cassidy points out that nations, political trends, and lifestyles are influence by nothing more than their economic circumstances. He notes that Marx shows that capitalism had achieved miracles greater than any in precapitalist history. When we compare air travel, railroads, electricity, television, and skyscrapers to the Egyptian pyramids and the Gothic cathedrals, it is easy to see what he means.

Marx also wrote about the inherent unfairness of capitalism—of the tendency for the owners to take more than the workers. In 1978, Cassidy says, typical chief executives of American corporations earned about 60 times more than their average workers. By 1995, after years of economic growth, chief executives earned 170 times more than their workers. Increasing amounts of money that might have gone for better wages go instead to company profits. And money in America continues to be redistributed from the poorest to the richest. In the 61 years from 1980 to 1996, the amount of total income that went to the top 5 percent of households grew from 15.3 percent to 20.3 percent, while the money going to the bottom 60 percent of households dropped from 34.2 to 30 percent (Cassidy, 1997).

So although Marx's ideas of what societies—especially the poorest people—might do to make the society fairer were not especially viable, his analyses of and predictions about capitalism may have been largely on target.

Managing the Economy—
the Influence of John Maynard Keynes

The theories of government's ability to manage the economy—cooling it off when it is too hot, growing too fast, and becoming too inflationary, or heating it up and making it more effective and more responsive to economic needs—come in part from the works of John Maynard Keynes (Pennant-Rea & Emmott, 1983).

In the U.S. system, Keynesian economic theory has governed American thinking for much of the time since the presidency of Franklin D. Roosevelt, which coincided with Keynes's writing and the popularization of his theories. In fact, even the free-enterprise-oriented, capitalist administrations of Ronald Reagan and George Bush tended to follow some of the fundamental teachings of Keynes. Despite the fact that authors such as Popple and Lieghninger (1993) call supporters of Keynesian economics liberals, the reality is that most public officials appear to embrace Keynesian approaches, treating them as valid economic principles rather than aspects of some political point of view.

Keynes, who was from England, visited the United States during the Great Depression of the 1930s (Burns, Peltason, & Cronin, 1995). He insisted that if people did not consume or invest enough, the national income would fall. He proposed that government find ways to increase expenditures on consumer goods and also investments in heavy industries such as steel and shipping facilities. If private business could not do it, government must, he said.

In many ways the 1930s New Deal programs were based upon Keynesian economic theory. Rapidly injecting money into the economy was one of the purposes of such employment and training programs as the Works Progress Administration and the Civilian Conservation Corps. After World War II the U.S. Congress passed the Employment Act of 1946, which was designed to provide mechanisms for managing the economy but also to stimulate the economy and to pursue high levels of employment (Dolgoff, Feldstein, & Skolnick, 1993). The act created the Council of Economic Advisors, one of the federal executive branch's primary mechanisms for monitoring and fine-tuning the economy. President Harry S. Truman, recognizing the need for the government to take steps to maintain the health of the economy and high levels of employment, proposed the legislation (Burns, Peltason, & Cronin, 1995). The policy of trying to guarantee employment to all employable people was reaffirmed in 1978 through the passage of the federal Humphrey-Hawkins Full Employment Act (Dolgoff, Feldstein, & Skolnik, 1993). The goal of full employment, by requiring the government to create jobs and employ those who would not otherwise be employed, has not been implemented or seriously pursued, according to Dolgoff, Feldstein, and Skolnik (1993).

The *multiplier* and *leverage* effects are among the concepts provided by Keynes. They are discussed in more detail in a following section on the money supply. The emphasis on consumption to stimulate economic growth, referred to above, is an example of the multiplier effect, and the emphasis on investment is an example of the leverage effect. Keynes also was one of the first to show how deficit financing can help government grow—that by borrowing in the short term, governments can expand their economies. He also showed the other side of the lesson—that when things are moving along well in an economy and the economy is close to inflation, governments best serve their people by contracting the money supply, by making it more difficult to borrow, and by reducing economic activity. Keynes was one of the first to show how governments, by public policy, are able to tune an economy in ways that make it possible to keep the economy in balance, so that most people are employed, goods and services are equitably distributed, there is sufficient growth, and there is only modest inflation.

As suggested earlier in this section, it appears that conservative and liberal politicians alike concur about the value of the Keynesian approach. His findings constitute something of a law in economics, a law that is operational. Historically, as discussed in chapter 2, the most severe economic crisis ever to hit the United States was the Great Depression of the 1930s. It was the policy of the New Deal, which began in 1933, to apply Keynesian theory to modern government. The economy did, in fact, expand, and the Depression did end, and since the 1930s there has never again been as severe an economic crisis as that one. Whether or not such economic disaster will occur in the future, despite efforts to prevent it, is unknown.

The basic concept of Keynesian economics is that money spent, whatever its source, becomes part of the Gross Domestic Product of the nation, and the larger the Gross Domestic Product, the larger the tax collections, the greater the availability of funds, and the likelihood of creating prosperity. Of course, excessive funds in the Gross Domestic Product can lead to inflation because, in the classic mode, too many dollars chasing too few products or services leads to increases in prices for those products and services and the increase may be inflationary. Inflation causes a loss of value of dollars and is a particularly negative result for people who live on fixed incomes, which are based on the value of funds.

As discussed earlier, the Federal Reserve can increase the interest rates in various ways and that increase in the interest rates tends to cool off the economy and reduce inflationary pressures.

The leverage and multiplier effects are also important in Keynesian theory. As mentioned earlier, the multiplier effect assumes that money will be inserted at the bottom of the economy and that it will "trickle up" through the economy and increase the Gross Domestic Product. The leverage effect works in the opposite manner but with similar effects. That is, when money is introduced at the highest levels of the economy, it subsequently "trickles down" through the rest of the economy and increases the Gross Domestic Product and improves the overall process of enrichment.

The identification of the "trickle-up" approach is largely with the Democratic Party, which tends to have a more positive approach to the role of government—that government can help solve problems in the society. So the Democrats were the architects of some of the programs discussed in this text such as Social Security, AFDC, the War on Poverty, Worker's Compensation, Unemployment Compensation, Medicare, and Medicaid—all of which are targeted to provide specific benefits to individuals and families but that also inject money into the economy in ways that are likely to enhance the Gross Domestic Product.

The Republican approach tends to be that of reducing the role of government—to leaving funds in the hands of citizens by avoiding the raising of taxes or by reducing taxes. Tax reduction or the avoidance of tax increases are classic ways of implementing the leverage effect that Keynes described. The leverage method that was used in recent years, particularly by President George W. Bush, was to reduce taxes and improve the economy through that mechanism.

Placing money in the economy through programs that serve the poor or that serve the elderly or working families is the classic "trickle-up" approach —money is spent immediately by those recipients of funds and it moves quickly through the economy and ultimately enriches those at the top such as industrialists and property owners.

So the net effect is the same because the top people in the economy, according to Keynesian theory, would spend the same funds to employ individuals and to provide services that require labor—so that both effects, leverage and multiplier, are likely to improve the economy when used correctly. Multiplier and leverage effects are also discussed later in this chapter.

There are political discontinuities about the use of the Keynesian formulations for improving the economy. For example, one of the earliest examples of using tax decreases to improve the economy was proposed by and implemented by President John F. Kennedy, a Democrat who followed two-term Republican President Dwight D. Eisenhower. He was elected in 1960 and assumed office in 1961. On the other hand, one of the major initiatives of President Bill Clinton, who assumed office in 1993, was to follow up on a campaign promise to reform "welfare as we know it," which led to the passage of the Personal Responsibility and Work Opportunity Act of 1996, which is described earlier in this text and which led to the development and implementation of TANF. Reducing welfare, requiring work, and generally cutting people from the assistance roles is a classic example of the use of the leverage effect as Keynes described it. That is, reduce the fiscal burden of government and let the money trickle through the economy as a way of building prosperity.

The other side of the Keynesian issue is whether or not the budget of the federal government should be balanced or in deficit, and if in deficit, to what extent. It is noteworthy that President Ronald Reagan, a Republican and an avowed conservative, proposed and implemented programs that led to very large fiscal deficits. President Bill Clinton, who followed eight years of President Reagan and four years of President George H. W. Bush, implemented programs that led to a budget that was not only balanced but that actually had a surplus.

Keynes would say that a budget deficit was not the problem that it is often perceived to be but that it can be a way of improving the economy. However, budget deficits may be inflationary. President George W. Bush, who followed eight years of the presidency of Bill Clinton and who assumed office in 2001, proposed policies such as two major tax reductions, including one rebate, to virtually all taxpayers, that led to some federal deficits. Those policies, combined with the overwhelming decline in the economy resulting from the terrorist attacks on September 11, 2001, as well as the wars in Afghanistan and Iraq, led to an elimination of the surplus that President Bush had inherited as well as the development of a deficit once again.

So while the Democratic Party has traditionally been accused of allowing for the development of deficits, it was the Republicans in more recent years who pursued policies that allowed deficits to develop. While the Republican Party has traditionally supported notions of balanced budgets as ideal public policy, in the most recent years it has been the Republican Party that has pursued deficits as a way of improving the economy.

But the differences in the approaches to the economy are also evidence that, as some would say, everyone is now a Keynesian. The most conservative presidents as well as the more liberal have supported Keynesian economic approaches. (It should be mentioned, of course, that the most recent Democratic president, Bill Clinton, would not consider himself a liberal, although he was called that by his Republican opponents. Actually, he became prominent as a Democrat with a different approach—a new approach that was more conservative than that pursued by Jimmy Carter and earlier Democratic presidents.)

These discussions of Keynesian economic theory and government spending are crucial because many times government's expenditures are for social welfare programs. Programs for creating jobs, providing housing and financial assistance, and improving education are among the solutions to social problems; at the same time they serve those in need, these solutions add money to the economy and thus stimulate it along the lines suggested by Keynes.

The tendency throughout the world is toward mixed economies that follow the Keynesian model, provide the humanity and protection of the socialist and communist approaches, and allow the relatively free activity of economic markets under the free enterprise system. In truth, most governments, particularly Western governments and especially the U.S. government, use a mixed approach. That is, in the United States, for example, there is a high degree of emphasis on capitalism, competition, and other manifestations of Adam Smith's free enterprise approach to government. At the same time, governmental attempts to improve the economy by speeding it up or slowing it down, following the theories of John Maynard Keynes, have been encouraged. There are also many examples of government involving itself directly in human services and the redistribution of wealth, which are in some ways Marxist ideas. Government in the United States is, thus, largely mixed—although the fundamental tenets underlying it support free enterprise and capitalism.

A contemporary Harvard University economist, John Kenneth Galbraith, who is in his nineties, presented some original ideas in his works on economic principles (Cassidy, 1998). Perhaps his most significant book is *The Affluent Society* (Galbraith, 1998). Galbraith wrote about the importance of public expenditures for the common good in such examples as roads and schools. The classical capitalist objective of making profit can readily disregard public expenditures for larger social objectives.

Taxation

One of the ways in which government affects social policy is through tax policy. By giving special advantages, for example, to social agencies and those who support them, government supports social welfare programs.

By definition, all taxation is a means for distributing the cost of government in ways that are considered just and fair by the government and its people. Taxes are not primarily a means for raising revenue, although that is typically the way we think of them. Instead, they are a way of raising revenue in a manner that citizens may believe to be rational and equitable (Snider, 1965).

Governments may simply take—and have taken—the property of citizens and use it for governmental operations. It may take people and force them to labor on behalf of the government. Taxes are simply a way of making the rules explicit and of trying to find a way that distributes the burden fairly and in line with beliefs of the society. In many ways taxes reflect the values of a nation's population. When we provide tax deductions for charities and charitable contributions, for health care expenditures, and for older people, we are expressing our belief in their worth over other kinds of activities and people.

Governments always make sure they have the money to do what they want to do. The questions are simply over how they will obtain that money, from whom they will obtain it, and in what amounts.

There are three general classifications of taxes—*proportional, progressive,* and *regressive.* R. Pennant-Rea and B. Emmott (1983), among others, claim that a proportional tax is blind to income, that it takes the same proportion of a wealthy person's funds as a poor person's. A flat 10 percent tax on all incomes, without regard to the circumstances of the taxpayer, would be a proportional tax, which is seldom used. It has been strongly supported by Steve Forbes, who has sought the presidency as a Republican. He calls his plan a "flat tax," which is proportional and which is discussed below.

Progressive taxes require people to pay on the basis of their wealth. The more money they have, the larger share of their money is paid in taxes, and, similarly, the lower their incomes, or wealth, the lower the taxes they pay. The U.S. federal personal income tax is a progressive tax. It charges higher rates at the upper levels of income and lower rates at the lower levels; in fact, people with the lowest incomes pay little or no personal income tax. The Earned Income Tax Credit gives money to low-income families through the tax system.

There is a bias in the income tax toward those who earn their money from working as opposed to those who earn their money from investments. Those who earn money from investments may pay a larger tax on their earnings than those who earn money from working. There is also a bias in favor of families. Those who support children and other family members pay fewer dollars in taxes than those who support only themselves. As noted, too, there is a bias in favor of those who give money to charitable causes. They pay lower taxes because they do not pay taxes on the amounts that they contribute to charitable causes. Thus, the income tax, like all taxes, reflects a variety of values and government goals.

A regressive tax is one that places its burden more heavily on lower-income people than on upper-income people. The favorite example used by those who write about tax policy is the sales tax, which is charged at a certain rate—

6 percent is a common amount—on purchases. Some say that the sales tax is fair because it charges everyone the same amount, that everyone faces an equal burden. In reality, however, the sales tax is regressive, because the lower one's income, the larger the percentage of one's earnings that is spent on items for which sales taxes are paid, such as food and clothing. People with great wealth spend smaller proportions of their entire wealth on items that they purchase in retail stores. They use much of their money for savings, investments, insurance, and the like, on which sales taxes are usually not charged. Therefore, there is a great difference in the percentage of one's income that is paid in sales taxes, based upon one's overall income. In some states sales taxes are not applied to necessities such as food, clothing, and shelter, which mitigates against the regressive nature of the sales tax; the lower-income families, who spend the largest parts of their incomes on such necessities, are not taxed on them, thus making the sales tax less regressive.

A taxation idea that became popular during the 1996 presidential campaign was the "flat tax," which was supported most strongly by candidate Steve Forbes but also had other adherents. The idea was to replace the progressive income tax, which is complicated and requires extensive effort to calculate for many people, with a single-rate tax for all taxpayers. Different supporters had different ideas about its amount and variations in its administration, but generally it was suggested that the rate be 15 or 20 percent. The inherent lack of progressivism in the tax would be compensated for with an exclusion for all taxpayers who earned less than a specified amount per year. Most calculations of the impact of the Forbes plan, at least, showed that it would greatly benefit the higher-wage earners and cost middle-income taxpayers more than the system that was in existence (Gibbs, 1996).

In 1993 President Bill Clinton said that his administration was considering using a Value Added Tax (VAT) as a means of financing his new health care reforms. The VAT, according to Pennant-Rea and Emmott (1983), is widely used in European nations, Mexico, and other nations but, thus far, not in the United States, Canada, and Japan. The VAT is somewhat akin to the Marxist notion of the value of labor. When a raw material is turned into a finished product, it is taxed every step of the route, from beginning to end, but ultimately only the consumer pays the tax. For example, a rancher sells a head of cattle to a packing house. That rancher pays the VAT of 10 or 20 percent but passes it along as part of the price to the packing house. The packing house sells the meat that it takes from the head of cattle to a food store and also pays the VAT and passes the tax cost along to the food store. The food store sells the product to the consumer, who pays the VAT and is the only participant who does not pass along the tax.

Ultimately, the VAT can quickly and easily raise extensive revenues for the government. The consumer pays what amounts to a large national sales tax.

Is the tax regressive? Perhaps it is, because it is applied to products at all stages of their manufacture. Lower-income people spend disproportionately more for products than upper-income people. This tax, however, is supposed to be easy to administer and raises revenues efficiently, and it could, in theory, replace all or part of the income tax.

Some suggest that the Social Security tax is regressive. Everyone pays the same rate on his or her earnings up to a maximum salary. The lower-income person pays his or her percentage, matched by a comparable amount from the employer, up to that maximum. The amount of one's earnings does not affect the rate paid, only the amount, thus the wealthier person pays only to the maximum and nothing above that. Social Security benefits, however, are related to one's earnings and the amount of one's contributions over time. Therefore, the lower-income worker can expect benefits upon retirement or if he or she ever becomes disabled, which are related to the amount paid into the system.

Some assert that Social Security is not a tax at all. They view it as an insurance premium that protects one against retiring in poverty, or losing income because of disability. It protects information from loss of all income when a worker dies. Participants receive the amount they should, based upon their contributions. Benefits are based on money paid in, not on the special needs of the beneficiaries. Some believe that part of one's Social Security payments should be invested by the payer. President George W. Bush is a proponent of that policy, which was a major public issue in 2005.

There are many other kinds of taxes. Some are called sin taxes. These taxes are placed on alcohol and tobacco, for example. The assumption is that government wants to discourage the use of these products and, therefore, makes them more expensive by applying extra taxes. There are also luxury taxes on such things as jewelry, expensive vehicles, boats, and other costly items. Taxes of this kind are based on the notion that people who can afford such luxuries ought to pay more in taxes than those who cannot afford such luxuries.

There are fuel and energy taxes as well. Governments that want to control the use of fuel and energy will raise the taxes on these commodities as a way of discouraging people from wasting energy. In some European nations gasoline costs three times as much as it does in the United States.

There are also a number of tax incentives, special breaks in tax structures, to encourage some kinds of purchases or behaviors and to discourage others. For example, some states exempt food and clothing from sales taxes. Others exclude medical care and prescriptions from the sales tax. These, again, are means for making the sales tax more progressive.

There are a number of ways in which government expresses its policies and preferences through the tax structure.

The Money Supply

The amount of money in circulation and the value of that money are also products of governmental policy. When government wants more money in circulation, it makes it easier for banks to borrow money from the federal government and make loans to citizens. The loaning of money by banks actually creates money and expands the money supply. The more money banks loan, the more money there is in the economy. When government wants to reduce the money supply and cut down the amount of money in circulation, it makes it more expensive and difficult for banks to make loans (Snider, 1965).

Government needs to control the money supply as a means of controlling inflation, which occurs when there is more money in the economy than there are available goods and services, or to spur economic growth when there is not enough money being invested in the economy. Increasing the interest rate slows down the economy and helps prevent or at least control inflation. Lowering the rate tends to lead to economic investment and growth.

In the United States the executive branch of government influences the money supply, often based upon the advice of the Council of Economic Advisors, a group of three appointed by the president with the consent of the Senate. In addition, the president annually must report to Congress on the nation's economy. The establishment of that report and the creation of the Council of Economic Advisors resulted from the passage of the Employment Act of 1946 (Burns, Peltason, & Cronin, 1995). Other entities, such as the Federal Reserve Board and the Department of the Treasury, also play significant roles in studying and molding the economy.

The process of creating money works by consumers and businesses borrowing money from banks for investment in capital growth. Banks are able to loan money based upon their assets and their reserve requirements. For example, if the bank has a current reserve requirement of 10 percent and it makes a loan of $10,000, it must have $1,000 in assets to back the loan. The other $9,000, however, is new money, and when the borrower pays back the loan, plus the interest, the bank now has greater assets. It actually created the $9,000 by the use of its account with the Federal Reserve Bank, an independent agency that is, in essence, a bank for banks. The bank can borrow more money from the Federal Reserve, which increases its assets, and makes more loans. The Federal Reserve makes it more costly for banks to borrow when it wants to restrict the money supply and less costly when it wants to expand the money supply.

Parenthetically, paper money and coins have very little to do with the amount of money in circulation. There is a great deal more money in circulation than there are bills or coins to cover it. Cash is simply a convenience that is used for some transactions. Most of the money in circulation is simply numbers in checking accounts that are transferred from one account to another (Snider, 1965). Little of the money people spend is cash. Instead, it is spent through writing checks. With the widespread use of credit cards there is even less need for cash. People charge their expenditures to their credit cards, they are billed for those expenditures, and they write checks to pay the credit card bills. In the whole process no cash ever changes hands. Again, money is created by banks when they make loans; the loans are generally made in the form of credit to a customer's checking account.

One of the ways in which the money supply increases is through expenditures. Government is a major spender of funds, along with businesses. Businesses spend to increase their profits. Governments spend most often to carry out their programs; however, they sometimes spend to improve the economy. When governments and businesses spend money on anything, they increase the supply of money in the economy. When governments spend money at the lower levels of the economy, by providing assistance to low-income people, for example, the money is spent almost immediately. As it circulates through the economy—to the stores in which the people spend the money, the banks where the stores deposit their receipts, the manufacturers or farmers who make the products that are purchased or grown—the amount of money is multiplied. Therefore, government jobs programs, cash assistance programs, and food stamp programs, in addition to improving the lives of people, are means to introduce more money into the economy. Putting money into the hands of any people puts money into the hands of all people. The effect of putting money into the economy through assistance programs stimulates what is referred to as the multiplier effect, a concept developed by Keynes.

The leverage effect (also a Keynesian concept), on the other hand, occurs when money is introduced into the economy "at the top"—by providing financial assistance, contracts, and other benefits to large corporations and to wealthy individuals. The money, once used, again moves through the economy, although not always as rapidly as when it is introduced at the lower levels of the economy. One of the approaches tried for increasing the resources at the top of the economy has been "supply side economics" (Pennant-Rea & Emmott, 1983), a central tenet of Reagan's early 1980s policy. When a major manufacturer or a very wealthy person is provided with a government contract or a tax cut or any other means of providing relief to the top of the economy, the theory goes, the money circulates and provides employment, and money in other forms, to everyone else.

Some people refer to the leverage effect as "trickle-down" economics: provide money to the top earners in the economy, and they will invest it in new production, purchases, and home construction, among other things; eventually those funds will trickle down to reach everyone else. Conversely, if you put the money into the base of the economy, such as assistance programs for disadvantaged people, the money will eventually "trickle up" to the wealthiest. Spending money simply adds to economic activity and wealth.

Of course, when governments spend more than they have or more than they can justify based upon the wealth of their nation, they cause inflation. That is, if they spend money that is not worth very much—given that the wealth of the nation determines what the money is worth—they cheapen the money and stall the economy. Inflation is simply devaluation of money; it is too much money chasing too few goods. When on a given day $100 purchases only half of what it would have been able to purchase a day or month earlier, the cost has been inflated and the money has lost half its value.

Inflation typically results when money no longer reflects the value of the nation's wealth. Simply printing money, without an adequate economic base to back the amount that is printed, leads to inflation.

Social policy is affected by monetary policy in many ways, and social policies influence the money system. In the simplest terms, when there is a large supply of money available, there are more resources for social services of all kinds, and governments are more likely to appropriate those funds for such services than they are when money is in short supply. Similarly, social programs usually benefit the lowest-income individuals and families in the nation most directly. Those individuals and families, of necessity, spend nearly all the money available to them. In some cases, through borrowing, they spend more money than they have available. The multiplier effect comes rapidly into play when the money is spent, and the trickling up through the economy is often dramatic. The ultimate result is often a stronger or at least more active economy as well as increases in tax revenues, often larger in amount than the social services expenditures were.

When the money supply contracts and interest rates increase, there is less investment by businesses, which often results in reduced employment. This, in turn, can cause greater social needs. In many ways social policies are a central factor in the operations of an economy and represent significant economic as well as social functions.

Deficit Financing

There is extensive discussion in the United States about the virtues and vices of federal deficit financing. Deficit financing is another form of governmental finance in which government borrows money and uses that money for its own operations. It is a tax because, ultimately, the money and the interest on the debt, which is paid to those who loaned the government money, are paid by taxpayers. According to the *Pocket Economist* (Pennant-Rea & Emmott, 1983), deficit financing is the act of allowing a budget deficit as a way of putting money into the economy and expanding the demand for goods and services. Governments may sometimes simply expand the amount of money in circulation, but, in the United States, the money is borrowed from lenders and paid back to them.

It should be noted that deficit financing is only an option for the federal government. Only sovereign, or autonomous, nations that control their own money supplies are able to add to the nation's economy through some of the mechanisms already discussed. Similarly, only sovereign nations—such as Germany and Mexico—can issue bonds to spur investment and participate in the kinds of borrowing and lending discussed in this section. Most state governments, by law, must operate on strictly balanced budgets. They must show that their revenue estimates will pay for their planned expenditures. If their revenue estimates fall short and less money is available than was anticipated when the budget was developed, they must reduce expenditures for the rest of the fiscal year so that it will end with a balanced budget.

Of course, some states are permitted to borrow—from retirement funds and other trust funds and from banks—but they must pay back the loans plus interest, just as they would pay for any other expenditure. Only the federal government may determine that it wants to borrow money and authorize itself to borrow and spend more through the issuance of bonds, treasury notes, and other financial instruments. State governments generally must spend only as much as they receive in taxes. If they need more money, they must borrow it from banks, just as families must.

Despite the criticism and expressions of concern, however, deficit financing is often a convenient and efficient way to improve a nation's economic situation. Like individual citizens, nations are able to do things through borrowing, which they could not do with cash. An individual might want to purchase a house and do so by borrowing money. Saving the money for the house, on the other hand, might require twenty years. Borrowing the money and paying off a mortgage may make it possible for the person to live in the house twenty years sooner. That is not terribly different from a national government borrowing money to undertake new projects without cutting back on other services and without waiting to save the money through tax revenues.

There is one essential difference between borrowing by a national government and individual borrowing: the individual must eventually pay back the money. Individuals and families ultimately die, while nations do not. One always hears, in discussions of deficit financing, that by borrowing money, we are mortgaging the quality of life of our children and grandchildren. That sounds reasonable, but, in reality, a nation's debt can go on forever. The children, grandchildren, great-great-grandchildren need not pay the debt back either. They can simply continue paying interest and borrowing more to pay off old debts, into infinity. The nation is not going anywhere and does not have the same constraints a family has.

This does not mean there are no consequences for nations that do not pay their debts. They may find it impossible to borrow, to buy the products of other nations, or even to sell their own goods on world markets. Nations that have become economically unsound have typically experienced widespread poverty, revolutions, and other severe problems. In addition, the interest payments on the debt are a major item in the national budget. Paying for the interest competes with all other demands for money, including social welfare programs. The national debt occupies a larger and larger share of the national budget and thus reduces the amounts of money available for appropriation for social needs.

It is important to note that deficit financing is far from a universally accepted idea. Many political figures campaign against it. There has been a national movement to introduce and adopt a new amendment to the U.S. Constitution that would require the government to operate with a balanced budget, the so-called balanced budget amendment (Burns, Peltason, & Cronin, 1995). At times the movement has been strong and popular, although, at the time this is being written, it is not often reported in the media as a change that is being actively pursued. Nevertheless, President Clinton campaigned on a promise to reduce the federal deficit over a period of several years and carried out fiscal measures to achieve that goal. Congress has also attempted to reduce the deficit through legislation, the most important of which has been the Graham-Rudman-Hollings bill, which focuses on balancing the budget.

In 1995, as part of the Republican Contract with America, additional efforts were made to eliminate the budget deficit over a period of years, efforts with which President Clinton continued to agree. However, the approach of Congress was to eliminate the deficit and cut taxes at the same time, largely through eliminating and reducing government programs. There was special emphasis on reducing social welfare programs. The president tended to oppose the depth of the social welfare reductions approved by Congress. The desire for a balanced budget became a major point of contention between the president and Congress in 1995 and 1996, resulting in deadlocks that closed down many federal agencies for periods of days and weeks. However, in 1997 Congress passed and Clinton signed the Balanced Budget Act, which was to provide for a balanced budget. In fact, the last federal budgets of the twentieth century were balanced.

Some observers point out that deficit financing has further policy implications. When the government operates through borrowing, who receives the interest? Generally, the debt is to other Americans, often the most wealthy Americans, who own the Federal Reserve notes and other fiscal instruments through their own investments. Therefore, the interest goes to the wealthy.

K. Phillips (1990) points out that during the presidency of Ronald Reagan the U.S. debt and deficit increased because taxes were reduced without a comparable reduction in spending. The borrowing, which was necessary, increased U.S. expenditures on interest paid on the debt, which went from $96 billion in 1982 to $216 billion in 1988. Because taxes were reduced at the same time, fewer dollars earned with that interest were repaid to the federal treasury as taxes. Phillips points out that the increase in the deficit combined with the decrease in taxes had a great deal to do with the U.S. redistribution of wealth that took place in the 1980s. During that time the wealthiest Americans had major increase in their incomes; the middle-income groups either stayed the same or experienced slight increases in wealth; while the lowest-income individuals, who have few investments and whose benefit programs were either reduced or not expanding, declined (Ginsberg, 1995). Therefore, it is clear that deficit financing has an impact on individual taxpayers and the distribution of the burden of paying for government services. The two political parties were once divided over deficit financing. However, both now pursue it as an economic strategy, at times.

The Budget Process

Economics and finance are such important components of social policy that they are central to much of the work done by the executive and legislative branches every year in the form of budgeting and budget preparation. The budget process continues throughout the year in the federal and state governments. (For a sound and detailed discussion of the budget process, see Burns, Peltason, & Cronin, 1995.) The budget process begins well before the end of the budget, or fiscal, year, which at this time is October 1–September 30 in the federal government and which varies among the state governments. The most common state fiscal year is July 1–June 30, although some use the calendar year as the fiscal year.

In the federal executive branch the president proposes a budget to the Congress each year, which is based upon the estimates and requests of all the government agencies. The executive branch has an agency called the Office of Management and Budget (OMB), which studies all of the budget requests and makes a recommendation to the president for the new fiscal year. The president proposes the budget, which is a massive document, to Congress, where it is again studied by a number of groups, especially the Senate Finance Committee and the House of Representatives Ways and Means Committee. Congress also has an agency called the Congressional Budget Office, which serves as something of an auditor and planner on financial matters.

The Office of Management and Budget and the Congressional Budget Office both have large staffs of experts on every phase of government. They carefully study the agencies' budget requests and try to determine the impact of those requests as well as the impact of any recommended changes in them. How many fewer people might be served, for example, if the budget for food stamps were reduced? What level of health care will be available with the recommended appropriation for Medicaid? The policy experts in these two offices are familiar enough with the programs to make knowledgeable recommendations for budget or appropriations levels. Those who work within the programs find that influencing the staff of these two organizations may be more significant in producing results than anything else they might do in trying to improve their programs.

Ultimately, the president's executive budget, which specifies both income and expenditures, is acted upon by Congress after careful study by the two committees. There is intense negotiation, and at times conflict, between the executive and legislative branches about the budget. In fact, it is the budget that has caused some of the conflicts between the federal executive and legislative branches. The tax increases passed by Congress and signed by President George H. W. Bush during his term of office were a source of conflict and of strong political maneuvering. In fact, the issue of taxes was probably the most widely discussed subject in the 1992 presidential campaign that followed. By 1993 President Clinton engaged in—and prevailed in—a major conflict with Congress over the economic program he was proposing for the coming fiscal year.

The president exercises some control over the budget with the veto power. However, the president must either accept and sign the budget or veto all of it. As discussed earlier, Congress passed a bill to provide the president with the "line item veto," which allowed Clinton, the only president to whom it applied, to pick and choose among the items in the budget, vetoing only some of them. However, the judiciary found the line item veto unconstitutional.

The federal budget also shows deficit financing such as the amount that will be borrowed, the amount of interest expected to be paid, and the overall balance sheet of anticipated revenues, expenses, borrowing, and deficits.

Budgets are essentially plans. Less money may come to the treasury from taxes than is anticipated, or more money may be raised. Agencies may not choose to spend all of the money appropriated for them, or they may receive some additional money during the fiscal year to carry out a specific objective or to avoid reducing services to clients.

The state budget process is in some ways similar to but also strikingly different from the federal process. For example, states in general must always present and operate under a balanced budget. It is a violation of the law in most cases for the state to operate in a deficit position. And in most states, as mentioned, the governor has line item veto power and can eliminate or reduce a specific budget item without vetoing the whole appropriations bill.

As in the national government, on the state level there are professional staffs in both the executive and legislative branches whose members know about all the various state agencies, study their budget requests, and help develop the final budget legislation. In most states it is the governor who presents the executive budget, which is, as it is in the federal process, the most important working document in the fiscal planning process. In a few states a board of the key elected officials develops and presents the budget on behalf of a kind of executive committee. Those are generally states with weak governors. Even in those states, however, the governor presents an executive budget, although it does not have the same importance as the executive budget has in states with strong governors. Even in the states with weak governors the governor has the line item veto power and exercises it often in creating the budget bill.

The bill that is finally passed is usually a combination of the executive budget and changes made to it by the legislative branch. Battles over the budget are so important that in many states, and at times in the federal government, the budget does not pass the legislative body and become law until the fiscal year ends. In those situations the state often passes a kind of bill called a "continuing resolution," which allows government to spend money at the same level as it did in the prior year for the functions specified in the now-expired budget. Failing to do so, which has happened from time to time, may mean that essential services are abandoned and that government employees are not paid for their services or required to work. Such situations usually last only a few days because they paralyze the government so that everyone works to resolve the problems and pass a budget.

An issue that often becomes critical in budget debates is the efficiency of government, or its avoidance of duplication of services. The Congressional Budget Office and many private groups, including lobbying groups, study the budgets of the state and federal governments and look for ways to eliminate waste and conserve funds. A popular book, *Government Racket* (Gross, 1992), summarizes the problems of duplication and waste in a variety of federal government programs.

In American state and national government there is nothing quite so fascinating as the ways in which presidents, governors, Congress, and state legislatures deal with the budget. It is the budget that contains the real details of social policy, and it is the budget that reflects what government wants to do and will do in a multitude of specific programs and procedures.

Conclusion

The levels of and the ways in which government finances itself have great impact on the levels of human services programs that government is willing to sustain. Spending money on social welfare programs may have a very positive impact on the economy through the multiplier effect. Spending too much may cause inflation, which is often harmful to everyone because, no matter how little or how much money they have, it is worth less than it would have been had there been less or no inflation.

It is important to understand that economic policy and social policy are closely connected and that government can increase and decrease the money available to citizens through its own policy decisions. Budget and finance policies are the highest form of social policy in some ways. In fact, there is no such thing as a social policy that does not have some financial implications. Therefore, understanding social policy also requires an understanding of economic policy. What is and is not done in the social policy field is always related to some form of economic issues.

Discussion Questions

1. Are social welfare programs more likely to have an impact through the "multiplier" or the "leverage" effect? Explain your answer.

2. This chapter suggests that the free market, classic economic theory of Adam Smith, is fundamental in the U.S. economy. Try to list three examples, not already used in the chapter, of the ways in which free market economic principles are followed in the U.S. economy.

3. Describe some of the ways in which the U.S. economy appears to be a "mixed" economy. Identify elements from all three economic approaches discussed in this chapter.

4. John Maynard Keynes is considered a giant in economic theory because of the contributions he made to showing governments how they might control their economies. In your own words, describe what you believe are some of the practical consequences of Keynes's economic discoveries.

References

Bullock, A., & Stallybrass, O. (1977). *The Harper dictionary of modern thought.* New York: Harper & Row.

Burns, J. M., Peltason, J. W., & Cronin, T. E. (1995). *Government by the people,* 16th ed. Englewood Cliffs, NJ: Prentice-Hall.

Cassidy, J. (October 20, 27, 1997). The next thinker: The return of Karl Marx. *New Yorker,* 248–289.

Cassidy, J. (November 30, 1998). Profile: Height of eloquence. *New Yorker,* 70–75.

Dolgoff, R. Feldstein, D., & Skolnik, L. (1993). *Understanding social welfare,* 3rd ed. New York: Longman.

Galbraith, J. (1998). *The affluent society,* 40th anniversary edition. Novia Scotia: Mariner Books.

Gibbs, N. (January 29, 1996). Knock 'em flat. *Time*, 22–27.

Ginsberg, L. (1987). Economic, political, and social context. In A. Ninahan et al. (Eds.), *Encyclopedia of social work*, 18th ed., xxxiii–xli. Silver Spring, MD: NASW Press.

Ginsberg, L. (1995). *Social work almanac*, 2nd ed. Washington, DC: NASW Press.

Greenberg, E. S. (1989). *The American political system: A radical approach*, 5th ed. Glenview, IL: Scott, Foresman, Little.

Gross, M. L. (1992). *Government racket: Washington waste from A to Z*. New York: Bantam.

Hirsch, E. D. (1993). *The dictionary of cultural literacy: What every American needs to know*. Boston: Houghton Mifflin.

Moreau, R. (April 12, 1993). The "Saigon virus": It's catching—business is booming in South Vietnam. *Newsweek*, 34–38.

Pennant-Rea, R., & Emmott, B. (1983). *The pocket economist*. Cambridge: Cambridge University Press.

Phillips, K. (1990). *The politics of rich and poor*. New York: Random House.

Popple, P. R., & Leighninger, L. (1999). *Social work, social welfare, and American society*, 3rd ed. Boston: Allyn & Bacon.

Smith, A. (1910). *The wealth of nations*. New York: Knopf (Everyman's Library). Original edition published in 1776.

Snider, D. A. (1965). *Economic myth and reality*. Englewood Cliffs, NJ: Prentice-Hall.

SIX

The Descriptive Component
Economic Assistance and Entitlements

A fundamental requirement for understanding social policy is understanding social programs. Throughout this book, programs—or, as they are sometimes called, provisions—are discussed as the outcomes of social policy. Problems are addressed through the development of policies, and programs are developed to implement the policies and resolve the problems.

In this book programs are discussed and described as examples of public policy and analysis and as benchmarks in the historical development of social welfare and social work. This chapter and the chapter that follows are designed to describe the basic categories of social welfare programs and certain facts about the programs to provide an understanding of the American social welfare system and the ways in which it operates.

Although social programs are an important part of overall American government and charitable activity, they are not as well known as one might expect among American citizens. It is critical, however, that human services workers, especially social workers, have a detailed and working understanding of social programs. In many ways social programs are the subject matter of social work and other human services professions, just as medicine is the subject matter of physicians and law the subject matter of attorneys. Social programs are what social and other human services workers use, in addition to their own professional skills for serving clients, to help people. A knowledge of social programs is indispensable for every kind of practice in every kind of situation, yet it must be understood that even the most experienced human services professionals cannot know the details of all the programs that are available to their clients at all times and in all places. Understanding that social policies, and thus, social programs are continuously being changed is important. Sometimes these programs are changed by an overhaul of an existing policy, such as the shift from the Aid to Families with Dependent Children (AFDC) to Temporary Assistance for Needy Families (TANF) as a result of the Personal Responsibility and Work Opportunity Reconciliation

Act (PRWOR) of 1996 (see table 1 for list of policy and program acronyms). More frequent, however, are the incremental changes made to policies over time. The Child Abuse and Treatment Act (CAPTA) and the Older Americans Act (OAA), as described in chapter 7, have been amended numerous times over the years, and both policies have implications for social work or human services practitioners.[1] In the past, it may have been a bit easier for human services and social workers to practice without a great deal of policy knowledge as services were a bit more straightforward, funding was streamlined, and fewer battles over resources for programs existed. However, a survey of workers in aging programs over a decade ago noted that knowledge of aging policies, specific legislation, and regulations was ranked as the top area needed for their jobs (Peterson, Wendt, & Douglass, 1991). The current unstable nature of support and the increasing complexity of policies such as TANF, Medicaid, Medicare, and Social Security require the human services worker to have specialized policy knowledge (Liebig, 1995). It will be very difficult for those working in the human services profession who do not have a solid knowledge of the relevant policies and programs pertinent to their field of practice. Inevitably these policies have the potential to impact not only the type of services they offer, but who they offer them to, for how long, and under what conditions. Sometimes a policy change can result in a dramatic shift in the kind of job the human services or social worker does. For example, a student who worked for the Georgia Department of Social Services as an AFDC caseworker once remarked that after the shift from AFDC to TANF what she did at work changed completely—from a counselor to an employment services worker! She said that it seemed like overnight the DSS office where she worked had been transformed into an employment agency rather than a department of social services. Clearly, many of these changes were the result of a new policy that placed emphasis on work and time limited public assistance. Learning about programs and keeping up with their development is, for the human services worker, the equivalent of the physician maintaining current knowledge about medical advances. Fortunately, due to the expansion of policy related materials available in libraries and especially on the Internet, for social workers with access, keeping up with the latest policy changes is much easier. The ways that social workers can keep up to date are included in chapter 9.

Table 1. Frequently Used Acronyms for Federal Policies or Government Agencies

FEDERAL POLICIES	
Acronym	*Policy*
ADA	Americans with Disabilities Act
AFDC	Aid to Families with Dependent Children

CAPTA	Child Abuse Prevention and Treatment Act
EITC	Earned Income Tax Credit
FMLA	Family and Medical Leave Act
HIPAA	Health Insurance Portability and Accountability Act
IDEA	Individuals with Disabilities in Education Act
OAA	Older Americans Act
PRWORA	Personal Responsibility and Work Opportunity Reconciliation Act
SSI	Supplemental Security Insurance
TANF	Temporary Assistance to Needy Families
WIC	Women, Infants and Children

FEDERAL AGENCIES

Acronym	Government Agency
ACF	Administration on Children and Families
AOA	Administration on Aging
CDC	Center for Disease Control
CMS	Center for Medicare and Medicaid Services
DOJ	Department of Justice
EEOC	U.S. Equal Employment Opportunity Commission
GAO	Government Accounting Office
HHS	Health and Human Services
NIMH	National Institute for Mental Health
OJJDP	Office of Juvenile Justice and Delinquency Prevention
SAMHSA	The Substance Abuse and Mental Health Services Administration
SSA	Social Security Administration

Familiarity with Social Programs

There are several reasons social programs are not as well known to the general public as other programs such as education and health care. First, information about social programs is not typically taught to students in elementary or secondary schools. In most cases students in higher education—unless they happen to be students of social work or social problems or policy courses in fields such as political science, psychology, and sociology—learn little about social programs. In college curricula there is usually no requirement for the study of such issues, although students may be exposed to them through elective courses or through the selection of specific social sciences as part of their basic undergraduate requirements.

For many social work students at the baccalaureate and graduate levels social work courses are the first in which they learn about such fundamental social services as Social Security, mental health programs, child welfare, and corrections.

Second, most Americans, especially younger Americans, do not have very much contact with social services systems. We all pay Social Security taxes and Medicare taxes. We may hear about or read about social services programs in the media, and we may even have relatives or friends who are recipients of social welfare programs and services. Yet, personal involvement with the social services is not a typical experience for healthy, relatively prosperous American young people and their families. Many people come to social agencies for the first time when they encounter a disabling personal or family crisis such as mental illness, unemployment, or severe physical illness and have no knowledge or skills for gaining access to the services that are available to them.

As other parts of this book demonstrate, the recipients of social welfare services are typically special groups, such as older people; young mothers who, because of lack of support from the fathers of their children, need financial assistance; children who cannot live with their own families and therefore become part of the foster care or adoption systems; aspiring adoptive parents; foster parents; people with a variety of physical and mental disabilities; and those who encounter difficulty with the law.

Even when they are all added together, the groups who receive social services constitute a relatively small proportion of the American society. More important, they are often isolated geographically and generationally from college students and many employed adults. At some point during their lives, most Americans have some contact with social programs—when they retire, when their parents are ill, when they become unemployed—but, so long as everything in their lives is satisfactory, most have little or no contact with social services programs or agencies.

Third, even political figures are reluctant to discuss social welfare programs in great detail during elections. Those who speak most about social welfare programs typically oppose them, using them as a surrogate enemy that stands for "government waste," poor economic policy, and a number of other negative indicators against which political campaigns may be launched. Consequently, a detailed knowledge of American social welfare programs is a requirement for most people who are newly exposed to the human services professions.

It is a practical impossibility to describe in detail all of the social welfare programs that operate in the United States. The programs are extensive and complex. Many who work in them full-time for decades do not know every detail of all of the programs in their own organizations.

A conscientious study of social welfare programs would include some comparative analysis of services in the United States with services in other nations. Adding the international dimension makes it even less likely that a human services curriculum would be able to describe comprehensively all of the relevant programs and services. Even if it were technically possible to do so, it would also be challenging because the programs are constantly changing through judicial, legislative, and executive actions, as chapters 4 and 5 suggest. But even if all the roadblocks to describing every program in detail were removed, doing so would probably prove to be so boring for most students that instructors and authors would not attempt such comprehensive descriptions.

Reference works such as the *Encyclopedia of Social Work,* 19th ed. (Edwards et al., 1995), *The Social Work Dictionary,* 3rd ed. (Barker, 1995), and *Social Work Almanac,* 2nd ed. (Ginsberg, 1995) provide the kinds of descriptive information on individual programs that can help students understand enough to write about them or bring them to the attention or benefit of their clients. Information and referral services operate in most communities so that those who are in need of services can find out what the services are and how they operate.

It is necessary for beginning students as well as those at any level of professional practice to remember that there are several broad categories of services. The eligibility rules and the nature of the specific services available to specific individuals or families vary considerably.

Table 2. Useful Policy Information Web Sites

Bureau of Justice Statistics	http://www.ojp.usdoj.gov/bis/
Census Bureau	http://www.census.gov/
Department of Justice	http://www.usdoj.gov/index.html
Federal Bureau of Investigation	http://www.fbi.gov/ucr/02cius.htm
Latest Federal Government Statistics	http://www.whitehouse.gov/news/fsbr.html
National Center for Health Statistics	http://www.cdc.gov/nchs/express.htm
The National Committee Vital and Health on Statistics	http://ncvhs.hhs.gov
Office of Juvenile Justice Delinquency and Prevention	http://ojjdp.ncjrs.org/
Social Security Programs	http://www.ssa.gov/SSA_Home.html
State Policy Documentation Project	http://www.spdp.org/index.htm

Table 2 (*continued*)

Statistical Resources on the Web (University of Michigan)	http://www.lib.umich.edu/govdocs/stats.html
2000 Greenbook, Committee on Ways and Means, U.S. House of Representatives	http://www.gpoaccess.gov
United Nations	http://unstats.un.org/unsd/databases.htm
U.S. Administration on Aging	http://www.aoa.gov/
U.S. Department of Health and Human Services, Administration for Children and Families	http://www.acf.hhs.gov/
Welfare Information Network	http://www.financeprojectinfo.org/win/
World Health Organization	http://www.who.int/whosis/

Exploring Social Welfare Programs

The federal philosophy since the early 1980s has been to give states more say in how they operate programs. The impact of devolution, or the shift of power from the federal to the state level, on the social welfare system has been lamented by many social work and human services professionals, primarily because they think that client rights were better protected when the federal government exercised more control over welfare programs (Schneider & Netting, 1999; DiNitto, 2003). The period between the Great Depression and the early 1960s has been termed "cooperative federalism," meaning that the federal and state governments shared responsibility for social programs more or less equally (Laslovich, 1993). However, beginning with the Nixon presidency, a new type of federalism or "new federalism" emerged. New federalism includes various types and forms of devolution, deregulation, decentralization, tax cuts, and reduction of big government (Conlan, 1998; Linhorst, 2002). All of these are examples of the ways some administrations have attempted to shift the responsibility of welfare from the federal government to the states. Table 17 (see page 290) highlights these strategies and the main arguments both for and against using such strategies. The general intent of the federal administrations from Nixon to the present has been to reduce the size of the federal government and increase the authority and decision making power of the states.

One of the strategies to emphasize devolution is through the use of block grants to states to solve a social problem. DiNitto (2003) defines block grants as "federal payments to state or local governments for general functions, such as health, welfare, education, law enforcement, and community development. The money must be spent for the general function of the block grant, but states and communities are free to decide specific uses for the funds" (51). Block grants generally give states more control over the federal funds they receive than do categorical programs, which have many more rules and regulations. Critics of block grants contend that the trade off for more state flexibility has been reduced federal funds. Further, decision making for social welfare programs typically has less support at the state level than at the federal level and fewer resources (DiNitto, 2003; Jansson, 2001). The Alcohol and Drug Abuse and Mental Health Services block grant, for example, provides funding to states to address needs for substance abuse and mental health services. The funding is given to states by the federal government in blocks (lump sums) and then local community organizations apply directly to states for funding of their programs.

Deregulation, another strategy of decreasing federal responsibility, refers to the elimination of governmental controls from industry, private and public. Privatization relates to the transfer of governmental responsibility to private sector, particularly when those private organizations are able to provide similar services or supplies at a less expensive rate (DiNitto, 2003). The privatization of any services, it has been argued, allows for more efficient, higher quality, and cost-effective services (Riedl, 2003). Decentralization refers to various means of allocating or transferring the authority and decision making responsibility from the central (federal) government to the state or local level. Rather than the program being controlled by one central organization, the program is controlled locally and thus is better able to react to specific circumstances in the community.

Characteristics of Social Welfare Programs
One of the complicated terms in social welfare is *entitlement*. According to Barker (1995, 121), an entitlement is "services, goods, or money due to an individual by virtue of a specific status." It is important to note that entitlements are provided as a right, not as charity. That is true not only of the benefits to which people contribute, such as OASDI, but also of assistance that is paid for with general governmental funds raised through taxes. A service is an entitlement because the laws establishing it say that people in a specific class are legally entitled to that service. Governments have no discretion over eligibility; if someone fits the defined status or class, he or she need only apply for the service to receive it. A good bit of thinking, especially conservative economic and political thinking, finds the concept of entitlements repellent. If one person is entitled to something, that means someone else is obligated to provide it, says Block (1986), among others. Others who are more supportive of welfare assistance, such as Peter Edelman (1997), believe that

entitlement is a perfectly good term. It simply means, says Edelman, who resigned from the Clinton administration because of his disappointment with the president's signing the new welfare law, that the state is entitled to funds that will benefit citizens who are entitled to the help. However, it is unlikely that the term will be used frequently in the future to describe assistance programs; it has too many negative connotations for those who were instrumental in developing and putting the new welfare law into effect.

As noted previously, when and if individuals meet specific eligibility requirements, they are thought to have a legal right to receive certain goods, services, or financial benefits; then they are thought to be *entitled* to these benefits. People may be eligible for programs, for example, because they are veterans, because their income falls below a certain level, because they are elderly, or because they are disabled. In some cases, if individuals were denied benefits, they might be able to sue in court to receive those services they were denied. Examples of typical federal entitlement programs in the United States include Medicare, Social Security, Medicaid, or programs for veterans. Some entitlement programs may be means tested while others are open to specific groups of people such as the elderly or veterans and do not require a special test of financial means. Typically, programs that involve a test of one's income to qualify for those benefits place a stigma on the recipients. It is difficult, at times, for policy makers to predict how much will be needed to pay for these entitlement programs, thus projecting costs for entitlement programs is no easy endeavor. If the economy is not doing well, for example, more people may fall into poverty, taxing unemployment insurance programs or welfare. However, programs are not simply at the mercy of the economy. For example, although many economists and policy analysts have predicted the impact of the growing number of elderly individuals in the United States on entitlement programs such as Medicare and Social Security, the elderly are quite a powerful lobbying group and proposals to make major changes to Social Security or Medicare programs are met with strong opposition.

Eligibility in Social Welfare Programs
People often assume that social welfare policies refer to only means-tested programs such as TANF. However, social welfare programs can be considered to be both entitlement and means-tested programs. In addition, sometimes in order to be eligible for a program individuals must also be "tested." Chambers (2000) notes that an analysis of the eligibility rules of social welfare programs should include asking three important questions:

(1) Who gets what?
    The people who will be able to receive the benefits of a program.
(2) How much?
    The level or amount of benefits that a person will receive.

(3) Under what conditions?
The personal circumstances that will qualify that person to receive benefits. For example, do they have to be poor, a certain age, disabled?

Further, Gilbert and Terrell (2002) refer to four conditions of eligibility: (1) attributed need, (2) compensation, (3) diagnostic differentiation, and (4) means-tested need.

Eligibility on the basis of attributed need refers to legislation targeted at groups based on needs. Examples of attributed need include help for people when they grow older and for health care for children who need it but whose families are not insured. Examples of such policies include the Older Americans Act or the Family and Medical Leave Act of 1992. Both the OAA and FMLA are policies that address needs of individuals based on normal life events such as aging, the birth or adoption of a child, or caring for an elderly family member. Such needs are considered a normal, expected part of life. Compensation, however, refers to legislation targeted at groups, organizations, or geographical areas based on needs for equity. For example, Social Security might be considered to be a compensatory policy because individuals pay into Social Security as they work and then begin receiving the benefits when they reach a certain age. Another example might be the Ryan White Care Act, which provides funds to areas in the United States that have high rates/risks for HIV/AIDS. Diagnostic differentiation requires some kind of diagnostic test to determine eligibility, such as eligibility for Medicare Home Health Care, which measures performance on Activities of Daily Living (ADLS) such as walking or bathing. In order to qualify for SSI, for example, one must be certified, which usually involves a number of assessments by doctors, social workers, nurses, or physical therapists.

A means test usually involves looking at the combination of an individual's assets and income in comparison to what government agencies believe he or she needs in order to determine eligibility of a particular benefit (Chambers, 2000; Barker, 1995). Often a great deal of work goes into determining the rules and regulations for eligibility. For example, the poverty thresholds are the official version of the federal poverty measure and are updated by the Census Bureau (U.S. Department of Health and Human Services Office of the Assistant Secretary for Planning & Evaluation, 2003). Mollie Orshansky, who worked for the Social Security Administration in the 1960s, is credited with the creation of the policy thresholds (Fisher, 1992). Currently, the thresholds are almost always used for statistical purposes, to report on the number of people living in the United States who are poor, for example (HHS, 2003). On the other hand, the poverty guidelines are developed to determine eligibility for some social welfare programs such as Food Stamps, School Lunch Programs, Head Start, and the State Children's Health Insurance Program.

Table 3. Examples of Federal Government Programs
That Use the Poverty Guidelines to Determine Eligibility*

Federal Agency	Program Examples
Department of Agriculture	Food Stamps, Special Supplemental Nutrition Program for Women, Infants, and Children (WIC), the National School Lunch and School Breakfast programs
Department of Energy	Weatherization Assistance
Department of Health and Human Services	Community Services Block Grant, Head Start, Low-Income Home Energy Assistance, Children's Health Insurance Program
Department of Labor	Job Corps, Senior Community Service Employment Program, National Farmworker Jobs Program
Legal Services Corporation	Legal services for the poor

* The description in the table is based on Gordon M. Fisher, "Disseminating the Administrative Version of the Federal Poverty measure in the 1990s," paper presented June 6, 1996, at the annual meeting of the Sociological Practice Association, Arlington, Va. Fisher, a program analyst in the Office of the Assistant Secretary for Planning and Evaluation in the Department of Health and Human Services, has been responsible since 1982 for preparing the annual update of the poverty guidelines. http://www.wisc.edu/irp/faqs/faq7.htm

The poverty guidelines are used for administrative purposes and are released each year by the Department of Health and Human Services (HHS) (HHS, 2004). The 2004 poverty guideline for a family of four is $18,500. This means a family of four must have more than that amount to be considered nonpoor. Contrary to popular belief, generally speaking most cash assistance programs in the United States do not use poverty guidelines to determine eligibility. In fact, eligibility for TANF varies quite a bit across states so a person might be eligible in one state and not in another. This is because states can use a combination of financial, categorical, and behavioral criteria to determine eligibility for TANF. This means that being poor is only one of the criteria for becoming eligible for TANF.

The largest and most important income maintenance program is Social Security, often called Old Age Survivors and Disability Insurance, or OASDI. OASDI is an example of a non-means-tested program. OASDI is available to

Table 4. 2004 HHS Poverty Guidelines

Number of people in family	Yearly income must be the same or below this amount to be considered in poverty
1	$ 9,570
2	$12,830
3	$16,090
4	$19,350
5	$22,610
6	$25,870
7	$29,130
8	$32,390
For each additional person, add	*$ 3,260*

Source: Federal Register, Vol. 70, No. 33, February 18, 2005, 8373–8375.

elderly, blind, and disabled individuals and to eligible members of their families. There is no income limit for receiving OASDI; even the very wealthy may receive it.

The amount of OASDI depends upon a variety of factors, including the length of time the person worked in employment for which Social Security taxes were paid, age, and income when he or she worked. In the case of families that are collecting benefits under the coverage of a deceased wage earner, the amount paid depends upon the factors already mentioned plus the number of children in the family who are eighteen or under.

The means of the recipient are not a factor in determining benefits, just as they are not a factor in receiving benefits from a private insurance policy. That is, the wealth or poverty of the recipient is not a factor in determining eligibility or the amount of the benefit. A very wealthy person may receive a significant amount of money in monthly benefits based solely upon his or her earnings, age, and the number of years payments were made to Social Security. A very poor person may receive no more than the legal minimum, no matter how great his or her needs may be. The specific amounts of OASDI change each year to reflect inflation. In 1997 the maximum amount was $14,976 per year for an individual and $22,464 for a couple (Bernstein and Ma, 1996). However, because benefits depend on one's earnings, the amounts vary. The average is much lower than the maximums. In contrast to OASDI, SSI has strict income and resource limits (Kauffman, 2002). In other words, in order to be eligible for SSI, an individual has to submit a record of income in order to prove they are poor enough to receive it.

Of course, there are regulations governing OASDI that prevent recipients from collecting maximum benefits while continuing to work for relatively high earnings during their early retirement years. And recipients who have other income must pay taxes on a portion of the OASDI benefits. Ultimately, therefore, wealth has some impact on the benefits one may retain after taxes. Yet to calculate the specific benefits, no means test is used.

Location and Operation of Social Welfare Programs

Another way to describe services is in terms of the level of government or the location in which they are provided. Generally, government or public services are provided at the federal, state, and local—which includes counties, regions, cities, and towns—levels. As indicated, some services are largely local, while others are national or statewide in scope. There is great variability within the United States in the kinds and levels of services provided.

In the United States many services are provided through joint financing by the federal and state governments. The services, however, are usually delivered at the local level—in countries, cities, or regions. Very few services are provided directly from the federal government. Social Security, Supplemental Security Income, some services to Native Americans, and veterans' benefits are the primary exceptions.

It is a truism of American government and the federal system, discussed in chapter 4, that services are largely financed by the federal government, partly financed by state governments, and delivered at local levels, although often by divisions of state government. Services may on occasion be financed by county or city governments with locally collected taxes. That is especially true of certain services that are relatively new in the social services system, such as domestic, violence shelters, rape crisis programs, and self-help groups as well as others that have not had the long history of mental health, corrections, mental retardation, and vocational rehabilitation services, which have long been established with financing from federal and state sources.

Another distinction made in describing the structure of services is whether the auspices of the services are religious or secular. Many of the social services provided to people in the United States are developed, administered, and financed by Roman Catholic, Protestant, Jewish, and other religious bodies. These services may include child care, counseling, financial assistance, health services, or any number of other aids to people who are in need. A variety of nonsectarian, or secular, organizations also provide human services. These include civic clubs such as Kiwanis, Lions, Rotary, and Civitan.

In addition, other nonreligious private, voluntary, charitable groups organize and deliver human services. Groups of people with special interests, such as parents of children with mental retardation, and advocacy groups, such as the Alliance for the Mentally Ill, which is composed largely of relatives of persons with mental illness, are also examples of nongovernmental, nonsectarian services.

There are also a large number of well-known organizations devoted to the resolution of specific personal or health problems, such as the March of Dimes, Cystic Fibrosis Foundation, the American Lung Association, Easter Seals, the National Association for Mental Health, and numerous others.

A detailed description of all the services and auspices under which services are provided is, of course, impossible because of the dynamic nature of social services. Services develop, go out of existence, combine with other services, change patterns, become affiliated with government agencies, and otherwise modify themselves or are modified periodically by others.

Financing of Social Welfare Programs

To pursue another theme that pervades this book, understanding the financing of human services is crucial to understanding the services themselves. Although this chapter has so far suggested that there is a clear distinction between governmental and nongovernmental or between public and private organizations, that distinction is more traditional or historical than it is real. As chapter 2 discusses, for much of human history there was no government involvement in human services. In the United States it was not until the 1930s that the federal government became involved in the organization and delivery of services to residents.

One of the least known but most important developments in the human services is the blurring of the lines between governmental and nongovernmental programs. Although the distinctions once were absolute, there are now many programs in which federal and other government funds are used to support nongovernmental services. These examples usually involve contracts or grants in which a government agency employs a voluntary program to carry out certain governmental functions or to achieve some of the objectives of a governmental program. Although that is more likely to be the case in personal social services—services other than those that are designed to assist people in maintaining their incomes, as described in chapter 7—that pattern can also be true in financial assistance programs. In some states, for example, the distribution of assistance checks and food stamps is handled by banks, finance companies, private check-cashing companies, or other financially oriented institutions. Governments pay the organizations a fee for carrying out those responsibilities, believing they save money and increase efficiency by doing so. Some refer to this trend as the "privatization" of services (Barker, 1995).

Some of the newer experiments in the food stamp program involve the use of electronically encoded cards that look and function like debit cards of the kind issued by corporations such as MasterCard or Visa. Instead of receiving a book of food stamps, the client receives a credit to his or her account each month. That account information is maintained in a central place. When the client purchases groceries with his or her food debit card, the amount of credit is reduced by the amount spent on the groceries. The cards are usually produced and maintained by a private corporation, as are the records and the special machines used in the food stores, under contract with the governmental agency responsible for food stamps.

Planning and Fund-Raising Agencies

There are also a number of agencies that are organized to serve other agencies. The United Way organizations, which are found in most communities, are perhaps the best example. They raise funds in a coordinated way to provide help to voluntary agencies in their communities. These fund-raising organizations have the support of local governments and business communities for a variety of reasons. First, they are usually able to raise money for less administrative cost than the dozens of agencies they represent would incur if they conducted their own campaigns. One single, efficient campaign is conducted each year on behalf of large numbers of individual voluntary member agencies. The agencies request amounts each year, and the United Way determines the amount it will attempt to raise for each. In turn, each agency agrees that it will not embark on public campaigns for funds but will instead contribute to the overall United Way effort.

United Way agencies also contribute to the rational financing of voluntary agencies by setting budgets that appear to be reasonable for the community. They try to ensure that the most important community needs are served and that the role of emotion in determining who receives what is minimized. For example, certain disabling conditions that largely affect children may have strong appeals in the community, even though the number of children affected is small. The "health" organizations established to deal with specific conditions may raise more money than their problems warrant in the community. When organizations are part of United Way fund-raising efforts, such problems are reduced. United Way board members put health problems in perspective so more-appropriate funding levels are provided. Combined campaigns reduce the amount of work time that might be devoted to raising funds for worthwhile causes by concentrating the whole effort on one campaign rather than on dozens of smaller efforts.

Typically, the United Way raises voluntary funds for most of the longest established local and national charities such as the YMCA and YWCA; Boy Scouts, Girl Scouts, and Campfire; family service agencies; and many others. Most of the services it supports are not income maintenance oriented, although a few, such as the Salvation Army, help individuals and families meet some of their fundamental needs through the provision of food, clothing, and lodging. As mentioned earlier, the United Way groups function as policy-making organizations in their communities.

Although they remain popular and important in communities, United Way organizations faced some serious problems in 1992, when it was reported that the chief executive officer of United Way America, the national coordinating body for all local United Ways, was paid an unreasonably high salary and was also spending the organization's money lavishly on his personal expenses. Several local United Way organizations withheld money from the national body and also scrutinized their own administrative expenditures to see if similar abuses might occurring. An excellent and detailed book on the United Way was written by E. L. Brilliant (1990).

Coordinating and planning councils also operate in many communities in ways designed to help those communities rationally and efficiently provide services without duplicating assistance to the same clients or groups of clients. Such organizations have a long social policy history oriented to the objective of avoiding the duplication of services. Readers will recall that avoiding duplication and the possible waste of limited resources have been preoccupations in social services for as long as those services have existed.

In the classic example of the centralized planning council, records are maintained on all of those who seek and receive services. Then, before an organization helps someone, it checks to determine whether or not the person has already received or is continuing to receive help. In some communities computer-stored records are used to investigate such possibilities.

However, because government provides most of the financial assistance that is available and government agencies are required to maintain and consult specific records on all those they help, the need for a community central registry has declined. Planning and coordinating councils are now more likely to devote their efforts to studying and trying to find the means for dealing with human need. Such groups may discover that there are special housing needs for abused spouses and may work to find a solution for them. Or they may find that the real need is for information on services and establishing an information and referral service to those who call. Or they may discover that, although there are ample services, those who need them most are confused by the application procedures or not received enthusiastically when they apply for help. Thus, the planning council may focus its efforts on providing "advocacy" services—on making sure someone is available to help applicants obtain what they need.

Some central planning efforts are focused on coordinating services rather than providing new services. In some cases central locations are developed so that an individual who needs help may apply for a variety of services in the same building or, ideally, with one application, which is then duplicated and distributed to all the programs and services with potential resources available to the client. Some central planning bodies provide case managers to clients

—people who coordinate the services that the client is receiving or ought to be receiving.

Program Descriptions

Income Maintenance / Anti-Poverty Programs

Income Maintenance services are those that help people with their basic financial requirements such as buying food, paying rent, paying for medical services, purchasing clothing, and meeting other fundamental needs. In the United States, income maintenance is subdivided in a variety of ways. The basis for most income maintenance programs in the United States is the Social Security Act of 1935, the development of which is described in chapter 2. These programs are sometimes referred to anti-poverty programs.

In the 1930s four welfare programs were established, and each of them was a state program that used federal matching funds—the amount depending upon the per capita income of the citizens of the state. Those four programs were Aid to Dependent Children, Old Age Assistance, Aid to the Disabled, and Aid to the Blind. In 1975 the three "adult categories" were integrated into a new federal assistance program, Supplemental Security Income, which provides for a standard assistance payment to people who are aged, blind, or disabled and who are also poor.

In 1996 Congress passed the Personal Responsibility and Work Opportunity Reconciliation Act, which represented major changes in the ways income maintenance is handled in the United States (see additional discussions in earlier chapters). The fundamental change in the new welfare law, which is the most significant change since national public assistance came into existence with the Social Security Act of 1935, has been to end the national character of the welfare program and turn substantial portions of it over the states.

Social Security. As previously discussed, Social Security was established as part of the Social Security Act of 1935. Basically, Social Security is a federal program designed to provide a source of income to retired workers. It also includes provisions for unemployment benefits. In order to be eligible for Social Security, a person must have paid into the Social Security system for a certain amount of time or have the necessary family relationship with the recipient. To be fully eligible, individuals must have paid into the Social Security system over ten quarters. In addition, Social Security benefits are tied to previous earnings, so poor recipients receive lower Social Security payments. Contrary to popular beliefs, Social Security was never designed to cover all of the necessary financial needs of retired individuals. Despite this, many elderly may try to depend either solely or primarily on their Social Security benefits to live. This is a problem because the amount does not cover the cost of housing, food, or medical care. Some have argued that Social Security, despite its status as an entitlement program, is experiencing a decline in public support. In other words, because more and more young people have come to believe that Social Security will not be there for them when they retire, they are less inclined to support paying for the program now. The cause for the erosion of this support may be related to the strain on the Social Security system as the baby boomers, who were born in the 1940s and 1950s and who are the largest group of people to be born in one era in American history, begin to access the system (Committee for Economic Development, Concord Coalition, & Center on Budget and Policy Priorities, 2003; Liebig, 1995).

The demographic imperative is well documented in both the research literature and popular media. U.S. society is aging in unprecedented numbers and it is estimated that older adults will comprise 20 percent of the population in 2030 (Kisor, McSweeney & Jackson, 2000; Administration on Aging, 2004). The baby boomers required more schools when they were at that age and more colleges when they were in higher education. Now they require more medical care and more Social Security.

Some Americans doubt that Social Security will be available to them when they retire. Part of this doubt may also be related to the growth and complexity of the Social Security system. Originally constructed as a fairly simple retirement plan in 1935, the Social Security system now encompasses many programs (Cutler, 1997; Schulz, 1996). Due to the fact that so many older adults are expected to start receiving their Social Security benefits, some have projected that the system will run a deficit in about fifteen years (Committee for Economic Development, Concord Coalition, & Center on Budget and Policy Priorities, 2003; Williamson, 1997). The administration of George W. Bush has expressed interest in the privatization of Social Security. That is, workers would invest all or part of their Social Security payments in private investments. Some people have suggested that allowing individuals to invest part of their Social Security contributions in stocks is a better way to prepare for retirement (Markoe, 2003). This allows for the individual responsibility and private control and expenditure of one's own funds. However, some researchers have expressed concern about any privatization plans for Social Security. In general Americans do not save money well and few do an adequate job of life course financial planning (Takamura, 1999). Privatization might also have a negative impact on women, low wage-workers, and minorities (Alliance for Worker Retirement Security, 2000; Kisor, McSweeny, & Jackson, 2000; Tanner, 1996, 2001). Women, minorities, and low wage-workers experience higher rates of poverty and are more likely to depend on Social Security benefits for the majority of their income (Tanner, 1996; Alliance for Worker Retirement Security, 2000; Kisor, McSweeney, & Jackson, 2000). The more income a person has, the more money he or she can place in pensions, private accounts and investments, and other retirement accounts (Tanner, 1996; Hudson, 2002). Unfortunately, many poor elderly have little leftover cash to save and invest (Hudson, 2002). At many times since the act was passed in 1935, adjustments have been required in Social Security payments and in benefits. If the program encounters great problems in the future, it is likely that it will be revised rather than abandoned. Because many Americans depend on or will depend on the program, at least in part for their income, eliminating it would be a cause of major social and economic problems for poor people, probably more costly to resolve than maintaining the existing system would be. The other problem with the privatization of Social Security is that it relies heavily on the market economy. The stock market can go up and down, and people can lose what they had invested, just as millions of Americans lost their retirement benefits when the market went down in 2001.

SSI (Supplemental Security Insurance). In 1972, the SSI program, or Title XVI, was added to the Social Security amendments. SSI is a program designed to provide income for poor individuals sixty-five or older and individuals who are blind or disabled *and* who meet federal income and resource levels. SSI replaced state-run programs of aid to the aged, blind, and disabled in the 1970s that varied greatly among the states (Kauffman, 2002). Funding for SSI comes from general revenues, and Social Security revenues come from payroll taxes. There are very strict income and resource limits used to determine SSI eligibility. The SSI payment is a uniform monthly benefit that is set by the federal government, but states can opt to supplement it if they choose. Thus, although some states subsidize their residents' federal SSI payments (from less than ten dollars in some states to several hundred dollars in others), the program relies primarily on federal financing. However, in some cases, receiving the state supplement can make a family ineligible for other programs that might assist them, such as food stamps. There are also strict limits on the amount of assets someone may have and also receive SSI. Those who have more than the maximum amount of assets, including cash and life insurance, must spend those assets before becoming eligible. This is commonly referred to as spend-down. The monthly SSI grant per individual in January 2004 was $564. For an eligible couple, the amount was $846.

Supplemental Security Income also covers some of the financial needs of children with disabilities, although their families may have relatively large assets. In the revised law (PRWORA), however, eligibility has been redetermined for many children with disabilities who were included in SSI before the change in the law. In 1997 some 95,000 children who had been receiving SSI lost those benefits. Many fell into a category of recipients eliminated when maladaptive behavior was eliminated as a reason for receiving the aid (Pizzagati, 1997).

Many of the children who lost their SSI benefits as a result of changes in the law also lost their Medicaid coverage. In the original Personal Responsibility and Work Opportunity Reconciliation Act of 1996, SSI and Medicaid benefits for immigrants were strictly limited. Even legal aliens who had not yet attained citizenship and who may have been receiving SSI for years were to be cut from the program in 1997. However, the 1997 Balanced Budget Act (National Association of Social Workers, 1997) rescinded those plans for legal immigrants who were living in the United States by August 22, 1996, the day the new welfare law was signed by the president. That change restored benefit eligibility to some 350,000 immigrants. However, later arrivals were not eligible for assistance, no matter what their legal status. The Balanced Budget Act also extended eligibility for assistance programs to seven years for legal immigrants who arrived after the new law passed. The assumption was that by the time that deadline had passed, the immigrants would have attained citizenship.

Public Assistance (AFDC/TANF). The program for families and children, which was originally known as Aid to Dependent Children and renamed Aid to Families with Dependent Children in the 1960s, was our federal-state-financed program. The state determined the amount of the grant, based on formulas for determining financing need—although few states paid what their own calculations determined would be the need level for a family with children. However, the program had a national character, and there were many rules and regulations that required all states to operate the program in similar ways. Standards for the amount of assets a family could own, for example, were set nationally. Rules on eligibility were clearly established. Mothers, married or single, widowed, or divorced, were eligible to receive assistance for themselves and their children if they met the poverty guidelines. Families of specific sizes were treated in the same way, no matter that their children might have been born while they were receiving aid. And families were eligible for help so long as they needed it until their youngest child was older than eighteen, even though they may have received help for many years. These features were controversial, and many American policy makers and critics said that AFDC, as it was operated, created dependency. There were strong efforts made to eliminate or revise it in major ways. President Clinton suggested, when he ran in 1992, that he would work toward the elimination of welfare as it then existed. Attacks on the AFDC program were also central to the Contract with America, discussed earlier, and to the thinking and writing of House of Representatives Speaker Newt Gingrich.

As previously discussed, in August 1996, President Clinton signed the Personal Responsibility and Work Opportunity Reconciliation Act of 1996. PRWORA made fundamental structural changes in the old AFDC welfare programs. Under the revised law, AFDC was eliminated and replaced with TANF (pronounced TANIF, Temporary Assistance for Needy Families).

The major change in the program lies in the delegation of administration and standards to the states in the form of block grants, with many fewer restrictions and requirements than the former AFDC program. Now states can exercise great latitude concerning the way in which the program will be administered, how much assistance families will receive, and what some of the requirements will be. The federal formula for helping states pay for welfare assistance to low-income families continued with states with lower per capita income receiving a greater percentage than states with higher per capita income.

However, the federal government also set some strict guidelines for the TANF program. The primary change, as well as the most dramatic, was the end of AFDC as a program of entitlement for those who qualified for it for as long as they were eligible to receive it. Under TANF a lifetime limit of five years of assistance was placed on families. That is, even if they remained poor for ten years or twenty, they could receive assistance only for five.

The new federal law also gives the states the right to make the time limits shorter. Several states cut the length of time families could receive assistance to no more than two years for a lifetime. The five-year federal limit is a maximum, not an entitlement or right. States may also refuse to add to the assistance of families that have additional children while they are receiving benefits.

The federal rules also allow states to exempt up to 20 percent of their recipients from the five-year limit if they choose to do so (some states do and some states do not). States may also, of course, provide any kind of level of benefits they choose to disadvantaged families.

The revised federal law also expands work requirements for assistance recipients and demands that every state place a substantial portion of their recipients in work sites within two years after they begin receiving assistance. Each year, the specific requirement for the percentage of clients working is increased. By 2002, 50 percent of the clients must be employed. The work requirements had been implemented into the assistance programs over a long period of time, beginning in 1981 with the Ronald Reagan administration, which allowed for community work experience for clients under specified circumstances if a state chose to exercise the option.

Some writers who opposed AFDC would probably not feel comfortable with or positive about the TANF program, either. George Gilder, in an article in *American Spectator* (1995), said that the AFDC system tended to make low-income women economically superior to low-income men and diminished the possibility that men who were not self-sufficient would become so. He says that the program drove men, especially African-American men, into socially and economically subordinate positions. Spending money to place low-income women in jobs and away from their children, as the AFDC program eventually did and the TANF program does, is expensive and requires massive government expenditures. He would have preferred a program that supported marriage and built male competence. He even raised questions about child support enforcement, something that is usually supported by both liberals and conservatives and by welfare reformers of every orientation, because it takes assets and opportunities away form men and gives more to women. Although he thought family allowances were the best solution, as is discussed in chapter 8, his basic belief, like Murray's (1994), is that all government assistance programs should be eliminated because they cause dependence rather than cure it.

Abramovitz says in the 1997 supplement to the authoritative *Encyclopedia of Social Work* that the replacement of AFDC and TANF could cause harm to poor and working class people, especially women and children. In her analysis of the reasons for the changes, Abramovitz compares the two programs and suggests the need for political action to overcome the threats to families resulting from the more restrictive TANF.

Even before the new welfare program had been in effect long enough to be evaluated, there were significant changes under way in assistance services for low-income people. President Bill Clinton noted that the welfare rolls had their largest drop in the history of social welfare programs. He said that caseloads fell by 3.1 million people between January 1993, when he assumed office, and April 1997, before the bill became law in July 1997 (Associated Press, 1997).

It is possible that the rolls decreased because new clients, believing they would not be eligible, did not replace the large numbers who left the program —as clients have done throughout the history of federally supported welfare assistance. The period during which the declines occurred was also one of great economic activity and job creation. President Clinton also noted that 12.5 million jobs had been created during his presidency. The availability of jobs often reduces the numbers of people who need and apply for financial assistance.

As the economic services associated with the Personal Responsibility and Work Opportunity Reconciliation Act began to be implemented, critiques in the media questioned the consequences of the massive changes the revised law made.

The possibility of requiring assistance recipients to work for their benefits began in 1981 under the federal budget Omnibus Budget Reconciliation Act. That act permitted the states to require clients to participate in community work experience programs. The author of this text, while serving as Commissioner of Human Services in West Virginia, led the implementation of those requirements in that state, an effort that received national and international coverage in publications such as the *Wall Street Journal* and *People* and on television networks in the United States and Great Britain. The idea was popular—put people to work for what they receive. In West Virginia we found that the clients were pleased with the opportunity to be employed. Most did not object to working for their benefits, and most preferred work to receiving assistance.

A number of studies on the implementation of work requirements help explain the complexities and costs of those efforts. Several are published by the Manpower Demonstration Research Corporation of New York, a major research organization dealing with welfare reform and work programs, which contracted with foundations and state governments to evaluate a variety of work initiatives. Another study is by O'Neill and O'Neill (1997), and yet another, edited by Garth Mangum and Stephen Mangum (1996), honors Sar A. Levitan, one of the major writers and scholars on work programs and other efforts to improve social policy for the disadvantaged.

Generally, studies of work programs, along with the experiences of Congress in attempting to implement its new legislation, show that such programs may have long-range advantages in that they make recipients of assistance independent and economically self-sufficient. In the short run, however, they cost government more than simply giving assistance because they require child care arrangements, training programs, supervision, job-finding tools, uniforms, workers' compensation coverage, and all of the other costs associated with working. Policy developers often overlook these additional costs, which are an important consideration in efforts to reduce dependency and increase participation in the work force.

Of course, all three of these income maintenance programs can work together. One family may have a Social Security recipient, for example, who may also be eligible for Supplemental Security Income because the Social Security payments are less than SSI would provide. In such a case the recipient would receive a combined payment of no more than the SSI payment level. The children in the family may also make them eligible for TANF in some states. The complexities of calculating the amounts of payments and the degrees of eligibility are great and often require specialized computer programs for definitive answers. The greater latitude given the states under TANF makes the calculation of income maintenance benefits even more complex.

The TANF program is outlined in the appendix, which contains a description of its major features. Several of those features are additional restrictions on assistance to low-income families, especially one-parent families. For example, women who are teenage mothers cannot receive assistance on their own if they are living independently. They must reside with their parents or in another approved adult residential situation. They must also be studying for a high school diploma or GED or be participants in some other state-approved educational or training activity. But states may, if they choose, deny benefits to any teen parent. States are given a bonus for reducing their illegitimacy rate. There are also special funds set aside for states that encounter large amounts of unemployment.

Although the Congress was set to reauthorize welfare in 2002 before the September 30 deadline, they failed to do so. At the time of this writing, welfare reauthorization is currently being debated. The promotion of marriage through welfare funds is currently a hot issue. Some have argued that the preservation of marriage should be central to welfare reform efforts (Fagan, Rector, Johnson, & Peterson, 2002; Fagan, Rector, & Noyes, 2003; Rector, 2001). Further Rector (2001) has noted that the "collapse of marriage is the principal cause of child poverty and a host of other social ills" including criminal behavior, abuse, drug and alcohol addiction, school drop out and welfare use (p. 63). While it is true that living in a female-headed family greatly increases a child's chance of living in poverty (Single-Rushton & McLanahan, 2003) and efforts to support married families are needed, other researchers disagree that marriage promotion is the answer to child poverty (Solot & Miller, 2002). Others have raised doubts about the effectiveness of marriage promotion programs (Fremstad & Primus, 2002). Despite substantial changes in welfare policy since 1996, child poverty still remains a significant social concern in the US. In fact, child poverty is significantly higher in the United States than is the rate in other industrialized countries. In 2000, approximately 12 million American children lived in poverty and 5 million of those in extreme poverty (National Center for Children in Poverty (NCCP), 2003). The poverty level in the US for a two-parent family of four is $18,400, which is not enough to provide a family with the basic necessities of life, according to many studies (NCCP, 2003). The delivery of social welfare programs, including TANF and job training programs, is also a controversial issue. Faith based initiatives involve using churches or other religious organizations to provide federally funded services such as substance abuse treatment, job training for TANF recipients or housing programs. Some argue that faith based initiatives could be unconstitutional in that they appear to favor people of one religious persuasion. Others have concerns that these efforts may violate the separation of church and state.

Child Support and PRWORA. There is an important federal-state program designed to locate parents who should be but are not paying child support. It is called the Child Support Enforcement Program, and it is required to operate in every state. The failure of families to receive adequate child support is the most important reason for their eligibility (Committee on Ways and Means, U.S. House of Representatives 1993). As part of PRWORA, TANF applicants are required to cooperate with the Child Support Enforcement Program if they qualify for TANF. The state can then attempt to find the absent parent and obtain support from that parent.

PRWORA also established a Federal Registry of noncustodial parents and required employers to report all new hires to the National Directory of New Hires. This new system created a better tracking system of child support orders, especially directed at tracking noncustodial parents that cross state lines. In order to be eligible for federal money for TANF, states had to create a state registry and a centralized system for the collection and distribution of child support payments. The law also expanded the ability of the states to withhold the incomes of noncustodial parents, to revoke their recreational, drivers or professional licenses for non-cooperation, and required that child support orders include health care insurance coverage. Paternity establishment were also expanded.

The Child Support program is also available to non-TANF families. For a small fee—as little as one dollar in some states—the program will attempt to locate the absent parent through Social Security numbers and other data provided by the parent receiving assistance if the absent parent's whereabouts are unknown; arrange for a court to determine the absent parent's child support liability; and enforce the court order with deductions from the absent parent's wages, tax refunds, and benefit payments. The objective is to get financial support for the child as well as to force absent parents to meet their obligations, sometimes through punishment such as fines and imprisonment.

The policy associated with child support programs is that legal parents or guardians of children are expected to pay for their care. In addition to the public programs for securing support payments that result from court orders, there is also a variety of private resources, such as certain businesslike organizations or attorneys who specialize in obtaining child support—that help families who are having difficulty receiving the support to which they are entitled.

Food Stamps and Anti-Hunger Programs. The Food Stamps Act was enacted in 1964 during President Lyndon B. Johnson's administration. Currently, approximately 19 million Americans receive food stamps each month, making food stamps an extremely important economic security program for poor families (Economic Research Service [ERS], 2003a). The Food Stamps program is a means-tested program and regulates what products recipients can and cannot buy. For example, recipients cannot buy paper products, alcohol, pet food, or cleaning products with food stamps. Historically, recipients received actual stamps, which they could use to buy groceries at participating stores, although many recipients now utilize electronic benefit transfer (EBT) cards that they can use like ATM or credit cards at participating stores.

PRWORA changed more than the family assistance program. It also instituted major restrictions on the provision of food stamps. Initially, some adult food stamp recipients without dependents were restricted to just three months of benefits every three years. Benefits for those adults in need of financial help were liberalized through changes in the law that were incorporated in the Balanced Budget Act (National Association of Social Workers, 1997). The 2002 Farm Bill restored food stamps to children and most legal immigrants who have lived in the United States for five or more years and received SSI.

The Special Supplemental Nutrition Program for Women, Infants, and Children (WIC) was established in 1972 as a special food program for low-income pregnant and breast feeding women, infants, and children up to age five who are determined to be at nutritional risk. Determining nutritional risk is quite complicated and usually entails considering such factors as birth weight, growth, the amount of iron in the diet, or anemia. The WIC program also refers participants to relevant health and social service agencies as they are needed. WIC serves about 7.5 million women and children each month, which ends up being about half of all infants born in the United States (ERS, 2003b).

Sometimes referred to as the "free lunch program," the National Lunch Act was enacted in 1946. Some lunch programs existed prior to this act; some were in place as early as during the Great Depression. Since 1946 the program has expanded, and in the year 2001, over 25.4 million children received their lunches through the program. If their families qualify, children are then offered free and reduced lunches. There has been some controversy associated with the school lunch program, most notably criticism about the stigmatization of children who receive free lunches; further, the nutritional value of the school lunches are said to be unhealthy, high in fat, and not sensitive to vegetarians or ethnic differences. There was an interesting controversy in the early 1980s about calling ketchup a vegetable as part of calculating the nutritional value of the lunches.

Earned Income Tax Credit. Another program for low-income people that is of growing importance is the Earned Income Tax Credit, or EITC. The EITC program was first passed in 1975 and then expanded significantly in 1996. Under the program, employed people with low earnings are able to receive the equivalent of cash income tax refund that may be significantly more than their overall tax payments. This is like the "negative income tax" proposed by the Friedmans (1980) as an alternative to assistance payments. It is estimated that about 5 million individuals (about half of those 5 million, children) are lifted out of poverty by the EITC (NCCP, 2003). Basically the EITC is a tax refund where the amount of the refund is determined by a family's income and size. For poor working families the amount could be as much as $4,000 because poor families can get back much more than they paid into the system. However, families must be aware of the EITC and apply for the refund in order to obtain this benefit. For more information on the EITC, refer to http://128.242.238.174/initiatives/fes/eitc.htm, sponsored by the Annie E. Casey Foundation's National Tax Assistance for Working Families Campaign.

Assets-Based Programs. An emerging idea in social welfare assistance is the assets-based approach, developed by Michael Sherraden (1991). Sherraden, who is a professor at Washington University's George Warren Brown School of Social Work in St. Louis, believes that low-income people can be helped through providing them with assets or savings that they can use for major purchases, home ownership, and education. Current programs focus on immediate spending for immediate needs. Assets approaches would give people long-term objectives and possibilities.

One of Sherraden's later ideas was for the development of Children's Savings Accounts (Curley and Sherraden, 1998), which would start children at birth with $1,000 and which could be augmented by contributions that could be fully tax refundable. The funds would receive interest or would be invested in securities. Over the years, children could develop assets that could help them with their adult years—and help break family poverty cycles. There is interest in Congress in such approaches, and the new welfare law of 1996 gives states the opportunity to try out such ideas.

The assets-based approach fits well with the popular and central concept of social work practice—strengths-based approaches (Chapin, 1995). R. K. Chapin is one of several theorists who have written about strengths approaches to serving clients (Chapin, 1995). Social workers have long found it useful to focus on client strengths rather than problems and, of course, assets-based services help build client strengths.

Housing Programs. The U.S. Department of Housing and Urban Development (HUD) operates three main housing programs that benefit low-income individuals and families. These are public housing programs, Section 8 voucher programs, and HUD subsidized housing programs. To be eligible to reside in a public housing authority (PHA) residence, individuals must meet the eligibility requirements. Rent is then subsidized and based on the person's ability to pay. HUD also manages the privately owned subsidized housing program. The Section 8 program is a voucher program or rental assistance program where recipients are able to locate housing in the private real estate market (Fuchs, 2002).

Housing issues are of increasing importance in the lives of working families as well as in the fight against poverty. Wages, or what people earn, have not increased as rapidly as housing costs. As a result, in some U.S. cities such as Los Angeles, housing affordability has reached crisis proportions. A study conducted in 1999 by the National Low Income Housing Coalition demonstrated that a worker would need to earn an hourly wage of $11.08 (or 215 percent of the U.S. minimum wage) to be able to afford a two-bedroom rental unit (Fair Market Rent) in the United States (Dolbeare, 2001). Put another way, a minimum wage worker would have to work about 86 hours a week to afford housing! In addition, low-income individuals tend to rent rather than own homes and often end up paying a disproportionate amount of their income for rent, which is often for low quality housing as well (Dolbeare, 2001; LA Crisis Housing Task Force, n.d.). The 2003 report was unfortunately, no less bleak than in 1999:

Millions of American families are unable to afford safe and decent rental housing. Wages have failed to keep pace with rental costs, rental costs have increased faster than costs of other basic needs, affordable rental housing is being lost to homeownership and market-rate rentals, and little or no new affordable housing is being built. As a result, these families are living in substandard conditions, are homeless, or are making choices each day to spend money on housing and do without health care, child care, or other basic necessities (Pitcoff, Pelletiere, Crowley, Schaffer, Treskon, Vance, & Dolbeare, 2003).

As the availability of low income and affordable housing continues to decline across the United States, along with continued reductions in housing expenditures at the federal, state, and local levels of government, the gravity of housing policy becomes apparent.

Workers Compensation Programs. Another of the important income maintenance programs in the United States is provided under the title of workers' (or, in some cases, workmen's) compensation. Those programs compensate working people and their families for illnesses, injuries, or deaths that are connected with employment. Each state has a program, but each state program (and the levels of compensation it offers) is different. In general, the programs are funded by taxes or insurance premiums paid by employers. In some states the government collects the fees and pays the benefits. In some states companies purchase coverage from private insurance companies, which administer the benefits. In yet other states there is a combination of state-operated and insurance company–operated programs.

Workers' compensation is paid to those who sustain injuries in connection with their work or who become ill because of that work. The coverage, however, is not only for industrial accidents or illnesses. Employees who are injured in auto accidents while they are on duty, for example, may be entitled to benefits such as payment for their medical care and financial support while they are recovering. If they are killed in the accident, their families may receive financial support. Industrial illnesses caused by environmental problems in the workplace and other factors may make workers eligible for health care and income maintenance assistance.

Workers' compensation is not means tested. That is, eligibility is based upon the fact that the worker was injured or killed in connection with work. That, and not the financial needs of the worker, is the criterion.

Pensions and Insurance. Self-employed people and those employed by others may also be covered for income maintenance and retirement pensions through publicly or privately financed insurance programs. In some cases individuals purchase their own coverage, and in others their employers pay all or part of the costs. Employees of government typically receive some kind of retirement benefits, and the same is true of most employees of large corporations and many other organizations. When the individuals retire, they receive pensions that may be combined with Social Security retirement. These pensions may be the basis for retirement and may, in many cases, be much larger than the Social Security benefits. Government assists with these programs through tax incentives. Private employers may deduct the costs from their taxes. Public employers operate the programs in part through appropriations. Employees usually contribute part of the costs, but they also receive tax incentives in that they may often exclude their payments from their taxable incomes and pay taxes on their contributions only when they retire and receive them. Retired people are typically in lower tax brackets than those who are working.

The federal government also provides for taxpayers to establish Individual Retirement Accounts through which some families are able to deduct contributions to a retirement plan from their personal income and thus pay lower income taxes. They may withdraw their contributions starting at age 59? without penalty—but there is a penalty for earlier withdrawals, with exceptions. They must begin withdrawing funds by age 70? to avoid penalties on their retirement accounts. A 1997 tax change increased the limits on the amounts families may earn and still deduct from their taxes their contributions to IRAs. A new program, called the Roth Individual Retirement Account, allows for some tax deductible contributions to IRAs and withdrawals from them without paying taxes on the money withdrawn. Congress has also allowed IRA holders to withdraw their funds before retirement age if they use them for home purchases or their children's college expenses. Withdrawals for other purposes incur penalties, as mentioned above.

There are also insurance plans that provide income to people who become disabled. These plans, which may also be paid by the employee and the employer or by one or the other, provide payments to workers when they are ill or injured and unable to continue working.

As is discussed earlier in this chapter, all of these programs may work together and may have some impact on one another. For example, the amount of workers' compensation payments may be deducted from the Social Security disability payments. All or some of the private or public resources of individuals are considered in their income tax payments.

Employment and Training Programs. Assistance to the unemployed is another example of income maintenance services. These are services administered by state employment services agencies with funds that are usually totally provided by the federal government with revenues collected from payroll taxes paid by employers. These programs provide unemployment compensation for those who are without work for a period of time, without regard to the assets of the unemployed—although they must report and deduct income received from other employment. Unemployment of the wage earner or wage earners is a financial disaster for most families. It is also a problem that affects a large number of families every year. In the 1990s the unemployment rate in the United States was low. In 1996, the average weekly unemployment benefit was $186. The range was $119 per week in Louisiana to $262 per week in Hawaii (Committee on Ways and Means, U.S. House of Representatives, 1996).

Those who collect unemployment compensation must have lost their jobs for reasons other than their own misconduct or unwillingness to continue working. Employees who misbehave on the job or resign voluntarily are not eligible. Generally, unemployment compensation continues until the recipient finds work or for twenty-six weeks, whichever comes first. In time of severe economic problems the federal government may extend the period of eligibility beyond twenty-six weeks.

There is also a human services element associated with unemployment compensation services. The unemployment agency makes referrals to jobs and training programs, which is a way of helping people overcome their unemployment problems. Those who are assisted must be available for work and must report to the unemployment office periodically to receive their compensation.

There are also many kinds of training programs that are financed by government and industry or, most typically, by a combination of government and industry efforts. Programs such as the Job Training Partnership Act provide federal training funds to states, which in turn use those funds to train or retrain workers. Some of that training is in the form of apprenticeship programs, other parts are in more-formal courses, and other portions are in work experience activities, in which trainees learn basic job skills by working for public and private employers. Some work experience programs are associated with TANF, which requires most recipients to work or participate in work training if they are physically able to do so and do not have infant children. There are efforts to involve the private sector heavily in such programs. Part of that involvement is in the training itself, and part is in the form of tax incentives. In some programs special federal tax benefits are provided to employers who hire assistant recipients.

General and Emergency Assistance. Federal programs are usually entitlements for people who meet specific needs requirements. Many of those who are desperately in need of help are not blind, disabled, or elderly, however, so they do not qualify for SSI; do not have children, so they do not qualify for TANF;

and are not recently unemployed, so they do not qualify for unemployment compensation—they are just poor. Many such individuals are women who have recently become single because their male wage-earning partners have left them or have died. If they are younger than Social Security age, have no work history, and have no disabilities, they do not qualify for the basic programs.

Therefore, there are many local and state general assistance programs that help people who need assistance, without regard to their characteristics other than poverty. Those programs vary dramatically from place to place. That is because there are no national standards for such assistance. State or local governments may provide whatever kinds of help they choose. Some states have regular, monthly assistance programs. Other states provide help only once and then for only one month's needs.

Emergency assistance is similar to general assistance in its variability, except that the federal government provides some help to the states for families that are in need of it. Under the current law, the federal government's block grants funds for family assistance can be used, if the states choose, for temporary or emergency assistance. Specific emergency assistance programs may include temporary housing, food, medical care, and other in-kind assistance as well as limited cash assistance.

Emergency and general assistance may be provided by county or other local governments or by the same agencies that provide TANF. Frequently, one of the tasks of the worker in the TANF program is to help needy clients connect with some of these limited assistance programs to help them overcome their immediate needs.

Health Care Programs

A major form of income maintenance is assistance with the financing of one's health care, especially when there are catastrophic, expensive medical needs. The two basic public health insurance programs in the United States are Medicare and Medicaid, which were established in 1965 under Title 18 and 19 of the Social Security Act. Both programs are administered by the Centers for Medicare and Medicaid Services (CMS, previously the Health Care Financing Administration, or HCFA), which is also responsible for the State Children's Health Insurance Program (SCHIP), the Health Insurance Portability and Accountability Act of 1996 (HIPPA), and the Mental Health Parity Act (MHPA) of 1996.

Medicare. Medicare is an insurance program to which employed people and their employers contribute. It is provided to three categories of individuals. First, it is provided to all people sixty-five years old or older, no matter how much, if anything, they have paid into the system. Medicare also covers some people under age sixty-five with disabilities (some SSI recipients) and individuals with End-Stage Renal Disease, which is permanent kidney failure that requires dialysis or a kidney transplant. Interestingly, until recently with the new passage of the new Medicare Prescription bill, Medicare benefits have remained relatively constant since they were originally implemented in 1966. Overall, Medicare focuses on acute illness and has not focused on funding long-term care. There are two parts of Medicare, Part A (Hospital Insurance) and Part B (Supplementary Medical Insurance). Part A covers most inpatient services and is an earned benefit that requires no premium. Part B is a voluntary benefit that individuals pay a monthly premium to use. Almost all elderly recipients of Medicare opt to purchase Part B. Generally speaking, Medicare does not fund prescription drugs, eyeglasses, or long-term care. For those who qualify, Medicare covers a limited short stay in a long-term care facility after a hospital stay. For individuals to qualify for Medicare nursing home coverage, that person must have been in the hospital for a minimum of three consecutive days, obtain documentation of the need for skilled nursing, and physician authorization.

Medicare is the largest public health insurance program in the United States, providing the major source of health care coverage for elderly and disabled persons. Since the 1970s there have been numerous attempts to control Medicare spending, which represents a large portion of all government spending. For example, in 1983 the Health Care Financing Administration (HCFA—now CMS) instituted the Prospective Payment System (PPS), which set limits on hospital reimbursement for inpatient care by establishing a set amount to be paid for each person's case depending on their medical condition or Diagnostic Related Groups (DRGs). In other words, there are specific guidelines for treatment based on the age, sex, and condition of a patient and complications of his or her illness. Thus, a person who was sixty years old and had a heart attack would be eligible for a specific amount and type of treatments for a set period of time. In 1997, the Balanced Budget Act also made substantial changes to the Medicare programs, an area of much discussion and contention between Congress and President Bill Clinton. Although Medicare is a federal government program, it is often administered by private insurance companies under contracts between the government and the companies, an example of the blurring of the private and public sectors that was discussed earlier in this chapter.

Before the program was initiated few older Americans enjoyed adequate health insurance. Today Medicare covers the majority of the elderly. Currently, however, Medicare is faced with several challenges. Solutions aimed at fixing Medicare must address: (1) the rising costs of spending on health care, (2) the growth in the number of Medicare beneficiaries, and (3) insufficient revenue contributions into the Medicare fund (Moon, 1999).

Long-term care is also a significant issue of concern, as it is estimated that about one of every three persons over sixty-five needs some form of care or assistance, and this translates into approximately 50 million caregivers in the United States (National Family Caregivers Association, 2000). However, very little formal support is given to caregivers, and state-level expenditures for institutional care far exceed resources allocated for informal caregivers. It has been estimated that the "free" services that family caregivers provide amount to approximately $257 billion per year (Arno, Levine, & Memmott, 1999). Elaine Brody (1985), a social worker, has termed the societal belief that families are unwilling to provide care for the elderly the "Myth of Abandonment." Clearly, the societal expectation that families should bear the significant financial and emotional costs of caregiving is present in current policy. In addition, these caregivers who care for both their own children and older relatives have been called the Sandwich Generation. A rationale for limiting resources for community and home-based services may be the woodwork effect. This argument stems from the notion that there is a hierarchy of assistance where individuals and family have responsibility before the government, as discussed in chapter 1, and that if the government provided expansive home-based services individuals would come out of the woodwork to access them and overwhelm the system.

In November 2003 the Medicare Prescription Drug Improvement and Modernization Act of 2003 was enacted. Enacting some of the most substantial changes to Medicare since 1965, this law adds $400 billion worth of prescription drug coverage to Medicare. The new law has been criticized by some who feel the coverage inadequate and others who note that the law basically funds private insurance and drug companies and will force many elderly into Medicare HMO programs. Others argue that the new law will provide important assistance to the elderly, some who pay one-third of their income for prescriptions.

Medicaid. Medicaid was enacted largely because of the inability of the states to provide adequate health care to the poor. Medicaid is provided to pay the costs of care for low-income people or people who would be of low income if they had to pay their own medical care costs. It generally is available to those who receive TANF and SSI as well as other people who would be eligible for TANF or SSI if they paid their own medical bills. The levels of coverage and eligibility vary, however, from state to state. For example, because of the variance from state to state in eligibility, an individual may be eligible for Medicaid in California and not in South Carolina. Medicaid operates as a vendor payment program, and states pay providers directly for services. However, providers who accept Medicaid must agree to accept the Medicaid payment rate, which is usually lower than private insurance reimbursement, and to accept Medicaid payments as payments in full. Thus, Medicaid is not always popular with private physicians, dentists, and private hospitals. This also facilitates the stigma some argue is associated with the Medicaid program. In most states Medicaid covers hospital care, physicians' services, some prescriptions, and nursing home care. The costs are paid by the federal and state governments, with the federal government providing half or more of the costs.

Medicaid is NOT necessarily provided to ALL poor people as, even under the broadest provisions of the federal law, Medicaid does not provide health care services unless an individual is in one of the eligible categories. In other words, low income is only one test for Medicaid eligibility. As Medicaid is a federal program with broad federal guidelines, states have the option to provide Medicaid to "categorically needy" or "medically needy" people. For example, under the medically needy program, states can provide Medicaid to people who would be eligible for Medicaid under the normal rules, except their income and resources are slightly above the guidelines established by the state. This is where the term *spend down* comes from: people qualify for Medicaid because their medical expenses cause them to be even with or just below the state's eligibility level. These are usually people who have health problems and have health insurance bills that bring their income level down to the point that they become eligible. Usually the state regulations for spend downs are quite expensive and complex, requiring recertification every quarter. Although states can design their own Medicaid programs, under federal guidelines, if a state has a Medicaid program they must provide some basic services including, for example, health services for children, inpatient services, outpatient services, laboratory and X-ray services, family planning, home health, physician services, rural health care services, or nursing home or skilled nursing care. The child health services are referred to as early and periodic screening, diagnosis, and treatment (EPSDT) services. Since Medicaid covers inpatient skilled nursing care, the Medicaid program plays a crucial role in the funding of long-term care. In fact, coverage of long-term care consumes a large portion of the total Medicaid budget. In 2001, Medicaid funded 41 percent of all costs for care of individuals in nursing homes and those receiving home health services in the United States (CMS, 2004). Total costs for Medicaid amounted to $34.4 billion for nursing home care and $3.1 billion for home health care (CMS, 2004). Obviously, as the population in the United States continues to age, costs for long-term care, home health care services, and nursing home care will continue to increase.

The federal government also makes disproportionate share hospital (DSH) payments to hospitals that provide inpatient services to a disproportionate number of Medicaid recipients or low-income persons. Sometimes states require small deductibles or co-pays for some Medicaid services. The amount the federal government pays for each state's Medicaid program is called the Federal Medical Assistance Percentage (FMAP). FMAP is determined annually by a formula that compares the state's average per capita income level with the national income average.

Medicaid and Medicare work together in many cases. For example, Medicaid supplements some Medicare recipients, and some people who are in need of health care may receive Medicare benefits for part of their costs and Medicaid benefits for the rest. People eligible for both Medicaid and Medicare are often referred to as dual eligibles. Medicaid, however, is always the payer of last resort.

There are several changes to Medicaid as a result of the PRWORA of 1996. TANF recipients were not automatically eligible for Medicaid, and states are now allowed to deny Medicaid to individuals who lose TANF because of failure to comply with work requirements.

There are many rules, regulations, and procedures that are required in the Medicaid and Medicare programs. For example, providers of services may bill Medicare recipients for the difference between the amounts Medicare pays and what the provider usually charges. It is a violation of federal law, however, for a provider to bill a Medicaid recipient for those additional amounts. Special efforts are made by the federal and state governments to hold down the costs of these expensive programs, a major public policy concern. There are also special efforts to prevent fraud or abuse of these programs, which have been problems in many parts of the United States.

State Children's Health Insurance Program (SCHIP). As part of the Balanced Budget Act of 1997, the State Children's Health Insurance Program (SCHIP) was enacted. SCHIP is a block grant provided to states to provide and expand children's access to health insurance and care. States were able to expand their current Medicaid programs, create new health care programs, or purchase services from private providers. According to CMS, between the period of 1988 and 1998, while the percentage of children covered by Medicaid increased, the percentage of children without any health insurance also increased (Centers for Medicare & Medicaid Services, n.d.). Many uninsured children reside in families with working parents, the "working poor," and are less likely to be covered by private or employer health insurance plans.

Health Insurance Portability and Accountability Act (HIPAA) and the Mental Health Parity Act (MHPA). Human services workers recognize that many people have mental health problems, which are often costly to treat. However, health insurance does not always cover mental health treatment. The federal government tried to deal with this by enacting the Mental Health Parity Act of 1996. The MHPA was enacted to help facilitate equality between coverage for mental health services and medical/surgical services. However, the MHPA is fairly limited in that it only prevents *group* health plans from enforcing annual or life limits on mental health benefits when they are lower than those for medical or surgical benefits (RAND, 2000). In other words, the law does *not* mandate mental health services be covered as part of a health insurance plan. In addition, the law only applies to group health plans with fifty or more workers. Individuals who purchase their own health care plans and those who work for small companies are not covered under the MHPA. Some people argue that even though the total cost of mental treatment goes up with mental health parity laws, the benefits still outweigh the costs. For example, because people will have better access to mental health treatment they will be less likely to miss work and be more productive. In addition, a healthier workforce combined with earlier access to preventive mental health treatment also has the potential to keep *overall* mental health costs down. Universal access to mental health treatment also has potential to reduce the stigma that is commonly associated with treatment (Levin, Hanson, Coe, & Taylor, 1998). However, more recent reports indicate that insurance coverage for individuals with mental health problems is still highly inadequate and that parity legislation has not necessarily increased access to or use of mental health services (Pacula & Sturm, 2000; RAND, 2000).

The Health Insurance Portability and Accountability Act of 1996 is also known as the Kennedy-Kassebaum Act. The two titles of HIPAA cover the portability of health insurance coverage (Title 1) and administrative simplification (Title 2). Title 1 protects the health care coverage of individuals (and their family members) due to employment changes or job loss. In other words, individuals who change or lose their jobs can have access to health care for the period between jobs. Title 2 of HIPAA involves the use of and treatment of health care data. The Department of Health and Human Services (DHHS) is responsible for establishing national standards and guidelines for handling electronic health care data. This is especially relevant to human services and social workers who work in medical settings who will have to be compliant with the HIPAA law. There are specific guidelines regarding the sharing of health care information and the protection of confidentiality of clients. Human services professionals and social workers are often considered "covered entities" under the HIPAA law. The National Association of Social Workers (NASW) was actively involved in the creation of the privacy regulations associated with HIPAA (Bateman, 2002).

Managed Care. Health care financing and its reform were, and still are or remain, social policy issues of major consequence throughout the 1990s. The costs of health care have grown rapidly; many people do not have and cannot afford private health insurance; the cost of public programs such as Medicaid and Medicare has increased; and there are strong desires among many policy-making groups to reduce health care costs. President Clinton, following through on a plan developed by his wife, Hillary Rodham Clinton, proposed a major reform in health care planning and delivery in 1994. However, strong opposition to the plan, especially among health care providers such as hospitals and health insurance companies, along with some concerns that the changes would lead to significant departures in the ways patients received health care and chose their physicians, caused the plan to fail passage in Congress.

The complexity and seeming irrationality of the health care system in the United States are still of concern. Hospitals and other providers often supply health care services to people who are not insured or who have no funds to pay for their own care. The cost of the free care is typically passed on to those who pay for their care privately or through private insurance companies. Consequently, there are examples of very high costs for simple medicines and medical supplies. A single aspirin tablet may be billed to patients at a cost of several dollars, although consumers know they can buy large bottles of aspirin for just a few dollars. The high charges reflect the cost of providing care to those who cannot pay themselves. It is an odd financial mechanism for the indigent, and it is also uneven because not all hospitals in all parts of the United States or even in all parts of any one state provide health care to those who are not able to pay for it themselves.

The solution that was most popular among many health care organizers and planners in the 1990s was "managed care." Managed care at is most basic is about controlling the who, what, when, where, and how of health care. More officially, "managed care entails interventions to control the price, volume, delivery site and intensity of health services provided, the goal of which is to maximize the value of health benefits and the coordination of health care management for the covered population" (American College of Cardiology, 1993). Basically the goal of managed care is to keep people out of the hospital, thus the renewed focus on preventative and outpatient care. The intention was to require patients to have their care rationally managed, often through the screening of a primary care physician—a general or family practitioner—rather than allowing them to go directly to specialists whose care they might prefer. Primary care such as that provided by a general or family practitioner is usually less expensive than that provided by specialists, whose fees are generally higher and who might use more tests and even hospitalization for something a primary care physician might handle through a simple office visit. The managed care approach is characteristic of efforts such as health maintenance organizations (HMOs), in which increasing numbers of corporations and other entities are enrolling their employees rather than providing them with open-ended health insurance that allows them to use whatever health care services they choose. These prepaid health care programs may hold down the costs of employee care. They also allow employers to plan for and predict the amount of their expenditures for employee health coverage.

There are valid arguments on both sides of the managed care debate, and the overall impact of pushing health care utilization down can be seen as both good and bad. For example, managed care has facilitated a renewed interest in primary preventive care and wellness, reduced the amount of inpatient care (the most expensive type of health care), created more innovative home health care, created more systematic use of medical protocols and guidelines, and emphasized greater use of evidence-based medical practice (Cohen, 2001). For example, consider the case of childbirth. Many years ago, after childbirth a woman might stay in the hospital up to one week or more. However, unless there are special circumstances that prevent it, most women are able to return home relatively quickly after childbirth. Currently, most insurance companies cover a forty-eight-hour stay in the hospital after a normal vaginal delivery and seventy-two hours after a caesarean section. The use of protocols and evidenced based practice has determined the range of appropriate medical services needed for childbirth.

Table 5. The Pros and Cons of Managed Care

PROS	CONS
Sets limits or prevents unnecessary services	Physicians and patients tend to dislike managed care programs, feel limited in their choices and options for medical care
Focused on preventative care	Endangers the health of patients
Reduced use of inpatient care	"Profit over patients" is the bottom line
Reduction of health care costs	Fewer people interested in medical profession
Fostered new innovative home health care	Fewer jobs for specialists
Emphasized evidenced based medical practice	"Gag rules," health care providers are prevented from full disclosure of treatment options to patients
Created systematic use of medical protocols and guidelines	No flexibility or ability to individualize treatment plans

Managed care also inhibits the use of unnecessary services. Consider the case of caesarean section, which is a surgery performed where a baby (or babies) is delivered through an incision in a women's abdomen and uterus. There is evidence that suggests that many caesarean sections in the United States are used for nonmedical reasons such as the convenience of the physician or mother. Caesarean sections are ultimately more expensive that vaginal deliveries and because they are a surgical procedure, managed care companies, by setting specific guidelines around the use of certain procedures based on specific criteria, attempt to limit misuse of this procedure when it is unnecessary.

The high cost of medical care in the United States is undeniable and the question of whether or not the United States can afford or should provide all citizens with as much health care as they want is an important question to consider. In countries with national health care or socialized medicine there are more limits on the health care available to individuals. On the other hand many Americans are unhappy with the status of managed care. Physicians, in particular, dislike managed care primarily because of the limits placed on care options that some argue also endanger the health of patients, the emphasis on cost rather than quality care ("profits before patients"), fewer jobs for specialists, and even declining interest in attending medical school (Cohen, 2001). Individuals enrolled in HMOs are often dissatisfied with their benefits and options for medical treatment. The movement to create a Patients' Bill of Rights is, in large part, due to dissatisfaction with managed care health plans. The managed care debate, in the meantime, is not likely to quiet. It is estimated that over 74 million Americans are enrolled in HMOs (National Center for Health Statistics, 1999). Growing dissatisfaction with health care insurance and costs has promoted many states to pass Patients' Bill of Rights. The NASW has a Mental Health Bill of Rights available on their Web site for those interested in exploring this topic further.

It is possible that managed care policies will become central to the efforts to reform health care payments services in the United States and that, at some point, most Americans will receive their health care benefits and coverage through a managed care organization such as a health maintenance organization.

When the Medicare and Medicaid programs were changed in 1995 in ways designed to hold down the increasing costs of those programs, one of the provisions was to encourage Medicare clients—primarily older adults—and state Medicare programs to use more extensively managed care, especially health maintenance organizations. There were also provisions to reduce the reimbursements for care to hospitals and other providers, such as nursing homes, although physicians were not expected to feel much impact on their own fees from these programs.

Conclusion

It is clear that publicly funded and administered human services are a complicated and extensive part of American community life. Understanding everything there is to know about these services is impossible, yet those involved with social work and related fields must be aware of the broad structures and categories that describe and govern the human services. Perhaps more important, one must be able to understand and analyze social policy in one's locality to better understand how to gain access to those services for clients.

This chapter has covered many of the public and voluntary, cash and in-kind, income maintenance programs found in the United States. These are, in many ways, the keys to social policy in the United States. Although human needs are numerous and varied, financial need is often a key ingredient of other kinds of needs, whether for mental health assistance, child protection, or health care. Financial assistance and income maintenance programs are thus fundamental to all social programs.

Discussion Questions

1. List and define three income maintenance programs that fall in the category of entitlements and three that do not.

2. What are some of the differences between means-tested and non-means-tested programs? Why do you believe both of these kinds of programs have been developed and maintained as part of the U.S. human services system?

3. This chapter describes a large number of income maintenance programs for many different groups of people. Do you think there are any gaps in the provision of assistance to Americans? If so, who are the people affected? Why would they be left out of the benefits available to people in need?

4. Visit the Social Security Administration online (http://www.ssa.gov) and choose "Calculate your benefits" on the homepage. You can use the calculators to estimate your potential Social Security benefit amounts using different dates for your retirement and possible earnings. While there, you may also investigate the history of Social Security.

5. Visit the State Policy Documentation Project at http://www.spdp.org/. Explore the TANF program components in your state. Compare your state to other states and comment on your results. Explore your state's eligibility rules, time limits, or work requirements. Does your state have less or more stringent TANF guidelines than other states? What are the maximum cash benefits allowed in your state's TANF program and how does that compare to other states?

6. Visit the Families USA Web site (http://www.familiesusa.org/) and click on the Medicare Road Show to listen to personal stories from seniors about Medicare, or explore other health care issues of interest.

References

Abramovitz, M. (1997). Temporary assistance to needy families. In R. L. Edwards et al. (Eds.), *Encyclopedia of social work*, 19th ed., Supplement, 1997, 311–330. Washington, DC: NASW Press.

Administration on Aging. (2004). *A profile of older Americans: 2003*. http://www.aoa .gov/prof/statistics/profile/2003/4.asp (accessed February 10, 2004).

Alliance for Worker Retirement Security. (2000). *Social Security reform: Confronting the challenges to women's retirement security.* http://www.retiresecure.org/articles.php?id=6 (accessed March 20, 2003).

American College of Cardiology. (1993). *Managed care primer.* Bethesda, MD: Author.

Arno, P., Levine, C., & Memmott, M. (1999). Economic value of informal caregiving. *Health Affairs* 18 (2), 182–188.

Associated Press. (July 6, 1997). President praises welfare overhaul. *State* (Columbia, SC), A7.

Barker, R. L. (2003). *The social work dictionary,* 5th ed. Washington, DC: NASW Press.

Bateman, N. (2002). Overview of HIPAA administrative simplification provisions [Electronic version]. *Mental & Behavioral Health: NASW Practice Update* 2 (3). Available at http://www.socialworkers.org/.

Bernstein, P., & Ma, C. (1996). *The practical guide to practically everything: 1997 edition.* New York: Random House.

Block, W. (1986). Private property, ethics, and wealth creation. In Berger, P. L. (1986) *The capitalist revolution: Fifty propositions about prosperity, equality, and liberty,* 107–128. New York: Basic Books.

Brilliant, E. L. (1990). *The United Way: Dilemmas of organized charity.* New York: Columbia University Press.

Brody, E. (1985). Parent care as a normative family stress. *Gerontologist* 25, 19–20.

Centers for Medicare & Medicaid Services (CMS). (n.d.). State Children's Health Insurance Program (SCHIP). http://www.cms.hhs.gov/schip/ (accessed February 12, 2004).

Centers for Medicare & Medicaid Services (CMS). (January 2004). Medicaid—A brief summary. http://www.cms.hhs.gov/publications/overview-medicare-medicaid/default4.asp (accessed March 26, 2004).

Chambers, D. (2000). *Social policy and social programs,* 3rd ed. Boston: Allyn & Bacon.

Chapin, R. K. (July 1995). Social policy development: The strengths perspective. *Social Work,* 506–514.

Cohen, J. J. (September 2001). A word from the president: Lessons from managed care. *Association of American Medical Colleges Reporter.* http://www.aamc.org/newsroom/reporter/sept2001/start.htm (accessed February 12, 2004).

Committee for Economic Development, Concord Coalition, & Center on Budget and Policy Priorities. (September 29, 2003). *No end in sight to rising deficits, experts warn.* http://www.cbpp.prg/9-29-03bud-pr.htm (accessed September 29, 2003).

Committee on Ways and Means, U.S. House of Representatives. (1992). *Overview of entitlement programs: 1991 green book.* Washington, DC: U.S. Government Printing Office.

Committee on Ways and Means, U.S. House of Representatives. (1993). *Overview of entitlement programs: 1993 green book.* Washington, DC: U.S. Government Printing Office.

Committee on Ways and Means, U.S. House of Representatives. (1996). *1996 green book: Background material and data on programs within the jurisdiction of the Committee on Ways and Means.* Washington, DC: U.S. Government Printing Office.

Conlan, T. J. (1998). *From new federalism to devolution: Twenty-five years of intergovernmental reform.* Washington, DC: Brookings Institution Press.

Curley, J. & Sherraden, M. (1998). *Policy report: The history and status of children's allowances: Policy background for children's savings accounts.* St. Louis, MO: Center for Social Development, Washington University in St. Louis.

Cutler, N. E. (1997). The financial gerontology birthdays of 1995–1996: Social Security at 60 the "Baby" Boom at 50. In M. Reisch & E. Gambrill (Eds.), *Social work in the 21st century,* 143–151. Thousand Oaks: Pine Forge Press.

Department of Health and Human Services Office of the Secretary. (2003). Annual update of the HHS poverty guidelines. *Federal Register* 68 (26), 6456–6458.

DiNitto, D. (2003). *Social welfare: Politics and public policy,* 5th ed. Boston: Allyn & Bacon.

Dolbeare, C. N. (2001). *Out of reach: The gap between housing costs and income of poor people in the United States.* National Low Income Housing Coalition. http://www.nlihc.org/oor99/index.htm (accessed February 5, 2004).

Dolgoff, R. & Feldstein, D. (2003). *Understanding social welfare,* 6th ed. Boston: Allyn & Bacon.

Economic Research Service. (2003). *Food stamp program.* http://www.ers.usda.gov/Briefing/FoodStamps/ (accessed February 10, 2004).

Economic Research Service. (2003). *The WIC program.* http://www.ers.usda.gov/Briefing/wic (accessed February 10, 2004).

Edelman, P. (March 1997). The worst thing Bill Clinton has done. *Atlantic Monthly,* 43–58.

Edwards, R. L., et al. (Eds.), *Encyclopedia of social work,* 19th ed., 1849–1855. Washington, DC: NASW Press.

Fagan, P., Rector, R., Johnson, K., & Peterson, A. (April 2002). *The positive effects of marriage: A book of charts* [Electronic version]. Washington, DC: Heritage Foundation.

Fagan, P. F., Rector, R. E., & Noyes, L. R. (June 16, 2003). *Why congress should ignore radical feminist opposition to marriage* (Executive Summary No. 1662) [Electronic version]. Washington, DC: Heritage Foundation.

Fisher, G. (1992). The development and history of the poverty thresholds. *Social Security Bulletin* 55 (4), 3–14.

Fremstad, S., & Primus, W. (January 22, 2002). *Strengthening families: Ideas of TANF reauthorization* [Electronic version]. Washington, DC: Center on Budget and Policy Priorities.

Friedman, M., & Friedman, R. (1980). *Free to choose: A personal statement.* New York: Avon.

Fuchs, F. (2002). Overview of public housing, HUD, federally subsidized housing and section 8 housing voucher programs. In National Center on Poverty Law (Eds.),

Poverty law manual for the new lawyer, 109–125. Chicago: National Center on Poverty Law.

Gilbert, N., & Terrell P. (2002). *Dimensions of social welfare policy,* 5th ed. Boston: Allyn & Bacon.

Gilder, G. (June 1995). End welfare reform as we know it. *American Spectator* 28 (6), 24–32.

Ginsberg, L. (1983). *The practice of social work in public welfare.* New York: Free Press.

Ginsberg, L. (1995). *Social work almanac,* 2nd ed. Washington, DC: NASW Press.

Hudson, R. (2002). Getting ready and getting credit: Populations of color and retirement security. *Public Policy and Aging Report* 12 (3), 1–2.

Jansson, B. (2001). *The reluctant welfare state,* 4th ed. Belmont, CA: Wadsworth Publishing.

Katz, J. L. (September 23, 1995). Senate overhaul plan provides road map for compromise. *Congressional Quarterly,* 2908–2911.

Kaufmann, J. (2002). An introduction to Old-Age, Survivors, and Disability Insurance and Supplemental Security Income. In National Center on Poverty Law (Eds.), *Poverty Law Manual for the New Lawyer,* 92–103. Chicago: National Center on Poverty Law.

Kisor, A., McSweeney, E., & Jackson, D. (2002). Social problems and policies and the elderly. In R. L. Schneider, N. P. Kropf, & A. J. Kisor (Eds.), *Gerontological social work: Knowledge, service settings, and special populations,* 2nd ed., 65–95. Belmont, CA: Brooks/Cole.

Kopp, M. A. (July 24, 1995). The family sufficiency act of 1995. *Washington Social Legislation Bulletin* 34 (14). Washington, DC: Child Welfare League of America.

LA Crisis Housing Task Force. (n.d.). *Housing crisis task force report.* http://housingcrisisla.ucla.edu/ (accessed February 5, 2004).

Laslovich, M. J. (1993). The American tradition: Federalism in the United States. In M. Burgess & A. G. Gagnon (Eds.), *Comparative federalism and federation: Competing traditions and future directions,* 187–202. New York: Harvester Wheatsheaf.

Levin, B. L., Hanson, A., Coe, R. D., & Taylor, A. (1998). *Mental health parity: 1998 national and state perspectives.* Louis de la Parte Florida Mental Health Institute, University of South Florida. http://www.fmhi.usf.edu/institute/pubs/parity/parity98.pdf (accessed February 10, 2004).

Liebig, P. S. (1995). Social policy and professional identity. *Generations* 19, 39–42.

Linhorst, D. (2002). Federalism and social justice: Implications for social work. *Social Work* 47 (3), 201–208.

Mangum, G., & Mangum, S. (Eds.) (1996). *Of heart and mind: Social policy essays in memory of Sar A. Levitan.* Kalamazoo, MI: Upjohn Institute.

Markoe, L. (November 18, 2003). Graham rolling out Social Security plan. *State* (Columbia, SC), A1, A6.

Moon, M. (1999). *Growth in Medicare spending: What will beneficiaries pay?* http://www.urban.org/url.cfm?ID=407788 (accessed March 3, 2003).

Murray, C. (1994). *Losing ground: American social policy, 1950–1980,* 10th anniversary edition. New York: Basic Books.

National Association of Social Workers. (October 1997). Budget law for '98 alters social programs. *NASW News,* 9.

National Center for Children in Poverty (NCCP). (2003). *Low-income children in the United States (2003).* http://www.nccp.org/pub cpf03.html (accessed February 12, 2004).

National Center for Health Statistics. (1999). Health: United States, 1999. http://www.cdc.gov/nchs (accessed February 23, 2004).

National Family Caregivers Association. (October 2000). *Caregiver Survey-2000* [Electronic version]. Kensington, MD: Author. http://www.nfcacares.org/ (accessed March 3, 2003).

O'Neill, D. M., & O'Neill, J. E. (1997). *Lessons for welfare reform: An analysis of the AFDC caseload and past welfare to work programs.* Kalamazoo, MI: Upjohn Institute.

Pacula, R. L., & Sturm, R. (2000). Mental health party legislation: Much ado about nothing? *Health Services Research* 35 (1), 261–273.

Peterson, D., Wendt, R., & Douglass, E. (1991). *Determining the impact of gerontology preparation on personnel in the aging network.* Washington, DC: Association for Gerontology in Higher Education.

Pitcoff, W., Pelletiere, D., Crowley, S., Schaffer, K. Treskon, M., Vance, C., & Dolbeare, C. N. (2003). *Out of reach 2003: America's housing wage climbs.* National Low Income Housing Coalition. http://www.nlihc.org/oor2003/ (accessed February 5, 2004).

Pizzagati, K. (September 1997). Children lose SSI benefits under new welfare law. *Children's Monitor,* 1997 Supplement, 4.

RAND. (2000). Are people with mental illness getting the help they need? http://www.rand.org/publications/RB/RB4533/ (accessed February 11, 2004).

Rector, R. (Summer 2001). Using welfare reform to strengthen marriage [Electronic version]. *American Experiment Quarterly,* 63–67.

Riedl, B. M. (February 12, 2003). *Ten guidelines for reducing wasteful government spending* (Executive Summary No. 1622) [Electronic version]. Washington, DC: Heritage Foundation.

Schneider, R., & Netting, F. (1999). Influencing social policy in a time of devolution: Upholding social work's great tradition. *Social Work* 44 (4), 349–357.

Schulz, J. (1996). Economic security policies. In R. H. Binstock & L. K. George (Eds.), *Handbook of aging and the social sciences,* 4th ed., 410–429. San Diego, CA: Academic Press.

Sherraden, M. (1991). *Assets and the poor: A new American welfare policy.* Armonk, NY: M. E. Sharpe.

Single-Rushton, W., & McLanahan, S. (July 2003). *For richer or poorer? Marriage as an anti-poverty strategy in the United States* (Working Paper No. 01–17–FF) [Electronic version]. Princeton, NJ: Center for Research on Child Wellbeing.

Solot, D., & Miller, M. (2002). *Let them eat wedding rings: The role of marriage promotion in welfare reform* [Electronic version]. Boston, MA: Alternatives to Marriage Project.

Takamura, J. C. (1999). Getting ready for the 21st century: The aging of America and the Older Americans Act. *Health and Social Work* 24 (3), 232–238.

Tanner, M. (July 26, 1996). *Privatizing Social Security: A big boost for the poor* (Social Security Choice Paper No. 4). Washington, DC: Cato Institute.

Tanner, M. (February 5, 2001). *Disparate impact: Social Security and African-Americans* (Briefing Paper No. 61). Washington, DC: Cato Institute.

U.S. Department of Health and Human Services Office of the Assistant Secretary for Planning & Evaluation. (September 11, 2003). *Information contacts and references on: The poverty guidelines, the poverty thresholds, and the development and history of U.S. poverty lines.* http://aspe.hhs.gov/poverty/contacts.htm#f (accessed November 10, 2003).

Williamson, J. (1997). A critique of the case for privatizing Social Security. *Gerontologist* 37 (5), 561–571.

Those who want current, detailed information on these programs may find what they need within current government documents, especially those published by the Social Security Administration. The series of House Ways and Means Committee "green books," three of which are cited above, provides one of the best compendiums of data on all entitlement programs. In addition, the annual "Statistical Abstracts," published by the Bureau of the Census, is a good source of information.

For additional information on the programs described in this chapter, see the above sources; R. L. Edwards et al. (Eds.) (1995). *Encyclopedia of Social Work,* 19th ed. Washington, DC: NASW Press; and L. Ginsberg et al. (Eds.) (1990). *Encyclopedia of Social Work,* 18th ed., 1990 suppl. Silver Spring, MD: NASW Press.

SEVEN

The Descriptive Component Continued
Special Care for Special Groups

Chapter 6 described the economic assistance services that are the foundation of social programs in the United States. This chapter describes the other side of social services—the personal social services, which R. L. Barker (2003, 324) says are designed "to enhance the relationships between people and their environments and to provide opportunities for social fulfillment. . . . [They] include counseling and guidance, development of mutual help and self-help groups, family planning, and services for older people and for children." Barker says that personal social services are those that do not provide money, health care, education, or housing.

Personal services are crucial, and developing and administering them is the focus of most professional human services jobs. They require high levels of professional skill because services are individualized to meet the requirements of a multitude of clients. The economic assistance programs described in the last chapter, for example, can make a dramatic difference in the lives of clients, but one has to know just what programs are available, how they can best be applied to a particular case, and what the limits are.

The care of people with special needs is a distinctive area of social policy in the United States. Although the poor have traditionally been viewed as the primary category of those with needs and the major subject of social policy, the vulnerable and disadvantaged include many subcategories of individuals such as widows, orphans and other dependent children, the elderly, people with mental and physical disabilities, those suffering from illnesses, people found guilty of breaking the law, and others. The establishment of the human services profession is part of that history of developing services for people with special needs.

Institutional Care

Institutional care has long been a factor in the social services for people who cannot care for themselves, as chapter 2 describes. According to C. A. Alexander (1995), in the eighteenth century a number of institutions were established for people with specific needs. A privately financed home for mothers and children was established in New Orleans by the Ursuline sisters, for example, primarily to care for survivors of Indian massacres and a small-pox epidemic. Dorothea Dix, an influential advocate for individuals with mental illness, was instrumental in the development of many institutions that cared for individuals with mental illness and disabilities during the mid-1800s (as discussed in chapter 2). She lobbied state governments fiercely in an attempt to provide more humane treatment for people with mental illness and those who lived in prisons. In 1884 she lobbied the federal government for the passage of the Land Grant Act, which although it passed in Congress, was ultimately vetoed by President Franklin Pierce, who believed that states, not the federal government, had the responsibility for the welfare of its citizens. The Land Grant Act would have set aside federal lands as a public endowment to be used to fund programs for individuals with disabilities and mental illness. Despite this, Dix accomplished a great deal in her lifetime, including playing a significant role in the establishment of over thirty mental institutions, many schools for those with mental disabilities, and schools for the blind and deaf.

Defining Institutions. The most traditional and basic definition of an institution is a physical space, usually a building, where an organization operates or conducts business. The human services profession primarily concerns itself with institutions that are dedicated to the residential care of individuals who require some amount of specialized care. This might include, for example, people with mental illness, people convicted of crimes, people in need of substance abuse treatment, or individuals who require around the clock medical care. Institutional care generally includes a residential component, can be long term or temporary, and includes a variety of social and medical services (Hutchison & McGill, 1998). Institutions can be either privately or publicly run, and some examples include state or county mental hospitals, group homes, residential treatment programs, prisons, nursing homes, private psychiatric hospitals, foster care homes, shelters, rehabilitation centers, and substance abuse treatment programs.

Trends in Institutionalization. Institutions are considered to be the most formal of settings in which to receive care. Historically, confinement within institutions was the most preferred and in some cases, the only option, for care of people that society thought were unfit, undesirable, or dangerous (Goffman, 1961). Sometimes this confinement of certain people may be necessary due to public safety such as in the case of some dangerous criminal behavior, but in other cases it may be due to a lack of supportive care within a community and a misunderstanding of the nature of mental illness or disabilities. Critics of institutional care note the negative impacts of segregating people away from the general population, the dehumanizing approach to care that sometimes occurs within institutions, and the stigma attached to people who are not considered "normal" and are unable to function well or live in the community (Hutchison & McGill, 1998; MacNeil & Teague, 1987; Meddaugh & Peterson, 1997; Shapiro, 1993).

The shift from public to private facilities and the de-emphasis on institutional care can be seen in most areas of services that many human services workers provide. Care for the infirm and aged, dependent children, youthful offenders, persons who are disabled, and persons with mental illness has moved from public to private resources. Some observers of social policy, as noted, refer to this shift as the privatization of services. With the exception of correctional facilities, overall there has been a decline in the number of people placed in institutional care. The number of those cared for by states has decreased and state institutions are smaller facilities than they were in the past. For example, only 2.1 million of the estimated 27–39 million Americans with disabilities live in institutions (Kaye, 1997). In addition, of the over 4 million children with disabilities in the United States, only 91,800 (2 percent) live in institutions (Adler, 1995). Public policy has swung in the private direction for a variety of reasons. Private care is often viewed as potentially more humane and, in some ways, less costly than public care. However, sometimes the care can be provided by contracts with private facilities and services, which can be cancelled or allowed to expire. When government builds facilities and staffs them with permanent employees, it takes on fiscal obligations that continue indefinitely and often expensively.

In addition, there have been trends when institutional care is emphasized or de-emphasized, depending on a variety of factors such as the costs of institutional services, the development of new treatment modalities or medication, the emergence of civil and human rights issues, and increased awareness of the need for more humane treatment methods. For example, prior to the 1970s, it was considered commonplace to confine people with mental illness and disabilities within institutions. During the 1970s the independent living movement gained momentum and programs and policies geared toward "mainstreaming" individuals with disabilities and mental illness were created. To mainstream a person means to place an individual in the most normal setting possible. For example, instead of placing a child in a special school for children with learning disabilities, the preference would be to keep that child in a regular classroom. Overall, the end result of both the move to private organizations and the de-emphasis on institutional care has resulted in fewer Americans living in institutions.

Results of Deinstitutionalization. Obviously, the growing knowledge of the high costs of institutional care and the promise of newer treatments and medication for people with mental illness and disabilities have all contributed to deinstitutionalization. Some argue that the deinstitutionalization of individuals from mental hospitals has contributed significantly to the problem of homelessness (Torrey, 1988). Indeed, it is estimated that up to a quarter of the homeless population in the United States has a serious mental illness as compared to 5–6 percent of the general U.S. population (Rosenheck, Bassuk, & Salomon, 1999). Others have argued that it is not that people with mental illness are no longer in institutions, but that the type of institution has changed—to jails and shelters (Barr, 1999). Ironically, it may be that the shift away from institutional care in mental hospitals into the community has, in the end, just shifted the mentally ill population into less humane institutions.

The use of institutional care has also varied within the field of child welfare (Downs, Moore, McFadden, Michaud, & Costin, 2004). For example, sometimes out of home care (foster care, adoption, group homes) for children has been the preference in the case of child abuse. Yet, at other times the preference has been the preservation of the family, reunification services, or kinship care (McFadden & Downs, 1995). Kinship care is usually when a relative or extended family member assumes the parenting duties for a child who is related to them. (For more information on kinship care, please refer to the Children's Defense Fund, Kinship Care Resource Kit, http://www.childrensdefense.org/childwelfare/kinshipcare/resourcekit/default.asp.) When child safety has been emphasized, institutional care is heavily used, but when family preservation is emphasized, focus is placed on supportive services provided within homes. Sadly, the most prominent use of institutions for children is incarceration for delinquent or criminal behavior. Even more troubling is that of the juveniles held in residential settings a disproportionate number of those are children of color. This phenomenon has come to be known as disproportionate minority confinement and is a problem of serious concern to human services workers, researchers, and civil rights advocates.

Funding for long-term care of the elderly and individuals with disabilities is another example of the complexity of institutional care. The "nursing home bias" describes the strong financial incentives to provide long-term care in nursing homes. The nursing home bias, in policy terms, means that institutional care in the United States is an entitlement, while in-home care lacks that status (Dautel & Frieden, 1999). There have been recently publicized cases that highlight families who are forced to place their older relatives or disabled family members in the care of the state because they cannot afford to keep them at home or provide them with the services they need, even though they might prefer to care for them at home. For example, thousands of parents are reported to have given up custody of their children so that the children can get access to quality mental health services and, in some cases, have even been pressured by states to do so (Pear, 2003). Many disabilities rights and caregiving advocates argue that some Americans end up living in institutions for the crime of being old, disabled. or unable to afford in-home services.

Regulating Institutions. It should come as no surprise then, that there have been various policies and Supreme Court cases that have addressed the issue of institutional care. The Education of All Handicapped Children Act of 1975 requires that children with disabilities be placed in the "least restrictive environment" possible (Douvanis & Hulsey, 2002; Mackelprang & Salsgiver, 1999). The *least restrictive environment* means that services should be provided in the most "normal" setting possible such as in one's own home or with a family. Table 6 provides examples of the continuum of services for children from least restrictive to the most restrictive. This has obvious implications in terms of the use of institutions. The Americans with Disabilities Act of 1990 (*Public Law*, 101–336, 1998), important civil rights legislation in the United States, states that "no qualified individual with a disability shall, by reason of such disability, be excluded from participation in or be denied the benefits of the services, programs, or activities of a public entity, or be subjected to discrimination by any such entity" (Title II, Section 20). In 1999, the Supreme Court issued their ruling on the *Olmstead v. L.C.* case. The ruling required that individuals with disabilities should be placed in the most integrative setting possible to meet their needs. In other words, the Court rejected the notion that states could enforce that people be placed in institutions. A precedent indicating the preference for community placement and treatment was established (Centers for Medicare & Medicaid Services, 2002). In 2001, President George W. Bush issued an Executive Order that promoted the use of community-based, as opposed to institutional, care for individuals with disabilities (U.S. Department of Health and Human Services Office for Civil Rights, 2003).

Clearly, one of the most persistent criticisms of institutional care is that it is the *most* expensive type of treatment available, no matter whether it is received in the hospital, prison, group home, or nursing home. In addition, the separation and confinement of individuals now seems counterintuitive to what is accepted "best practices" in the treatment of individuals with mental illness, disabilities, or even, some argue, for people convicted of less serious drug crimes. Some argue for a philosophy of "harm reduction" for dealing with substance abuse issues in society. They argue that jail is not an effective way of eliminating the many social problems drugs cause society. Community treatment programs are the preferred way to treat drug abuse rather than jail in such a model. Overall, most human services workers now understand the importance of keeping families together and giving people the opportunities to maintain social connections and develop their potential in the most humane, least restrictive setting possible.

Table 6. Continuum of Services from Least to Most Restrictive

Least Restrictive

Child Living at Home with Parents
Child Living with Relative
Foster Family Home
Specialized Foster Family Home
Group Home
Private Child Welfare Institution
Shelter
Mental Health Facility
Correctional Facility

Most Restrictive

Source: Adapted from Proch and Taber (1987).

Licensing Policies

One of the major elements of social policy is the control of facilities of care, such as hospitals, day care, nursing homes, and foster care. It is the policy of all the states to license facilities that care for children as well as the aged and other groups. Each state's licensing laws and procedures are different, but the essential features of all cover specific elements of the facilities' operations. These include

1. Fire and other safety controls. Facilities must comply with fire prevention strategies, have extinguishers available, store hazardous materials properly, be constructed in ways that will allow people to exit burning areas safely, organize regular fire drills, and avoid dangerous structural features and materials that may cause injury or death. Such arrangements are, of course, especially important when institutions house vulnerable groups such as children, people with disabilities, and older people.

2. Public health inspections to ensure properly maintained food preparation areas, environmental safety, general good health practices, and general cleanliness.

3. Programs that can help residents with their problems or basic needs. These parts of the licensing process usually involve human services professionals

who try to ensure that there are sufficient numbers of qualified staff and that facilities operate programs that can educate, develop, and treat or maintain the morale of residents. A facility that has no program beyond eating, sleeping, and watching television—which many do not—may find its license threatened.

Operating a facility without a license is a violation of the law, so facilities treat the licensing requirements seriously. In some states, however, facilities that are operated by religious bodies are not subject to the licensing requirement. The belief is that the children's home or facility for the aged is a "church" and, as such, is not subject to state regulations. Of course, that is not a constitutional issue. A facility that provides care for people, no matter what its sponsorship, is not automatically constitutionally exempt from state regulation—just as the profit-making business enterprises of a nonprofit organization are subject to taxes, even though the nonprofit organization itself may not be. An anomaly of social policy in some states is that religiously affiliated human services facilities are legally exempted from licensing laws. Many of those facilities are of high quality and would have no difficulty in meeting licensing requirements; others may operate in ways that are detrimental to their residents.

Child Welfare

What Is Child Welfare?
The Child Welfare League of America, which is one of the largest, oldest, and most respected child welfare organizations in the United States, list six values pertinent to ensuring that every child is able to reach his or her potential and promoting the well-being of every child.

1. Every child and every youth has value to society.
2. Every child and youth is entitled to nurturance, protection, the chance to develop to his or her full human potential, and opportunities to contribute to the common good.
3. The family and the child welfare system both have specific responsibilities, but society at large shares the responsibility for promoting healthy human growth and development.
4. Children and youth thrive, or fail to thrive, in the context of families, kinship systems, and communities. Our work must recognize and value these connections.
5. The agencies and organizations that comprise CWLA have come together because we share a common mission and because we value interdependence: We know we are stronger together than alone.
6. The shared values that bind this learning organization include openness, trust, accountability, and a commitment to continuous quality improvement. (Child Welfare League of America [CWLA], 2004)

Child welfare/advocacy organizations have contributed significantly to our understanding of child welfare issues and policies. Each year the Child Welfare League of America develops a legislative agenda that lists the policy priorities that are relevant to America's children. Individuals can also sign up to receive their legislative updates, information and publications, and statistics on a variety of child welfare topics. The Children's Defense Fund (CDF) was founded by Marian Wright Edelman and the mission of the CDF is to Leave No Child Behind by working to ensure that every child has a healthy, fair, safe, and moral start in life (Children's Defense Fund [CDF], n.d.). The Annie E. Casey Foundation, another important child advocacy organization, focuses its work on disadvantaged children and their families. One of their most well known contributions is the publication of annual Kids Count data that reports on the status of child well-being at the national and state level. Kids Count data is available to private citizens and policymakers and can be used to determine whether or not the well-being has improved or declined. This data can ultimately be used to help advocate for more responsive public policy and programs (Annie E. Casey Foundation [AECF], 2004b).

It is important to note the holistic approach to child welfare of the organizations just discussed. Many people in the public think of child welfare as primarily about dealing with the problems of child abuse and neglect. While it is true that child abuse is a social problem that must be contended with, others have argued that child abuse is the "red herring" of child welfare (Lindsey, 2003). In other words, the belief that child abuse should be the central focus of child welfare ignores all of the other, possibly related factors that could ultimately prevent or at least significantly reduce the problem of child abuse. True child welfare, some argue, should be about reducing or eliminating poverty, supporting families, and dealing with other social problems that are related to child abuse. Lindsey (2003), for example, points out the difference between child neglect, which is about improper care of children, and child physical abuse, which is about causing physical harm to children. He notes that in neglect cases many children are removed because their parents have economic difficulties that make it difficult for them to adequately provide for their children and that child removal should not be based on money. Thus, the "child saving" focus negates the importance of dealing with the many other important needs of children and their families such as health care, quality education, or living without poverty.

Awareness of the many social problems faced by children today is important for human services workers to consider because the children they serve are likely to experience many problems other than child abuse. Child poverty, for example, is a growing concern. According to 2003 Kids Count data from the Annie E. Casey Foundation, 17 percent of all children (about 12 million) live in poverty (AECF, 2002) and 12 percent have no health insurance (AECF,

2004a). For a look at key indicators about the well-being of children in America, the CDF publishes twenty-five key facts about American children that highlight many other concerns related to children.

25 Key Facts About American Children

1 in 2 will live in a single parent family at some
    point in childhood.
1 in 3 is born to unmarried parents.
1 in 3 will be poor at some point in their childhood.
1 in 3 is behind a year or more in school.
1 in 4 lives with only one parent.
2 in 5 never complete a single year of college.
1 in 5 was born poor.
1 in 5 is born to a mother who did not graduate from high school.
1 in 5 has a foreign-born mother.
3 in 5 preschoolers have their mother in the labor force.
1 in 6 is poor now.
1 in 6 is born to a mother who did not receive prenatal care in the first
    three months of pregnancy.
1 in 7 has no health insurance.
1 in 7 has a worker in their family but still is poor.
1 in 8 lives in a family receiving food stamps
1 in 8 never graduates from high school.
1 in 8 is born to a teenage mother.
1 in 12 has a disability.
1 in 13 was born with low birthweight.
1 in 15 lives at less than half the poverty level.
1 in 24 lives with neither parent.
1 in 26 is born to a mother who received late or no prenatal care.
1 in 60 sees their parents divorce in any year.
1 in 139 will die before their first birthday.
1 in 1,056 will be killed by guns before age 20.

© 2001 Children's Defense Fund.
Source: *The State of America's Children Yearbook,* 2001.

Broadly defined, then, child welfare should refer to all of the aspects of society essential for the enhancement of the well-being of children. Human services workers may be aware of Maslow's "hierarchy of needs," which provides a nice framework for thinking holistically about child welfare and helps conceptualize a more comprehensive view of what children need to develop into healthy, productive adults.

Physiological
Survival
Children need: food,
sleep, clothes, shelter,
health care

Safety
Children need: security,
freedom from abuse

Belongingness
Children need: to love and be loved, and
their parents need the support to do this well

Esteem
Children need: approval, respect, acceptance, dignity

Self-Actualization
Children need: opportunities to reach their full potential

Figure 1. Holistic View of Child Welfare Utilizing
Maslow's Hierarchy of Needs

Brief History of Child Welfare

Children have traditionally been the focus of many of the resources provided for personal social services. Although it may be difficult for current readers to imagine, children were not always treated as a special group by society, as if they were any different from adults. Although they are obviously smaller, weaker, and less skillful, generally, than adults, children were not always considered a population group with special needs and requiring special care; that concept is relatively new, a development from late in the last century. The New York Society for the Prevention of Cruelty to Children was established in 1875 and encouraged the growth of other child saving societies across the United States (Downs et al., 2004). An excellent and fascinating book about child abuse policy is *Making an Issue of Child Abuse* by Barbara Nelson (1984). In the early 1960s, Dr. Henry Kempe published an important work where the term "battered child syndrome" was first used. Kempe and his colleagues used new technology (at that time), the X-ray, to document the horrors of child abuse. For the first time it was possible to notice old injuries that children sustained due to a lifetime of physical abuse. The work of Kempe and others spawned some of the first mandatory child abuse reporting laws in many states. Reports of child abuse since then have dramatically increased, most notably with the passage of the Child Abuse Prevention Act of 1974. In 1975 there were just over 300,000 reports of child abuse; in the year 2000 there were about three and a half million reports (Lindsey, 2003).

Although there is discussion later in this chapter of the special services for people with physical, mental, and behavioral disabilities, the general pattern in child welfare is to treat children as children. A juvenile delinquent is not a special species of humanity but is, the child welfare policies of the nation assert, a child with special behavioral problems. That is, a child is first a child; special characteristics or problems are considered secondary issues.

The movement in child welfare has gone from protection of individual children from abuse or neglect to preserving families. It is now federal law that states that accept federal money for children's services (and all do) have programs that work intensively toward the preservation of families. The idea is that families are the best location for children and can best nurture children. However, some families need help in freeing themselves from abusive or neglectful behavior or in preventing such behavior. The family preservation programs such as Homebuilders provide vulnerable families with services from professionals, usually master's level social workers. Those workers spend several hours each week with the family, providing both "hard" and "soft" services. Hard services are concrete kinds of help, such as food, cash assistance, food stamps, health care, housing, clothing, and other tangible aid. The soft services are primarily education and counseling for families that have trouble appropriately and effectively raising their children. Workers who visit their families carry out activities ranging from helping them repair their cars or clean their houses to assisting in resolving conflicts between parents and between parents and children.

Children constitute a large population group everywhere in the world. In the United States some 18 percent of the population was under seventeen years old in the year 2002 (U.S. Department of Commerce, Bureau of the Census, *Statistical Abstract of the United States,* Washington, D.C., 2003). More than one third of the members of the National Association of Social Workers (NASW) are involved in serving children and their families (Ginsberg, 1995). The following section highlights some child welfare policies in more detail.

Child Labor. Even prohibitions against children working with the same kinds of circumstances as adults are relatively new developments. Not only was there no social policy prohibiting child labor in earlier U.S. history, but in some ways it was encouraged. P. J. Day (1997, 146) noted that child labor was "viewed as beneficial to both child and society, teaching the sanctity of work and the evils of idleness." Although there were concerns earlier, policies to end child labor were not in effect until the twentieth century. In certain industries, such as mining, children were prized because they could reach places that larger workers could not reach, and since they were not responsible for supporting families, they could be paid lower salaries than adults. If they were injured or killed in industrial accidents, the impact, it was felt, would not be as great as if a principal family wage earner, such as a father or mother, had been injured or killed. Many early social workers and settlement workers advocated for the abolishment of child labor, including Jane Addams, Robert Hunter, Lillian Wald, Julia Lathrop, and Florence Kelley. The National Child Labor Committee was formed in 1904 to document the extent of the problem of child labor in the United States. The photographs of Lewis W. Hine documenting child labor in the United States from 1908–1912 can be viewed at http://www.historyplace.com/unitedstates/childlabor/. There are some interesting political cartoons from that time period that highlight some perspectives of child labor from a historical perspective.

Many of the states have had laws against child labor for much of their history. Yet there was no federal prohibition against it until the early twentieth century; in 1916 the U.S. Congress passed a law called the Child Labor Act to forbid interstate commerce in goods that were manufactured by children. The bill was declared unconstitutional by the Supreme Court, however, in 1918 (Alexander, 1995).

The Fair Labor Standards Act (FLSA) of 1938 regulates child labor in nonagricultural (nonfarmwork) industries. (Current FLSA standards are available at the U.S. Department of Labor Web site: http://www.dol.gov/dol/compliance/comp-flsa-childlabor.htm.) Most states have enacted laws that prohibit child labor including restrictions on the number of hours and days eligible children can work, the types of work or jobs children can perform, and mandatory school attendance—therefore protecting children's educational opportunities.

Child labor is reemerging as an American social problem. Dumaine (1993) describes several examples throughout the United States of current problems with illegal child labor. He suggests that employers are hiring children for long hours and to do dangerous work in fast food restaurants, garment factories, in grocery stores, or door-to-door night sales of items such as candy. In recent years there has been substantial concern about the extent of illegal child labor in the United States and its effects on the health and development of children (Dumaine, 1993; Hedgers, 1996; Kruse & Mahony, 1998; National Child Labor Committee, 1994; National Institute for Occupational Safety and Health Child Labor Working Team, 1997; Tucker, 2000; U.S. General Accounting Office, 1991, 1992). The most dangerous and difficult work for children is agricultural work and it is also the least regulated and protected by law (Tucker, 2000). Children who work in the fields, for example, might carry heavy produce, spend long days (up to twelve hours, which is well over the legal limit) picking or planting in the agricultural fields, and work late into the night or in very bad weather conditions. A 1998 study estimated that almost 150,000 children work illegally, over the hourly limit, and in dangerous jobs every week; and annually almost 300,000 work illegally at least once in the United States. Sadly, many of these children earn an average of just $1.38 per hour, which is below the minimum wage (Kruse & Mahony, 1998).

The Children's Bureau and Policy Concerns for Children. Congress established the Children's Bureau in 1912 (Alexander, 1995) to work toward the protection of the rights of children and to promote children's well-being. Despite the Supreme Court invalidation of the Child Labor Act, the Children's Bureau was given directives to prohibit federal contractors from using child labor (Jansson, 1997), another example of executive branch policy making that worked even though the legislative and executive branches were unable to implement the same policy.

The Children's Bureau, one of the oldest of the federal agencies that deals with human services, has throughout its long history monitored the problems of children in the United States and advocated better treatment of young people. Its creation followed the precedent-setting 1909 White House Conference on Children, the first to be held (Alexander, 1995); these were continued for the rest of the century in some form although the national, high-profile conferences were dropped during the presidency of Ronald Reagan. That first conference was initiated under the sponsorship of another Republican president, one of the most innovative in all American history and an activist, Theodore Roosevelt. These conferences pushed for programs that eventually led to the Social Security Act and many other reforms.

Current children's services are many. In fact, most of the money spent for human services in the United States is devoted to improving the well-being of children. The largest and most expensive of these efforts is, of course, public education. Substantial amounts are also spent on the economic assistance included in the TANF and OASDI programs, among others.

Trends in Child Welfare Services

The major programs providing help to children, apart from financial assistance and education, are called child welfare services, which fall into several different categories. In every category, however, it is fundamental to child welfare policy that the focus is on the well-being of the child. The best interests of the child, always and without question, are supposed to be the fundamental concern of those who administer child welfare policies, including agency personnel and the courts. The goal is that the best interests of the child be served, even when his or her interests may conflict with the wishes of parents, relatives, and other interested parties. And very often the child's best interests are the same as those of the child's caregivers. One of the recent social policy themes that permeates child welfare is that children ought to be able to remain with their families—biological, adoptive, or any other kind—

whenever possible. But a related policy theme is that children should be removed from abusive family situations when a satisfactory resolution and reunification cannot be expected, so the child may be placed with another family on a permanent basis. Obviously, delaying proper care for children too long is equivalent to denying children their childhoods. Waiting too long can mean waiting until near adulthood, when having a satisfactory childhood is no longer a possibility.

Child Protective Services

The most important of the categories of child welfare is child protective services, which is a collection of services provided to children who are in danger of neglect or abuse by their parents or others who are caring for them. In every state there are child protective services provided to children whose need comes to the attention of the child protective agency. Children who require protective services fall into a number of categories, such as those who are victims of physical abuse, sexual abuse, medical neglect, emotional and psychological maltreatment, and neglect.

In 2001 there were approximately 5 million reports of child abuse made to Child Protective Services (CPS) agencies in the United States (U.S. Department of Health and Human Services Administration on Children, Youth and Families [US HSS ACYF], 2003). Once a case is reported it can be either "screened in" or "screened out." When a case is screened in it means that an investigation of that case was warranted. Although screened out cases are also given referrals for help such as food pantries or parenting classes on occasion, there was not enough evidence to suggest that an investigation was needed. Over a quarter of the cases that were screened in were substantiated, or found to be real cases of abuse or neglect that required some kind of intervention (US HSS ACYF, 2003). The rest of the screened in cases were found to be at no risk for abuse, the abuse did not occur, or there was not enough evidence to prove the case. The following is a list of some of the categories used by the National Clearinghouse on Child Abuse and Neglect Information to determine the status of child abuse investigations. These categories also vary somewhat by state because of different state laws.

Table 7. Definitions of Some of the Categories Used

Substantiated	This is the most serious category. This means that the claim of maltreatment of risk for maltreatment was found to be true.
Indicated or Reason to Suspect	This means that the claim of maltreatment could not be substantiated by law but that there is "reason to suspect" that the maltreatment did occur or that the child is at risk for maltreatment.

Unsubstantiated	This means one of two things:
	1. It was determined that no maltreatment occurred *or*
	2. There was not enough evidence to establish that maltreatment occurred or that there was no risk for maltreatment.

Source: Adapted from US HHS ACYF (2003).

Fundamental to the concept of child protective services is that children are vulnerable and, therefore, in need of special protection by society. That idea emanates from the twentieth-century redefinition of children as a special category of people, just as the laws against child labor emerged from a new cultural ideal that children should not work, especially in dangerous occupations. Although child welfare and child protection are state and local government functions, substantial amounts of federal funds are provided to the states to help them with that work.

Informing the Authorities about Child Abuse and Neglect. In recent years there have been large increases in reports of child maltreatment. Miringoff (1995), for example, says the problem of child abuse has grown more extensive almost every year since 1970. In 2001 alone there were millions of reports of child abuse, which amounts to approximately 50,000 reports per week at CPS agencies (Lindsey, 2003; US HHS ACYF, 2003). This makes some sense because public knowledge of the problem has also expanded and the media regularly report on child maltreatment cases. Greater public awareness has led to more reporting of suspected abuse and neglect. The legal requirements in almost every state now compel those who have contact with children—such as nurses, physicians, social workers, teachers, and other professionals—to report promptly to the state child protective services agency any suspicions they have about possible neglect and abuse. Failing to do so, in most states, is a crime, and a professional who fails to report a suspected case could be fined or imprisoned. These professionals who must report child abuse are sometimes referred to as "mandated reporters." In 2001, these mandated reporters (teachers, police officers, social service workers, nurses, and physicians) made more than half of all child abuse reports (US HHS ACYF, 2003). In all states any person can make such a report and cannot be charged with making a false report, even if his or her suspicions are unfounded. Thus, the social policy is that the government seeks the widest possible range of reports, which can be culled and rejected when appropriate. Some have argued that this is not good policy because it wastes a great deal of money on investigations that are not needed and has the potential to violate the legitimate rights of parents who sometimes must suffer through unnecessary and embarrassing investigations (Besharov & Barth, 1994).

When a report is made, the child protective services agency—which is often a division of the same social services organization that provides TANF and food stamps—is required to investigate the report, often within a day. The investigation attempts to uncover whether the complaint is legitimate or unfounded. In some situations reports are made mistakenly because the observer thinks a child is being abused or neglected when, in reality, a family has merely punished and not abused a child. Or perhaps the child suffers from an illness or has sustained an injury that appears to be the result of maltreatment but is not. Sometimes the child protective services system has been used by an angry relative, former spouse, or a neighbor as a means to retaliate against parents for some reason. No matter what the suspicions of the child protective agency or worker, however, in most states a complaint must be investigated.

When a report is confirmed and neglect or abuse is verified, the protective services agency and its worker may exercise one or more of several options for dealing with the problem. Parenthetically, the popular media often suggest that child protective matters are investigated and addressed by law enforcement agencies; in truth, almost all such investigations are handled by the child protective services agency staff. Police departments are more likely to report the problem to child protective agencies rather than investigate them. Much of the involvement of law enforcement officers is in visits to homes under circumstances that may appear to be dangerous. In those cases, when the worker has reason to believe that there might be an assault by a parent or caregiver, the police may be asked to come along to protect the worker. It is true that most forms of abuse and some forms of neglect are crimes. Occasionally a child's caregiver may be arrested and tried for such a crime, yet those cases are only a small fraction of the many handled every year. Even child sexual abuse and abuse that leads to serious physical injury are not always handled within the criminal justice system. Child welfare matters of almost every kind are treated as confidential everywhere in the United States. Court proceedings are secret, reports by child welfare workers may not be divulged, and the names of the children and their families are kept out of the press.

The options that may be used in indicated cases of maltreatment, which are spelled out in some detail in the agencies' policy manuals, include the following:

1. Counseling with the household, in which the worker talks with household members about the nature of the problem and helps them plan to avoid future incidents of maltreatment.

2. Emergency removal of the child or children. If the children in the household appear to be in imminent danger, they may be removed to an emergency

shelter, which may be a group home, an institution, or another household that receives children for temporary, emergency protection.

3. Foster care. One of the solutions often used is foster care, which is temporary care in another home. The foster parents may be relatives of the child or strangers who are recruited and paid by the protective services agency.

4. Long-term or permanent substitute care. It is the philosophy and strategy of child welfare services programs to place children in as few different substitute care arrangements as possible. Child welfare workers believe that the well-being of children is compromised when they move from one foster home to another. Therefore, their preference is for longer-term care with a single family so that, if a child is removed from his or her household, there is placement in only one other home until, and if, the child may be returned. If the child cannot be returned, there is often an effort made to make the foster home placement permanent or to arrange for the child's adoption.

5. Referral to specialized services. When it appears to be potentially useful, members of the household are referred to counseling and mental health services to help them overcome their problems associated with caring for the child or children. In some cases, especially neglect cases, caregivers may be referred to financial assistance agencies so that they can better meet the material and health needs of the child through programs such as TANF, food stamps, Medicaid, and public housing.

6. Termination of parental rights. In cases in which it is doubtful that the family can improve, the agency may take steps to call upon the courts to terminate legally the rights of the caregivers to be guardians of the child so that the child can be placed in a more permanent foster care arrangement or be adopted. The Adoption and Safe Families Act of 1997 emphasizes the safety of children and the promotion of adoption or other permanent homes for children who cannot remain with their parents. New time limits were established for the termination of parental rights and a new emphasis on kinship care was established. It is now a federal law that states must take steps to terminate parental rights based on how long a child has been in foster care.

Table 8. Major Legislation Related to Child Abuse Prevention, Foster Care, and Adoption

Year	Law
1974	Child Abuse Prevention Act
1975	Title XX of Social Security Act
1978	Indian Child Welfare Act
1980	Adoption Assistance and Child Welfare Act
1988	The Child Abuse Prevention, Adoption, and Family Services Act
1993	The Family Preservation and Support Services Act

Table 8 (*continued*)

1994	Multi-Ethnic Placement Act
1996	Personal Responsibility and Work Opportunity Reconciliation Act
	Interethnic Adoption Provisions
1997	Adoption and Safe Families Act
1999	Foster Care Independence Act
2000	Strengthening Abuse and Neglect Courts Act
	Child Citizenship Act
	Intercountry Adoption Act
2001	Promoting Safe and Stable Families Amendments
2003	Keeping Children and Families Safe Act

Reports on Specific Types of Abuse. In 2001 there were 903,000 child abuse victims. Of these, the majority were cases of neglect, followed by physical abuse, sexual abuse, and other forms of maltreatment. Table 9 highlights these abuse categories, their definitions and examples, as well as the total number of child victims in 2001.

Table 9. Victims of Child Abuse in 2001

Type of Abuse and Definition of Abuse
Total Number of Child Victims in 2001 and Percent of All Victims*

Neglect

Failure by the caregiver to provide needed,	516,635
age-appropriate care although financially	(57.0)
able to do so or offered help to provide care	

Other Abuse

Other types of abuse coded as other.	174,937
Depends on the state law: for example,	
"abandonment" might be counted as "other"	(19.5)

Physical Abuse

Physical acts that produced or could	168,278
have produced physical injury to the child	(18.6)

Sexual Abuse

The involvement of the child in sexual	88,830
activity to provide sexual gratification or	(9.6)
financial benefit to the perpetrator (some	
examples: molestation, sexually exploitative	
activities, pornography, incest, rape)	

Psychological Maltreatment

Acts or omissions that caused, or could   61,778
have caused, conduct, cognitive, affective,   (6.8)
or other mental disorders (emotional
neglect, psychological abuse, mental injury
are examples)

Medical Neglect

Failure to provide for the appropriate health 17,665
care for the child although financially able   (2.0)
to do so or offered financial or other help
to provide health care

Source: Definitions and data from US HHS ACYF (2003).

*The percentages total more than 100 percent because some children may have
been victims of more than one type of maltreatment.

Overall most studies reveal that over half the children who require protective services have been neglected rather than abused. In many cases, however, children suffer from a combination of maltreatments, which is one of the reasons it is often difficult to isolate neglect from abuse. In general, younger children are the ones most often neglected, and older children the ones most often physically abused (National Center on Child Abuse and Neglect [NCCAN], 1993; US HHS ACYF, 2003).

Another critical social policy is that children should not languish in temporary care—that they should either be returned to their households or placed permanently with foster or adoptive families. In 2001, approximately 2 million children and their families received some kind of preventative services from child protection services. Preventative services are usually given to parents of children who are at risk for abuse (US HHS ACYF, 2003). Over half of the child abuse victims also received post-investigative services, which are services given to families who either accept them voluntarily or who are mandated by courts to accept them to keep their children safe (US HHS ACYF, 2003). Approximately 250,000 children were placed in foster care due to child abuse in 2001. Families are permitted, by social policy found in the state statutes, to have a period during which they may try to improve the care of their children, often through the services offered to them. When they are unable or unwilling to improve, the children may be removed. These policies are underscored in the 1997 Adoption and Safe Families Act.

The whole area of protective services, including removal of children from their homes, has become controversial in recent years. There is a national organization, Victims of Child Abuse Laws, or VOCAL, which says it has members in every state and some other nations who are battling public agencies because, VOCAL claims, they are targeting parents who discipline their children but are not abusers, yet have been charged as such (Zupan, 1993). Media reports about discontented parents who believe the protective services system has harmed them are common. These protests have become more frequent as the number of reports and other activities by the system to combat child abuse and neglect have grown.

Foster Care. Foster care is used when it is deemed that children cannot remain safely at home. The foster care system has been criticized for many reasons; it is expensive, sometimes abuse occurs within the foster care system, and research has found that children who remain in foster care for a long period of time often suffer negative emotional and developmental consequences. The term *foster care drift* refers to children who were moved from one placement to another with little hope of being reunited with their parents or being placed in a permanent home. Sometimes, before some of the newer policies were enacted, children could remain in the foster care system for many years. Currently, the average length of stay in foster care is thirty-three months (U.S. Department of Health and Human Services Children's Bureau [US HSS CB], 2003).

In 2001 there were,

542,000 children in foster care
290,000 children who entered foster care
263,000 children who left foster care
126,000 children in foster care waiting to be adopted
65,000 children in foster care whose parents' rights
   were terminated
50,000 children adopted from the public foster care system
20,000 children who aged out of the foster care system at
   18 years of age (US HHS CB, 2003)

There is a disproportionate number of children of color in foster care. Several factors have been identified that increase the chances of a child entering foster care: children who have been prior victims of child abuse, victims of sexual abuse, and children under four years of age (US HHS CB, 2003). African-American children were forty-two times more likely and American Indian children fifty-five times more likely than white children to be placed in foster care (US HHS CB, 2003). Thus, the most prominent child welfare program offered to disadvantaged minority children "is removal from their family and placement in foster care" (Lindsey, 2003, 60).

Table 10. Racial/Ethnic Status of Children in Foster Care in 2001

Black Non-Hispanic	38%	204,973
White Non-Hispanic	37%	203,222

Hispanic	17%	89,785
Unknown/Unable to Determine	3%	17,235
American Indian/American Native, Non-Hispanic	2%	10,106
Two or More Races Non-Hispanic	2%	11,479
Asian Non-Hispanic	1%	3,649
Hawaiian/PI Non-Hispanic	0%	1,551

Source: US HHS CB, 2003.

There are many different kinds of foster care placements available for children. These include shelter homes, long-term foster care, specialized foster homes, treatment foster homes, and residential group care (Downs et al., 2004). Shelter homes, also called emergency foster care, are usually used on a short term basis during assessment of a child's home setting. Long-term foster care is used for children when adoption is not a viable option. Specialized foster homes are provided to children who have special needs and require special care such as children with HIV or mental or physical disabilities. Foster parents in such homes usually have specialized training. Treatment foster homes, sometimes referred to as therapeutic foster care, are homes where treatment is provided by specially trained families for children who would otherwise have to live in residential treatment or group homes. Residential group care usually involves round the clock care for children in a residential facility. These facilities can focus on different areas depending on the population they serve: for example, treatment (psychiatric, drug, and alcohol), protection, and corrections. Kinship care, which is care provided by a relative or extended family member, is also a growing practice priority.

A former foster child, Kevin Sieg wrote about his experiences in *Newsweek* (1998). He described his life in foster care, which resulted from his mother's serious mental illness—he had never met his father. He said he began his life as an orphan in 1987, when the state removed him from his biological mother and explained that orphans are not necessarily people whose parents have died but that the term also includes people who have been separated from their parents for other reasons.

He describes some of his conflicts with his various foster parents and the abrupt end of his care because he had "aged out" at eighteen. Now a student at the University of Akron, Sieg's story is one of the most moving about the realities of foster care for some children. He says he survived the system but that many other foster children are not so lucky.

Group Care for Children. One of the substitute care arrangements used for children who cannot live with their caregiver families is group care, which is provided in a number of forms by many different groups. The traditional group care service for children was the orphanage, which generally cared for children whose parents had died. In modern American society there are few true orphans, largely because of the extension of the adult life span. For decades there has been no need for orphanages in the traditional sense of the concept.

One of the issues in the Contract with America of 1994 (Gillespie & Shell-has, 1994) was major reforms in the care of children who could not satisfactorily live with their biological families. Proposals were made to replace foster care with orphanages. *Orphanages* was probably a general term for group care of various kinds. However, once it was understood how much more expensive group care is than foster care or even adoption, the subject was quickly dropped. Adoption assistance is endorsed in the Contract with America, and adoption assistance has been, for a long time, one of the major strategies of professionals in human services. Government assists adoptive families financially so they can adopt the child.

There have been, however, consistent needs for some group care to serve children who cannot live with their families or in substitute families. Therefore, over the years many of the orphanages that did not go out of existence when there were no more orphans to serve changed their function to that of providing care for children who were not able to live at home. These facilities, which house varying numbers of boys and girls, are typically used for children who cannot live with relatives or in foster homes. Many such children are placed in group care because, for instance, they are one of a group of siblings who do not want to be separated from one another; because they are older and, therefore, more difficult to place in foster homes; or because they have behavioral or emotional problems that make it difficult for them to be placed in private homes.

Group care homes have various kinds of organizational structures. Some have their own schools, for example, while others send their children to public schools. Some are religiously affiliated, following the tradition of the orphanages from which they came, while others are operated by nonsectarian community boards. Others may belong to governments and are operated by counties, cities, or states. Most carry out fund-raising to pay for any costs that are not otherwise covered. Many of the children in group care facilities, however, are supported by state child welfare agencies, which provide a fixed monthly stipend to the facility for caring for the children. In some states the facilities are paid the audited cost of caring for the children. In others the state provides a flat amount, often the same as is paid to the foster parents who maintain children in their homes. The balance of the cost of caring for the children, which is often more than the direct costs of foster parents, is obtained from donations, endowments, or the sponsoring organization such as a church or civic group.

Modern group care is expensive for several reasons. Group care facilities require paid employees twenty-four hours per day along with the operation and maintenance of buildings, which is also expensive. Those who study caring for people who cannot care for themselves have begun to believe that in almost every case large institutional or group care is not the first choice. Not only is it expensive, but it is typically less desirable in human terms—more familylike care is preferable.

There are many interesting policy issues associated with group care, many of them dealing with money, which, as noted, is a central feature of social policy. For example, many children in group care also attend the local public schools, even though their official residences may be in other communities. Where does the state per-child education allocation go—to the district that is the official residence or the district in which the group facility is located? For another example, what are the legitimate costs that public agencies ought to pay for children, beyond food and shelter? Should the public pay for their school pictures, Scout dues, prom dresses, class rings, and football game tickets, just as parents typically do for their children? In many cases these issues are resolved informally, with voluntary contributions. Some agencies cover certain of these costs as a matter of policy.

Small group homes also are operated for children who need group care. These may house as few as two or three children. Care is provided by houseparents, whose profession is the operation of the small group home. In some cases therapeutic or specialized foster care homes are developed to house children with severe emotional or physical problems. In those cases the adult caregivers earn their living by serving as substitute parents; that is their sole employment. Small group homes are used in particular with children who have physical or mental disabilities or histories of juvenile delinquency. They often arrange for care and treatment by social workers and psychologists as well as routine medical services.

Family Preservation. Evaluation of intensive family preservation programs indicates that they are highly successful. In the most successful programs, almost all of the families stay together and none of the children have to be placed in foster care. And even in the less successful programs, rates of maintaining families and keeping children in their own homes may be as high as 70 percent. Although the costs of intensive family preservation are great, because of the small caseloads carried by workers, the long-term cost may be less expensive than providing children with substitute foster care, mental health services, or care in group homes and other facilities. If it is also better for the children, which most child experts now believe it is, family preservation services may also prevent future problems such as unemployment, incarceration, or desertion by people who were not reared satisfactorily. For some, family preservation is a controversial matter. They are concerned that the emphasis on family preservation—keeping the child with the biological parents—may work against the health and well-being of the child. (This discussion of family preservations is taken from the book *The Family at Risk* by Marianne Berry [1997].)

Adoption. Through the 1990s the number of adoptions each year has hovered around 120,000 annually (Flango & Flango, 1994) and about 2 percent of all U.S. children are adopted (Child Welfare League of America, 2003). There are several different kinds of adoption procedures that vary by the formality of arrangements, whether they are conducted with or without an agency, and whether the agency is public or private. The majority of adoptions are by relatives and are sometimes referred to as *kinship* or *stepparent* adoption (U.S. Bureau of the Census, 1991). In many states adoption by relatives is not handled through agencies at all, even though adoption by strangers might be. In many cases those relatives are stepparents who merely formalize their parent-child relationships. In other cases children are adopted by their grandparents or other relatives. Many times these family members already are the child's primary caregivers and have been for a long time. When adoptions are handled without the services of an agency, they are generally referred to as *informal adoptions.* The rate of *formal* kinship adoption has been increasing since the late 1980s due to policy shifts that placed foster care children in kinship foster care, which was then finalized into adoptive placements (National Adoption Information Clearinghouse, 2003). *Private agency adoptions* are when children are adopted into nonrelative homes usually through some kind of profit or nonprofit agency. When children who are a part of the public child welfare system are adopted these are referred to as *public agency adoptions. Independent adoptions* are when children are placed in nonrelative homes. Lawyers, doctors, or the birthparents themselves handle most of these adoptions. The number of children adopted from other countries has also been increasing. In 1999, 16,396 children were adopted from countries outside the United States (CWLA, 2003; National Adoption Information Clearinghouse, 2003). The countries with the largest number of children adopted were China, Russia, South Korea, and Guatemala (CWLA, 2003).

Transracial adoption is also a controversial issue in the field of adoption. Transracial adoption is when parents adopt a child of a different color or ethnicity. The National Association of Black Social Workers concerned with the increase of transracial adoptions during 1972, issued a statement opposing transracial adoption. Most of the arguments against transracial adoption relate to cultural preservation issues. In other words, some doubt the abilities of different race parents to understand or prepare children of a different race/ethnicity to cope with racism and discrimination. Others argue that children adopted into homes where they are "different" can suffer from emotional problems. They also argue that agencies have not done enough to recruit and retain minority foster care and adoptive parents so that the claim that there are not enough homes is unfair. In contrast, some argue that the benefits of children in an adoptive, permanent, and loving home outweigh the problems children of color encounter as they remain in the foster care system. Efforts to recruit minority adoptive and foster care placements are conducted in most states, either by public or private agencies. Many social workers of all colors and ethnicities believe that the primary criterion should be the quality of the adoptive home and the needs of the child, rather than the color or ethnicity. But such issues are controversial and policies vary among the states. Most recently the issue of adoption by gay and lesbian parents has received a great deal of attention in the media. Some states have laws banning adoption by gay and lesbian parents. Other states, however, recruit and use gay and lesbian families as foster care providers. For an interesting look at adoption history in the United States visit the Adoption History Timeline available at http://www.uoregon.edu/~adoption/timeline.html.

Public and governmental concern about children spending their lives in less than desirable foster care led to a new federal legislation with the Adoption and Safe Families Act of 1997 (Public Law 105–89). The legislation encourages states to terminate parental rights as early as practicable, when the possibilities of reuniting families with children seem remote. States are provided opportunities to receive financial help as an incentive to more rapidly remove children from foster care and place them with adoptive families. There is also emphasis on "special needs" adoptions, which involve children with disabilities, minority children, and older children. In addition, the new law provides help with criminal records checks on potential foster and adoptive parents. This is part of the effort to achieve permanent homes for children who would not otherwise have them.

Child Day Care

For several complex social, political, and economic reasons child day care for preschool-age children has taken on new importance in American social policy. Increasing numbers of children require care outside of their homes during the day. Policies requiring TANF recipient families to work or train for work have also accelerated the need for day care. Child care generally consists of different arrangements that caregivers make for the care of their children during the hours in which they work. Although this sounds like a simple task, in reality, securing high quality and reliable childcare is a struggle for most American parents. There are two general kinds of day care in the United States: care in centers and family day care. The first is familiar to most Americans; the second is also widely used. Parents, often mothers who have their own preschool-age children, care for others' children during the day. Many families have used such arrangements for years.

The U.S. government has never enacted large-scale government-assisted child care (Downs et al., 2004). Some have argued that this is because of conflicting values regarding the role of women in society, the reticence of government to interfere with family life, the diversity of families in the United States, and beliefs about the negative consequences to children separated from their mothers for long periods of time (Downs et al., 2004). Whatever the reason, the state of day care in the United States is quite insufficient in comparison to the need. The three biggest myths about child care are that (1) babysitting is all that is needed, (2) it is easy to take care of children who are not your own and it does not require special skills, and (3) there is no need to regulate childcare providers and facilities (Downs et al., 2004). Family day care has been and commonly continues to be called by some, "babysitting." In some cases the family day care providers are relatives of the children they are taking care of. However, recent research has questioned the quality of kinship care by relatives (Ehrle, Geen, & Clark, 2001). For most parents, finding and keeping child care that is located close to their homes, of good quality, and reasonably priced is quite difficult.

The United States has long been an industrial nation with a large labor force, which has always included large numbers of women, many of whom have needed day care or after-school care for their young children. Over half of working mothers contribute half or more of the total household income (CDF, 2003).

Usually, the older children are, the more likely they are to be in day care. During the last forty years, however, the biggest increase has been in the number of working mothers with preschool-age children and infants. Infant and preschool care is the most difficult and the most expensive type of care. Approximately 8.7 million preschool-age children were in some kind of day care arrangement in 1999 (Sonenstein, Gates, Schmidt, & Bolshun, 2002). Most children ages six to twelve who have working parents stay with their relatives (23 percent), in after school programs (15 percent), and in family day care (11 percent). However, about 10 percent of children remain alone (Sonenstein et al., 2002). These children who take care of themselves after school are sometimes referred to as "latchkey" kids. These children typically remain at home unsupervised after school, waiting for their parents to return home from work. It is estimated that there are anywhere from 3 to 5 million children who spend time without adult supervision every week in the United States, and the chance of being home alone increases as children age (Capizzano, Adelman, & Stagner, 2002; Downs et al., 2004; U.S. Bureau of the Census, 1994). This is important as research has documented that children left alone are much more likely to become injured, have behavioral problems, and engage in risky behaviors such as smoking and alcohol and drug use (Vandivere, Tout, Zaslow, Calkins, & Capizzano, 2003).

Often people are surprised when they find out how much child care costs in the United States. Day care costs range from about $4,000 to $10,000 per child, annually. In comparison to how much it costs to attend public college in most states, day care costs usually come out on top; in every state, the average cost of infant care is higher than tuition at a public college (Schulman, 2000; Waits et al., 2001; Wertheimer, 2003). Obviously, for low-income people, this represents a large chunk of their income. In addition, low-income people often end up paying more for substandard care (Schulman, 2000; Wertheimer, 2003).

Table 11. Costs of Child Care in Comparison to Public College Tuition

Area	Four Years in Child Care Center	Four Years of Public College Tuition
Boston, MA	$42,199	$16,048
St. Paul, MN	$35,699	$15,464
Seattle, WA	$28,600	$12,604
Cumberland County, ME	$26,919	$16,232
Denver, CO	$23,712	$10,740
Los Angeles, CA	$23,705	$10,436
Kansas City, MO	$22,776	$14,200
Orange County, FL	$19,925	$8,088
Urban Areas in WV	$19,552	$9,348
Dallas, TX	$19,032	$9,728
Tucson, AZ	$18,634	$8,632
Birmingham, AL	$15,828	$10,484

Source: Adapted from Schulman (2000).

Child Care Policies

As previously noted, the United States has not instituted large-scale government-assisted child care programs. Most low-income families rely on federal and state funding for child care. The major source of funding for low-income families comes from the Child Care and Development Block Grant (CCDBG), which currently serves about 2 million children in the United States. The CCDBG provides money to states for funding child care programs for TANF recipients. Many states, faced with serious budget crises, have cut child care programs and funding of the CCDBG (CDF, 2004; Downs et al., 2004). It has been estimated that only one out of every seven children eligible for funding under the CCDBG receive this benefit (CDF, 2004). Currently there are over half a million children on waiting lists. Sixteen states have changed eligibility criteria that eliminate many families from receiving assistance, and nine states cut funding for after-school programs and prekindergarten programs (CDF, 2004).

Some families also receive assistance for child care through the Dependent Care Tax Credit that allows families to deduct a part of what they spend on day care from their taxes. This is helpful to some families, particularly working poor families; however, it does not assist families who have incomes so low that they do not pay taxes. The Family and Medical Leave Act of 1993 offers some assistance to caregivers. Under this law full-time workers can get up to twelve weeks of leave for the birth or adoption of a child, care of an ill child or family member, or personal illness. However, the leave is unpaid and only employers with fifty or more employees are mandated to comply with the law. Some have argued that the FMLA is financially smart because it allows for individuals to take leave without losing their jobs. Caregiving and parenting are generally normal events and it seems reasonable that policies should be somewhat responsive to the needs of the families that work for them (Kamerman, Gambrill, & Mason, 1994). Finally, Head Start is another federal program that offers assistance to low-income families who need child care. Head Start is administered on the local level and consists of early childhood development programs for low-income children. Head Start was initiated in 1966 as a part of President Johnson's War on Poverty and was one of the original CAPs, or Community Action Programs. The philosophy of most Head Start programs is to provide comprehensive programming that improves the developmental outcomes of low-income children (Downs et al., 2004). Early Head Start programs for children under three years of age and their parents were established in 1994 (Downs et al., 2004).

Nutritional Assistance to Child Care Facilities
In addition to financial payments and training for centers and family day care providers, under some arrangements in some states food or cash to purchase food is provided to day care programs, including family day care centers. Food or money for food is provided through the U.S. Department of Agriculture to group child care facilities. The policy is to make nutritional assistance available to the children and to facilitate group care and day care services without adding financial burdens to the institutions or families. Of course, the primary purpose of Department of Agriculture programs is to maintain the food production capacities of the nation and to ensure that the farming industry is sustained. Purchasing and redistributing surplus food is a by-product of those policies. Payments are provided under the same agency, the Food and Nutrition Service, which operates the food stamp program.

Policies and Services for People with Mental Illness

One of the more complex areas of social services for people who need help is the care of the mentally ill. As chapter 2 points out, institutions for the mentally ill were an innovation and reform in the nineteenth century. Before the development of the asylum movement, the mentally ill might be incarcerated along with prisoners who had violated the law. They could be chained and even executed. The segregation of the mentally ill and the provision of humane treatment to them in asylums was a major reform pursued by Dorothea Dix and other advocates. The history of care for the mentally ill in America has been described in a fascinating, classic work by A. Deutsch (1949).

In later years, the mental hospital reform movement became its own problem, because such institutions were found to fall short of high-quality, humane care for the large population of Americans with mental illness.

Who Are People with Mental Illness?

Although this section has discussed people with mental illness as if they were a single group of people, that is not the case. They include those who are diagnosed with existing mental illness, those with behavior problems, those who abuse or are addicted to substances such as alcohol and other drugs, as well as older people who suffer from dementia and children with mentally disabling conditions. Some mentally ill people are defined as dually diagnosed; that is, they may be addicted to alcohol or other drugs and also diagnosed as mentally ill, or they may experience mental illness as well as a developmental disability such as epilepsy.

One of the key policy sources in defining mental illness and its treatment is the *Diagnostic and Statistical Manual of Mental Disorders* (4th ed.) of the American Psychiatric Association (1994). The manual specifies and codes mental illnesses. It is the basis for billing insurance companies and government agencies for mental health services as well as for separating those who are mentally ill from those who are not. Although it was not designed to serve as a policy manual, it has, in effect, become one.

The Evolution of Treatment of Mental Illness

In the twentieth century another famous reformer, Clifford Beers, became an important figure in mental health. His book, *A Mind That Found Itself,* written in 1908, following his own recovery from mental illness, spoke about inhumane treatment by the staff within punitive asylums—the very organizations that were originally designed to improve the treatment of the mentally ill and make it more humane (Beers, 1953; Quam, 1995). Beers helped organize state, national, and international organizations concerned with mental illness, which evolved into such groups as the National Association for Mental Health.

The social policy for much of the twentieth century had been to place mentally ill people in mental institutions, where they could be safely treated for their conditions. Yet as Beers and others reported, the institutions presented new kinds of mistreatment of that vulnerable population. In the 1960s other students of mental illness and mental health studied and wrote about the poor, often punitive treatment to which the mentally ill were subjected. One of perhaps the two most important works was *Asylums* (Goffman, 1961), which described, on the basis of a participant's observation, the social structure of a major mental hospital. The portrait's truth was persuasive. It demonstrated that treatment for patients in such institutions was unlikely to be a high priority. The second work, *The Myth of Mental Illness* (1961), by psychiatrist Thomas Szasz, effectively questions whether there is actually something that can be called mental illness in the same sense that a physical condition is illness. This book, and several that followed, challenged the mental health system in the United States, especially the system of committing people to institutions without their consent.

A development in the 1960s and the years that followed was a series of court cases that challenged the involuntary commitment aspect of the mentally ill laws that had for so long been the basis of social policy covering the mentally ill. One of the most important, *Wyatt v. Stickney* (1972), was a federal Alabama case that held that a person could not be confined in a mental hospital against his or her will unless treatment was provided to that person. It became clear that the mental health policies, as they had operated, could no longer continue because many mental hospitals had neither the programs nor the personnel to provide the treatment required. The states also discovered that supplying treatment to their mental patients was much more expensive than the essentially custodial care that had been provided for much of the history of the asylum movement. Therefore, many states began discharging patients who, prior to the court cases and the community mental health legislation, might have spent the balance of their lives in mental hospitals. The new requirement was that the mental health system and the mental hospitals become treatment centers designed to help and not simply restrain or isolate the mentally disabled.

Meanwhile, treatment had become more of a possibility with the development, beginning in the 1950s, of sophisticated drugs that could be used with severely mentally ill people in place of mechanical restraints, locked cells, and other artifacts of past methods. It became increasingly possible, because of these new drugs, for more people with mental illnesses to live in the community and carry on near-normal lives.

Not all mentally ill people, even though they may or may not need hospital care, can live unsupervised in their communities. Therefore, there have been small group facilities established for the mentally ill, often operated by private individuals who house several patients who might otherwise be in hospitals; these facilities are not terribly different in structure from the small group homes described for children who cannot live in their own homes. In many cases the adult residents pay for their care with payments from Supplemental Security Income or Social Security Disability, for which they are eligible because of their disabilities. This is another form of the movement toward private rather than public care for vulnerable people.

Although some observers continue to believe that mental illness is simply a metaphor for socially unacceptable behavior (Szasz, 1961), there appears to be strong societal acceptance of the idea that mental illness is, in fact, an illness and that it is treatable; psychoactive drugs have increasingly provided means for treating the kinds of behavior defined as mental illness. In recent years there have been many trends that have had an important impact on the mental health field: (1) an increase in research and understanding of the brain and behavior; (2) the emergence of innovative and effective mental health treatments, (3) changes in the way U.S. society organizes and pays for mental health care, and (4) increased advocacy by consumers of mental health services and their families (US HHS, 1999). For example, the National Alliance for the Mentally Ill has worked steadfastly to reduce the stigma of mental illness, to educate the public about mental illness, and to advocate for more responsible and responsive policies for the mentally ill. The recent Mental Health Parity Act, as discussed in chapter 6, is an example of such legislation.

Other observers have been bitter critics of the social policy to remove mental patients from hospitals, a process that is called *deinstitutionalization*. E. F. Torrey (1988) is one who insists that the removal of such individuals is directly related to the problem of homelessness. It is one of the ironies of current U.S. policy that many persons who would have once been held in mental hospitals because they have symptoms of mental illness are now residing in homeless shelters, which are typically not as attractive or humane as today's mental hospitals. In addition, as discussed earlier in this chapter, many of the homeless mentally ill also reside in jails, arguably less humane than shelters. Mental hospitals, especially after they were required to provide treatment to their patients, became so expensive that it was in the interest of the state governments to reduce their populations. Therefore, some observers believe that the whole shift from hospital to community services is an effort to save money more than an effort to preserve the rights and enhance the well-being of the mentally ill.

D. Mechanic's 1989 book is devoted solely to the whole issue of mental health and social policy. His book and other literature on the same subject are of increasing importance because it is clear that mental health is currently less a problem of medicine and treatment than it is a problem of social policy —for instance, policy about such fundamentals as deinstitutionalization.

Another important book is Elliot Liebow's (1993) *Tell Them Who I Am.* Liebow, an anthropologist, worked closely with homeless women in shelters and centers near Washington, D.C. Such shelters have in some ways replaced mental hospitals in housing people with mental problems. Although he does not specifically identify the women he met as mentally ill, Liebow notes that those who do need mental health services are not likely to receive or be able to effectively use them. He writes, "Even if one can overcome the initial problem of locating such persons and persuading them that they need what the program offers, there remains the even more difficult problem of getting those persons to remain in one place long enough to receive continued treatments over time" (41–42).

Not all groups react the same to the use of mental health services. Some research suggests that many minority groups are uncomfortable with, distrust, or fear the mental health system and are reluctant to receive mental health treatment (Lin, Anderson, & Poland, 1997; Neighbors, 1997; Neighbors & Taylor, 1985). Evidence also suggests that certain ethnic groups have been overdiagnosed with certain mental illnesses, for example, diagnosing African Americans with schizophrenia as opposed to mood disorders (Neighbors, Trierweiler, Munday, Jackson, Thompson, Binion, & Gomez, 1999; Trierweiler, Neighbors, Munday, Thompson, Binion, & Gomez, 2000). This is important due to the stigma attached to illnesses such as schizophrenia. In addition, the relatively new field of ethnopharmacology suggests that some of the drugs used to treat mental illness may have different effects on different ethnic groups (US HHS, 1999). Many experts emphasize the importance of cultural sensitivity in dealing with minority group clients. Bertha Holliday, director of the American Psychological Association's office of ethnic-minority affairs, says that therapy is not embedded in African-American culture. Some African Americans can't afford it or don't have insurance, and others fear the stigma. While some use clergy for therapy, others consult psychics and astrologers. The suicide rate for young African-American males is high, reflecting an increase in this decade and one element of the seriousness of mental health problems in the African-American community. Dr. Linda James Myers of Ohio State University says that drug and alcohol use in the community is in part a reflection of people's efforts to medicate themselves for depression. African Americans are also concerned about showing weakness when they live in rough neighborhoods. There is something of a taboo about therapy in such areas, an additional reason for the resistance to it (Leland, Samuels, Rosenberg, & Springer 1997).

Many social work clients are members of minority groups, including African Americans. One of the strategies for dealing with a number of personal and family problems such as child and spouse maltreatment, delinquency, and crime is referral to mental health services. However, if minority clients are unwilling to or unable to use those services, the strategy is clearly not likely to be worthwhile. Mental health services providers, who include many members of minority groups, need to find alternative ways for dealing with mental illness among their clients, especially those who are culturally resistant to what they presently offer.

Community Mental Health Centers

Perhaps the major current policy response to the issues of mental health and mental illness has been a series of statutes establishing and financing a network of community mental health centers. That development was initially a product of President John F. Kennedy's New Frontier program. The statutes on community mental health were passed in 1963, 1975, and 1980. Those Community Mental Health Acts established local services for the mentally ill and were part of the virtual revolution in the care and treatment of the mentally ill that began in the 1960s. D. Chambers (1993), in his social policy analysis text, provides a detailed discussion of the community mental health legislation and policies.

By the 1990s community mental health centers dotted the United States to the point that virtually every citizen was covered by a program. The programs are generally less accessible to those in rural areas than those who live in cities, but the services are still available, to some extent.

Community mental health programs provide for mental health counseling, prescription drugs, "club houses" for people to spend their days in, hospitalization in community hospitals for people who require it for short periods of time, employment referral and training, and community education about mental health problems. Today's community mental health centers typically provide screening for those who appear to need mental hospitalization. The effort is to prevent commitment to an institution and to serve the patient in the community instead.

Policies and Services for People Who Are Disabled

People with disabilities have been a long-standing concern of social policy, even before the development of programs such as Social Security. Those who are blind, deaf, and physically handicapped are provided protection and services through a variety of statutes and programs such as Social Security, Supplement Security Income, and Medicaid. Their right to accessible public facilities is guaranteed by the Americans with Disabilities Act, which was passed by Congress in 1990, during the presidency of George H. W. Bush.

Another population group whose care has evolved over the years is people with developmental disabilities, a category that generally includes people with mental retardation, autism, cerebral palsy, and epilepsy. Historically, each of those groups has been handled in ways that are comparable to those used with the mentally ill. In the past they have been restrained, isolated, punished, and killed. There have also been major changes in the care of the developmentally disabled toward deinstitutionalization and a shift from public to private care, as in the case of the mentally ill and juvenile offenders. Over the past several years there has been a remarkable reduction in the number of persons with mental retardation housed in state facilities. There have, however, been almost comparable changes in private facilities. Clearly the movement has been from state institutions, which were typically large, to smaller community institutions.

A series of statutes and court decisions has also begun more aggressively to protect the rights of people with disabilities, including those with physical handicaps, to live lives as close to normal as possible. The policies of the nation now require schools to enroll and serve students with disabilities in public schools and higher education programs (sometimes in special classrooms for all or part of the day), require transportation companies to provide service to those who need special help, and require that public buildings be accessible to all.

Persons with developmental disabilities may also be provided with a variety of community services such as day centers, recreation programs, special education activities, and various other programs to enhance their lives and well-being.

People with disabilities, including the mentally and developmentally disabled, are eligible, as the preceding chapter makes clear, for Supplemental Security Income if they are of low income. Those who have worked prior to becoming disabled—who tend to be mentally or physically disabled, since developmental disabilities begin, in many cases, at birth—may receive OASDI.

Recipients of SSI are usually eligible for food stamps and for social services provided by state human services agencies as well. These may include chore services and homemaker services to help clients and their families handle their everyday living situations more effectively, as well as transportation assistance. They are also normally eligible for Medicaid to help pay the costs of their health care.

Criminal Justice System
Youthful Offenders
Children who have had difficulty with the law pose a special set of social policy issues. Child welfare specialists tend to include juvenile offenders with children who face other problems and to view them as people who are in

need of treatment or supervision rather than punishment. In U.S. tradition a child who violates the law is not treated as a criminal; in fact, the assumption is that a child is not capable of knowing that he or she is violating the law—that the concept of crime is one that children do not fully comprehend. There are, of course, exceptions. Children who commit what would be serious crimes if they were adults, such as rape, armed robbery, and murder, are in some states treated as adults and may be punished as adults, including capital punishment. Most legally established juvenile offenses would be considered crimes if they were committed by adults. Because of the age of the perpetrator, however, the acts are not considered criminal. Cases are heard in special courts. Policies prohibit releasing the names or photographs of the children who are involved. Sentences for offenses are not viewed as punishment but rather as a means of controlling children's behavior, rehabilitating children, and treating them so that they learn not to commit future crimes.

Status offenders are young people who commit acts that may be forbidden for children but are not offenses when they are committed by adults. These are sometimes referred to as nondelinquent or not criminal offenses. Status offenses include such acts as consuming alcohol, engaging in sex, staying on the streets past a specific curfew, being out of control of parents or guardians, truancy, or running away. A delinquent or criminal offense is one that is illegal for both adults and children. Some examples of criminal offenses include person offenses (battery, rape, homicide), property offenses (theft, arson), and drug offenses. A commonly used term in juvenile justice is adjudication. Adjudication refers to the court process that determines if a child has committed the crime with which he or she is charged. An adjudicated youth is one who has been convicted of the offense. When youth offenders have been adjudicated they are usually given three possible dispositions: committed, where they are placed in a facility as a result of the court sentence; detained, where youth are held before the adjudication hearing or in between placements or wait to be transferred to adult criminal court; or diversion, where youth are sent directly to a facility or treatment center instead of court. For a diagram of case flow in the juvenile justice system, visit http://ojjdp.ncjrs .org/ojstatbb/structure_process/case.html.

The Office of Juvenile Justice and Delinquency Prevention (OJJDP) was established in 1974 as a result of the Juvenile Justice and Delinquency Prevention Act (JJDPA). The JJDPA created grants for delinquency prevention programs and is the main source of federal funding provided to states to improve their juvenile justice systems and programs. The JJDPA has been amended and reauthorized many times since 1974. The main premise of the JJDPA, however, is to keep children from having contact with adult offenders. Currently, there are four core standards and protections that states must comply with in order to receive federal funding. These core protections are deinstitutionalizations of status offenders (DSO), adult jail and lock up removal, "sight and sound" separation, and address disproportionate minority confinement and are highlighted in table 12. All of these stress the priority placed on keeping children out of jails and adult facilities. Research has documented that children who are placed in adult facilities are at high risk for committing suicide and being abused.

Table 12. Four Core Protections for Juvenile Offenders

Deinstitutionalization of *Status Offenders (DOS)*	Children who are status offenders cannot be held in secure detention or confined. Treatment is the preferred practice for handling status offenders and can include participation in counseling and mentoring programs, community based services, residential treatment in a group home, or alternative education.
Disproportionate Minority *Confinement (DMC)*	All states must assess and implement a plan to address the disproportionate number of minority youth in facilities.
Adult Jail and Lock-Up Removal	Children cannot be held in adult jails or lock up except for specific and limited time periods.
Separation—"Sight and Sound" *or Lock Up (due to the exceptions above)*	Children who are placed in adult jails are prohibited from "sight and sound" contact with adults.

Although there is a decreasing emphasis on institutional group care for juveniles, national data reflect an increase in the numbers of children who are being held in facilities. Small group homes and foster care are used for youthful offenders, just as they are for children who cannot live with their biological families. Some of these facilities are private rather than public, and, as can be seen in other forms of care discussed in this chapter, there has been a shift from the public to the private.

The total number of children in custody has increased. Of all youth in juvenile facilities in the United States for 1999, approximately 109,000 were juvenile offenders being held in facilities; this is 81 percent of *all* youth in residential placement in the United States (Office of Juvenile Justice and Delinquency Prevention [OJJDP], 2002). However, many states and federal legislation have been "cracking down" on youth crime, making it much easier to prosecute juveniles as adults, which may account for the increase in youth in custody.

Unfortunately, harsher sentencing laws and greater abilities of states to prosecute juveniles as adults further compound the problem of disproportionate minority confinement. Disproportionate minority confinement continues to be a significant issue; for example, in 1997, three out of four juveniles who entered state prisons were minority youth and over one-third of those were in prison for nonviolent offenses (Males & Macallair, 2000). In half of the states in the United States, the ratio of minority youth to majority youth in custody is 3.3 to 1 (OJJDP, 2002). The number of girls who commit crimes has also been increasing. In 1997, almost 750,000 girls were arrested, which accounts for 26 percent of all juveniles arrested annually (Acoca, 1999). The increase in the number of girls arrested is greater than that for boys. Evidence suggests that female offenders may appear different than their male counterparts and require specialized care not widely available in most states (Acoca, 1999; American Bar Association & National Bar Association, 2001). Current treatments are not necessarily responsive to the special needs of girls who suffer from sexual and physical abuse, mental health problems, and substance abuse.

Adults in the Criminal Justice System
An area of work for human services professionals, including social workers, is work with criminal offenders. Again, for much of human history, law violators were simply punished for their behavior. The assumption was that people were conscious of their own misbehavior and chose to commit any illegal acts. Therefore, punishment was the appropriate response. As time has passed, however, social policies have changed. Perhaps the most important of the changes has been the assumption that physical punishment is not the appropriate response to all misconduct. In fact, the Bill of Rights to the U.S. Constitution forbids cruel and unusual punishment. Incarceration and isolation from the larger community are acceptable, partly as the kind of punishment that can be imposed on those who violate the law and partly to protect the public from law violators. Capital punishment—the death penalty—is also permitted in many states.

Policy alternatives to imprisonment, such as probation and early releases, such as parole, have required human services workers to supervise and otherwise monitor offenders while they are serving their probationary periods. Even prior to sentencing, many courts rely upon professional workers to study convicted offenders and assess the best sentences for them in terms of community justice and the possibility of preventing them from committing future offenses. Incarceration in prisons, although not as expensive as mental hospitalization, is still a costly alternative. When it is possible, social policy suggests the need for community care of offenders so they may be employed and so they are able to pay their own living costs. That trend is another example of the shifting of responsibility from the government to other resources. Although the trend is not as pronounced in adult corrections as it is in some of the other fields discussed in this chapter, some states are experimenting with contracting with private vendors to run all or a part of their corrections systems.

Current social policies have led to employing human services professionals in positions dealing with probation and parole programs as well as within corrective institutions themselves. There are a number of social problems and social justice issues related to the U.S. justice system. These issues include the following:

The total number of people in the U.S. criminal system (people in jail, in prison, on parole or probation) has increased dramatically in the last two decades. The total number of people in the criminal justice system is about 6 million, which is three times greater than in 1980 (Parkin, 2002; Wagner, 2003). The United States accounts for half of all the 8 million people in prisons across the world (Schiraldi & Ziedenberg, 1999). The irony of these dramatic increases in the prison population is that they have occurred during a time when crime has been declining; in fact, the U.S. crime rate has been going down since the mid 1990s. Some have argued this is due to the war on crime and drugs that includes harsher sentences, especially for those who have committed nonviolent offenses.

African Americans are disproportionately represented in the criminal justice system in the United States. Although African Americans account for 13 percent of the total U.S. population, they account for one half of all U.S. prisoners (Parkin, 2002). In 2000, one out of every three African American men was in the criminal justice system and half of all women in prison were minorities (Greenfield & Snell, 1999). African American women are seven times more likely than white women to go to prison in their lifetimes (Greenfield & Snell, 1999). As noted previously in this chapter, minority youth are also overrepresented in the juvenile justice system.

There are some serious social justice concerns associated with these trends. For one, since many states take away the right of people to vote when they have been convicted of a crime, almost 1.5 million African American men can no longer vote, thus removing political power from a particular group of people (Schiraldi & Ziedenberg, 1999). Upon release from prison, many prisoners find it difficult to find jobs due to their criminal records and in some cases are banned from receiving cash assistance.

There has also been a significant increase in the numbers of women in prison. Women are most often incarcerated for economic crimes such as forging checks or using credit cards illegally. Eighty percent of women in prison have incomes below $2,000 per year and 90 percent of prisoners are single mothers

(Ruiz, 2002). Of those women convicted of violent offenses, most reports indicate that these crimes were in defense of their children (Ruiz, 2002). The prison sentences given to wives who kill their husbands are two times longer than for husbands who kill their wives (Ruiz, 2002). The fact that many of the women prisoners are single mothers also poses special concerns. About half a million children in the United States have mothers in prison and about 5 percent of all women who go to prison are pregnant when they enter the system (Greenfield & Snell, 1999). Newborns are removed from women prisoners after twenty-four hours, and some contend this causes potentially lasting harm to both the mothers and their babies (Chicago Legal Aid to Incarcerated Mothers, 2000). The fact remains that historically very few women went to prison, and therefore, in large part, the criminal justice system is based on a male dominated model. While some states have experimented with innovative systems of care for women prisoners and their children, these programs are not the norm. Sadly, since almost all of the women in prison are single moms, many of their children are placed in state custody and enter the foster care system, putting them at further risk. Evidence also suggests that women prisoners are at great risk for HIV infection and sexual abuse and rape (Maruschak, 1999). For more information on parents in prison visit the following Web site: http://www.fcnetwork.org/read.html.

As noted previously, large numbers of prisoners have problems with illegal drugs. Some advocates and scholars argue for a philosophy of "harm reduction" for dealing with substance abuse issues in society. They argue that jail is not an effective way of eliminating the many social problems drugs cause society. Community treatment programs are the preferred way to treat drug abuse rather than jail in such a model. Part of the increase in the prison population is due to the War on Crime and War on Drugs. As a result, the number of non-violent offenders in prison has increased dramatically (Greenwood, Rydell, Abrahamse, Caulkins, Chiesa, Model, & Klein, 1994; Shichor & Sechrest, 1996). In addition, people who are incarcerated often suffer from mental disabilities, especially mental retardation and mental illness. Barr (1999) argues that many individuals in prison who have mental illness never receive the care they need. Many also have learning disabilities. Such inmates often benefit from the services of human services workers who can help prisoners overcome or cope more effectively with their problems.

Long prison sentences, which have been associated with public policies designed to reduce drug use and abuse, have created an elderly prison population. It is not unusual for state and federal prisons to house inmates in their senior years, which creates a need for the kinds of health and human services other elderly people require (Harbert & Ginsberg, 1990).

The death penalty has also emerged as a hot policy topic. In 2003 there were sixty-five total executions (U.S. Department of Justice Bureau of Justice

Statistics, 2004). Texas, Oklahoma, and North Carolina are the states with the highest number of executions while California, Texas, and Florida have the highest number of inmates on death row (Death Penalty Information Center, 2003). Regionally, the South accounts for 89 percent of the executions in the United States. Racial disparity exists in the use of the death penalty, and African Americans are sentenced to death at higher rates and individuals guilty of murdering a white person are more likely to be sentenced to death than if the victim is black (Death Penalty Information Center, 2003; Dieter, 1998). In 2003, for example, no white person was sentenced to death for the murder of an African American (Death Penalty Information Center, 2003). In 2003, Illinois Governor George Ryan commuted the death sentences of all 171 individuals on death row in prisons in Illinois (Death Penalty Information Center, 2003). Governor Ryan responded in part to the work of journalism students at Northwestern who began to investigate another death penalty case in the early 1990s. He cited concerns with the application of the death penalty in several of the cases he commuted. His efforts were applauded by death penalty opponents and angered many others who thought his blanket approach was too lenient (Flock, 2003). Public support of the death penalty has declined, part of which is likely due to the media attention on the issue of fairness in sentencing and the use of DNA to exonerate some convicted criminals. Ten individuals who were previously on death row were freed or exonerated in 2003, some as the result of DNA testing or findings of improper police or judicial treatment (Death Penalty Information Center, 2003). The use of the death penalty for juvenile offenders also remains controversial.

There have been significant increases in prison costs and prison construction. In fact, direct expenditures for most criminal justice functions including police, corrections, and legal have all increased significantly. In 1999 the total cost of incarcerating individuals in state and federal jails was $39 billion and costs were expected to reach over $41 billion in 2000 (Schiraldi & Ziedenberg, 1999). In addition, it is estimated that in 2000, the United States spent over $25 billion to incarcerate over 1 million *non*violent offenders (Schiraldi & Ziedenberg, 1999). In fact, the United States spends twice the amount to incarcerate nonviolent offenders (affecting 1 million individuals) than is spent on the entire welfare budget (affecting 8 million individuals) (Schiraldi & Ziedenberg, 1999). In addition, most states have seen significant increases in the construction of prisons and most states spend more on prison construction than on construction of colleges (Justice Policy Institute, 2002). Between 1984 and 1994, twenty-one prisons were constructed in California as opposed to one state college and in New York the state prison budget increased by over $700 million and the higher education budget fell by over $600 million (Justice Policy Institute, 2002). The privatization of prisons, not unlike the other institutions, is also a controversial issue. Proponents of privatization of the prison system argue that it allows for a more efficient and cost-effective way of handling criminals (Loux, 1996). Others have argued that prisons-for-profit pose some serious ethical issues, most notably the issue of prisoner rights and use of prison labor (Geis, 1987; Shichor & Sechrest, 1996).

Crime Victims

In terms of crime victims, men and women were approximately equally divided. The largest percentage of crimes were committed against young people, with a rate (number per 100,000) of 55.1 for those twelve to fifteen, 55.8 for sixteen to nineteen year olds, and 44.7 for twenty to twenty-four year olds. As people age, they are much less likely to be victims of crimes. For ages thirty-five to forty-nine the rate was 22.4 per 100,000 people.

In 2002, black people had a rate of 27.9 crime victimizations while whites had 22.8, and Hispanics had a rate of 23.6.

Household income is also a major factor. The lower the household income the more likely a family is to be a crime victim. Those with less than $7,500 had a rate of 46.6 while those with $75,000 had a rate of 18.5.

In terms of property crimes, however, such as burglary, car theft, and other kinds of thefts, the rates are approximately similar for all income levels—170–185 per 100,000 people (Encyclopedia Britannica, 2004).

Domestic violence remains a significant social problem that has only recently received a policy response. The Violence Against Women Act of 1994 was enacted to address the failure of states to deal with violent crimes committed against women. The law provided federal funding to states to promote domestic violence prevention grants. It had several titles that addressed safe streets and homes for women, civil rights, equal justice in courts, stalking, and special protections for immigrant women and their children. The act was reauthorized in 1996 and 2000.

Programs for Older Adults

Another special group that has traditionally been the target of social policy is the elderly. Older adults are probably the most diverse population in the United States. That is, the aging process affects different people in different ways. Health and economic status, mobility, and appearance all vary dramatically from person to person, within and among age groups. Some seventy year olds are healthier than some forty year olds; some sixty year olds need to retire, while some eighty year olds continue full-time employment. Given those variations in circumstances, it is not surprising that there are difficulties in developing social policies that make sense for the total population of older people.

The Older Americans Act was hailed as a significant piece of legislation. The establishment of the Administration of Aging (aging network) and the goal to better coordinate public services and resources to the elderly was and is a significant contribution of the OAA. The OAA, which was passed in 1965, provides funds to the states for the establishment and operation of various programs for older people. Those programs include low-cost meals; home-delivered food; the operation of local senior centers, which sponsor education, recreation, and health programs; transportation services; telephone reassurance (in which older people who live alone receive daily telephone calls to determine whether or not they are all right); and many other activities and forms of assistance chosen and designed, in part, by older people themselves. By policy the funds are allocated and administered through state commissions on aging and local-area agencies on aging. Conscious efforts are made to ensure that the programs meet the needs and interests of the elderly. In general, as previously noted in chapter 6, most of the programs for the elderly are contained in the Social Security Act and the OAA, and these two programs provide the core of services to the elderly (Carlton-LaNey, 1997). Despite this, current funding is not sufficient to cover the broad and comprehensive services needed for the elderly, resulting in a "symbolic gesture of commitment to elders" (Carlton-LaNey, 1997, 287), and numerous amendments to the OAA have led to a scatter shot approach to services for the elderly (Kisor, McSweeney, & Jackson, 2000). However, the OAA has also had to keep pace with a growing and changing population of older adults. As the needs of the older population have shifted from "meals on wheels" to long-term care, some have criticized the OAA for not responding to the changes (Hudson, 1995). Issues related to transportation and housing are also important policy issues for the elderly. A comprehensive plan for housing and transporting the elderly in the United States has never been in place, despite the growing demand for such policies. In addition, caregiving has emerged as an important policy topic for all Americans. Despite the fact that caregiving will be a fairly normal experience for most Americans, policy initiatives have lagged behind this need. Caregiving affects not only the elderly but their families, employers of caregivers, and society as a whole. For an excellent resource on the OAA, visit Administration on Aging (2002).

Some programs for older adults have been characterized by patronization and treatment of senior citizens as if they were senile. In his popular 1995 novel, *The Rainmaker,* John Grisham describes a law student's visit to a senior citizen center. The young man's impressions are familiar to those who have visited similar centers in the United States. In his novel, Grisham calls the center "the Cypress Gardens Senior Citizens Building," although he notes that there are no flowers or greenery around. The staff director deals with the aging clients by alternately shoving people into their seats when they stand and hugging and patting them. She leads song, helps serve food, chastises those who want alternatives to the served meal, introduces programs, and

230

generally directs the activities of the older people as if they were children. In many cases, senior adults are so lacking in positive activities and positive social opportunities that they tolerate, without complaint, the authoritarian direction of their "leaders."

In 1995 *Consumer Reports* magazine conducted a study of nursing homes. In their study, they report that 40 percent of nursing homes have violated the Centers for Medicine and Medicinal Services standards of patient care. Some 16,000 nursing homes, about 86 percent, are certified by that organization.

The magazine describes the quality of care of thousands of nursing homes as poor or questionable at best and says that serious health conditions such as bedsores, assaults on patients' dignity, and the use of physical restraints were present in many of them. They also found that food served in the nursing homes was frequently unsanitary. They said too that some homes hide their inspection reports and, because they have strong political influence, are allowed to stay open, even when state governments find them in violation of standards.

A reporter for the magazine visited fifty-three nursing homes and twenty-seven "assisted living or board and care" facilities ostensibly to find a home for her mother. She found that the statistics conveyed the facts about such homes. One posted its negative survey too high for anyone to read. They also posted it horizontally when it was printed vertically. Another posted its surveys of conditions, but the posted survey was three years old.

The *Consumer Reports* study implies that many homes get by with inadequate and even inhumane care by staying heavily involved with public policy and by making contributions to political candidates who help them overcome criticisms or negative action.

Consumer Reports gave scores to the national home chains, ranking them from best to worst, so that consumers could make decisions about the best facilities for themselves.

Low-income elderly people are eligible for SSI, as are the mentally and physically disabled. They may also receive the social services that disabled people may obtain through state human services agencies. An important distinction between social services and income maintenance is that the latter is an entitlement, while the former is not. Agencies may provide their social services on a discretionary basis because they have only limited funds and are not required to spend them equally on all clients, which is the case for economic assistance entitlement programs.

Other Services

Many other policies establish agencies and programs for the benefit of Americans. It is beyond the scope of this book to catalog all of them, and as has been suggested, they change so frequently that it is not productive to try to develop an exhaustive listing.

Some of the more important programs that are part of the social policy of the United States and are designed to improve the well-being of individuals in the nonfinancial assistance realm include

1. Community Action Programs, which are outgrowths of the War on Poverty or Economic Opportunity Act of 1964, discussed in chapter 2.

2. Vocational Rehabilitation, which finances programs in each state, largely with federal funds, to train or retrain people for employment. Many of the beneficiaries have physical or mental disabilities.

3. Family service agencies, which provide family counseling, some adoption services, consumer credit counseling, and counseling services for employees under contract with employers, among other services that vary with each local family service agency.

4. Informal education and recreation agencies such as Boys and Girls Clubs, Jewish Community Centers, YMCAs and YWCAs, Boy Scouts, Girl Scouts, Campfire, Big Brothers and Big Sisters, and a variety of comparable organizations that are local.

5. There are also many self-help organizations, including the Alliance for the Mentally Ill, Alcoholics Anonymous, programs for parents of children with disabilities, and similar organizations for people facing other problems.

6. Employee Assistance Programs, which operate in government agencies and corporations to help employees with personal problems such as alcohol and drug abuse, marital difficulties, and other forms of counseling and assistance.

7. Veterans' services, which are provided to veterans of various war eras. They include health and mental health care; pensions, especially for those injured during wars; education grants; and various other benefits, some of which are means tested.

In addition to the government and nonprofit agencies that have been discussed in this chapter, there is also an array of proprietary, businesslike organizations that provide human services. These include private practice counseling services and hospitals for those who are facing personal problems.

Conclusion

This chapter has provided information on the current operations of many of the most important human services, especially those that are targeted for special groups of people with special needs. The services delineated are not, by and large, entitlements, as are those described in the preceding chapter. They are, however, widely available to those who need them. They represent what some call the personal social services in that they help people with their personal, functional problems rather than their economic needs. They constitute a critical part of U.S. social policy and represent the nation's specific efforts to address tangible human problems with appropriate policies and programs.

Discussion Questions

1. Contrast the services provided to persons with mental illness with those provided to older adults.

2. What are some of the ways in which the services described in this chapter are different from the entitlements discussed in the last chapter?

3. Discuss some of the factors that have caused offenders against the law and the correctional system to become a concern of social policy.

4. Analyze some of the reasons for the shift from institutional or group care of children, mentally ill people, and offenders to community or family care.

5. Visit the National Center for Policy Analysis (http://www.ncpa.org/). On the left side of the page, click on "Both Sides." Once there, choose a topic from this chapter of interest to you (for example, crime). Read both sides of a particular issue. What are the main perspectives of each side? How do these sides influence policy? Do you think one side is more congruent with social work values and ethics? Why or why not?

6. Visit the Statistical Briefing Book at the Office for Juvenile Justice and Delinquency Prevention (http://ojjdp.ncjrs.org/) and investigate statistics on juvenile crime. Is what you find congruent with public perception of juvenile crime?

7. Explore the Drug Policy Alliance Web site (http://www.lindesmith.org/reducingharm/). Investigate some of their key topic areas and consider the following questions. Is jail the best approach to deal with the problems that drug use cause society? What is a harm reduction approach and do you think it has more potential to thwart the drug problem? Which approach is more congruent with professional values and ethics?

8. For an interesting look at adoption history in the United States visit the Adoption History Timeline available at http://www.uoregon.edu/~adoption/timeline.html. Explore many of the issues, both historical and contemporary, related to adoption.

References

Acoca, L. (1999). Investing in girls: A 21st century strategy. *Juvenile Justice* 6 (1), 3–13.

Adler, M. (January 1995). Disability among children [Electronic version]. *ASPE Research Notes*, 10. http://aspe.hhs.gov/daltcp/reports/rn10.pdf (accessed February 10, 2004).

Administration on Aging. (2002). *Selected highlights: Side by side comparison of 1992 and 2000 amendments to the Older Americans' Act (OAA).* http://www.aoa.gov/about/legbudg/oaa/legbudg_oaa_2000_sidebyside.asp.

Alexander, C. A. (1995). Distinctive dates in social welfare history. In R. L. Edwards et al. (Eds.), *Encyclopedia of social work,* 19th ed., 2631–2647. Washington, DC: NASW Press.

American Bar Association & National Bar Association. (May 1, 2001). *Justice by gender: The lack of appropriate prevention, diversion, and treatment alternatives for girls in the justice system.* Washington, DC: American Bar Association & National Bar Association.

American Psychiatric Association. (1994). *Diagnostic and statistical manual of mental disorders—DSM IV.* Washington, DC: American Psychiatric Association.

Annie E. Casey Foundation (AECF). (2002). *Children at risk: State trends 1990–2000.* http://www.aecf.org/kidscount/c2ss/summary.htm (accessed February 20, 2004).

Annie E. Casey Foundation (2004a). *Kids Count 2003 data book online: Profile for United States.* http://www.aecf.org/cgi-bin/kc.cgi?action=profile&area=United+States (accessed February 20, 2004).

Annie E. Casey Foundation. (2004b). *Welcome!* http://www.aecf.org (accessed February 20, 2004).

Barker, R. L. (2003). *The social work dictionary,* 4th ed. Silver Spring, MD: NASW Press.

Barr, H. (1999). *Prisons and jails: Hospitals of last resort.* New York: Correctional Association of New York and Urban Justice Center.

Bastian, L. D. (October 1992). *Bureau of Justice Statistics: Criminal victimization, 1991.* Washington, DC: U.S. Department of Justice.

Beck, A., et al. (May 1992). *Bureau of Justice Statistics: Survey of state prison inmates, 1991.* Washington, DC: U.S. Department of Justice.

Beck, A. J., & Gilliard, D. K. (1995). *Bureau of Justice Statistics bulletin: Prisoners in 1994.* Washington, DC: U.S. Department of Justice.

Beers, C. W. (1953). *A mind that found itself.* Garden City, NY: Doubleday.

Berry, M. (1997). *The family at risk: Issues and trends in family preservation services.* Columbia: University of South Carolina Press.

Besharov, D., & Barth, D. (1994). Debate 16: Limiting abuse reporting laws. In M. Mason & E. Gambrill (Eds.), *Debating children's lives: Current controversies on children and adolescents,* 285–297. Thousand Oaks, CA: Sage Publications.

Bumiller, E. (August 26, 2003). Bush "compassion" agenda: An '04 liability? *New York Times,* A1.

Capizzano, J., Adelman, S., & Stagner, M. (2002). *What happens when the school year is over? The use and costs of child care for school-age children during the summer months* (Occasional Paper No. 58). Washington, DC: Urban Institute.

Carlton-LaNey, I. (1997). Social workers as advocates for elders. In M. Reisch & E. Gambrill (Eds.), *Social Work in the 21st Century,* 285–295. Thousand Oaks, CA: Pine Forge Press.

Centers for Medicare & Medicaid Services. (2002). *Americans with Disabilities Act/Olmstead decision.* http://www.cms.hhs.gov/olmstead/default.asp (accessed February 11, 2004).

Chambers, D. (1993). *Social policy and social programs: A method for the practical public policy analyst,* 2nd ed. New York: Macmillan.

Chester, B. (1995). Victims of torture and trauma. In R. L. Edwards et al. (Eds.), *Encyclopedia of social work,* 19th ed., 2445–2452. Washington, DC: NASW Press.

Chicago Legal Aid to Incarcerated Mothers (2000). *Women in prison fact sheet.* Chicago: Author.

Child Welfare League of America (CWLA). (2003). *Adoption fact sheet.* http://www.cwla .org/programs/adoption/adoptionfactsheet.htm (accessed February 17, 2004).

Child Welfare League of America (2004). *Mission statement.* http://www.cwla.org (accessed February 20, 2004).

Children's Defense Fund (CDF). (2001). *25 key facts about American children.* http://www .childrensdefense.org/data/keyfacts.asp (accessed February 19, 2004).

Children's Defense Fund. (February 2003). *Quality child care helps parents work and children learn.* Washington, DC: Author.

Children's Defense Fund. (March 2004). *Low-income children and families suffer as states continue to cut child care assistance programs.* Washington, DC: Author.

Children's Defense Fund. (n.d.). The Children's Defense Fund mission statement. http://www.childrensdefense.org/ (accessed February 20, 2004).

Committee on Ways and Means, U.S. House of Representatives. (1996). *1996 green book: Background material and data on programs within the jurisdiction of the Committee on Ways and Means.* Washington, DC: U.S. Government Printing Office.

Dautel, P. J., & Frieden L. (1999). *Consumer choice and control: Personal attendant services and supports in America.* Houston, TX: Independent Living Research Utilization Program.

Day, P. J. (1997). *A new history of social welfare,* 2nd ed. Englewood Cliffs, NJ: Prentice Hall.

Death Penalty Information Center. (December 2003). *The death penalty in 2003: Year end report.* Washington, DC: Author.

Deutsch, A. (1949). *The mentally ill in America: A history of their care and treatment from colonial times,* 2nd ed. New York: Columbia University Press.

Dieter, R. C. (June 1998). *The death penalty in black and white: Who lives, who dies, who decides.* Washington, DC: Death Penalty Information Center.

DiNitto, D. M. (1995). *Social welfare: Politics and public policy,* 4th ed. Englewood Cliffs, NJ: Prentice-Hall.

Douvanis, G., & Hulsey, D. (2002). *The least restrictive environment mandate: How has it been defined by the courts?* (Report No. ED-99–CO-0026). Arlington, VA: Council for Exceptional Children. (ERIC EC Digest #E629)

Downs, S., Moore E., McFadden, E., Michaud, S., & Costin, L. (2004). *Child welfare and family services,* 7th ed. Boston: Allyn and Bacon.

Dumaine, B. (April 5, 1993). Illegal child labor comes back. *Fortune,* 86–91.

Dumaine, B. (April 5, 1993). Legal child labor comes back. *Fortune,* 86–95.

Ehrle, J., Geen, R., & Clark, R. L. (2001). *Children cared for by relatives: Who are they and how are they faring?* (Policy Brief B-28). Washington, DC: Urban Institute.

Faust, T. N. (April 2003). Shifting the responsibility of untreated mental illness out of the criminal justice system [Electronic version]. *Corrections Today.*

Fender, L., & Shaw, D. (1990). *The state of the states' children.* Washington, DC: National Governors' Association.

Flango, V., & Flango, C. (1994). *The flow of adoption information from the states.* Williamsburg, VA: National Center for State Courts.

Flock, J. (January 13, 2003). *"Blanket commutation" empties Illinois death row: Incoming governor criticizes decision.* http://www.cnn.com/2003/LAW/01/11/illinois.death .row/ (accessed February 20, 2004).

Geis, G. (1987). The privatization of prisons: Panacea or placebo? In B. J. Carroll, R. W. Conant, & T. A. Easton (Eds.), *Private means—public ends: Private business in social service delivery,* 76–97. New York: Praeger.

Gillespie, E., & Shellhas, P. (1994). *Contract with America.* New York: Random House.

Gilliard, D. K. (1993). *Bureau of Justice Statistics bulletin: Prisoners in 1992.* Washington, DC: U.S. Department of Justice.

Ginsberg, L. (1995). *Social welfare almanac,* 2nd ed. Washington, DC: NASW Press.

Goffman, E. (1961). *Asylums.* New York: Anchor.

Greenfield, L. A., & Minor-Harper, S. (March 1991). *Bureau of Justice Statistics special report: Women in prison.* Washington, DC: U.S. Department of Justice.

Greenfield, L. A., & Snell, T. L. (1999). *Women offenders* (Bureau of Justice Statistics Bulletin, NCJ 175688). Washington, DC: Bureau of Justice Statistics.

Greenwood, P. W., Rydell, C. P., Abrahamse, A. F., Caulkins, J. P., Chiesa, J., Model, K. E., & Klein, S. P. (1994). *Three strikes and you're out: Estimated benefits and costs of California's new mandatory-sentencing law.* Santa Monica, CA: RAND.

Grisham, J. (1995). *The rainmaker.* New York: Doubleday.

Harbert, A., & Ginsberg, L. (1990). *Human services for older adults: Concepts and skills,* 2nd ed. Columbia: University of South Carolina Press.

Hedgers, S. J. (September 23, 1996). The new jungle. *U.S. News and World Report,* 35–44.

Hudson, R. (1995). The Older Americans Act and the defederalization of community-based care. In P. Kim (Ed.), *Services to the aging and aged: Public policies and programs,* 45–75. New York: Garland.

Hutchison, P., & McGill, J. (1998). *Leisure, integration, and community,* 2nd ed. Toronto, ON: Leisurability Publications.

Jansson, B. S. (1997). *The reluctant welfare state: A history of American social welfare policies,* 3rd ed. Pacific Grove, CA: Brooks-Cole.

Jansson, B. S. (1999). *Becoming an effective policy advocate: From policy practice to social justice,* 3rd ed. Pacific Grove, CA: Brooks-Cole.

236

Justice Policy Institute. (2002). *Cellblocks or classrooms? The funding of higher education and corrections and its impact on African American men.* Washington, DC: Author.

Kadushin, A., & Martin, J. A. (1988). *Child welfare services,* 4th ed. New York: Macmillan.

Kamerman, S., Gambrill, E., & Mason, M. (1994). In M. Mason & E. Gambrill (Eds.), *Debating children's lives: Current controversies on children and adolescents,* 285–297. Thousand Oaks, CA: Sage Publications.

Kaye, H. S. (1997). *Disability watch: The status of people with disabilities in the United States.* Oakland, CA: Disability Rights Activists.

Kisor, A., McSweeney, E., & Jackson, D. (2000). Social problems and policies and the elderly. In R. L. Schneider, N. P. Kropf & A. J. Kisor (Eds.), *Gerontological social work: Knowledge, service settings, and special populations,* 2nd ed., 65–95. Belmont, CA: Wadsworth Brooks/Cole.

Kruse, D., & Mahony, D. (March 1998). *Illegal child labor in the United States: Prevalence and characteristics* (Working Paper No. 6479). Cambridge, MA: National Bureau of Economic Research.

Leland, J., Samuels, A., Rosenberg, D., & Springen, K. (July 14, 1997). "Don't show weakness": Black Americans still shy away from psychotherapy. *Newsweek,* 60.

Liebow, E. (1993). *Tell them who I am.* New York: Free Press.

Lin, K. M., Anderson, D., & Poland, R. E. (1997). Ethnic and cultural considerations in psychopharmacotherapy. In D. Dunner (Ed.), *Current psychiatric therapy,* 2nd ed., 75–81. Philadelphia: W. B. Sanders.

Lindsey, D. (2003). *The welfare of children,* 2nd ed. New York: Oxford Press.

Loux, S. (1996). *Prison privatization in Pennsylvania.* Harrisburg, PA: Commonwealth Foundation for Public Policy Alternatives.

Mackelprang, R., & Salsgiver, R. (1999). *Disability: A diversity model approach in human service practice.* Pacific Grove, CA: Brooks/Cole.

MacNeil, R. D., & Teague, M. L. (1987). *Aging and leisure: Vitality in later life.* Englewood Cliffs, NJ: Prentice-Hall.

Maguire, K., & Pastore, A. L. (Eds.). (1995). *Bureau of Justice Statistics sourcebook: Criminal justice statistics—1994.* Albany, NY: Hindeland Criminal Justice Research Center.

Males, M., & Macallair, D. (2000). *The color of justice: An analysis of juvenile adult court transfers in California.* Los Angeles: Building Blocks for Youth.

Maruschak, L. M. (1999). *HIV in prisons 1997* (Bureau of Justice Statistics Bulletin, NCJ 178284). Washington, DC: U.S. Department of Justice.

Mayer, J. (June 5, 1995). The justice file: Rejecting Gina. *New Yorker,* 43–51.

McFadden, E. J., & Downs, S. W. (1995). Family continuity: The new paradigm in permanence planning. *Community Alternatives* 7 (1), 39–59.

Mechanic, D. (1989). *Mental health and social policy,* 3rd ed. Englewood Cliffs, NJ: Prentice-Hall.

Meddaugh, D., & Peterson, B. (1997). Removing powerlessness from the nursing home. *Nursing Homes* 46 (8), 32–36.

Miringoff, M. L. (1995). *1995 index of social health: Monitoring the social well-being of the nation.* Tarrytown, NY: Fordham Institute for Innovation in Social Policy.

National Adoption Information Clearinghouse. (2003). *Adoption: Numbers and trends.* http://naic.acf.hhs.gov/pubs/number.cfm (accessed February 19, 2004).

National Center on Child Abuse and Neglect (1993). *National child abuse and neglect data system, working paper 2: 1991 summary data component.* Gaithersburg, MD: National Center on Child Abuse and Neglect.

National Child Labor Committee. (1994). *Child labor in the 90s: How far have we come?* New York: Author.

National Institute for Occupational Safety and Health Child Labor Working Team. (August 1997). *Child labor research needs: Recommendations from the NIOSH Child Labor Working Team.* Washington, DC: U.S. Department of Health and Human Services.

Neighbors, H. (1997). The (mis)diagnosis of mental disorder in African Americans. *African American Research Perspectives* 3 (1), 1–11.

Neighbors, H. W., & Taylor, R. J. (1985). The use of social service agencies among black Americans. *Social Service Review* 59, 258–268.

Neighbors, H. W., Trierweiler, S. J., Munday, C., Jackson, J., Thompson, E., Binion, V., & Gomez, J. (1999). The psychiatric diagnosis of African Americans: Diagnostic divergence in clinician-structured and semi-structured interviewing conditions. *Journal of the National Medical Association* 91 (10), 167–175.

Nelson, B. (1984). *Making an issue of child abuse.* Chicago: University of Chicago Press.

Nursing homes: When a loved one needs care. (August 1995). *Consumer Reports,* 518–527.

Office of Juvenile Justice and Delinquency Prevention (OJJDP). (October 2002). *OJJDP statistical briefing book* [Electronic version]. http://www.ojjdp.ncjrs.org/ojstatbb/ (accessed February 27, 2004).

Parkin, D. (2002). Throwing away the key: The world's leading jailer [Electronic version]. *International Socialist Review,* 21. http://www.isreview.org/issues/21/prisons.shtml (accessed March 5, 2004).

Pear, R. (September 1, 2003). Mental care poor for some children in state custody. *New York Times,* A1.

Petit, M. R., & Curtis, P. A. (1997). *Child abuse and neglect: A look at the states. 1997 CWLA stat book.* Washington, DC: CWLA Press.

Proch, K., & Taber, M. A. (1987). Alienated adolescents in foster care. *Social Work Research and Abstracts* 23 (2), 9–13.

Quam, J. K. (1995). Beers, Clifford Whittingham (1876–1943). In R. L. Edwards et al. (Eds.), *Encyclopedia of social work,* 19th ed., 2573. Washington, DC: NASW Press.

Roberts, A. R. (1995). Victim services and victim/witness assistance programs. In R. L. Edwards et al. (Eds.), *Encyclopedia of social work,* 19th ed., 2440–2444. Washington, DC: NASW Press.

Rosenheck, R., Bassuk, E., Salomon, A. (1999). Special populations of homeless Americans. In L. B. Foburg & D. L. Dennis (Eds.), *Practical lessons: The 1998 National Symposium on Homelessness Research.* Washington, DC: U.S. Department of Housing and Urban Development and U.S. Department of Health and Human Services.

Ruiz, D. S. (2002). The increase in incarcerations among women and its impact on the grandmother caregiver: Some racial considerations. *Journal of Sociology and Social Welfare* 29 (3), 179–197.

Schiraldi, V., & Ziedenberg, J. (1999). *The punishing decade: prison and jail estimates at the millennium.* Washington, DC: Justice Policy Institute.

Schulman, K. (2000). *The high cost of child care puts quality care out of reach for many families.* Washington, DC: Children's Defense Fund.

Shapiro, J. P. (1993). *No pity: People with disabilities forging a new civil rights movement.* New York: Random House.

Shichor, D., & Sechrest, D. K. (Eds.). (1996). *Three strikes and you're out: Vengeance as public policy.* Thousand Oaks, CA: Sage Publications.

Sieg, K. (October 26, 1998). My turn: Growing up a foster kid. *Newsweek,* 20.

Sonenstein, F. L., Gates, G., Schmidt, S. R., & Bolshun, N. (2002). *Primary child care arrangements of employed parents: Findings from the 1999 National Survey of America's Families* (Occasional Paper No. 59). Washington, DC: Urban Institute.

Szasz, T. S. (1961). *The myth of mental illness.* New York: Harper & Row.

Third World Traveler. (n.d.). *Prison watch.* http://www.thirdworldtraveler.com/Prison System/Prison System.html (accessed February 29, 2004).

Torrey, E. F. (1988). *Nowhere to go.* New York: Harper & Row.

Trierweiler, S. J., Neighbors, H. W., Munday, C., Thompson, E., Binion, V., & Gomez, J. (2000). Clinician attributions associated with the diagnosis of schizophrenia in African American and non–African American patients. *Journal of Consulting and Clinical Psychology* 68, 171–175.

Tucker, L. (2000). *Fingers to the bone: United States failure to protect child farmworkers.* New York: Human Rights Watch.

U.S. Bureau of the Census. (1990). *Statistical abstract of the United States: 1990,* 110th ed. Washington, DC: U.S. Government Printing Office.

U.S. Bureau of the Census. (1991). *Statistical abstract of the United States: 1991,* 111th ed. Washington, DC: U.S. Government Printing Office.

U.S. Bureau of the Census. (1994). *Who's minding the kids?* (Statistical Brief 94/5). Washington, DC: U.S. Government Printing Office.

U.S. Bureau of the Census. (1995). *Statistical abstract of the United States: 1995,* 115th ed. Washington, DC: U.S. Government Printing Office.

U.S. Department of Health and Human Services (US HSS). (1999). *Mental health: A report of the Surgeon General—Executive summary.* Rockville, MD: U.S. Department of Health and Human Services, Substance Abuse and Mental Health Services

Administration, Center for Mental Health Services, National Institutes of Health, National Institute of Mental Health.

U.S. Department of Health and Human Services Administration on Children, Youth and Families (US HHS ACYF). (2003). *Child maltreatment 2001.* Washington, DC: U.S. Government Printing Office.

U.S. Department of Health and Human Services Children's Bureau (US HHS CB). (2003). The AFCARS report: Preliminary estimates for FY 2001 as of March 2003. http://www.acf.hhs.gov/programs/cb/publications/afcars/report8.htm (accessed February 19, 2004).

U.S. Department of Health and Human Services Office for Civil Rights. (2003). *New Freedom Initiative—Disability most integrated setting—The Olmstead decision.* http://www.hhs.gov/ocr/mis.htm (accessed February 20, 2004).

U.S. Department of Justice, Bureau of Justice Statistics. (January 7, 2003). http://www.ojp.usdoj.gov/bjs/glance/tables/incrttab.htm (accessed on January 8, 2004).

U.S. Department of Justice, Bureau of Justice Statistics. (2004). In 2003, 65 inmates were executed, 6 fewer than in 2002. http://www.ojp.usdoj.gov/bjs/glance/exe.htm (accessed March 17, 2004).

U.S. General Accounting Office (GAO). (1991). *Child labor: Characteristics of working children* (GAO/HRD-91–83BR). Washington, DC: Author.

U.S. General Accounting Office. (1992). *Child labor: Information on federal enforcement efforts* (GAO/HRD-92–127FS). Washington, DC: Author.

U.S. House of Representatives, Select Committee on Children, Youth, and Families. (1989). *No place to call home: Discarded children in America.* Washington, DC: U.S. Government Printing Office.

Vandivere, S., Tout, K., Zaslow, M., Calkins, J., & Capizzano, J. (November 2003). *Unsupervised time: Family and child factors associated with self care* (Occasional Paper No. 71). Washington, DC: Urban Institute.

Wagner, P. (2003). *The prison index: Taking the pulse of the crime control industry.* Cincinnati, OH: Prison Policy Initiative and Portland, OR: Western Prison Project.

Waits, L., Monaco, M., Beck, L., & Edwards, J. (September 2001). *Regional child care trends: Comparing Georgia to its neighbors.* Atlanta: Georgia Health Policy Center.

Wertheimer, R. (May 2003). *Poor families in 2001: Parents working less and children continue to lag behind* (Research Brief). Washington, DC: Child Trends.

Wyatt v. Stickney. (1972). 493 F. Supp. 521, 522.

Zupan, F. H. (March 31, 1993). Critics organize against "heavy-handed" DSS. *State* (Columbia, SC), 3B.

EIGHT

Analyzing Social Policies and
Models for Policy Analysis

Fundamental to understanding and working with social policy is the ability to analyze policies. In human services education, especially social work education, the emphasis in social policy curricula is on learning to analyze policies effectively and accurately. One cannot deal with policies as a practitioner or even intelligently apply social policy without a clear, systematic understanding of what the policies are and how they operate. Policies, in many cases, regulate what practitioners do on a day-to-day basis, including determining who the clients to be served will be, what the nature or type of service or benefit offered will be, or even how long services will be offered. It is also important for practitioners to be able to tell if the policy works well—does it meet its goals and objectives? Armed with tools to evaluate policies, practitioners will have a better sense of where to intervene or advocate for policy change.

Part of the competence of a professional is systematic knowledge of one's roles and the reasons for one's work. In the human services the simple following of rules and regulations, which implement social policy, minimizes the role of the professional. Jansson (1994) refers to this as the "myth of autonomous practice," or the idea that no social worker can really work independent of the many policies that can impact practice on a daily basis. One should know why the policy is being applied, the social values the policy reflects, the alternative ways in which the policy might be applied, and alternative effectiveness of the policy. Human services professionals should think and act beyond their daily tasks to the larger concepts of social change and human services delivery planning. Thinking beyond the day to day also helps workers avoid feelings of burnout as they avoid preoccupation with the service role of agency work (Schneider & Lester, 2001).

The Educational Policy and Standards documents, called EPAS, that govern accredited baccalaureate and master's social welfare policy and services curricula, for example, state that students must be taught to understand and analyze policies (Council on Social Work Education, 2003). Such an emphasis on policy analysis can be traced to Boehm's 1959 study of and recommendations for the social work curriculum. Volume 12 of the landmark thirteen-volume study of what social work education should teach and what social workers should know was written by Irving Weissman (1959), who was then a professor at the Tulane University School of Social Work in New Orleans. *Social Welfare Policy and Services in Social Work Education* standardized the policy curriculum area. These early concepts were developed by an eighteen-person panel of social work educators, organization leaders, and federal officials (Weissman, 1959). They based their ideas on their own thinking and experiences as well as on an examination of course outlines from many of the schools that were teaching social work at the time.

As an analytic framework, the study presented a three-part model for understanding and evaluating social policy. The model presented by Weissman and his colleagues said that there were three elements necessary for understanding social welfare policy and service: (1) problem, (2) policy, and (3) provision.

Their theory was that policies developed from the understanding and definition of social problems. *Problems,* Weissman (1959) wrote, were those situations that could not "be worked out with available resources institutionalized in society" (32). *Policy,* then, "refers to the process of social decision-making by which a course of social action is determined, formulated and promoted . . . as well as the product of that process" (32–33). In other words, once a problem is identified and agreed upon as a problem, society determines policies that are designed to deal with the resolution of the problem. The way in which the policy is implemented is defined as *provision,* which deals with making resources available to meet social problems or implement policies (Weissman, 1959). Clearly, one of the first systematic models for understanding social work and social welfare was Weissman's three-part model. It is interesting and perhaps historically significant that three-part analytical models were well regarded in social work. In fact, the most fundamental conceptualization of the social casework, or direct practice, approach that was originally developed by Mary Richmond and later defined more specifically by G. Hamilton (1940) had three phases—study, diagnosis, and treatment. That conceptualization was widely used at the time of the *Social Work Curriculum Study* (Boehm, 1959) and was likely to have influenced the model chosen by those who developed the concept for social welfare policy and services. In more recent years, as this chapter will demonstrate, much more detailed and comprehensive models have been developed for policy analysis. Similar expanded conceptualizations of direct practice are also now used (Meyer, 1987).

The fundamental reasons for the emphasis on policy analysis in social work education are discussed in chapter 1. To serve people effectively, social work believes that it, in the corporate sense of the whole profession, and its individual practitioners must influence social policies—that policies are a major tool for helping those in need. Most of the current textbooks on social policy place their greatest emphasis on policy analysis.

Elements of Understanding

R. L. Barker (2003) says policy analysis consists of "systematic evaluations of a policy and the process by which it was formulated. Those who conduct such analyses consider whether the process and result were rational, clear, explicit, equitable, legal, politically feasible, compatible with social values, cost-effective, and superior to all the alternatives, in the short term and in the long term" (330). Effectively analyzing policies presupposes various kinds of knowledge. One cannot analyze social policy by simply understanding and applying a policy analysis framework. Instead, one must have some knowledge of the public policy-making process, politics, public opinion, public finance, the structure and function of the social welfare system, and economics. That is why policy analysis is only one of the components of understanding social policy, as it is discussed in this book. One needs the background information provided by the other components of understanding social policy as well as the learning associated with other areas of the curriculum, especially research and human behavior and the social environment.

Distinguishing between Policy Analysis and Policy Evaluation
Some authors have attempted to differentiate between policy analysis and policy evaluation. Analysis involves the explanation and investigation of a social problem and the many alternatives and possibilities for solving the problem (Wharf & McKenzie, 1998). Policy evaluation, which is similar to program evaluation, focuses on an assessment of effectiveness of a particular policy—does the policy work? It is quite easy to confuse these terms, both because the terms are often used interchangeably and because different models often incorporate elements of analysis and evaluation within them. As Popple and Leighninger (2004) note, "policy analysis is used to refer to everything from the processes citizens use to familiarize themselves with issues prior to voting, to a multi-year, multimillion dollar project to set up and evaluate programs utilizing different types of financial assistance approaches" (41).

Many policy analysis and policy evaluation models exist across many academic and professional disciplines including social work, political science, and sociology. These models vary on a number of different domains and this section will focus on explaining and describing what many of these domains are. The end of this chapter will focus on a brief description of several models typically used in social work and human services education.

Content and Process. Some of the models focus more on the content or subject matter of social welfare policies while others focus on the various processes associated with policy making. In education, the value of content versus process knowledge is frequently debated. Some argue that content knowledge has a short "shelf life." In other words, it is not easily retained and quickly becomes obsolete. In policy terms, content knowledge in its most basic form may be referred to as the who, what, and where of policy while process knowledge is referred to as the how. Some argue that a purely content oriented model, while it will offer a good description of the various parts that make up a policy, will not tell much about how a policy is made in the real world. The content approach to policy has been referred to as a "textbook" approach (Nakamura, 1987) to public policy and some have argued such approaches are less useful for policy research and education (Jenkins-Smith & Sabatier, 1993).

Prigmore and Atherton (1986) note that "most writers on social welfare policy have traditionally taken an ideological position on a social problem, often poverty, or have directed their attention toward some goal, such as income maintenance or health provision, and then devoted the discussion to interpreting or defending their position. More recently, a growing number of writers have addressed the analysis of social welfare policy as a process without necessarily infusing it with a specific ideological stance" (48). Thus, process models take into account the various influences that play into the policy-making process and are concerned with how a policy came to be. In this sense, then, process models are more interactional or relational as significant weight is given to the realistic consideration of the political environment and the many political players (special interest groups, politicians, advocacy groups) involved. Because process models focus on the how, models that incorporate process elements tend to be more dynamic, flexible, and potentially less predictable. By focusing on what is measurable and logical, content models may appear more empirical and quantitative (Popple & Leighninger, 2004). However, while content models are useful in that they assist in helping people get a mental picture of the various components that make up policies, they are not as helpful for creating and considering the possible policy alternatives (Popple & Leighninger, 2004).

Rational and Political Approaches to Policy Analysis, Process, and Evaluation. Models may also focus on a rational or political approach to the policy process. Many models approach policy analysis from a rational standpoint. Implicit in this approach is the assumption that policy making is a rational, logical, and measurable endeavor. Those critical of a rational approach to policy analysis accuse it of being naïve and too heavily focused on idealism (Prigmore & Atherton, 1986). They also note that such an approach places false hope in objectivity and is an ineffective manner in which to view policy in the real world (Lindblom, 1964; DiNitto, 2003). As DiNitto (2003) remarks, "the idea of rationalism involves the calculation of all social, political, and economic values sacrificed or achieved by a public policy, not just those that can be measured in dollars" (4). DiNitto (2003) expanded Lindblom's earlier work by conceptualizing the "conditions" of rational policy models and pointing out the extreme difficulty in meeting such conditions. For example, consider some of those:

1. Members of society must agree on a uniform set of values and these values must be given equal consideration.

2. Members of society must agree on a problem definition.

3. Members of society must agree to do something about a social problem.

4. Members of society must identify and consider all of the possible policy alternatives, the consequences of those alternatives (costs, benefits, quality), and project into the future possible successes or failures.

Now, one should consider some of the above conditions in the "real world" as it is known. Is it possible to meet each of these conditions? As will be discussed in further detail below, it is virtually impossible to get people in a society to agree on a universal standard of values. Further, as was discussed previously, it is also highly unusual to have universal agreement on the cause or consequences of a social problem. Due to all of the political, economic, and social forces that shape policy it is also very, very difficult to project into the future the possible impact of a policy on a social problem, even when the most sophisticated statistical procedures are employed. DiNitto (2003) and Lindblom (1964) favor the idea of "political rationality," where a policy is successful because it generates enough support to become a law. A political approach refers to a more dynamic and process oriented version of policy analysis that asserts that in an increasingly complex and political environment, policy change might best be undertaken in small or incremental steps. Proponents of a political approach note that it is extremely difficult to undertake an exhaustive look at the various options and cost/benefits of policy options. They argue that such endeavors might, in fact, waste valuable time and resources. As a result, a complete overhaul of current policies and fewer policy options are considered. The preference becomes to enact small changes in the policies that currently exist, or incrementalism. The focus becomes the continuing political struggle over the concerns and problems as a result of poverty and other social problems (DiNitto, 2003). This struggle involves mediating among contrasting goals and objectives, problem definition, approaches to problem resolution, existing programs and policies, policy solutions, and decision making (DiNitto, 2003).

Common Elements in Policy Analysis Models
It is worthwhile to note that any usable policy analysis framework will include several dimensions. There are many common elements frequently included in policy analysis models. These include problem formulation and identification,

historical analysis of social problems and responses, assessment of values and ethics, description of the various elements or "ingredients" of a policy, assessment of feasibility, discussion of alternatives, and evaluation. The following will describe these elements further. Many of the models that will be discussed at the end of this chapter contain one or more of these various elements. Accounting for both process and content, and rational and political elements, makes many of these models interesting hybrids. The chart below highlights some of the contrasting themes.

Table 13. Contrasting Themes of Policy Models

• Rational	• Political
• Content oriented	• Process oriented
• Descriptive	• Prescriptive
Describes the elements or ingredients of policy, policy elements seen as "choices" of policy	*Describes the "how" or "how to" of policy*
• Empirical	• Value laden
• Predictable	*Multiple viewpoints*
Outcomes can be known and predicted	Policy outcomes can be "guessed" but outcomes are uncertain
• Logical	*Social problems are socially constructed; there are various viewpoints, values and possible solutions.*
• Neutral, objective	• Non-neutral, subjective
The most logical option will be chosen, despite "personal" objections	*Recognizes conflict inherent in policy process, special interests*

Problem Identification. Mark Twain once said, "For every complex problem, there is a simple answer, which is wrong." This is a good starting point to begin a discussion of problem identification in policy making. In chapter 3 the various ways of defining social problems were discussed at length. Obviously important to the policy process is defining the problem. This is largely because the solution designed for a problem (the policy) is contingent upon how the problem is defined. Causes of social problems are never universally agreed upon, thus even the first phase of policy analysis is often a contentious process. Consider the following description of two different perspectives on policy responses to the problem of poverty and welfare.

A variety of conservative social policy analysts have advocated major changes in social welfare and concluded that existing social welfare policies caused more problems than they cured. Prominent among these analysts is Charles Murray, whose book *Losing Ground* (1994) was highly influential in the passage of the 1996 welfare reform legislation that, as previously discussed, eliminated Aid to Families with Dependent Children and replaced it with Temporary Assistance for Needy Families. Murray argues that the AFDC program and federally financed welfare assistance in general caused poverty and dependency. By allowing low-income people to receive welfare assistance without working, the nation created a new welfare culture. Young women, married or not, Murray said, could receive help simply by having a child. Many chose not to marry and had children in order to receive assistance from government that would allow them to live independently, have families, and set up their own households.

Other writers, policy makers, and voters agreed with Murray or had reached similar conclusions even before he wrote his book. Milton and Rose Friedman (1980) said that the then-current welfare system as well as the whole Social Security program were examples of poor public policy that ought to be changed. Herrnstein and Murray (1994), in their book *The Bell Curve,* suggested that the nation could be moving toward a "custodial" state. In other words, the government welfare system had grown to such extent that it was responsible for the well-being of too many people who should be responsible for themselves and not reliant on government support. Newt Gingrich (1995), the former Speaker of the House of Representatives, also was persuaded that major changes were needed in the public assistance system, and he described in his book those that he thought necessary. He and most of these others didn't like means-tested programs—or direct federal help of any kind.

All of these analysts also believed that federal welfare assistance was inappropriate and that the lowest level of government and the political entity closest to the citizenry should provide that assistance. They also believed that states should be able to set up any kind of welfare assistance program they chose but that federal involvement in such efforts was incorrect. In this they were much like the earliest thinkers about federal relations with citizens.

In contrast, others argue that the economic conditions of poor people have more to do with structural conditions such as job loss, unemployment trends, and residential segregation of the poor from mainstream society. Wilson (1987) argues that structural conditions (i.e., unemployment trends in cities, regional economic restructuring of job opportunities) had created serious problems associated with poverty concentrated in certain areas that he called the "underclass." While Murray, as noted above, claimed that the welfare state encouraged women to have children out of wedlock, Wilson, among others, noted that the main reason for the decline in marriage had more to do with long-term spells of unemployment, lack of education and job skills for poor men, and high levels of incarceration and mortality (Bulcroft & Bulcroft,

1993; Burnbridge, 1995; Tucker & Mitchell-Kernan, 1995; Wilson, 1987). As a result, many poor women find the men available to them as "unmarriage-able" (Edin & Lein, 1997; McLaughlin & Lichter, 1997). Similarly, Massey and Denton (1993) argue that residential segregation creates restricted economic opportunities for poor people, making it difficult for them to obtain jobs. Poor communities are also less able to advocate for themselves on a political level due to increased neighborhood disorganization and disenfranchisement (Massey & Denton, 1993). In cities with increasingly shrinking tax bases, civic and social organizations end up with far fewer resources to improve neighborhoods or the lives of residents (Gibbs, 1998). Schiller (1995) argues that the idea that poor people do not have the desire or drive to remove themselves from poverty assumes that all poor people do not value becoming economically secure and is simply contrary to what is known about the lives of poor people. In addition, numerous studies have demonstrated that poor women respect marriage the same as middle-class women (Bulcroft & Bulcroft, 1993; Carlson, McLanahan, & England, 2003; Jones & Luo, 1999; McLoyd, Cauce, Takeuchi, & Wilson, 2000) and, in fact, may be making more sound economic choices by not marrying (Edin, 2000a, 2002b: Edin & Lein, 1997). There is little empirical support for the idea that women choose to remain unmarried to collect welfare benefits.

Finally, in a recent and interesting book, *Nickel and Dimed: On (Not) Getting By in America* (2001), Barbara Ehrenreich explores poverty among working Americans. As part of a journalistic report, Ehrenreich took minimum wage jobs in fields such as house cleaning and table waiting in restaurants to see if and how she could survive. In her book she discusses the difficulty in obtaining housing if earning a minimum wage. She experienced apartments that were not rentable; the only available housing for many low wage earners is in motels, which will take people for short periods of time with advance payment. Transportation posed similar problems because of the lack of access to public transportation in many of the places she worked. She also worked in retail companies such as Wal-Mart. Her descriptions of attempting to survive in minimum wage work vividly illustrate the plight of low-income people and low wage earners in the United States—the groups that constitute the majority of people who live in poverty.

The preceding examples provide a brief glimpse into the complexity associated with problem definition. Obviously, depending on the explanation chosen above, the policy response will be different. Finally, in addition to the identification and definition of the problem there are other aspects key to understanding and identifying the problem of concern. These include factors such as the origins of the problem—when did this problem emerge and why? One must also consider how widespread the problem is, how many people are affected by the problem (scope), and if any groups are differentially impacted by the problem. Frequently, "outgroups" in society (children, women, minorities) are affected differently by social problems (Jansson, 2003).

Historical Perspective. Sometimes models stipulate a historical evaluation of a social problem. For example, is the social problem a new problem, or is it an old problem that is reemerging (Karger & Stoesz, 2002)? Consideration of the historical context of social problems and policy responses also allows for an assessment of previous policy precedents (Karger & Stoesz, 2002). In addition, often policies are amended and change considerably over time due to various political, economic and social events. Thus, a consideration of how these policies managed the social problem over time is also an important component of historical analysis. Finally, conducting a careful analysis of the historical background of a policy can "curb the tendency to reinvent the wheel" (Karger & Stoesz, 2002, 32), or put another way, keep one from making the same mistake twice.

Goals. Many policy models include discussion of the goals of policy. Consideration of the logic of the policy goals is part of this process. Contemplation of the long, short, primary, secondary, manifest, or latent goals of a policy is also relevant (Jansson, 2003). Jansson (2003) notes that often secondary goals are mistaken for primary goals and refers to this as "goal displacement." A savvy policy analyst will consider the problem of goal displacement seriously. For example, suppose a policy that redesigns and streamlines services for children with disabilities has just been passed. The primary goals were to improve services for children, increase efficiency, and reduce costs. Reducing costs, while important, is secondary to the more important goal of improving children's services. In addition, a careful evaluation of the goals is also warranted—can the goals be measured and eventually known once data is collected (Chambers, 2000)?

Sometimes the goals of a policy may be understated or overstated depending on the nature of the goal. Every policy usually has explicitly stated goals. These goals are generally the goals that are likely to sound the best to the public. Goals related to behavioral control are generally understated whereas goals related to the betterment of society are overstated. Dolgoff and Feldstein (2003) use the example of food stamps to highlight the ways that goals can be under- or overstated. Perhaps the most prominent and well-known goal of the food stamp program is to help low-income people achieve a balanced diet and improve their nutrition. Another goal of food stamps is to expand the market for food produced by American farmers by increasing the buying power of low-income people. The third goal, and one that is certainly understated, is to control the behavior of food stamp recipients. Recipients of food stamps cannot buy whatever they want at the grocery store. In fact, there are specific and strict guidelines regarding what people can purchase.

Certainly this final goal is understated and might even be considered a negative consequence of the policy.

Values, Ethics, and Special Lenses. To varying degrees, many of the models also consider how congruent the policy is with the values and ethics of a profession, or evaluate the policy using a special "lens." Consistency with the Social Work Code of Ethics, for example, is an element in some policy analysis models. Issues related to fairness, equality, and social justice are also important. Some models offer a special lens from which to consider a policy such as feminist perspectives or racial and ethnic perspectives (Wharf & McKenzie, 1998). Wharf and McKenzie (1998) refer to this as the "SCRAPS" test—where policy analysis focuses on an assessment of issues related to sexism, classism, racism, ageism, and poverty. The acronym refers to the fact that women, people who are poor, minorities, and the elderly are frequently thrown the "scraps" (Flynn, 1992). For example, some believe using a feminist lens to look at policies is important because, "in a patriarchal society, male authority permeates every institution: In the polity, men hold most appointed and elected offices and make laws, decisions, and policies; in the economy, men have control of capital, resources, and the production and distribution of goods and services; in religion, men hold the highest offices, dictating moral standards of society; and in the family men make major decisions as 'heads of the house'" (Day, 2003, 9). Consideration of the extent to which a policy attempts to address past injustices and oppression is also relevant. Since policies are very "context sensitive," it is not unusual for them to have competing priorities (Karger & Stoez, 2002).

Rational models, DiNitto (2003) argues, assume that all values can be known and agreed upon, yet, as previously discussed, that is not realistic. If so, the analysis of competing values seems highly relevant. Day (2003) dedicates an entire chapter to the assessment of values.

As Kahn (1973) notes, usually major policy changes are made based on values and political perspectives, not on assessment of effectiveness. Other authors also emphasize the importance of individual or personal analysis of one's values, ethics, and opinions about policy and that the combination of personal feelings and insights in connection with empirical data can make the policy process more meaningful (McInnis-Dittrich, 1994; Prigmore & Atherton, 1986) Policy goals are often chosen based on values and values are used to help define problems, and when people's values are threatened, they are more likely to mobilize for change (Day, 2003).

If one takes one of the most controversial social policy issues of the last three decades—abortion—the issues may be clearly seen. The debate over abortion is, fundamentally, over two value questions: When does life begin, at birth or at the moment a sperm and an ovum unite? And are there justifiable social limits on the rights of a woman over her body and its functions? Those with opposite value positions are arrayed against each other on the issue. The "pro-choice" position is favored by those who believe women have authority over their own bodies and bodily functions as well as by those who want women to be as free as men to make their own plans and live their own lives. On the other side are some who believe abortion is a form of murder (because they believe life begins at conception, not at birth); some aspiring adoptive parents, who believe abortion has reduced the number of children available for adoption; and a variety of others. Analyzing the issue of abortion, and any other issue, requires some effort to investigate the decisions that led to its implementation or to its rejection.

Description of the Ingredients of Policy. Many models frequently describe the structural components or the "ingredients" of a social welfare policy (Dolgoff & Feldstein, 2003; Gilbert & Terrell, 2002; Chambers, 2000). Gilbert and Terrell (2002) refer to this as the "choices" of social policy: the who, what, and how much of social policy. Policies determine the forms of benefits, services, and regulations. Thus, a good description of policy includes the basics about these various forms. For example, will the benefit be counseling, cash, regulations, vouchers, or tax credits? The degree of selectivity or universality of a program is also related to the ingredients of policy. A program is selective when eligibility is determined by specific criteria, usually by the individual financial means of the recipients, as in TANF. A universal program is generally open to anyone in a certain class or category, such as Social Security (Dolgoff & Feldstein, 2003). Determination of eligibility for benefits and level of administration must also be contemplated. For example, will the policy be administered by the state, federal, or local government? Finally, the method of financing the benefit must also be considered.

Table 14. Common Descriptive Elements of Policy

Analysis Models	
	Common descriptive elements:
	Who gets what and why?
	What do they get?
	How do they get it?
	How will it be paid for?
	Where will it be located?
	Who will administer it?

Feasibility. An assessment of the feasibility of the policy is also an important element of a policy analysis model. Feasibility refers to the "workability" or viability of a policy. This is sometimes referred to as the "bodies, bucks, and buildings" assessment. Are there enough people with expertise to implement

251

the policy, is there enough money to finance it, and are there enough resources (building, space, technology) to run it? The following describes various domains of feasibility.

Table 15. Assessing the Types of Feasibility

Feasibility Type	Requirements
Financial/economic	Sufficient funds, now and in the future
Legal	No legal challenges
Political	Conducive political environment
Empirical	Empirical evidence supports policy
Administrative	Mechanisms in place to implement and administer policy
Public	Overall general public in support of policy

Financial/economic feasibility: Basically, economic feasibility involves asking the question: Is there enough money or a reasonable plan for funding the policy, currently and in the future? A policy may have the perfect political environment and enjoy public support, but if there is no money to fund a policy then there is not much one can do. Sometimes policies are passed and money is not available to fund them. These are sometimes referred to as "unfunded mandates." An unfunded mandate is a requirement imposed by the federal, state, or local government with no funding to pay for it. Everything costs money, even if it is a charitable effort directed by volunteers. Such fundamentals of program operation as postage, telephone costs, and transportation are always required. If all the funds are donated, that is the answer to how the program is financed. But financing is always a factor and is probably the first series of questions one must answer when analyzing policies. Whatever one is examining—the human services that are to result from the policy, the relationship between the extent of the funding and the actual impact it will make, or the priorities of the agency or government that develops the policy—money is at the heart of any analysis.

Legal feasibility: Sometimes policies are passed that are then shortly declared illegal or unconstitutional. Thus, it may be important to ask the question: Is this policy legal and will it be challenged in court? Prigmore and Atherton (1986) note that if a policy is likely to have a legal challenge, then it is unlikely the policy is equitable and just. For example, November 5, 2003, President George W. Bush signed the partial birth abortion ban into law. Almost immediately judges in the states of California, New York, and Nebraska suspended and blocked the law. Due to the complexity of the abortion issue and these subsequent legal challenges, the future of the law is less certain.

Much of the struggle with abortion issues continued to play out during the confirmation hearings of President Bush's judicial nominees.

Political feasibility: Before a bill becomes a law, it obviously will require a fair amount of political fuel to keep it going. Policies that take advantage of key time periods, or "windows," are more likely to get legislation passed. For example, the Safe Schools Act was passed quickly after the Columbine school massacre, and the U.S. Patriot Act was passed quickly after September 11. The Columbine massacre, in which twelve students were killed by fellow students, launched public outcry regarding the problems of school violence (Vossekuil, Fein, Reddy, Borum, & Modzeleski, 2002). The U.S. Patriot Act (officially, the Uniting and Strengthening America by Providing Appropriate Tools Required to Intercept and Obstruct Terrorism Act of 2001) significantly expanded the ability of government and law enforcement to spy and search. Despite the fact that many similar aspects of the Patriot Act had been previously rejected (some repeatedly) by Congress, the September 11 tragedy opened the door to dramatic changes present in the Patriot Act. The passage of the Patriot Act was so quick that a thorough legislative history of the law is lacking (American Library Association [ALA], 2003). Despite the potential to significantly thwart the constitutional freedoms of Americans, there was very little debate, discussion, or public hearings related to the act in either the House or Senate (American Civil Liberties Union, 2003; ALA, 2003).

Amidei (1991) also notes that there are several factors that increase the political feasibility of a policy: that it is introduced early in the legislative calendar; that it has multiple sponsors; that it has bipartisan, gubernatorial, or presidential support; that it has open hearings (the more people hear about the issue, the more likely they are to support the policy, especially when the open hearings involve testimony from celebrities, such as Michael J. Fox's testimony on Parkinson's Disease); and that the bill has amendments (there is more potential to compromise and trade the content of legislation to generate support).

There are some examples of times when political feasibility either kept a bill from becoming a law or cost a candidate the election even when the policy was in need of a serious revision. Sometimes even the mere mention of messing with a particular policy can be a form of political suicide. For example, candidates for political office have had difficulties with Social Security, which appears to many to be a dispensable source of funds that can be cut to reduce deficits without hurting anyone too badly. President Reagan made some suggestions to change the Social Security system early in his presidency but quickly abandoned the position, although he made some changes in benefits for college-age survivors of recipients—they were essentially eliminated from receiving Social Security payments. He was also able to implement a tightening of eligibility requirements for persons with physical and mental disabilities. Keep in mind, however, that those targets were young people and people with disabilities, who are not as effective advocates as the elderly. President Bill Clinton's administration spoke of taking action to waive the annual cost of living adjustment for Social Security beneficiaries and of increasing the income taxes on the benefits they receive. Social Security is a costly program, and the Social Security Trust Fund, which holds the payments employees and employers make, has generally contained large amounts of money. Members of Congress, advocacy groups for the aging, and others protested strongly against any reductions, and the Clinton proposals were abandoned. Those moves would have their major impact on elderly people. After strong protests, some of them by members of Congress, the proposals were abandoned. They were reproposed in 2004 by Alan Greenspan, head of the Federal Reserve.

Social Security is difficult to reduce for several reasons, as any clear analysis would demonstrate. First, its principal advocates are older people, who are effective in influencing elected officials because they can articulate the issues that affect them and are also more likely to vote than other population groups. Older people and their organizations also strongly protect Social Security because, over the past decades, it resolved one of the most critical problems in the United States—the poverty of older adults. Although they are not all wealthy now, before Social Security was improved and stabilized in the 1970s and 1980s, the elderly were the poorest group in the nation. After the reforms, that was no longer true. The levels of benefits were increased, and the annual cost-of-living adjustments kept those benefits from being eroded by inflation. Furthermore, older people often feel financially vulnerable because most of the means available to younger groups to prevent future poverty—such as seeking better-paying work or setting up pension plans for their retirement—are not available to them. They feel trapped because they are subject to public policy decisions that are beyond their own control. A critical analysis makes it clear to most elected officials that threatening Social Security will often literally be self-defeating.

Empirical feasibility: Empirical feasibility involves consideration of the evidence in support of the policy, asking the question: Is the policy based on empirical evidence and as much verifiable information as possible? Of course, as suggested earlier in this chapter, this involves the assumption that policy making is a rational process and that the potential outcomes of a policy can be known. Most likely, determining empirical feasibility involves making the best guess possible, using empirical evidence to draw logical conclusions and project into the future. Obviously, one should not naïvely assume, however, that just because the evidence points to the "most logical" policy response that the policy will be supported by the public or politicians. As discussed previously, a lot depends on what people believe are the causes and consequences of the problem the policy is attempting to address.

Administrative feasibility: Just because a policy is enacted into law does not necessarily mean that it can be easily implemented and administered. Therefore, consideration of how the policy will be administered and implemented is another component of feasibility assessment. Consideration of any barriers that may get in the way of policy implementation and assessment of the logic of the goals and service delivery plan are also important (McInnis-Dittrich, 1994).

A person from another culture, for example, might develop an analysis of a social policy and a strategy for changing it that might objectively appear reasonable but might be horrendously inappropriate and unattainable. For example, when one of the authors of this text was a state human services commissioner in the 1970s, when his staff told him about a budget crisis in the line item for providing services to adults, it was suggested that they make some simple modifications of the "chore services" program, which paid people to provide cooking, cleaning, and personal care for adults with disabilities in their own homes. The staff suggested that they simply tell those chore services providers who were relatives of chore services recipients that they would no longer pay them for their help. It seemed reasonable that relatives ought to take care of one another without the state paying them. Because it seemed to be a worthwhile policy that ought to be well understood by all parties, including legislators, it was decided to announce it to the chore services providers and recipients.

As the policy was implemented more was learned about the issue than was previously known. First, it was discovered that half the chore service providers were relatives. In other words, half of the people who were receiving the services were being helped by their relatives. Second, it was learned that the providers had chosen, or had been persuaded, to supply care for their disabled grandparents or aunts or uncles or cousins in lieu of working in the regular economy. If they were not paid, they would have to quit providing services to their relatives. The families wanted their disabled family members to remain at home, which they could do only with financial help. The state had an interest in maintaining the arrangements as well, because care in the clients' own homes was much less costly than nursing home or institutional care. Other relatives, legislators, the press, and other groups pointed to the impropriety and wastefulness of the policy change. A reasonable-sounding policy proved totally unreasonable, and it was quickly abandoned.

Public feasibility: Policy analysis usually involves specific examinations; for example, one of the classic policy analysis questions is "Who benefits, and who loses?" In order to successfully pass and then implement a policy change, the public—or at least a majority of the public—must be in support of the policy. As discussed previously, politicians sometimes avoid "hot topic" issues, even when something needs to be done about an issue, simply because to mess with it would cause them too much political fallout. Since there is a general, usually correct assumption that every social policy helps some individuals and groups and also costs some individuals and groups, it is important to consider who the "winners" and "losers" of a policy change are. What are the costs to the losers? Often these costs can be translated into money. President Clinton, for example, early in his term of office, laid out that proposition clearly ("Economic sales," 1993): he said that there were sacrifices needed to render the American economy healthy and that the sacrifices would be greater among those who had benefited most during the Reagan and Bush administrations. Those were the wealthiest Americans, whose proportion of American income increased dramatically during those years (Ginsberg, 1998), as opposed to the least wealthy and lower-middle-income groups, whose incomes declined or remained steady. His policy would, he suggested, help all wage earners by reducing the budget deficit and the interest on national debt while it would disproportionately hurt the highest wage earners. Seldom are matters so clearly stated.

This can be highlighted using an example from one of the authors' experiences in state government. During one exceptionally cold winter the administration learned that many people were being forced to choose between heating and eating. They could not afford both adequate food purchases and the utilities or heating fuel to stay warm. Energy costs had increased dramatically because of conflicts in the Middle East. Illness and death seemed the potential consequences for many residents. Thus there was an effort to develop a policy that would require the utility companies to provide low-income people with lower-cost service. Utility rates, however, were set in the state—and in all states—by regulatory commissions that allow the electric and gas companies to charge on the basis of their costs. If they gave reduced costs to low-income families, those reductions would be passed on as increases to higher-income families. In effect, a tax would be imposed on some for the benefit of others.

Fortunately, the federal government has maintained a program for home heating assistance called the Low Income Energy Assistance Program. The funds are appropriated from the regular tax revenue of the government and given to the states on the basis of their weather; states with the coldest climates and the longest winters receive more funds per low-income person than warmer states. Less directly, that program is still one in which people pay taxes that are redistributed to low-income people, but the principle is the same: *In any policy decision, some people benefit, while others pay.* The utility companies also provided means for their customers to make voluntary contributions that would be applied to the utility bills of low-income people.

Alternatives. Several policy models encourage the consideration of the policy "alternatives" or other possible responses to the social problem of interest. Generating these alternative solutions to the problem involves using the "thought experiment," or taking a policy to its most logical conclusion using the best estimate of the potential effects (Popple & Leighninger, 2004, 60). Another consideration may be the degree to which a policy will be based on a residual or institutional framework. A residual approach to social welfare policy is based on the notion that social welfare policy is a "necessary evil" and should be secondary to the market economy (working) (McInnis-Dittrich, 1994; Dolgoff & Feldstein, 2003). Residual approaches take a "consumption approach" (the benefit or service is warranted until the person uses it and then no longer needs it) and are reactive to social problems (McInnis-Dittrich, 1994). Institutional approaches, on the other hand, are based on the notion that social welfare is a permanent, normative, and regular function of a society and its government (Dolgoff & Feldstein, 2003). The institutional approach views social welfare programs as part of preventative effort designed to deal with social problems and a legitimate use and function of the government. Institutional approaches are more preventative, focusing on long range goals and objectives, while residual approaches are more of a "Band-Aid" approach to social welfare.

What are the alternative approaches to solving the problem or implementing programs that could be solutions? If government wants to make it possible for parents, especially mothers, to work outside their homes, should government set up a national day care program? Should government give money to parents to purchase day care from centers or in-home providers? Or should government provide vouchers to parents that can be used only for day care? What, the next question becomes, are other alternatives, and what are the strengths and weaknesses of the alternatives? For example, if government gave money to families, some might simply keep the money and use it as a substitute for employment outside the home. Or they might use the money to pay a relative (like the chore services providers described earlier), who would then care for children rather than working outside the home themselves with their new money. A cash approach has many more possibilities than other approaches. Yet cash payments may not be viewed as being in the best interests of the families, children, or society. Setting up a network of day care facilities could assist in educating children, screening them for health problems, and gaining access to their parents for educational and other activities. In fact, Head Start is in part a day care program that achieves some of those other advantages.

Dolgoff and Feldstein (2003) refer to other considerations of alternative policy forms such as minimal versus optimal, public versus private, selective versus universal, or charity versus right. The issue of selectivity versus universality is an important policy debate. Will the program and benefits be available to all or will these benefits be offered to a select group or class of people? Dolgoff and Feldstein (2003) offer an excellent discussion of the differences between and strengths and weaknesses of universal and selective programs. A universal program is defined as one that is widely available. Usually one must be a member of a certain group of people (such as the elderly) or live in a particular area (such as rural areas), but overall the program is available to all of those within a category. In contrast, a selective program is one where an individual must be determined eligible to receive benefits, most often determined by some kind of means test, diagnostic criteria, or a combination of both. There are strengths and weaknesses of designing programs that are universal or selective in nature. Universal programs, because they are open to more people, enjoy broad support, making these programs much harder to cut, and create cohesiveness in society because recipients of services are not pitted against nonrecipients. In addition, recipients of selective programs have fewer advocates and tend to be stigmatized and isolated. Selective programs also avoid "creaming" while universal programs limit the potential for the "notch effect." The notch effect happens when people lose benefits or services as their conditions improve, sometime making their situations worse. Creaming occurs in universal programs, most often when people who do not really need the services get them, thus taking the "cream" off the top. Table 16 highlights some of the contrasts between the universal and selective programs.

Table 16. Contrasting Universal and Selective Programs

Selective Programs	Universal Programs
Limit cost	Limit stigma
Based on principle that only those who need a program receive benefits	Programs are universal, everyone has access
Avoid creaming	Avoid "notch effect"
Stigmatized and isolated	Broad constituency recipients
More corrupt—encourages cheating to get resources	Less corrupt—avoids cheating because everyone has access
Money not spent on those who do not need services	Less financial waste on administration of program
More bureaucracy, to determine eligibility	Less bureaucracy

Selective Programs	*Universal Programs*
Pits recipients versus nonrecipients	Creates cohesiveness nonrecipients of services

Source: Based on material in Dolgoff and Feldstein (2003).

Latent Consequences. Most policy analysis models include consideration of latent consequences that are sometimes also referred to as unintentional consequences. Sometimes as the result of a policy or program unexpected effects might occur. These effects can be intentional or unintentional or positive or negative. Generally speaking, policy designers are hoping for positive effects and avoiding negative consequences. For example, some might argue that job training programs might help people get jobs, which will then enhance their self-esteem and improve their self confidence and personal relationships (Dolgoff & Feldstein, 2003). This would be an example of a positive latent or unintended consequence—where the latent consequences (enhanced self esteem, etc.) are generated although they were not part of the policy goal. On the other hand, some have argued (Murray, 1994) that welfare programs, although not designed to do so, actually create disincentives for people to work. Others might argue, for example, that providing sex education or distributing condoms might increase the sexual activity of teens. McInnis-Dittrich (1994) provides an example of a possible unintended consequence of the food stamps program. Since food stamps do not cover other necessities that a person might need (diapers, trash bags, etc.), this might create an incentive to illegally sell food stamps in order to have the cash necessary to cover the costs of other necessities.

Perhaps the primary overall objective of policy analysis is to develop policies that have the results or consequences that they are designed for and that avoid results that are not intended. Unintended consequences are the nightmare of policy makers, who may set out to solve a problem such as developing a new catastrophic health insurance program with Medicare, as Congress did in 1988. The costs were to be financed largely from additional taxes on upper-income elderly people. Advocates for the new program appeared to approve of it partly because many older people thought they would be receiving new coverage for nursing home care. When they discovered that their taxes increased and that there was no nursing home care included, the elderly rebelled and demanded that the program be repealed, which Congress did in 1989 (Ginsberg, 1990).

Unintended consequences are always a social policy concern that is just below the surface of policy making. If the federal government provided health insurance coverage for all citizens, as had been proposed by the Clinton administration, would the policy increase the use of health care so greatly that the costs for everyone would rise prohibitively? If Temporary Assistance for Needy Families benefits are increased to a more generous level, will assistance compete with low-wage employment and, in turn, reduce the labor force and the amount of tax revenues? If TANF benefits are reduced, will children suffer? When involuntary commitment procedures for public mental hospitals were made more restrictive, was an unintended consequence creation of the problem of homelessness? Those who work with social policies always want to achieve specific objectives. They also try to analyze their policies so that they will know about and perhaps be able to avoid unintended consequences.

Evaluation. As discussed previously, although there are some differences between policy analysis and evaluation, most policy analysis models include some form of evaluation. Some form of program evaluation, designed to determine the program's impact, is generally part of any proposal for a program. The evaluative information is used to improve the program or as a basis for canceling the program in the future. Evaluating policy can include an assessment of several components: for example, adequacy, accessibility, cost, coherence, quality, or effectiveness. How will we learn what the policy is achieving?

The most basic form of policy evaluation asks the simple question: Does the policy do anyone any good? Of course, although the question may be simple, the answer is not necessarily simple. As noted previously, it is often quite difficult to determine the effectiveness of a policy; changes may be small and difficult to measure, and sometimes something other than the policy can be responsible for policy change (a good economy, for example) (Chambers, 2000). As DiNitto (2003) notes, policy problems are simply beyond the analytic capacities of human beings, mainly because these are rooted in values and special interests.

Sometimes measuring the effectiveness of a policy depends on the goals used to measure the success or failure of a program. For example, if one considers an evaluation of TANF, there might be several outcomes to choose from: the percentage of families no longer living in poverty, the number of people leaving the welfare rolls, or the number of former recipients working (or working and not living in poverty!). Obviously, then, political factors may also play into the research process as well.

A friend of one of the authors, who conducts policy evaluations in Washington, D.C., refers to the three-legged balancing act of policy: access, quality, and cost. According to this person, balancing these three components is the key to a good policy and is most like policy in the real world. Often, individuals assume that more money is needed; however, there can be instances in which more money does not translate automatically into better quality programs or programs that people will be able to have access to. Assessing the quality of services and programs from the perspective of the recipients is also an important element of evaluation. Balancing the costs of services, the quality of those services, and the ability of people who need those services to gain access to them is the key to good policy. In the real world, however, it is often quite difficult to design policies and programs that can balance all three of these elements well.

Figure 2. The Three-Legged Balancing Act of Policy

Adequacy generally "refers to the desirability of providing a decent standard of physical and spiritual well-being, quite apart from concerns for whether benefit allocations are equal or differentiated according to merit" (Gilbert & Terrell, 2002, 76). Dolgoff and Feldstein (2003) refer to two types of adequacy, horizontal and vertical. Horizontal adequacy refers to the coverage of the policy—does the policy reach the targeted population? Vertical adequacy refers to the amount or quality of the services each recipient receives. A policy could be horizontally adequate by reaching a lot of people but not be vertically adequate by not providing quality services. A policy might also be vertically adequate by providing high quality services, but only to a small number of people. Horizontal adequacy can also be referred to as access: Do the people who need it have access to the policy? Vertical adequacy can also be thought of as a measure of quality: Are the benefits or services the recipients receive of high quality?

Another dimension of policy evaluation includes an assessment of coherence (Dolgoff & Feldstein, 2003). Does the policy logically fit in with other current social policies and programs—or is it incompatible with current practices? An evaluation of the logic between the stated goals, the problem, and the expected outcomes is another form of assessing coherence.

Financing. Finances are also always a subject of discussion in any policy analysis model, as every policy enacted will require money. How much will the policy cost? How will the funds be raised to pay for it? And what else might have to be eliminated to make the policy affordable? Thus, consideration of the financial aspects of a policy is perhaps one of the most relevant components of policy analysis. The costs of social welfare policies are frequently the subject of a great deal of debate by the public, politicians, and the media. One of the components related to financing has to do with equity. Is the program equitable in terms of its input (what money and resources are put into it) and output (what people get out of the program)? When people feel as if they are paying for a program and not receiving benefits, this can often be a rather contentious problem. Some have argued, for example, that the shift from federal to state level means that poor people end up paying more for the programs they receive. Is the policy or program a priority use of money?

Another aspect of financing is the issue of efficiency. Dolgoff and Feldstein (2003) refer to two kinds of inefficiency—cost and benefit. Cost inefficiency happens when a great deal of money is spent on the administration of a policy—running the program. Benefit inefficiency refers to the problem where large amounts of benefits (money, services, etc.) go to people who do not necessarily need them—or who are not the original recipients of the policy as it was originally designed.

Another very common technique of policy evaluation includes an analysis of what is commonly known as the cost-benefit ratio or cost-effectiveness evaluation. In this type of analysis, a ratio of the tangible and intangible benefits of a program and all of the costs of a program should equal a good "return," or investment, to society. In such a model, the better the outcomes at the most reasonable "price," the better the investment. Does the cost of the policy, one asks, provide commensurate benefits? One example of applying that concept is in determining eligibility for assistance programs such as Temporary Assistance for Needy Families and food stamps. Those who study aid programs know that most of those who are certified as eligible are, in fact, eligible. There are a few fraudulent claims that can be prosecuted through the law enforcement systems. There are also several cases in which people are slightly, almost technically, ineligible because they neglected to report some earnings or a gift or because the value of their property increased and they did not report it. The cost of eliminating *all* of the ineligible applicants—down to the last fraction of a percent—is not viewed as beneficial enough to justify the cost. Eliminating all ineligible clients costs a great deal more than eliminating almost all of them, especially all that only slightly exceed the eligibility guidelines. Another way to express it is to say that such an intense effort is not likely to be cost-effective, because it costs more than it is worth.

Another example of cost-benefit analysis was offered in 1995 by *Consumer Reports* ("Nutrition reform," 1995), which analyzed the potential consequences of reducing expenditures on nutrition programs through making them block grants to the states rather than federal entitlements.

Cost/Benefit Ratio		Return
Tangible and intangible benefits of the program *Costs of the Program*	=	Society Benefits
Example— Women, Infants, and Children (WIC) Benefits *Tangible: improved nutrition, improved development outcomes of children* *Intangible: women more likely to receive prenatal care* Costs spent to run WIC programs	=	Improved outcomes for pregnant women, low-income children, fewer costs in the long run due to improved nutrition and health

Figure 3. Example of Cost-Benefit Analysis

Consumer Reports ("Nutrition reform," 1995) quotes President Richard Nixon about the importance of adequate nutrition for children and workers and then cites a report by the General Accounting Office, which said, "every $1 spent on WIC produced Medicaid savings of between $2 and $4." The article goes on to say that adequate diets for pregnant women and children can prevent the expenditure of much more money to deal with severe health problems in later years. The magazine suggests that the increased malnutrition problems and long-term social and economic costs should be considered in the whole discussion of reducing federal expenditures.

Examples of Frameworks for Analysis

There are many social work and social science frameworks of models for analyzing social policies. None is universally accepted or used in social work. Most include similar elements, although the emphases differ from model to model. All of these frameworks vary, and all are much more complex than the "problem, policy, provision" model proposed by Weissman in 1959.

The models differ in length. Some contain just a few elements, as the specific illustrations in this chapter demonstrate, while others include a larger number of elements. Some focus more heavily on philosophical and value issues while others place more emphasis on finances. Some place more emphasis on quantification than others. All, however, if systematically and carefully applied, should give the analyst a better understanding of the policy that is being analyzed than possible without a systematic model.

Most of the models follow, to some extent, the general features of the scientific method as Hirsch, Kett, and Tretil (1973) describe it: (1) careful observation; (2) education of natural laws (in the case of the social sciences and human services, reviewing what knowledge has been developed and what questions have already been answered through, for example, a review of the existing literature); (3) formation of hypotheses or generalizations (in the case of social policy, of specific policy solutions designed to deal with the issues being addressed); and (4) experimental or observational testing of the validity of the hypotheses, or policy solutions. In addition, the problem, policy, and provision triad (Weissman, 1959) is in some ways an abbreviated version of the scientific method. For example, Tropman (1987) suggests that there are five phases to the policy cycle:

1. Problem definition
2. Proposal development
3. Decision phase
4. Planning and program design
5. Programming and evaluation

In one way or another the policy analysis models described in this chapter deal with some of the phases specified by Tropman. The models tend to incorporate the approaches of other models, even though they do so in different frameworks and with different language. Einbinder (1995) has also added to basic concepts of policy analysis.

Midgley (2000) notes that there are four main approaches to conducting research on social welfare policy. These are (1) *understanding* the nature of policy making and implementation, (2) *describing* the social conditions/problems and social policies that have been used to react to the social problems, (3) *explaining* social problems and the emergence of social welfare policies that have attempted to impact or solve these problems, and (4) *evaluating* the policy outcomes and effectiveness of specific welfare policies. Variants of these approaches will be explored further in the next section.

Examples of Policy Analysic Models

As suggested, there are many examples of policy analysis outlines and models. Most require the analyst to answer a series of questions about the policy. Often, the result of answering these questions is considered an analysis of the policy. The following sections describe some currently used policy analysis models. Table 18 highlights the following models to be discussed. As noted previously, different policy analysis models tend to emphasize different dimensions. Although these models may not fit exclusively within the categories used in the table and in the narrative below, they were chosen based on their overall focus. Popple and Leighninger (2004) use three broad categories to describe the various approaches to policy analysis, and these categories will be used to frame the discussion of the following models and to organize the models in table 18. These are descriptive models, process models, and evaluative models. Another category has been added to this section that is referred to as "hybrid" models. These are models that incorporate description, process, and evaluation in their frameworks for analysis.

Descriptive Models

The difference between process and content models was discussed at the beginning of the chapter. Basically, descriptive models are content models where the focus is primarily on a description of the basics of a policy. Such models often provide a very detailed process for considering elements related to eligibility, financing, and administration of programs. Sometimes these models explore the possible forms or choices of policy, and these models are sometimes referred to as "choice" models. They are called choice models because they examine the many possible options that are available to policy planners (Popple & Leighninger, 2004). The policy is seen as a series of choices about the various forms the policy can take. Often these models take great care to consider the many possibilities for and approaches to policy and program design. Examples of such models include Gilbert & Terrell (2002), Burch (1999), Chambers (2000), Dolgoff & Feldstein (2003), and Dobelstein (2003).

Neil Gilbert and Paul Terrell were at the University of California, Berkeley, School of Social Welfare when they developed their policy analysis concepts in *Dimensions of Social Welfare Policy*. Actually, the 1992 volume is the third edition of a book that was published in two earlier editions by Gilbert and Harry Specht, who are deceased. The model is one of the most widely used in social welfare policy analyses. Gilbert and Terrell published a fifth edition in 2002.

Their book is primarily an explication of their model, which focuses on the process of policy development, or formulation. They present and develop a basic four-part framework that describes what they term the four dimensions of social welfare policy. Tied to these four dimensions are three "axes" that they refer to as the values, alternatives, and theories that underline these dimensions. In other words, the four dimensions are related to the who and what and where of policy while the three axes refer to the why.

1. Four Dimensions of Social Policy
   What are the bases of social allocation?

What are the types of social provisions to be allocated?
What are the strategies for the delivery of these provisions?
What are the methods of financing these provisions?

2. Three Axes That Underlie the Four Dimensions
   Values
   Alternatives
   Theories

Gilbert, Specht, and Terrell (1992) attribute the development of their model in part to Eveline Burns, who was one of the architects of Social Security and who, for many years before her death, was a leading writer and thinker about policy development. Burns's four questions were narrower because they focused on issues of Social Security, including a variety of financing assistance programs (Burns, 1949). Gilbert, Specht, and Terrell (1992) explain that they wanted to develop an analytic framework that could cover the larger spectrum of the entire social welfare field.

The first dimension, the bases of social allocation, is described as the "who" of social welfare—the same "who" as in the "who wins" issue described earlier. They also describe the various alternatives, values, and theories that could apply to this who. This "basis" is much more complicated than it seems. For every possible group to be served there are alternative approaches. As pointed out, one of the persistent conflicts in social welfare history and social policy theory is over how one might best help financially disadvantaged individuals. One group of approaches would provide assistance directly to those individuals, with revenues collected in the form of taxes from the nondisadvantaged. Another group of approaches would suggest providing money, tax relief, or other advantages to the affluent, who would, in turn, attempt to earn more by expanding or creating new businesses. Actually, these two approaches are both always being used in the United States to some extent. TANF is an example of helping disadvantaged individuals directly. Tax reduction and depreciation allowances for businesses are the opposite approaches. The first, as will be recalled, is popularly known as "trickle-up" theory, based on the idea that the disadvantaged will receive their help and spend it so that it will ultimately reach all levels of the economy, including the top, where businesses will use their new earnings to begin new enterprises or expand their existing ones. The second is called "trickle-down" theory, in which top earners use their wealth to expand, thus creating jobs, and ultimately the added wealth trickles down through all levels of economy.

This example represents all three of the axes used in this model. Two alternative approaches exist for examining the serving of the disadvantaged. First, there is the issue of *values,* such as are revealed by such statements as "People deserve to be helped directly when they are in need" and "People should not be helped directly, but growing employment in a growing economy will

266

provide for them." Second, there are *theories* about how money is distributed in an economy. In fact, both of these approaches, these ways of looking at the problem, have worked and continue to work in different ways at different times, just as both the trickle-up and trickle-down theories have been correct at times. The differences are probably in degrees rather than absolutes and in what the values of proponents and opponents are.

Gilbert, Specht, and Terrell make a valuable contribution to social policy analysis by defining their axes because they show that, almost always, there are many alternative ways of achieving a social policy objective; because they explain that social policy is not simply a technical concern but one that is affected by values and beliefs; and because they show that theoretical considerations and theories are also part of the process of social policy analysis.

The second element of the framework, the types of social provisions to be allocated, deals with what is actually done. The various ways in which child care would be provided is an example of the types of social provisions that could be applied when serving the who, or parents, in that case. Social provisions are the "what" element of the "who wins" questions. Who wins? What is the issue? The what can be financial assistance, day care, mental health counseling, nutrition assistance, housing, family planning, health care, and almost anything else that can be assumed under the social policy rubric. The three axes of alternatives, values, and theories are also applied in analyzing a policy or issue.

The third element, the strategies for delivering the provisions, is the "how" of social policy analysis. The strategies, however, are not programmatic but, rather, administrative in nature. An example might be the way in which financial assistance has been delivered to low-income people with disabilities. Chapter 2 shows that in early history, counties, through institutional care in many cases, served that group. When the provision of assistance evolved from assistance in kind, such as housing and food, to assistance in cash and from "indoor" to "outdoor" relief, the delivery strategy changed too. In the original version of the Social Security Act, the economically disadvantaged disabled received assistance through a matching program of federal and state funds that was administered by the states, as chapter 5 describes. Each state had a different payment level, based upon its appropriations. In 1972, the Supplemental Security Income system was established; it provided the national standards and set provisions for its administration by the U.S. Social Security Administration. So the delivery system has changed from local to state to federal government.

Medical insurance for the low-income population with disabilities, however, has not been handled in the same way. Had the disadvantaged disabled been incorporated into Medicare, which is principally for people sixty-five and older, they would have received medical insurance in the same way and through the same federal agency as Social Security beneficiaries. Yet they were not. Instead, the states are essentially required to cover SSI recipients through their Medicaid programs, which are financed with state and federal funds and administered by the states. To help them meet their nutritional needs, food stamps are available to almost all SSI recipients. The food stamp program is another delivery system. The stamps are provided at no cost to the states by the U.S. Department of Agriculture. The states, in turn, provide the stamps to the individuals and families who are eligible for them.

Housing for the disadvantaged disabled population is delivered in a variety of other ways, many of them with some federal financing but, in most cases, with local administration. As can be seen from the example, the delivery systems are varied, even for meeting the basic economic, food, housing, and health needs of special populations. For each delivery mechanism it is necessary to discuss the three axes of alternatives, values, and theories.

The fourth dimension is the financing of the services, or provisions, which is also affected by the three axes. Some of the variations in financing have been discussed already. One might recall that Social Security's social insurance and Medicare are financed by employee and employer contributions, which are held in trust funds. Those who benefit tend to believe that they are fully entitled to what they receive—that they paid for it. Other programs, especially those designed for people who cannot pay for their own, are financed through general tax revenues.

How programs are financed is often the most interesting of the policy analysis discussions. In recent years there have been many artful examples of financing good works by taxing perceived evils. Some suggest that health care for people who are cigarette smokers ought to be financed by cigarette taxes, for example, so that those who cause their problems also pay for treating them. In North Dakota, nonprofit organizations are permitted to support their own human services, or to finance those of other organizations, by sponsoring gambling. The net revenues from the gambling are then used to support the services (Conrad, 1990). In other cases, "luxury taxes" on expensive items such as automobiles, boats, furs, and the like are dedicated to paying for services to the disadvantaged. In other situations, services are paid for through full or partial fees for those services. Community mental health centers, family service programs, day care centers, leisure time and recreational programs, and many others are financed in whole or in part by fees that the recipients of the services pay. Whatever the arrangements, however, it is always important to examine the nature of the financing that is used or planned for the services. Finances are a crucial part of any social policy analysis, if not the most crucial part.

The previous brief examples show how alternatives, values, and theories are important in decisions about the financing of social provisions. There are many alternative ways to finance services, and the alternatives chosen are products of the values as well as the theories of those who make the decisions.

Another useful model of policy analysis is explicated in Hobart Burch's 1991 book, *The Why's of Social Policy: Perspective on Policy Preferences*, which he wrote with the assistance of Donna G. Michaels. His model follows a thorough analysis of social welfare and social policy issues, which are the bases for his book. The four steps of analysis he proposes are

1. Identify the issue
2. Analyze what exists
3. Determine what should be
4. Decide what is possible

Burch points out that if there is no concern about an issue, there is, in effect, no issue. He suggests moving from there to existing resources and services to the ideal state of what should be. Then he suggests that the analyst decide what is possible—what can actually be done, considering all of the constraints on public support and money. Developing lists of alternative solutions helps the process of choosing the possible solutions to the issue or problem.

Donald L. Chambers (2000) presents a policy and program analysis system in his book *Social Policy and Social Programs*. He defines the elements of his analysis process as "operating characteristics," which he believes are essential to the operation of any social policy or social program. They are

1. Goals and objectives
2. Forms of benefits or services delivered
3. Entitlement (eligibility) rules
4. Administrative or organizational structure for service delivery
5. Financing method
6. Interactions among the preceding elements

Chambers's book explicates his "operating characteristics" in detail and defines the subtypes or concepts associated with each, as well as the criteria for evaluating and appraising them. He also provides an example of applying his model to specific policies—the U.S. community health centers legislation. His book is thorough and detailed, and many find it useful for analyzing social policies. Chambers's approach has sometimes been referred to as a value critical/analytic descriptive approach to policy analysis. This is because the model considers values and theories related to how the social problem of concern is understood. The model focuses on the ideology that underlies various definitions of the problems and how that might impact financing, service delivery, policy goals, and the rules and benefits offered to potential recipients. Chambers also conducts a fairly extensive examination of the evolution of events surrounding the social problem of concern. Unlike other models, Chambers's model also spends a great deal of time discussing issues related to the judicial context of policy making and addresses issues related to legal feasibility.

Dolgoff and Feldstein (2003) highlight a policy analysis model with three main components: structural, alternative program characteristics, and evaluation. The structural components examine the various "ingredients" of a policy, such as the needs, goals, administration, and financing of a policy. The alternative program characteristics examine the various forms that the policy might take; for example, Is the program designed with a residual or institutional approach in mind? Is the policy designed as a right that people are entitled to or is it designed as a charity? Finally, the evaluation component considers issues related to adequacy, cost, coherence, and latent consequences. The following is an outline of the model.

1. Structural Components
   What are the needs and goals?
   What is the benefit?
   Who is eligible for the benefit, and how is eligibility determined?
   How is the policy paid for?
   Who administers the benefit program?
2. Alternative Program Characteristics
   Is the policy residual, institutional, or developmental?
   Is the policy set up as a right or as a charity?
   Does the policy provide minimal or optimal benefits?
   Is the policy set up to be selective in nature or universal?
   What is the nature of the benefits? What is offered to recipients?
   Is the program public or private?
   Where will the program be centralized or localized?
   Who will deliver the services—professionals or non-professionals?
   If the policy fails to reach its objectives, is it because there were not enough resources or because the program was not designed properly?
3. Evaluation
   Is the policy adequate?
   Is the policy affordable? Cost effective?
   Does the policy make sense?
   What are the potential latent consequences?

As discussed previously in this chapter, Dolgoff and Feldstein's model focuses heavily on consideration of the alternative program characteristics. Using the model encourages one to think critically about the possibility for program design—and the pros and cons of these possibilities. Most students will find their discussion of selective versus universal programs helpful when evaluating policies. In addition, the model assesses the level of administration and centralization of a program, which allows for a better understanding of the complex relationships (joint federal-state programs, for example) between different levels of government and their roles in social programs.

Andrew W. Dobelstein (2003) developed a model for policy analysis and the essential elements of it. He says those elements are

1. Identifying, understanding, or clarifying the problem
2. Identifying the location for policy decisions
3. Specifying possible solutions (alternatives)
4. Estimating or predicting the impact (outcomes) of those solutions on different populations

Similar to Gilbert and Terrell (2002), Dobelstein offers three caveats to his four elements. These are: values, public domain, and environment. He also emphasizes that these four elements and three caveats can be examined by using the three different theoretical models of policy analysis: a behavioral or rational model developed by Herbert Simon (1964), a criteria-based model developed by James Gallagher and Ron Haskins (1984), and an incremental model developed by Charles Lindblom (1964). Dobelstein explains all three models and applies them to examples in his book. Simon's and Lindblom's models are in Gore and Dyson's *The Making of Decisions* (1964). Dobelstein's model is actually quite complicated, particularly his section on cost-benefit analysis, and the analysis is certainly at a more advanced level. Due to this, his model is particularly useful if one is interested in conducting a more in-depth analysis or research on a particular policy.

Process Models

Models that emphasize process are much more interested in the interpersonal and interactional elements of policy making and focus less on specific policy content. In other words, process models focus on the how and why of policy creation, while also accounting for and considering the perspectives of the stakeholders invested in the policy of interest. As Popple and Leighninger (2004) state, "the focus of this analytical approach is on the interactions of the many political actors, which include public officials, bureaucrats, media, professional associations, and special interest groups representing those likely to be affected either positively or negatively by a policy" (54). The idea is that if a person understands the policy process, or how a policy comes to be, they may also understand the content of the policy in a new, more meaningful, and nuanced manner. Evaluation of implementation involves looking at the details of the policy to determine whether the policy is not working because something is wrong with the policy or if it is not working because it is not being implemented well. Dolgoff and Feldstein (2003) pose the "resources or engineering problem"—did the policy fail because it was poorly designed or because there were not enough resources to see it through?

Process models inevitably focus on a more realistic assessment of policy since a purely scientific evaluation of a policy is rather difficult. Therefore, process models also focus on the other influences and interests in the policy-making process that have the potential to thwart the success of a policy.

For example, Jansson's primary thrust in social policy is to educate people to practice the discipline, an orientation that is discussed later in this chapter. He also, however, includes extensive discussion of analytic skills in his book *Social Welfare Policy: From Theory to Practice* (1994) and presents a straightforward model that includes three steps:

1. Analyzing the presenting problem
2. Finding a policy remedy that will effectively address the problem
3. Convincing other persons to accept the recommendations

When he explains his three steps, Jansson includes the kinds of issues cited by others who present analytic models, such as developing and presenting data to explain the problem and solutions to it, examining alternative policy solutions, and making choices. Although Jansson's emphasis is on practice skills, he offers some important insights into elements of social policy that are often overlooked, especially the nonrational components of the subject (Jansson, 1994). Some human services workers are puzzled when they encounter opposition to or strong support for policies that do not appear to be in the interests of those on either side. Jansson devotes a part of his book to understanding some of the nonrational factors that have an impact on policy; the roles played by emotion, sentiments, prejudices, and power in the development of policy are important in any effective analysis. He places significant emphasis on specific practice skills and the "doing" of policy making —using the skills of policy practice—analytical, political, interactional, and value clarifying skills (Wharf & McKenzie, 1998). Jansson's approach is highly relevant to practitioners as it focuses on the "issues on the ground" (Wharf & McKenzie, 1998). Such a focus keeps practitioners connected to policy.

Similarly, Flynn (1992) offers three models for what he terms "small scale policy" analysis, one that focuses on content of policies and another on value elements and a final model on process elements. The first models are similar to the descriptive models described above; the content model focuses on a description of the policy; and the value model explores policy alternatives. The process model, however, focuses on the policy-making process itself and evaluates potential for policy change. An outline of this model follows:

1. Policy and social problem
2. Milestones in policy processes
   Charter and legitimacy
   Action-system
   Key participants

3. Interest group relationships
   Power and influence
   Salience of issue
   Inter-group activities
4. Process resources
   People power
   Technology
   Finances
   Time
5. Congruence with desired values
6. Recommendations

According to Flynn (1992) thinking about the milestones in the policy process involves a basic assessment of the players, plan, and problem involved in the planning of policy process. This approach focuses on the fact that policy exists in the real world, with time constraints, and often with specific tasks to be accomplished. Does the policy make sense; is there a legitimate link between the ideology and end goals? Assessing the relationships of interest groups involves an examination of the nature of those interested and involved in the policy issue and the level of involvement of those groups in the process. The process resources component assesses the resources necessary in any policy-making endeavor. The final element evaluates the extent to which the policy is congruent with the preferred values of the profession.

In DiNitto's (2003) most recent edition of her text, there is a focus on the political nature of policy analysis and policy making. She notes that "social welfare policy arises out of conflict over the nature of the problems confront society, and what, if anything, should be done to solve them" (7). She rejects rationalism as a useful paradigm for understanding social policy in the real world. Similarly, Prigmore and Atherton (1986) reject the naïve nature of policy making. The idea is that policy makers naïvely do not evaluate the unintended consequences of policies that are usually designed to serve a particular interest group.

Charles S. Prigmore and Charles Atherton of the University of Alabama presented a useful analysis model in the second edition of their 1986 text *Social Welfare Policy: Analysis and Formulation*. An outline of their model follows.

Considerations Related to Values
   Is this compatible with contemporary style?
   Is this compatible with important and enduring cultural values?
   Is this compatible with social work values and ethics?
Consideration of Influence
   Is this acceptable to those in formal decision making positions?
   Does this satisfy relevant interest groups?

Knowledge Considerations

Is the policy based on tested knowledge?
Is this policy workable in the real world?
Does this create few problems for the public and beneficiaries?

Elements Related to Costs and Benefits

Is this policy reasonably effective?
Is this policy going to be efficient?

In 1997 they revised their model, which suggests a number of "factors" that can be used to consider a proposed policy or to evaluate one that already exists (C. Atherton, personal communication).

These political and value considerations follow:

1. *Is the policy compatible with contemporary administrative themes or style? That is, is the agency head, mayor, governor, or president likely to support it?*
Consciously or unconsciously, most administrators become identified with certain long-term themes as well as distinct policy styles. They are more likely to be receptive to policy and program proposals that are compatible with those themes, since they are likely to be the things that got them elected or made them popular. Increasingly, however, administrators are becoming more conscious of public relations than they used to be, and one must be prepared for them to abandon principle for public opinion. One must recognize this without too much cynicism. Looked at one way, administrators, as public servants, *ought* to be sensitive to public opinion and shift with it when it appears to have legitimacy.

2. *Is the policy appealing to the appropriate legislative body? That is, is the agency board, city council, state legislature, or Congress likely to follow the policy in decisions or legislation?*
Legislators generally are less concerned with overall themes or styles but tend to be more sensitive to their perceptions of current public opinion than administrators are. Only the most well-entrenched politician can afford to ignore the frequent shifts in public opinion. Agency boards, which are often self-perpetuating, are different from elected legislative bodies since *usually* they are not as subject to public scrutiny as are publicly elected legislative bodies. The conventional wisdom is that voluntary and nonprofit agencies are more flexible. In reality, a self-perpetuating board may be the hardest group in which to induce change because it is not accountable to the election process.

3. *Does the policy satisfy relevant interest groups (professional associations, citizen lobbies, business associations, and civic groups)?*
It seems simpler to combine all interest group politics in one factor for teaching purposes, but in reality there may be great diversity of interests that get

masked in so doing. On a given policy, there may be a number of relevant interest groups to be considered.

Practical Considerations

1. *Is there any good research or practical trial that suggests that the policy is both "doable" and effective?*

Practical trials (e.g., pilot programs or a local program that does on a small scale what you might like to do on a larger scale) are probably more useful exemplars than some of the more esoteric research reports that may involve more artificial conditions. Your case may be strengthened if you can find a demonstration project that supports a new policy proposal.

2. *Is the policy efficient? Or, if the cost is too high, can the case be made that the outcomes justify the cost?*

Efficiency includes cost-effectiveness. It is now generally recognized that we do not live in a world of unlimited resources, and welfare is only one of a number of interests competing for money. While social workers may believe that, say, a shelter for battered children is badly needed, city government may think that it is more important to build a new fire station. Voluntary contributors may think that more good can be done for more people by providing a new library. It is important, therefore, when evaluating existing programs and proposing new ones, to consider how much a service costs and how well it works.

Cost-effectiveness is not the only value that matters. For example, it probably is not cost-effective to recommend an annual mammogram for all women over fifty. It is cheaper (from strictly a monetary point of view) just to treat the diagnosed cases of breast cancer. The savings in both the quality and span of life, however, justify the higher cost of annual mammograms. The conscientious policy analyst should recommend a cost-effective policy only when it will yield the same as or better results than the existing policy.

If a better policy costs more, the policy activist will probably be better off spending her or his time justifying the expense rather than in either denying or concealing the cost by deceptive rhetoric.

It is also important to realize that there may be some services and programs that one would like to offer in an ideal world but that would be judged by the public as simply too costly under any circumstances.

3. *What consequences can be reasonably anticipated if an organization or government adopts a new policy?*

Policy analysis and formulation is more of a craft or art than any form of "science." Not all outcomes of a policy change can be anticipated. This is, in part, because policy deals with what have been described as ill-structured problems rather than puzzles. Puzzles usually have only one right answer. Ill-structured problems involve choices between better answers or worse ones and thus clearly involve trade-offs. For example, if a city considers rent controls as a way to keep rents affordable, it may keep rental costs down for the existing tenants. On the other hand, there may be a lessened incentive for investors to build additional housing if they cannot recover their increasing costs and make a profit. The result can be a shortage of available low-cost housing as population pressure increases.

Evaluative Models

Descriptive and process models have been described and all emphasize, to some extent, some evaluative components. McInnis-Dittrich (1994) highlights three main approaches to policy research: research on the policy-making process, research on the causes and consequence of policy, and research that prescribes policy solutions. The most common type of policy research is summative policy research, or research that details the impact of a policy on a particular problem.

This type of policy evaluation is usually more formal and in nature and involves the systematic collection and analysis of policy data. The findings are then reported and fed back to the interested parties for assessment and recommendations. Such models emphasize a more rational or empirical approach to policy analysis and rely on more traditional research methodologies. Policy evaluation studies, for example, are often commissioned by individuals to examine specific policy issues and are often conducted by governmental agencies such as the Government Accounting Office (GAO) or other policy think tanks often located in Washington, D.C., such as the Heritage Foundation. Einbinder (1995) says that policy analysis uses fundamental social science research methodologies, many of which she says are not taught to social work students at the baccalaureate or graduate levels. For example, some policy analysts utilize quantitative and qualitative evaluations, such as multiple regression, a statistical technique; case studies; and meta-analysis, which she describes as a "quantitative method of summarizing the results of existing outcome research" (1852). She also says that micro-simulation techniques may be useful in determining the consequences of a policy. She suggests that statistics and a sound understanding of economics are important tools for policy analysts. In fact, the use of both quantitative and qualitative methodologies in the policy evaluation process allows for the assessment of nuanced information—such as the perspectives of clients, workers, and the public. Needs assessments, which often determine the scope and impact of a problem, often result in recommendations for policy change—these types of evaluations are prescriptive in nature.

Policy evaluation, like the policy process, is also not necessarily a rational process. Even empirical evaluations of policy involve consideration of values and ethics—this approach is related to evaluating the process of policy making (Popple & Leighninger, 2004; DiNitto, 2003). DiNitto notes that policy evaluation is both a rational and political activity. Just as in the rational model of policy making, assumptions of rational evaluation must assume the goals, objectives, and policies are clear and that there is a clear link between the benefits of a policy and the intended goals (DiNitto, 2003). So, although policy evaluation may "resemble rational, scientific inquiry . . . it can never really be separated from politics" (424). Lindblom (1964) refers to this as "partisan policy analysis." However, the merits of good policy evaluation, just as program evaluation, should not be underestimated. As Schnedier and Lester (2001) note, "the importance of rational, logical argument and solid facts should not be minimized even though there are limits" as findings and information from such studies can be used to advocate for change or make the case to retain services and benefits that are working as intended (258).

Thus, the evaluation need not be simply logical and quantitative to qualify as evaluation. As assessment of the ethical issues is also an important component of evaluation (Popple & Leighninger, 2004), and as discussed previously, many analysis models do include an assessment of the values and ethics both implicit and explicit to the policy. Is the policy based in moral or ethical practice?

DiNitto (2003) discusses social policy analysis under the rubric of program evaluation. She focuses on the impact of social policies, on learning about the consequences of policies. In her discussion of the process of evaluation, she makes the important distinction between understanding what social policy "outputs" (what the provisions are) and how it "impacts" (what the effects of the policy are on the target population and the larger society). Although DiNitto focuses on government policies and provisions, the principles of program evaluation that she suggests also apply to nongovernmental organizational policies and provisions. As her model for program evaluation, DiNitto incorporates a model proposed by P. H. Rossi and H. E. Freeman (1989). They suggest that an evaluation deal with several questions:

Consideration of Design

Is the problem correctly conceptualized?
What is the extent of the problem, and where is the target population?
Does the program design fit with the objectives?
Is there an underlying coherent rationale?
Are there efforts to maximize the chances of success of the provision?
What are the real or projected costs?
What is the benefit, as related to the costs?

Considerations Related to Monitoring

Does the service reach the population targeted?
Is the program being delivered as it was designed?

Considerations Related to Program Utility

Is the program reaching its goals?

Is something other than the program causing the positive results?
How much does it cost, and how much does it benefit the recipients?
Is this program the most efficient alternative?

McInnis-Dittrich (1994) offers another model of policy analysis. Her model is written specifically for practitioners and is particularly useful for assisting practitioners to think about evaluating policy. She uses the letters of *analysis* as the eight elements in her model.

Approach. A brief description of the methods used in the current or proposed policy.

Need. What need does the policy attempt to address?

Assessment. What are the program's or policy's strengths and weaknesses?

Logic. Does the proposed or current policy logically address the connection between the need and a means of solving the problem?

Your reaction. From your professional experience, does the policy seem effective?

Support. What is the financial support for the program?

Innovation. What provisions have been made for changing the program if necessary?

Social justice. Does the program address the important issue of social justice as expressed by society and the social work profession?

Iatridis (1994) writes about policy analysis and offers a model based upon the word *science,* which consists of seven steps.

S   The sociopolitical environment. What is the societal context of the problem, the ideological and social justice implications?

C   Causes. What caused the problem and what information does literature provide about causation?

I   Intervention approaches. What other needs are unmet?

E   Establish and rank recommendations. What are the recommendations for the change, the pros and cons, and their possible impact on needs?

N   Narrative. The step involves listing and explaining programs and plans that can be converted into action along with the resources needed and any criteria to be used for evaluating success.

C   Characteristics. What are the cost, prerequisites, problems, training requirements, and monitoring steps needed in the implementation of the policy?

E   Evaluation. This involves determining whether or not, or to what extent, the goals and objectives have been reached.

Barusch (2002) offers an analysis model that considers some descriptive elements, assessment of costs and benefits, and an evaluation that is specific to issues of social justice. She contends that good policy should emphasize justice over charity and that issues of unfairness and injustice have the potential to undermine social bonds and nations, as social justice issues are both "personal and political" and ultimately affect everyone.

What are the costs and/or benefits under consideration?
Who bears the cost, who receives the benefits, and what is the relationship between these two entities?
Is anyone who is affected by this policy being labeled "other," and does everyone affected by this policy have an equal voice?
What are the rules, both formal and informal, that govern who receives and who pays? Is this policy fair?

Hybrid Models

The following frameworks emphasize both evaluation and process. Some also offer a bit of description as well, but primarily, the focus is on understanding the process of policy making and policy evaluation. The following examines some of these models further.

The final models to be described in this chapter focus on multiple components (process, description, evaluation) usually by taking the user step-by-step from problem identification, to consideration of political aspects of policy environment, and finally to an evaluation and recommendation phase of policy analysis (Karger & Stoez, 2002; Wharf & McKenzie, 1998; Popple & Leighninger, 2004). Since this chapter has already detailed the nature of descriptive, process, and evaluative models, this section will primarily highlight the components of three models that incorporate descriptive, process, and evaluative components.

Wharf and McKenzie (1998) propose a five-step model including problem identification and specification, value assessment, assessment of alternative policy forms, assessment of feasibility, and recommendations.

Problem Identification and Goal Specification
Problem description, nature, and scope
Assessment of needs and strengths
Causal factors, assumptions, theories, and historical evaluation
Targets for change and goals
Key interest groups and their power and influence
Identification of Value Criteria
Adequacy, effectiveness, efficiency, impact on rights, social justice, and special lens evaluations
Assessment of Alternatives
Consider policy alternatives, and collect data to assess alternatives
Feasibility Assessment
Legality of policy

Resources
Public and political support
Logic of policy
Recommendations
Evaluation of policy

Karger and Stoesz (2002) proposed a model with four sections. Part one evaluates the historical background of a policy; part two, the social problem; part three describes policy; and part four conducts a policy analysis.

Historical background of the policy
Problems that created the need for the policy
Description of policy
Analysis of policy
Goals
Feasibility (political, economic, administrative)

Finally, Popple and Leighninger (2004) offer a highly detailed model and note that many policy analysts probably select different parts of the model depending on their interests and purposes for policy analysis.

1. Description and overview of policy and problem
    i. Description of policy
    ii. Nature of problem policy targets
    iii. Context of policy
    iv. Analysis of choice elements and policy alternatives
2. Historical analysis
    i. Analysis of previous policies and programs enacted
    ii. Analysis of how the policy/program responses evolved over time
    iii. Assessment of past approaches
    iv. Assessment of the extent to which the current policy response has incorporated past "lessons learned"
3. Social analysis
    i. Description of problem (detailed)
    ii. Description of theoretical explanations implicit and explicit in policy
    iii. Value assessment
    iv. Description of goals (stated, unstated)
    v. Explanations for the link between the problem and goals
4. Economic analysis
    i. Macroeconomic analysis—potential effects on economy
    ii. Microeconomic analysis—potential effects on behavior
    iii. Cost/benefit analysis

5. Political analysis
   i. Analysis of major stakeholders
   ii. Assessment of policy legitimacy
   iii. Assessment of rational, incremental, or conflict change
   iv. Assessment of implementation
6. Policy or program evaluation
   i. Evaluation of policy/program outcomes
   ii. Analysis of unintended consequences
   iii. Analysis of cost effectiveness
7. Recommended changes

Policy Analysis Models—a Summary

In the end, good policy analysis models incorporate both elements of content and process, rely on empiricism when possible, and include analysis of feasibility, efficiency, quality, access, and ethics. Since policy analysis is not pure science, objective, or value free, and in the end, potentially biased, then what is it? Perhaps policy analysis is "as much an art as it is a science" as Popple and Leighninger (2004, 60) claim. As it may be impossible to know with absolute certainly that a policy works or fails because of the policy alone, the next best option "means simply taking a program, either real or imaginary, and—as systematically as possible, based only on logical thought—analyzing the likely effects" (60).

Only some of the policy analysis models that have been developed and published are included here. There are others, and more are probably being created. They are important because it is necessary for social workers to be able to analyze social policies realistically and effectively. Because social policies are the heart of the practice of the human services professions, understanding what those policies are and developing the capacity to think about and suggest alternatives to them is a requirement for human services professionals.

Any one of the models presented here will help such professionals develop a sophisticated understanding of a given policy. Mastering one or more of them will help professionals achieve an even more sophisticated understanding. Then, when encountering a new policy, program, or problem, the professional will be able to examine it and think through its merits, possibilities, and deficits.

Policy analysis methods are critical to the well-informed professional because policies are the essential building blocks for resolving human needs and solving social problems. Without the capacity to critique policies or proposals for policies objectively and systematically, human services professionals may be encouraged to pursue approaches to problems that may not achieve the desired goals, may cost too much, or may conflict with strongly held public values. There are times when complex human problems such as substance abuse are under discussion. Invariably, simplistic policies will be proposed—lock up all of the users, give life sentences to all "pushers," legalize illegal drugs, and expand treatment facilities. The sophisticated human services professional is able to evaluate all of these as well as think through alternatives that may be more comprehensive and more effective. The professional who wants to influence policy decision makers must be able to dispassionately convince them of the value of a specific policy. Doing so requires the capacity to analyze and communicate about politics in persuasive ways.

Conclusion

This chapter has presented information on the policy analysis process. It has suggested some of the elements that may be included in policy analysis. The analytical component is only one of the six necessary for a thorough understanding of social policy.

Social policy analysis is a dynamic tool that can be applied and reapplied to any social problem, policy, or provision. As such, it may be the most useful of the skills that one may learn from this book or from the study of social policy.

Discussion Questions

1. Select a current social problem, policy, or program and analyze it with one of the models presented in this chapter. Answer all of the questions listed in the model to the extent possible with the information available on the item to be analyzed. If you want more detailed information on the model, consult the source, which is listed in the references.

2. Some social policy specialists suggest that if one were to learn only one of the components of social policy, it should be policy analysis. Do you agree or disagree? Justify your answer.

3. What do you think about political versus rational perspectives as they relate to policy making? Which perspective makes the most sense to you? Which would you find the most useful in understanding policies?

4. Think of a current policy and examine it in terms of unintended and intended consequences.

5. Discuss the roles that alternatives, values, and theories play in the analysis of social policy. What are some examples of each, relative to a specific problem, policy, or program?

6. I. Weissman (1959) proposed a three-part model for understanding policy. Do you agree or disagree with the assumption that the current models of policy analysis, such as those discussed in this chapter, are really just expanded versions of Weissman's model? Justify your answer.

References

American Civil Liberties Union. (March 20, 2003). *How "Patriot Act 2" would further erode the basic checks on government power that keep American safe and free.* http://www.cdt.org/security/patriot2/030320aclu.pdf (accessed August 14, 2003).

American Library Association (ALA). (2003). *Resolution on the USA Patriot Act and related measures that infringe on the rights of library users.* http://www.ala.org/Template.cfm?Section=IF•Resolutions&Template=/ContentManagement/ContentDisplay.cfm&ContentID=11891 (accessed August 14, 2003).

Amidei, N. (1991). *So you want to make a difference: A key to advocacy.* Washington, DC: OMB Watch.

Barker, R. L. (2003). *The social work dictionary,* 5th ed. Washington, DC: NASW Press.

Barusch, A. S. (2002). *Foundations of social policy: Social justice, public programs, and the social work profession.* Itasca, IL: F. E. Peacock Publishers.

Boehm, W. (1959). *Social work curriculum study.* New York: Council on Social Work Education.

Bulcroft, R., & Bulcroft, K. (1993). Race differences in attitudinal and motivational factors in the decision to marry. *Journal of Marriage and the Family* 55, 338–355.

Burch, H. A. (1991). *The why's of social policy: Perspectives on policy preferences.* New York: Praeger Publishers.

Burch, H. A. (1999). *Social welfare policy analysis.* New York: Haworth Press.

Burnbridge, L. (1995). Policy implications of a decline in marriage among African-Americans. In B. Tucker & C. Mitchell-Kernan (Eds.), *The decline of marriage among African-Americans: Causes, consequences, and policy implication,* 323–344. New York: Russell Sage Foundation.

Burns, E. (1949). *The American Social Security system.* Boston: Houghton Mifflin.

Carlson, M., McLanahan, S., & England, P. (2003). *Union formation in fragile families* (Working Paper No. 01–06–FF). Princeton, NJ: Center for Research on Child Well-being.

Chambers, D. L. (2000). *Social policy and social programs: A method for the practical public policy analyst,* 3rd ed. Boston: Allyn & Bacon.

Conrad, K. L. (1990). Charitable gambling in North Dakota. In L. Ginsberg et al. (Eds.), *Encyclopedia of social work,* 18th ed., 1990 suppl., 94–96. Silver Spring, MD: NASW Press.

Council on Social Work Education. (2003). *Handbook of accreditation standards and procedures,* 5th ed. Alexandria, VA: Author.

Day, J. P. (2003). *A new history of social welfare,* 4th ed. Boston: Allyn & Bacon.

DiNitto, D. M. (2003). *Social welfare: Politics and public policy,* 5th ed. Boston: Allyn & Bacon.

Dobelstein, A. W. (2003). *Social welfare: Policy and analysis,* 3rd ed. Pacific Grove, CA: Brooks/Cole.

Dolgoff, R., & Feldstein, D. (2003). *Understanding social welfare,* 6th ed. Boston: Allyn & Bacon.

Economic sales pitch under way. (February 7, 1993). *State* (Columbia, SC), 3A.

Edin, K. (2000a). Few good men: Why poor mothers don't marry or remarry. *American Prospect* 11 (4), 26–31.

Edin, K. (2000b). What do low-income single mothers say about marriage? *Social Problems* 47, 112–133.

Edin, K., & Lein, L. (1997). *Making ends meet: How single mothers survive welfare and low-wage work*. New York: Russell Sage Foundation.

Ehrenreich, B. (2001). *Nickel and dimed: On (not) getting by in America,* New York: Metropolitan Books.

Einbinder, S. D. (1995). Policy analysis. In R. L. Edwards (Ed.), *Encyclopedia of social work,* 19th ed., 1849–1855. Washington, DC: NASW Press.

Flynn, J. (1992). *Social agency policy: Analysis and presentation for community practice.* Chicago: Nelson Hall.

Friedman, M., & Friedman, R. (1980). *Free to choose: A personal statement.* New York: Avon.

Gallagher, J., & Haskins, R. (1984). *Policy analysis.* New York: Ablex.

Gibbs, J. (1988). *Young, black and male in America: An endangered species.* New York: Auburn House.

Gilbert, N., Specht, H., & Terrell, P. (1992). *Dimensions of social welfare policy,* 3rd ed. Englewood Cliffs, NJ: Prentice-Hall.

Gilbert, N., & Terrell, P. (2002). *Dimensions of social welfare policy,* 5th ed. Boston: Allyn & Bacon.

Gingrich, N. (1995). *To renew America.* New York: HarperCollins.

Ginsberg, L. (1990). Introduction. In L. Ginsberg et al. (Eds.), *Encyclopedia of social work,* 18th ed., 1990 suppl., 1–11. Silver Spring, MD: NASW Press.

Ginsberg, L. (1998). *Conservative social welfare policy: Description and analysis.* Chicago: Nelson-Hall.

Gore, W. J., & Dyson, J. W. (Eds.). (1964). *The making of decisions: A reader in administrative behavior.* New York: Free Press.

Hamilton, G. (1940). *Theory and practice of social work.* New York: Columbia University Press.

Herrnstein, R. J., & Murray, C. (1994). *The bell curve.* Glencoe, IL: Free Press.

Hirsch, E. D., Jr., Kett, J. F., & Tretil, J. (1993). *The dictionary of cultural literacy: What every American needs to know,* 2nd ed. Belmont, CA: Wadsworth.

Iatridis, D. (1994). *Social policy: Institutional context of social development and human services.* Belmont, CA: Wadsworth.

Jansson, B. S. (1994). *Social welfare policy: From theory to practice.* Belmont, CA: Wadsworth.

Jansson, B. S. (2003). *Becoming an effective policy advocate: From policy practice to social justice,* 4th ed.. Belmont, CA: Brooks/Cole.

Jenkins-Smith, H. C., & Sabatier, P. S. (1993). The study of public policy processes. In P. A. Sabatier & H. C. Jenkins-Smith (Eds.), *Policy change and learning: An advocacy collation approach,* 1–9. Boulder, CO: Westview Press.

Jones, R., & Luo, Y. (1999). The culture of poverty and African-American culture. An empirical assessment. *Sociological Perspectives* 42, 439–458.

Kahn, A. (1973). *Social policy and social services.* New York: Random House.

Karger, J. H., & Stoesz, D. (2002). *American social welfare policy: A pluralist approach,* 4th ed. Boston: Allyn & Bacon.

Lindblom, C. (1964). The science of muddling through. In W. J. Gore & J. W. Dyson (Eds.), *The making of decisions: A reader in administrative decisions,* 155–169. New York: Free Press.

Massey, D., & Denton, N. (1993). *American apartheid.* London: Cambridge University Press.

McInnis-Dittrich, K. (1994). *Integrating social welfare policy and social work practice.* Belmont, CA: Wadsworth.

McLaughlin, D. K., & Lichter, D. T. (1997). Poverty and the marital behavior of young women. *Journal of Marriage and the Family* 59, 582–594.

McLloyd, V., Cauce, A., Takeuchi, D., & Wilson, L. (2000). Marital processes and parental socialization in families of color: A decade review of research. *Journal of Marriage and the Family* 62, 1070–1093.

Meyer, C. H. (1987). Direct practice in social work: Overview. In A. Minahan et al. (Eds.), *Encyclopedia of social work,* 18th ed., 409–422. Silver Spring, MD: NASW Press.

Midgley, J. (2000). The definition of social policy. In J. Midgley, M. B. Tracy, M. Livermore (Eds.), *The handbook of social policy,* 3–10. Thousand Oaks, CA: Sage.

Murray, C. (1994). *Losing ground: American social policy, 1950–1980,* 10th anniversary edition. New York: Basic Books.

Nakamura, R. (1987). The textbook policy process and implementation research. *Policy Studies Review* 7 (1), 142–154.

Nutrition reform: How much will it cost if kids go hungry? (June 1995). *Consumer Reports,* 380.

Popple, P. R., & Leighninger, L. (2004). *The policy-based profession: An introduction to social welfare policy analysis for social workers,* 3rd ed. Boston: Allyn & Bacon.

Prigmore, C. S., & Atherton, C. R. (1986). *Social welfare policy: Analysis and formulation,* 2nd ed. Lexington, MA: Heath.

Rossi, P. H., & Freeman, H. E. (1989). *Evaluation: A systematic approach,* 4th ed. Newberry Park, CA: Sage.

Schiller, B. (1995). *The economics of poverty and discrimination.* Englewood Cliffs, NJ: Prentice Hall.

Schneider, L. R., & Lester, L. (2001). *Social work advocacy: A new framework for action.* Belmont, CA: Brooks/Cole.

Simon, H. (1964). A behavioral model of rational choice. In W. J. Gore & J. W. Dyson *The making of decisions: A reader is administrative decisions,* 119. New York: Free Press.

Tropman, J. E. (1987). Policy analysis: Methods and techniques. In A. Minahan et al. (Eds.), *Encyclopedia of social work,* 18th ed., 268–283. Silver Spring, MD: NASW Press.

285

Tucker, M. B., & Mitchell-Kernan, C. (Eds.). (1995). *The decline in marriage among African-Americans.* New York: Russell Sage Foundation.

Vossekuil, B., Fein, R., Reddy, M., Borum, R., & Modzeleski, W. (2002). *The final report and findings of the Safe School Initiative: Implications for the prevention of school attacks in the United States.* Washington, DC: U.S. Department of Education & U.S. Secret Service.

Weissman, I. (1959). *Social welfare policy and services in social work education.* New York: Council on Social Work Education.

Wharf, B., & McKenzie, B. (1998). *Connecting policy to practice in the human services.* New York: Oxford Press.

Wilson, W. J. (1987). *The truly disadvantaged.* Chicago: University of Chicago Press.

NINE

Practicing Social Policy

Thus far this book has focused on the ways in which human services workers can best understand social policy. The five components described here for comprehending social policy—the ways in which it is developed, its impact, and its outcomes in the forms of social provisions or programs—are historical, social problems, public policy, descriptive, and analytical. Yet there is a sixth component that is of growing importance in the human services field. That component is the practice of social policy—the actual involvement in making and implementing social policy.

For many human services workers as well as for those who write and teach about social policy, the discipline is something that one does rather than something that one simply studies. Wyers (1991) notes that policy practice involves practitioners across the range of practice areas from those in direct individual practice with individuals to those engaged in work with communities and organizations. Although some workers believe that policy practice is for those engaged in work with communities and organizations, ultimately policy practice is the responsibility of all social workers (Wyers, 1991; Schneider & Lester, 2001). Although the literature on human services workers as practitioners of social policy is relatively new, in fact, human services workers have been policy practitioners for the whole history of modern welfare. In particular, policy practice is a natural component of social work and is rooted in the history of the social work profession (Haynes & Mickelson, 2003; Schneider & Lester, 2001). There have been influential policy practitioners throughout history in the human services fields such as Jane Addams, Jacob Riis, Mary Richmond, Robert Hunter, and Harry Hopkins among others. Several social policy scholars argue for the importance of preparing social workers for work in the practice of social policy (Jansson, 2003; Schneider & Lester, 2001; Haynes & Mickelson, 2003; Abramovitz & Bardill, 1993). Recently, the ability of and need for human services practitioners to influence state policy has been emphasized (Schneider & Netting, 1999; DiNitto, 2003), and there is also an emerging interest in equipping students with the new tools of electronic advocacy (Hick & McNutt, 2002).

Although the field of social work has an extensive and rich history of advocacy and reform, one of the continuing debates in the field of social work involves the extent to which social work should involve itself in direct practice with individuals versus social action that leads to the promotion of social change and reform (Specht & Courtney, 1994; Haynes & Mickelson, 2003). Social work academics, practitioners, and students frequently debate the relationship between social work and policy practice and the relative role the field should have in policy reform (Schneider & Lester, 2001; Abramovitz & Bardill, 1993; Haynes & Mickelson, 2003). Some authors are highly critical of the field of social work and have written that social work has "failed" as it has abandoned the mission to serve poor and oppressed populations (Specht & Courtney, 1994; Piven & Cloward, 1994; Abramovitz, 1988; Reisch & Andrews, 2001), and different explanations and examples of this debate can be found in various policy textbooks (Haynes & Mickelson, 2003; Schneider & Lester, 2001). Some of this criticism may be valid as fewer social workers are involved in politics and policy advocacy than in direct practice and are not well engaged in the policy-making process (Ezell, 1993). Others argue that overconcern with the professionalization of social work as opposed to social justice is to blame (Gil, 1998; Piven & Cloward, 1975; Sarri, 1992; Specht & Courtney, 1994; Wagner, 1990). Many human services workers feel uncomfortable about their role in the policy-making process and do not feel comfortable with their policy practice skills (Ezell, 1993; Schneider & Lester, 2001; Haynes & Mickelson, 2003). Overall most social work programs do not offer as many courses on policy practice as on clinical practice issues, and students receive less education on the skills related to policy practice (Piven & Cloward, 1975; Haynes & Mickelson, 20903; Schneider & Lester, 2001; Kaminski & Walmsley, 1995). However, polarizing direct practitioners and practitioners involved in indirect work is not very useful for the workers who are involved with clients on a day-to-day basis as it implies that direct practitioners do not care about broader change and that practitioners working for social reform are not interested in helping individuals who have immediate needs. This chapter explores and clarifies the many roles and possibilities of policy practice. The truth is that there are multiple policy practice arenas and levels of involvement available for those interested in policy practice.

Despite this debate, from a professional standpoint, the practice of policy is clearly mandated by the NASW Code of Ethics and by the Educational Policy and Accreditation Standards (EPAS) of the Council on Social Work Education. Further, human services workers, because of their frontline experiences with clients, can often provide valuable insight into the policy-making process and may underrate their abilities to influence policy.

Excerpts from the Code of Ethics

6.01 Social Welfare

Social workers should promote the general welfare of society, from local to global levels, and the development of people, their communities, and their environments. Social workers should advocate for living conditions conducive to the fullfillment of basic human needs and should promote social, economic, political, and cultural values and institutions that are compatible with the realization of social justice.

6.04 Social and Political Action

(a) Social workers should engage in social and political action that seeks to ensure that all people have equal access to the resources, employment, services, and opportunities they require to meet their basic human needs and to develop fully. Social workers should be aware of the impact of the political arena on practice and should advocate for changes in policy and legislation to improve social conditions in order to meet basic human needs and promote social justice.

(b) Social workers should act to expand choice and opportunity for all people, with special regard for vunerable, disadvantaged, oppressed, and exploited people and groups.

(c) Social workers should promote conditions that encourage respect for cultural and social diversity within the United States and globally. Social workers should promote policies and practices that demonstrate respect for difference, support the expansion of cultural knowledge and resources, advocate for programs and institutions that demonstrate cultural competence, and promote policies that safeguard the rights of and confirm equity and social justice for all people.

(d) Social workers should act to prevent and eliminate domination of, exploitation of, and discrimination against any person, group, or class on the basis of race, ethnicity, national origin, color, sex, sexual orientation, age, marital status, political belief, religion, or mental or physical disability.

Source: NASW Code of Ethics (1999)

Figure 4. Excerpts from the NASW Code of Ethics Related to Policy Practice

There is a renewed interest in advocacy in the field of social work (Ezell, 2001; Haynes & Mickelson, 2003; Schneider & Lester, 20901; Jansson, 2003; Hick & McNutt, 2002). Due to continued devolution and federal and state budget realities, advocacy is emerging as an important tool for human services workers (Schneider & Netting, 1999). Practitioners well trained in the skills of policy practice will better be able to protect the benefits and services that are vital to many oppressed and vulnerable clients served by human services workers (Ezell, 2001).

Practitioners with access to E-mail and the Internet will find a variety of e-mail newsletters, legislative alerts, or publication alerts that will help them keep in touch with current "hot topics" relevant to their field of practice. Merely subscribing to these lists or new alerts can provide practitioners with current and relevant information. It is also possible to subscribe to policy alerts that update the practitioner on legislative action, progress, or status of particular bills.

Table 17. Understanding Strategies for the Reduction of Federal Responsibility for Social Welfare Programs

Strategy & Definition	Arguments For	Arguments Against
Devolution *Shift of power from the federal (central) government to the state or local level*	• Local & state governments are in the best positions to know what policies and programs they need • Reduced bureaucracy at federal level • Less money spent at the federal level	• Fewer federal protections to benefits & services • Less accountability to poor clients • Less monitoring of program outcomes
Deregulation *Removal of rules and regulations (example: health & safety standards, environmental protection standards*	• Avoids the "red tape" & restrictions on businesses • Fewer regulations will: *encourage a free market economy* *allow for more efficient business practices* *lead to more competition ower prices*	• Federal agencies and organizations become limited in their ability to monitor important issues (public safety, civil rights, environmental protections) • Creates opportunities for "moral hazard," corruption
Privatization/ Centralization *Transfer of governmental responsibility from public to private ownership*	• Public enterprises have no incentives to be efficient • Private organizations are able to provide more efficient, higher quality and cost effective services	• Private companties are not accountable to the public for their services • Profit, not people, is usually the bottom line in private organization

Strategy & Definition	*Arguments For*	*Arguments Against*
Privatization/ Centralization (*continued*)	• Avoidance of high over-head costs associated with paying state or federal salaries	
Block Grant A *"block" of money, in this case, a federal payment, granted by the federal government. General guidelines are provided to the recipients of the money.*	• Allow for local or state governments to creative and flexible— to experiment with different programs based on local needs • State or local governments have more control with the money they receive	• State governments are typically less supportive of social welfare than at the federal level • State governments have fewer resources than the federal government • An overall reduction in federal funds for social welfare programs
Decentralization	• State and local governments are empowered because they are more involved in the creation of social welfare programs • Under this arrangement the regional/local entities may make significant policy choices that are not subject to review and veto by the central authority • Brings the authority and decision-making about programs and services closer to the point of service or action	• Programs that are centralized are easier regulate, monitor, and organize • Evaluation of program outcomes is easier when the program is centralized • Fewer incentives for the local government to be responsive to individuals in need • The individual is left to the mercy of the "group," some local regions may have more conservative policies, so an individual served served locally might receive fewer benefits

Defining Policy Practice

Practicing social policy, generally speaking, involves advocacy. Although advocacy and policy practice are not necessarily equivalent, advocacy is an important component of policy practice. There are many different and varied definitions of policy practice and advocacy. Many people mistakenly view policy practice simply as advocacy. While policy practice certainly involves advocacy it is not the only aspect of policy practice. In addition, many individuals also assume that policy practice involves only working with federal or state laws. However, some authors assert that there are a wide variety of policies that might include, for example, personal policies, agency policies, and state and federal policies (Pierce, 2000; Barusch, 2002; Schneider & Lester, 2001). Personal policies are the personal guidelines that an individual utilizes to assist them in ethical decision making. Agency or administrative policies are those that govern a particular organization and may directly affect what a human services worker does day to day as well as the kinds of services or benefits received by clients. Wharf and McKenzie (1998) note that these include the "policy's impact on rights, statuses, and social justice, including the ability of service users to be self-determining" (57). It is possible that some policies sometimes get in the way of the provision of services or access to those services. As Barusch (2002) notes, "social workers engage in policy practice when they strive to master the laws and regulations that govern the services they provide to clients" (375). Of course state and federal policies refer to legislation, or laws, that may govern the programs and services offered by many human services professionals.

One of the keys to good policy practice is the avoidance of an inactive or reactive role in the policy-making process. Practitioners who are inactive tend to minimize or ignore the impact of policy on their practice and might be generally unaware of the policies that are relevant to their practice or even their day-to-day lives. A reactive practitioner, then as the term implies, mainly reacts to policies as they happen, ultimately becoming passive recipients of the policies that shape what they do or what their clients receive. In such cases there is a "preoccupation with the service role" (Schneider & Lester, 2001, 81). Not surprisingly then, reactive approaches to policy tend to be remedial or Band-Aid approaches to social problems, primarily because there is little time to anticipate or plan the best possible policy response for a social problem. If practitioners are prepared and proactive, they avoid minimizing the importance of policies or having a delayed reaction to badly designed, ineffective, and damaging policies (Pierce, 2000). In the end, proactive approaches help practitioners anticipate future policy outcomes and consider a wider variety of alternative policy approaches to solve social problems (Haynes & Mickelson, 2003). Perhaps the most important rationale for a proactive approach is that without it, poor and oppressed clients remain underserved or inadequately served (Haynes & Mickelson, 2003).

Policy practice, in most cases, is not and should not be neutral. Neutrality implies objectivity and rationality and, as discussed in chapter 8, rarely is policy making rational. In policy making, practitioners must identify personal values and ideology as well as that of opponents. Such work requires taking a personal position on issues. As Haynes and Mickelson (2003) note, "one potentially negative consequence of emotional neutrality is that it may induce social workers to deny or repress emotional experiences or emotional reactions. The isolation and suppression of emotions, however, may only serve to thwart justifiable anger and frustration at the social inequities that clearly are at the root of many client problems" (57). In fact, neutrality can be a significant barrier to effective policy practice (Schneider & Lester, 2001). Practitioners must realize that policy practice involves taking a stand against oppression and inequality and a stand for social justice (Haynes & Mickelson, 2003; Schneider & Lester, 2001; Freirer, 1990; McCormick, 1970). Neutrality, of course, does not mean adversarial; in fact, practitioners may choose strategies based on the nature of the problem and opposition to the problem.

Jansson (2003) notes that it is possible to surmount cynicism by developing policy-advocacy skills and that these skills can be used in organizational, community, and legislative settings (67). Further, Jansson (2003) suggests three interlocking rationales that justify policy practice: value/ethical rationale, analytical rationale, and political rationale. For example, the profession of social work implies values specific to social justice. Understanding policies and their impact on clients and on the services provided is also critical. Finally, even with clear and justified value positions and a thorough analysis of relevant policy issues and recommended changes, if one is unable to organize and bring about political support for these changes, these changes will not go far. Thus, these three rationales work together to serve as impetus for policy practice.

Policy Practice Types and Skills
Several authors note different typologies of and skills needed for policy practice. For example, Jansson (2003) notes four types of policy practice and advocacy: (1) ballot based, (2) legislative, (3) analytic, (4) troubleshooting. Schneider and Lester (2001) divide advocacy into four types: client, cause, legislative, and administrative. Haynes and Mickelson (2003) also discuss many of the previous typologies in addition to social work involvement in political action committees, political campaigns, and as politicians. In a comprehensive literature review on advocacy, Schneider and Lester (2001) noted over ninety different definitions of advocacy, including legislative advocacy or lobbying, speaking for a client, advocating for changing an agency policy, or running for office. They offer a definition of social work advocacy as "the exclusive and mutual representation of a client(s) or a cause in a forum, attempting to systematically influence decision making in an unjust

or unresponsive system" (65). A cause can be an issue or social problem of concern. They note that the social work advocacy relationship is exclusive and mutual. In other words, the relationship is equal and reciprocal, based exclusively on the needs of the client(s) or cause.

As noted previously, Jansson (2003) says that policy advocacy offers workers a chance to make a difference about some of the issues important to the worker and the clients they serve. The practitioner can choose from a wide variety of policy practice activities and may choose to work on the organizational, community, or legislative levels. For example, say that human services workers currently working as direct service or frontline workers decided that they wanted to do something about child welfare programs. They could choose to advocate for an individual client, a group of clients, a change of policy within the agency or a change of state or federal policy, to organize child welfare workers or clients, or to seek a leadership position where they could have more power to influence child welfare programs. Say for example, they chose the last strategy—to seek leadership positions. These workers could choose to seek leadership positions within the agency in which they work, where they would have more influence on agency policies. Alternatively they could choose to run for local office, or serve on a state board. Finally they could choose to run for office at the state or federal level. Obviously the level of personal involvement and the type of advocacy will depend on the needs of the client(s) and the personal interest and commitment of the human services worker to a particular issue or cause. The following section provides an overview of some of these policy practice types and discusses some of the skills associated with these types of practice.

Analytic Policy Practice
One of the primary tools of the policy practitioner is the development of factual information about the nature and extent of social problems. To be effective in understanding problems and in developing solutions for them, policy planners must conduct research or be aware of and use the research conducted by others on specific social problems and solutions. Analytic policy practice generally involves assessment and analysis of current and potential policies similar to what was discussed in chapter 8. Generally, this involves conducting research on policies and their outcomes, collecting data, and presenting research findings to policy makers and the public (Jansson, 2003). This involves analyzing information about policies in order to best decide about policy options. Human services practitioners in advocacy organizations or policy think tanks often conduct this work. Such organizations typically manage information about social problems or policies in attempt to provide information to policy makers and the public to advocate for particular policy issues (Jansson, 2003).

Legislative bodies, executive branch officials, and other decision makers in the policy-making process want to know the facts about problems and solutions before they make decisions. Therefore, policy practitioners are regular students of public documents, governmental statistical reports, and other sources of facts about human beings and issues affecting their lives. Major employers in the practice of social policy are think tanks and other policy study groups and institutions. Some of the most prominent are the Brookings Institution, the Institute for Policy Studies, the American Heritage Foundation, the American Enterprise Institute, the Center for Budget and Policy Priorities, and the National Center for Policy Analysis. There are hundreds of these around the nation, many of which receive funds from foundations and most of which are tax-exempt because they are engaged in study rather than in lobbying or politics. These groups are often important sources of information about social policies; executive and legislative branches call upon them for their data and their ideas.

Electoral Advocacy

In its most basic form, when human services workers organize to elect or remove certain individuals in elected office, this is ballot-based or electoral advocacy (Jansson, 2003; Haynes & Mickelson, 2003). Perhaps the simplest form of electoral advocacy is voting. Sadly, some human services workers do not vote and often do not know who their elected officials are. Informed voters, at the most basic level, are advocating for something! Involvement in electoral advocacy can also involve fundraising for political candidates, devising campaign strategies, organizing voters, working with the media, conducting research on voters (polls), running focus groups with voters to determine their stance on issues and their needs, registering people to vote, and writing policy issue papers (Haynes & Mickelson, 2003; Jansson, 2003). Many of the skills that human services practitioners already utilize are easily transferable to electoral advocacy settings such as generating solutions to complex problems, establishing rapport with people, managing angry individuals, empowering disenfranchised populations, working with small and large groups, and providing mediation and negotiation (Haynes & Mickelson, 2003; Jansson, 2003). Other skills that are important, but possibly less familiar are working with the media, developing press releases, preparing candidates for the media, and conducting or planning for press conferences (Jansson, 2003). Individuals actively working on a political campaign might utilize such skills.

Human services workers may also be involved with political action committees or PACs. PACs are organizations used to collect money and then support political candidates that support the PACs relevant issues (Haynes & Mickelson, 2003).

Table 18. Models Described in Chapter 8

Model Focus: Descriptive

Gilbert & Terrell (2002)	Dolgoff & Feldstein (2003)	Chambers (2000)	Dobelstein (1996)	Burch (1991)
• What are the bases of social allocation?	**Structural Components**	• Goals and objectives	• Identifying, understanding, or clarifying the problem	• Identify the issue.
• What are the types of social provisions to be allocated?	• Assessment of needs and goals, benefit, eligibility, financing, administration	• Forms of benefits or services delivered	• Identifying the location for policy decisions	• Analyze what exists.
• What are the strategies for the delivery of these provisions?	**Alternative Program Characteristics**	• Entitlement (eligibility) rules	• Specifying possible solutions (alternatives)	• Determine what should be.
• What are the methods of financing these provisions?	• Is the policy residual, institutional, or developmental?	• Administrative or organizational structure for service delivery	• Estimating or predicting the impact (outcomes) of those solutions on different populations	• Decide what is possible.
• What values, alternatives, and theories underlie these four dimensions?	• Is the policy right vs. charity, minimal vs. optimal, selective vs. universal?	• Financing method		
	Evaluation	• Interactions among the preceding elements		
	• Adequacy			
	• Cost effective, affordability			
	• Coherence			
	• Latent consequences			

Source: Model categories adapted from Popple and Leighninger (2004).

Table 18. Models Described in Chapter 8

Model Focus: Descriptive

Gilbert & Terrell (2002)	Dolgoff & Feldstein (2003)	Chambers (2000)	Dobelstein (1996)	Burch (1991)
• What are the bases of social allocation? • What are the types of social provisions to be allocated? • What are the strategies for the delivery of these provisions? • What are the methods of financing these provisions? • What values, alternatives, and theories underlie these four dimensions?	**Structural Components** • Assessment of needs and goals, benefit, eligibility, financing, administration **Alternative Program Characteristics** • Is the policy residual, institutional, or developmental? • Is the policy right v. charity, minimal v. optimal, selective v. universal? **Evaluation** • Adequacy • Cost effective, affordability Coherence sequences	• Goals and objectives • Forms of benefits or services delivered • Entitlement (eligibility) rules • Administrative or organizational structure for service delivery • Financing method • Interactions among the preceding elements	• Identifying, understanding, or clarifying the problem • Identifying the location for policy decisions • Specifying possible solutions (alternatives) • Estimating or predicting the impact (outcomes) of those solutions on different populations	• Identify the issue • Analyze what exists • Determine what should be • Decide what is possible

inger (2004).

Flynn (1992)

Policy and Social Problem

Milestones in Policy Processes
- Legitimacy
- Action-system
- Key participants

Interest Group Relationships
- Power and influence
- Salience of issue
- Intergroup activities

Process Resources
- people power
- Technology
- Finances
- Time

Congruence with Desired Values

Recommendations

...senting problem
...ng a policy remedy that will
effectively address the problem
- Convincing other persons to accept
the recommendations

...nterest

...ns
...od research or practical
...suggests that the policy is both
...able" and effective?
- Is the policy efficient?
- What consequences can be reasonably
anticipated if an organization or government adopts a new policy?

Latent ... Popple and Leigh

Model Focus: Evaluation

DiNitto (2003)	McInnis-Dittrich (1994)	Iatridis (1994)	Barusch (2002)
Consideration of Design • Is the problem correctly conceptualized? • What is the extent of the problem, and where is the target population? Does the program design fit with the objectives? • Is there an underlying coherent rationale? • Are there efforts to maximize the chances of success of the provision? • What are the real or projected costs? • What is the benefit, as related to the costs? **Considerations Related to Monitoring** • Does the service reach the population targeted? • Is the program being delivered as it was designed? **Considerations Related to Program Utility** • Is the program reaching its goals? • Is something other than the program causing the positive results? • How much does it cost, and how much does it benefit the recipients? • Is this program the most efficient alternative?	Approach—a brief description of the methods used in the current or proposed policy Need—What need does the policy attempt to address? Assessment—What are the program's or policy's strengths and weaknesses? Logic—Does the proposed or current policy logically address the connection between the need and a means of solving the problem? Your reaction—From your professional experience, does the policy seem effective? Support—What is the financial support for the program? Innovation—What provisions have been made for changing the program if necessary? Social justice—Does the program address the important issue of social justice as expressed by society and the social work profession?	S—Sociopolitical environment C—Causes I—Intervention approaches E—Establish and rank recommendations N—Narrative C—Characteristics E—Evaluation	• What are the costs and/or benefits under consideration? • Who bears the costs, who receives the benefits, and what is the relationship between these two entities? • Is anyone who is affected by this policy being labeled "other," and does everyone affected by this policy have an equal voice? • What are the rules, both formal and informal, that govern who receives and who pays? • Is the policy fair?

Hybrid Models

Karger & Stoesz (2002)

Historical background of the policy

Problems that created the need for the policy

Descriptions of the policy

Analysis of the policy
• Goals
• Feasibility (political, economic, administrative)

Wharf & McKenzie (1998)

Problem Identification and Goal Specification
• Problem description, nature, and scope
• Assessment of needs and strengths
• Causal factors, assumptions, theories, and historical evaluation
• Targets for change and goals
• Key interest groups and their power and influence

Identification of Value Criteria
• Adequacy, effectiveness, efficiency, impact on rights, social justice, and special lens evaluations

Assessment of Alternatives
• Consider policy alternatives, and collect data to assess alternatives

Feasibility Assessment
• Legality of policy
• Resources
• Public and political support
• Logic of policy

Recommendations

Popple & Leighninger (2004)

Description and overview of policy and problem
• Description of policy
• Nature of problem policy targets
• Context of policy
• Analysis of choice elements and policy alternatives

Historical analysis
• Analysis of previous policies and programs enacted
• Analysis of how the policy/program responses evolved over time
• Assessment of past approaches
• Assessment of the extent to which the current policy response has incorporated past "lessons learned"

Social analysis
• Description of problem (detailed)
• Description of theoretical explanations implicit and explicit in policy
• Value assessment

Economic analysis
• Description of goals (stated, unstated)
• Explanations for the link between the problem and goals
• Macroeconomic analysis—potential effects on economy
• Microeconomic analysis—potential effects on behavior
• Cost/benefit analysis

Political analysis
• Analysis of major stakeholders
• Assessment of policy legitimacy
• Assessment of rational, incremental, or conflict change
• Assessment of implementations

Policy or program evaluation
• Evaluation of policy/program outcomes
• Analysis of unintended consequences
• Analysis of cost effectiveness

Recommended changes

Many organizations do not lobby directly but, instead, organize specialized subsidiary groups that have lobbying as a primary purpose. In the same way organizations that lobby often cannot make contributions to political candidates, corporations cannot make political contributions either. Therefore, there are many PACs that have the solicitation and distribution of political contributions as their primary purpose. Such organizations collect money from the members of the specialized group. They have boards of directors that determine how the contributions they collect are distributed to candidates. PACs are important in influencing elections and, in fact, in the legislative process. Legislative and executive branch members who receive funds from PACs are assumed to be more likely than others to support legislation favored by the organizations or industries that have supported them financially.

On the far end of the spectrum from simply voting, human services workers may serve as elected officials. Many social workers are currently serving as elected officials at the federal, state, county, and city level. Many others have been elected to school boards. As noted in table 19, there are a total of 174 social workers serving in elected offices across the country. In addition, currently six social workers serve in the U.S. Congress, including two senators and four representatives. Senator Barbara Mikulski was elected to the Senate in 1986 and is the third highest-ranking member of the Democratic Leadership within the Senate. She also serves as the dean of Senate women. Elected in 2000, Senator Debbie Stabenow became the first woman from Michigan elected to the U.S. Senate.

Table 19. Examples of E-mail Alert Lists

AARP Citizen Advocate Registration	http://www.capitolconnect.com/aarp/recruitment/Registration.asp
OMB Watch	http://www.ombwatch.org/article/articlesttic/11/1/7/
National Health Council Advocacy Page	http://www.nationalhealthcouncil.org/advocacy/adv index.htm
American Association of Geriatric Psychiatrists' Action Alerts, Legislative Action Center	http://www.aagponline.org/advocacy/default.asp
American Association of Housing and Services for the Aging, Advocacy and News Alerts	http://www.aahsa.org/
Friday Alerts from the Alliance for Retired Americans	http://www.retiredamericans.org/fridayalerts.htm
Children's Defense Fund Action Council	http://www.cdfactioncouncil.org/

Table 19 (*continued*)

Human Rights Campaign Action Center	http://www.hrcactioncenter.org/actioncenter/join.html
Sierra Club	http://www.sierraclub.org/email/
Annie E. Casey Foundation E-mail Newsletters	http://www.aecf.org/lists/
American Federation of Teachers	http://capwiz.com/amft/issues/?style=D
National Education Association—Legislative Action Center	http://www.nea.org/lac/index.html
Center for Budget and Policy Priorities—Alerts	http://www.cbpp.org/alerts.htm

Table 20. Examples of Some Policy Think Tanks

Alliance Defense Fund	http://www.alliancedefensefund.org/
American Association of Retired People	http://www.aarp.org/
Annie E. Casey Foundation	http://www.aecf.org/
Benton Foundation	http://www.benton.org
Brookings Institution	http://www.brook.edu
Cato Institute	http://www.cato.org
Center for Budget and Policy Priorities	http://www.cbpp.org
Center for National Policy	http://ncpa.org
Child Trends	http://www.childtrends.org
Child Welfare League of America	http://www.cwla.org/
Children's Defense Fund	http://www.childrensdefense.org/
Heritage Foundation	http://www.heritage.org/
Institute for Policy Studies	http://www.pps-dc.org/
Kaiser Family Foundation	http://www.kff.org
National Center for Children in Poverty	http://www.cpmnet.columbia.edu/dept/nccp
National Center for Policy Analysis	http://www.ncpa.org
National Health Care Council	http://www.nationalhealthcouncil.org/
Urban Institute	http://www.urban.org
Welfare Information Network	http://financeprojectinfo.org/win/

Obviously elected officials have significant power to influence social welfare policy. They may draft legislation and participate on legislative committees.

Cause or Class Advocacy

Of course, human services workers may also become political activists, a role that is at times, more adversarial to the government. Political activists may engage in lobbying and organizing coalitions and more direct actions such as protest marches or civil disobedience. (For information about civil obedience please visit http://www.actupny.org/documents/CDdocuments/CDindex .html.) Some argue that political activism is the role most congruent with the social work profession and that social work, in its desire for professionalism, has abandoned a more radical approach to practice social change (Gil, 1998). They argue that human services workers have become a part of a system that serves to regulate and control oppressed people (Piven & Cloward, 1994; Abramovitz, 1988, Reisch & Andrews, 2001; Specht & Courtney, 1994). Further, they suggest that as opposed to advocating for change of the broader social structures, human services workers have become a part of those structures. Obviously most human services workers do not arrive at work with a desire to regulate and oppress people; most have a sincere desire to assist people. What is critical, however, is that human services workers remain knowledgeable about and aware of the systems in which they work and are ever vigilant about current or potential changes in policies that impact both their clients and the work they do on a daily basis. As Jansson (2003) says, "Social workers are even more morally deficient than other professionals if they do not engage in policy-sensitive and policy-related practice, because they occupy a unique position in the human services system" (Jansson, 2003, 36).

Cause, or class advocacy, involves the presentation of the cause of a client(s) (Pierce, 2000; Schneider & Lester, 2001) and "consists of those purposive efforts to change specific existing or proposed policies or practices on behalf of or with a specific client or group of clients" (Ezell, 2001, 23). Historically and contemporaneously, political activism and cause advocacy has been and can be an effective means of social change, and many human services workers have been a part of such efforts. In the late 1960s and early 1970s, the National Welfare Rights Organization (NWRO), founded by George Wiley, organized thousands of welfare recipients to advocate for social justice (Kotz & Kotz, 1977). What was notable about the NWRO was that it transcended racial, class, and gender concerns to form coalitions that advocated for broader social change and a more responsive welfare system. The notion of collectivity and entitlement served to thwart the stigma of utilizing public welfare services and, in fact, demanded fair and humane treatment for the individuals using such services. As Toney (2000) notes, "NWRO's impact extended far beyond money and legal rights. By asserting that the right to welfare is akin to a civil right, and that women and poor people deserve to be treated with dignity and respect, NWRO was the first movement to create a distinct political identity among poor black women" (Toney, 2).

Cause advocacy has merit, and the recent and emerging interest in developing social and human capital as well as community and economic development is reminiscent of the work of advocacy organizations in the past. Social capital refers to the relationships individuals have with one another that help them along in life. Human capital includes personal characteristics of an individual that enables him/her to participate productively in society. Currently one will find human services workers volunteering for or working for activist organizations such as the Human Rights Campaign (HRC), Amnesty International, The Sierra Club, National Organization for Women (NOW), Association of Community Organizations for Reform Now (ACORN), or Act-Up. Act-Up is an organization that advocates for people who have AIDS by conducting direct actions and demonstrations. The Sierra Club is a grassroots environmental organization, NOW advocates for the rights of women, and HRC advocates for equal rights for gay, lesbian, bisexual, and transgendered individuals. And finally, ACORN advocates on behalf of low and moderate income families. Table 23 lists a few examples of activist organizations; however, there are many such organizations that are involved in a wide variety of topics and issues that are not included on this list. In addition, the Advocacy Institute (http://www.advocacy.org/) has many resources, publications, tools, and information on advocacy skills.

Table 21. Number of Social Workers Serving as Elected Officials, 2003

	Total
U.S. Congress	6
State Legislature	44
County or Borough	17
City or Municipality	62
School Board	35
Other	10
Total	**174**

Source: Data from the National Association of Social Workers (2003), http://www.socialworkers.org.

Activist organizations and the human services workers within those organizations engage in capacity building primarily through public education, lobbying, and organizing. Sometimes, as in the case of the American Civil Liberties Union (ACLU) or the Southern Poverty Law Center (SPLC), litigation is used to work on issues related to civil rights and social justice. For example, the Southern Poverty Law Center uses law suits in an attempt to thwart the efforts of or shut down supremacist organizations and to promote social justice. In 1979, for example, a case was filed against the YMCA in

Montgomery, Alabama, that refused to allow two African-American children to attend one of their summer camps. In the early 1980s SPLC filed a suit that protected Vietnamese fisherman in Texas from members of the Texas KKK threatening them and burning their boats. Further, as recently as 2000 the SPLC worked on a case to improve the health care provided to inmates with mental illness in Alabama. For more information about the work of the SPLC and ACLU as well as obtain more detail about specific legal cases, visit the Web sites listed in the table above.

Administrative Advocacy

Sometimes agency policies do not serve human services workers or their clients well. In such cases administrative advocacy, which involves the promotion of change from within, may be called for. Such advocacy allows for changing or addressing agency regulations that harm or otherwise do not serve clients (Schneider & Lester, 2001). Pierce (2000) refers to this type of advocacy as organizational policy making. Sometimes human services workers find themselves working in environments where there is a preoccupation with the direct service role and in situations where employees are discouraged from conducting advocacy (Jansson, 2003).

Administrators in such agencies may be stereotyped as conservative, uncaring bureaucrats who are out of touch with the lives of the clients and the jobs of the frontline workers. However, some administrators and long-term employees make changes through their work. In particular, a strong administrator can make many vital changes to policies. Some of the reticence on the part of administrators, especially those in federal and state agencies, may be related to the Hatch Act. The Hatch Act limits and regulates the political activities in state federal and nonprofit agencies (Haynes & Mickelson, 2003). However, the Hatch Act is primarily related to partisan political activities, usually not lobbying or advocacy, so some of the reticence may be a misperception or misinterpretation of this law (Haynes & Mickelson, 2003). Another issue has to do with not acting in conflict with agency boards or superiors. If an agency has a particular position, it is not easy to oppose that position.

The skills associated with administrative advocacy can be varied but include tasks such as changing or modifying the mission, goals, and programs of an agency, taking advantage of changes in leadership within an agency to advocate for change, taking or initiating leadership positions within the agency, working the governing boards, creating or modifying internal advocacy programs or policies, and mobilizing or organizing a protest (Jansson, 2003; Schneider & Lester, 2001). Skills and strategies for administrative advocacy should involve the inclusion of clients in inputs about agency policy including organizational decision making when possible. Often misinformation about access to and eligibility for social welfare programs services serves to isolate and stigmatize the recipients of such services. The use of activism to counter such misinformation can be a galvanizing event, as the saying there are "strengths in numbers" goes. Further, human services workers who are open to researching the effectiveness of themselves as practitioners, as well as the programs in which they work, ultimately make themselves more account-able to the clients they serve. Informing clients of policy changes that impact their services and benefits—and legislation currently being debated—can also be a form of administrative advocacy. Providing clients with information about how to appeal unfavorable decisions and file complaints and who to contact is also a form of advocacy. Jansson (2003) notes that "the ethical social worker has to engage in brokering, liaison and case advocacy to help . . . rather than limiting self to narrow clinical services" (36). For some human services workers, policy sensitive practice is to practice with a general sense of the possibility that, at times, clients encounter negative consequences related to the nature of policies and that, on occasion, may need assistance (Jansson, 2003). Policy practice, when approached from a strengths or empowerment perspective, particular within agencies, can often best serve clients. If human services workers find themselves working within agencies that function well and clients are well served, then they can continue to provide those services. Just knowing that as a human services worker one can be an advocate when needed is empowering to both the worker and the client (Flynn, 1992) and "if providers and receivers of human services apply and analyze the substan-tive content of policies affecting them of those whom they represent, they are empowered" (Flynn, 1992, 1).

Client Advocacy

Client advocacy is "built on the philosophy that seeks to protect, enforce, and ensure clients' rights, entitlements, resources, services and benefits" (Schnei-der & Lester, 2001, 152). Many of the strategies as described in administra-tive advocacy can also be used when advocating for individual clients. As previously discussed, the recipients of public social welfare services, such as TANF recipients, are often vulnerable. Many times they are misinformed or uninformed about the services they may qualify for and frequently have their rights violated. Client advocacy involves assisting clients to gain access to the services to which they are entitled and informing them of their rights and other services for which they may be qualified. Client advocacy may also involve changing programs to be more responsive to the needs of recipients. Human services workers can use a variety of empowerment-based skills to assist clients to learn to advocate for themselves. Sometimes the human ser-vices worker may advocate on the behalf of clients. The Guardian Ad Litem program, for example, which operates in many states, provides advocacy serv-ices to children who are part of the court system due to alleged abuse and neglect. Part of the responsibility of a Guardian Ad Litem is to ensure that

302

the services entitled or mandated to children and families are carried out. The Guardian Ad Litem also monitors all relevant events in the care of children, and the advocacy effort is rooted what is in the best interest of the child. The Children's Aid Society located in New York has an Office of Public Policy and Client Advocacy that provides legal advocacy to children and their families. For more information about their work, visit their Web site available at http://www.childrensaidsociety.org/legaladvocacy/opopca/. Sometimes encouraging clients to testify on behalf of themselves is an important policy practice skill and is often very empowering to clients. Personal experiences may even be more effective at persuading policy makers than expert testimony in some cases (McInnis-Dittrich, 1994).

Empowerment through Public Policy Education

Human services workers through public policy education can use the information and knowledge they have attained from practice to inform society on key issues. This type of practice emerged from the "Citizen social worker model" during the 1950s (Haynes & Mikelson, 2003). Skills related to this type of practice might include consultation to clients, agencies, or other professionals, teaching, or the provision of expert testimony or knowledge (Haynes & Mickelson, 2003).

Electronic Advocacy

As the use of computers has expanded by both the public and the government alike, new advocacy tools and avenues for advocacy have emerged. "Electronic advocacy refers to the use of high technology to influence the decision making process, or to the use of technology in an effort to support policy-change efforts" (Hick & McNutt, 2002, 8). Some tools of technology are already quite familiar to many and are referred to as "traditional electronic advocacy" and include the use of television, radio, and fax alerts to influence policy (Fitzgerald & McNutt, 1999). In contrast, emergent electronic advocacy refers specifically to the utilization of Web-based technologies to influence policy. This may include the use of E-mail, online research, surveys, petitions or polls, or creating online dialogue on policy issues through discussion groups, chat rooms, and list services. In many states it is now possible to submit testimony electronically, and more policy information is available online than ever before. Whether it is called electronic advocacy or one of its many other names (NetActivism, e-advocacy, cyberactivism) this area of practice has certainly emerged as a significant and important element of policy practice. As Hick and McNutt (2002) note, "the development of information and communications technology (ICT) has vastly transformed the capacity of social work agencies, community organizations, social movements, and groups of concerned people to build coalitions and networks and to advocate for causes, principles, and other people" (4).

Legislative Advocacy

Another significant task in the practice of social policy is influencing legislation or, as it is often called in the United States, lobbying (which is also discussed in chapter 4). The job of the lobbyist is to work for the passage of legislation that is favorable to the organization that person is representing. Most of the national social welfare organizations have legislative representatives, many of them in Washington, whose job is to influence the U.S. Congress; other legislative representatives work in the states, where they influence state legislation. Such familiar organizations as the National Association of Social Workers, the American Public Human Services Association, the Child Welfare League of America, and similar groups have Washington representatives or legislative specialists who are, in fact, lobbyists. J. Figueira-McDonough (1993) points out that several social work scholars have proposed that all social workers be educated in lobbying and has also written about ways in which lobbying itself might be taught in social work curricula. In fact, many social workers and other human services workers are employed as lobbyists for voluntary and governmental organizations.

Lobbying involves the promotion of opposition of pending legislation or changes to legislation. When one lobbies, he or she is usually promoting a viewpoint on specific legislation. Lobbying can occur directly or more indirectly through grassroots organization (Smucker, 1999). Direct lobbying involves making direct appeals to policy makers. This could include testifying on a particular bill, public speaking, negotiation, and compromising with legislators. Grassroots organization involves mobilizing larger groups of people and public interest in an issue and might include, for example, coalition building, organization of protests, and mobilization efforts on behalf of a policy issue (Smucker, 1999). Since legislative advocacy often involves lobbying and testimony, skills related to the preparation, composition, and delivery of arguments on behalf an issue are important to this area of policy practice (Barusch, 2002; Jansson, 2003; Schneider & Lester, 2001). An important element of developing sound arguments and preparing for testimony involves a thorough understanding of opposing ideologies and arguments (Barusch, 2002; Jansson, 2003). Barusch (2002) refers to this as "perspective-taking," where one considers the issue from a perspective different from one's own. Developing a receiver profile involves consideration of counterarguments so that one can "speak to the audience" and is a part of this process. Many authors provide rules for and examples of how to provide testimony and written documents (Jansson, 2003; Schneider & Lester, 2001).

Sometimes practitioners must decide on the best strategy to take to engage in policy advocacy. Schneider and Lester (2001) suggest three strategies: collaborative, campaign, and contest. The first step in determining what strategy to use is to determine what kind of groups must be convinced to support your plan. One such group might consist of people who are simply in need of information, that already share values, and are likely to agree with your proposal if they obtain additional information. The second group might be neutral and consist of individuals who need additional information and probably a bit more convincing to agree with your policy plan. The final group, are those clearly opposed to your plan. After you place your opponents in one of these three categories, you can then match the group type with a strategy best suited to work with that group of people. Figure 5 illustrates this process.

Figure 5. Electing Advocacy Strategy (adapted from Schneider & Lester, 2001)

Collaborative strategies are best used when opposition to the issue is low and consists primarily of information sharing, problem solving, and negotiation of changes and solutions to the problem. In collaborative strategies the risk to the human services worker is low. Campaign strategies are utilized when there is medium to high opposition with groups who do not necessarily share the ideals and values of your solution. Such a strategy relies a bit more on persuasion, utilizing facts and briefing papers to convince, education, and catering to self-interests of the opposing side. The risk to the social worker in such a strategy is medium to low. The final strategy, contest, is utilized when the opposition to your plan is highly oppositional, nonsupportive, and at times openly hostile. In such cases, the plan becomes to attempt to change behavior (votes, support on an issue) as opposed to beliefs. Obviously this strategy is more adversarial, confrontational, and sometimes involves forcing those opposed to comply with what is desired. In such approaches the risk to the human services worker is higher.

As discussed in chapter 4, lobbying is a normal, perhaps necessary, part of public policy making in the United States. For some, lobbying has a reputation as a sort of sinister practice involving people who pursue special interests in not quite legitimate ways. Some people believe that lobbyists use bribery and other kinds of inappropriate influences to win their organizations' objections.

Although it is true that lobbying is always about the pursuit of specialized interests, the use of inappropriate lobbying techniques or bribery is unusual. It is not well understood in American life that special interests include a range of concerns and that not all of them are selfish. In fact, all lobbyists pursue their objectives from some sort of idealistic point of view. Most organizations sincerely believe in their purposes and pursue their legislative objectives hoping the result will be beneficial to the people they represent. The National Rifle Association, whose activities many in the social services community would consider in negative terms, believes it is pursuing an important social goal by making it possible for citizens to purchase and own weapons for personal defense, sports, and hunting with a minimum of governmental interference. The defense industry, too, believes in its efforts to protect the American people from foreign enemies. The tobacco industry believes that its lobbying preserves the rights of tobacco users as well as the economic well-being of tobacco farmers and tobacco product manufacturers. So all lobbyists, including those who pursue social welfare goals, view themselves as pursuing worthy goals on behalf of citizens.

Most Americans are members of organizations that lobby, although they may not know it. Churches, the American Automobile Association, conservation groups, professional and trade associations, and most other large national organizations lobby. Being able to join organizations and help them finance their lobbying is a basic right having to do with free speech and freedom of association.

Methods of Lobbying. The methods and techniques used by lobbyists are not as self-serving or pecuniary as is often supposed. Many times the primary task of the lobbyist is to draft or analyze legislation so that lawmakers can best introduce it or to explain legislation that has been proposed by others. Much of the legislation that is ultimately passed in the United States, in both

Congress and state legislatures, is originally drafted by lobbyists. The lobbyists for the American Association of Retired Persons (AARP), for example, propose specific changes in Social Security that would benefit older adults. That legislation is received by members of Congress who are interested in Social Security legislation and who, in turn, incorporate the AARP ideas into bills that are introduced into Congress. Often the member of Congress or a committee of Congress will modify the bill that has been drafted by the lobbyist, but, in some cases, the bill is introduced, acted upon, and made law without many changes at all.

In other circumstances, lobbyists testify before legislative committees on the impact of a given policy proposal or law. Often, because of his or her deep involvement in the specific area, the lobbyist has more detailed information on the consequences of a piece of legislation than do the members of Congress or others who must act on the legislation.

In other cases lobbyists mobilize support for or opposition to a piece of legislation that involves their organization's interests. They do so by asking their members to telephone, telegraph, and write to their representatives in Congress or the state legislatures opposing legislation that could be detrimental to their organization's interests or in support of legislation that pursues those interests.

Lobbyists have other methods, including those that win support from legislators, such as inviting legislators for meals and receptions, helping to obtain campaign support for legislators who are facing re-election campaigns, and inviting legislators to speak at organizational conferences, which may help them gain votes and may also earn them honoraria. Many groups also sponsor receptions and banquets to which legislators are invited. These are methods commonly used by lobbyists, including those who represent social welfare organizations.

Special interest groups for which lobbyists work are not always private organizations, and not all lobbyists are representatives of nonprofit associations of people with legislative concerns. Although they are not usually called lobbyists, the executive branch agencies also have employees who carry out extensive lobbying activities. Every department of government at the federal or state level has an interest in the activities of legislatures. In fact, their interests may be greater in some cases than those of any voluntary association or organization. Federal executive branch agencies have official designated legislative liaisons who are, in many ways, lobbyists. Their full-time job is to answer questions from legislative bodies, testify to their legislative committees, and pursue the legislative objectives of their agencies. Many state government executive branch agencies have similar personnel with similar responsibilities. The programs, budget, and even the survival of executive branch agencies depend, in large measure, on their ability to influence their legislative bodies. Therefore, most agencies actively press for their points of view and their programs.

It is important to point out, parenthetically, that the use of the general term *lobbyist* and the legal definition of a lobbyist may differ. Most legislatures do not define executive branch personnel as lobbyists and do not require them to register as such, which they do require of private organization lobbyists.

As suggested, most of the lobbying in the United States is carried on by voluntary associations representing specific interests or activities. There are public policies dealing with how extensive lobbying activities may be. There are also public policies dealing with the tax status of organizations that lobby. Whether or not an organization lobbies has some impact on its tax-exempt status. For example, a tax-exempt voluntary national human services organization is limited in the amount of its resources it may use for lobbying purposes.

Lobbying the Executive Branch. Not all lobbying is carried on in the legislative branch of government. In fact, some observers think that the most effective kind of lobbying takes place within the executive branch instead. The executive branch has great influence over the legislation that is ultimately passed by legislative bodies, their primary influence being in the kinds of legislation they propose. Much of the legislation that is ultimately passed by these bodies originates in the executive branch. Therefore, the priorities and specific policies of the executive branch greatly influence what is ultimately passed. Lobbyists who want to have an impact on legislation often start by attempting to influence the executive branch proposals that are made to legislatures. The weight of the opinion of the executive branch agency has great significance for any legislative body, as does the work of the executive branch lobbyists, who are often consulted by the legislative bodies and their committees.

Persuading the executive branch agency to propose or support the legislative priorities of an interest group is often the most useful expenditure of that group's time and resources. If the group can persuade the commissioner, director, any chief executive office, or any others with the ability to influence the organization's policy to support the organization's priorities, they may accomplish what they want much more readily than if they tried to influence the legislature directly. Such lobbying activities are not always difficult; in many cases the interest group's and the executive branch agency's priorities may coincide. It is also not unusual for a lobbying group to prepare legislation for an executive branch agency to modify and introduce as its own contribution to solving a social problem.

Policy Interpretation

There is another role in which policy practitioners function, and that is as interpreters of policies that already exist. Most large human services organizations, especially those that are connected with government, employ full-time units that answer policy questions for workers in the field. In programs such as TANF and Medicaid, for example, which have very complicated rules that may not clearly cover every possible situation, policy experts are available to answer questions from workers about the applicability of certain policies. How much of the income of all the family members has to be considered as part of the resources available to a family applying for family assistance? How does one determine the actual value of a collection of guns, which might be considered a resource in calculating eligibility? What are the employment requirements for a mother with a child who is chronically ill and whose family is receiving TANF? Questions such as these are asked and answered every day in public social services agencies and in large voluntary agencies as well. Many human services professionals practice their professions as policy experts. Because TANF is different in each state, the roles of public agency employees in developing and interpreting regulations are more important than ever. The federal rules have largely been dropped, so the states must fill in the gaps with their own clear and legal rules and regulations.

Policy units in large public agencies also analyze and evaluate legislation as it develops. Typically, during a legislative session, or even between sessions, when bills are being proposed for introduction, the policy unit of the department analyzes how much the bill will cost, what impact it will have on other services, and how it might be implemented by the agency. It also makes suggestions about the reactions of the agency to the legislation, sometimes going so far as to "oppose" or "support" bills, an action that does not fit most agencies, in which the chief executive officer is appointed by the governor. By definition, the agency supports the governor's program, whatever that program happens to be, even if the staff or the leadership of the agency might generally support or oppose the legislation. In other situations, in which the agency is controlled by a commission and is not directly under gubernatorial authority, the agency may be freer to take specific policy positions on legislation.

Jansson (2003) refers to policy interpretation as "trouble shooting," where practitioners work with existing programs in an attempt to improve them or to suggest changes as needed. Haynes and Mickelson (2003) refer to this area of policy practice as "monitoring the bureaucracy," where practitioners keep abreast of new program and policy regulations and respond to calls for input and making sure the policy works as intended.

Implementing Legislation

Often the most important element of the practice of social policy is the implementation of policies by executive branch agencies. Again, there are thousands of human services workers around the country whose job it is to translate legislation into operational rules and regulations for the executive branch agencies that employ them.

Legislation is often not extensively detailed or concrete and, therefore, cannot easily be used to implement a policy or carry out a program. The legislation may be broad in scope and only suggestive of specific activities in which executive agencies will engage, though this is not always true. Some legislation is highly specific and detailed and, therefore, is easier to implement.

For the most part, legislation, to be implemented, needs at least some fine-tuning and often much hard work, and this requires policy specialists in executive branch agencies. Assume, for example, that a legislative body has passed a statute that deals with the requirement to provide services such as food and shelter to the homeless. How will the program be operated? If voluntary organizations are to receive contracts from the government to provide such services, what organizations are eligible? How will they be paid? Who will handle their payments? What kinds of statistics will they keep, and what forms will they use for keeping these statistics? What health and safety standards will shelters be required to maintain if they are to receive public funds for caring for the homeless? These are only some of the issues that would arise out of the passage of such legislation.

As B. S. Jansson (1990, 380) says, "Enacted policies are merely paper directives, that is, abstract guidelines and objectives that reflect the preferences of the framers of policies, who have often balanced value, political, and analytic consideration when constructing them." Thus, the implementation stage of policy-making process is a highly dynamic process that involves several levels of government, administrators (high and mid-level), direct practitioners, and clients (Jansson, 2003; DiNitto, 2003).

Oversight agencies, or agencies that monitor policy implementation, can sometimes provide a pivotal role in implementation. Unfortunately, however, oversight agencies that do not provide technical assistance to agencies leave some agencies "hanging in the wind" without the necessary support to assist them with compliance (Jansson, 2003; DiNitto, 2003). Some authors suggest several strategies for intervening in or reforming the policy implementation process (Schneider & Lester, 2001; Jansson, 2003; Flynn, 1992).

Conclusion

This chapter has shown the ways in which social policy is more than a single subject of study. It is a whole field of human services practice—what some human services workers do as their primary employment.

310

Policy practice will likely continue to expand as a field because of the growing importance of policy in the creation and delivery of human services. The practice roles for human services workers in policy range from simple tasks of explaining to coworkers what policy means to drafting new policies. It is likely that in the future, increasing numbers of those employed in the areas of social services and human services will be policy practitioners.

Discussion Questions

1. What state or federal policies affect the work conducted in an agency where you have worked or are currently working? Do these policies all seem reasonable, and if not, how are they not working and how might you consider changing them?

2. Consider a time when you encountered unfair practices or treatment of individuals. Consider some of the possibilities for doing something about those practices as discussed in this chapter. Which would be the most effective? Why?

3. Visit Project Vote Smart (http://www.vote-smart.org/) and find the quiz "Who represents me?" and fill it out. After taking the quiz explore the voting records and issues of your representations. Did you know all of your representatives? Were you aware of their stance on issues that are important to you professionally and personally? Is this important knowledge for you on a personal level? Professional level?

4. Work on developing a "receiver profile" as Barusch (2002) notes. Consider an issue that is important to you and consider all of the counterarguments to your argument. Does this help you consider your issue from a different perspective and would this change the way you approach testimony on that issue?

5. Visit the Center for Medicare and Medicaid Services (CMS). What is your opinion about their abilities as an oversight organization? Can you get statistics there that evaluate the effectiveness of any policies that they oversee? Is there information available regarding compliance and implementation of their policies?

References

Abramovitz, M. (1988). *Regulating the lives of women.* Boston: South End Press.

Abramovitz, M., & Bardill, D. (1993). Should all social work students be educated for social change? *Journal of Social Work Education* 29 (1), 6–18.

Amidei, N. (1991). *So you want to make a difference: Advocacy is the key.* Washington, DC: OMB Watch.

Barusch, A. S. (2002). *Foundations of social policy: Social justice, public programs, and the social work profession.* Itasca, IL: F. E. Peacock Publishers.

DiNitto, D. (2003). *Social welfare: Politics and public policy,* 5th ed. Boston: Allyn & Bacon.

Einbinder, S. D. (1995). Policy analysis. In R. R. Edwards et al. (Eds.), *Encyclopedia of social work,* 19th ed., 1849–1855. Washington, DC: NASW Press.

Ezell, M. (1991). The political activity of social workers: A post Reagan update. *Journal of Sociology and Social Welfare* 20, 81–97.

Ezell, M. (2001). *Advocacy in the human services.* Belmont, CA: Brooks/Cole.

Figueira-McDonough, J. (March 1993). Policy-practice: The neglected side of social work intervention. *Social Work* 38 (2), 179–188.

Fitzgerald, E., & McNutt, J. (1999). Electronic advocacy in policy practice: A framework for teaching technologically based practice. *Journal of Social Work Education* 35 (3), 331–341.

Freire, P. (1999). A critical understanding of social work. *Journal of Progressive Human Services* 1, 3–9.

Gil, D. (1998). *Confronting injustice and oppression: Concepts and strategies for social workers.* New York: Columbia University Press.

Haynes, S. K., & Mickelson, S. J. (2003). *Affecting change,* 5th ed. Boston: Allyn & Bacon.

Hick, F. S., & McNutt, G. J. (Eds.). (2002). *Advocacy, activism, and the Internet: Community organization and social policy.* Chicago: Lyceum Books.

Iatridis, D. (1995). Policy practice. In R. L. Edwards et al. (Eds.), *Encyclopedia of social work,* 19th ed., 1855–1866. Washington, DC: NASW Press.

Jansson, B. S. (1994). *Social welfare policy: From theory to practice,* 2nd ed. Belmont, CA: Wadsworth.

Jansson, B. S. (1999). *Becoming an effective policy advocate: From policy practice to social justice,* 3rd ed. Pacific Grove, CA: Brooks-Cole.

Jansson, B. S. (2003). *Becoming an effective policy advocate: From policy practice to social justice,* 4th ed. Belmont, CA: Brooks/Cole.

Jenkins-Smith, H. C., & Sabatier, P. S. (1993). The study of public policy processes. In P. A. Sabatier & H. C. Jenkins-Smith (Eds.), *Policy change and learning: An advocacy collation approach,* 1–9. Boulder, CO: Westview Press.

Kahn, A. J. (1993). *Issues in American social policy: The substantive and research challenges for social work doctoral education.* Paper presented at Group for the Advancement of Doctoral Education Annual Conference, St. Louis, MO.

Kotz, N. & Kotz, M. (1977). *A passion for equality.* New York: Norton.

McCormick, M. (1970). Social advocacy: A new dimension in social work. *Social Casework* 51, 3–11.

McInnis-Dittrich, K. (1994). *Integrating social welfare policy and social work practice.* Belmont, CA: Wadsworth.

Pierce, D. (2000). Policy Practice. In J. Midgley, M.B. Tracy, M. Livermore (Eds.), *The handbook of social policy,* 53–63. Thousand Oaks, CA: Sage.

Piven, F. F., & Cloward, R. (1975). Notes toward a radical social work. In R. Bailey & M. Brake (Eds.), *Radical social work,* vii–xlviii. New York: Pantheon.

Piven, F. F., & Cloward, R. A. (1994). *Regulating the poor: The functions of public welfare.* New York: Pantheon.

Reisch, M., & Andrews, J. (2001). *The road not taken: A history of radical social work in the United States.* Philadelphia: Brunner-Routledge.

Sarri, R., & Meyer, C. (1992). Is social work inherently conservative—designed to protect vested interests of dominant power groups? In E. Gambrill & R. Pruger (Eds.), *Controversial issues in social work,* 39–51. Boston: Allyn & Bacon.

Schneider, L. R., & Lester, L. (2001). *Social work advocacy: A new framework for action.* Belmont, CA: Brooks/Cole.

Schneider, R., & Netting, F. (1999). Influencing social policy in a time of devolution: Upholding social work's great tradition. *Social Work* 44 (4), 349–357.

Smucker, R. (1999). *The nonprofit lobbying guide,* 2nd ed. Washington, DC: Independent Sector.

Specht, H., & Courtney, M. (1994). *Unfaithful angels: How social work has abandoned its mission.* New York: Free Press.

Toney, M. (2000). Revisiting the National Welfare Rights Organization. *Color Lines* 3 (3), [Electronic version]. http://www.arc.org/C_Lines/CLArchive/story3_3_09 .html (accessed February 12, 2004).

Tropman, J. E. (1987). Policy analysis: Methods and techniques. In A. Minahan et al. (Eds.), *Encyclopedia of social work,* 18th ed., 268–284. Silver Spring, MD: NASW Press.

Wagner, D. (1990). *The quest for a radical profession: Social service careers and political ideology.* Lanham, MD: University Press of America.

Wharf, B., & McKenzie, B. (1998). *Connecting policy to practice in the human services.* New York: Oxford Press.

Wyers, N. (1991). Policy-practice in social work: Models and issues. *Journal of Social Work Education* 27(3), 241–250.

APPENDIX

A Comparison of the Aid to Families with Dependent Children and Temporary Assistance to Needy Families Programs

The following summary was prepared by the American Public Welfare Association (now the American Public Human Services Association), National Conference of State Legislature, and the National Governor's Association in September 1996. It compares the Aid to Families with Dependent Children (AFDC) program to the Temporary Assistance to Needy Families (TANF) program that replaced it in 1997 under the provisions of the Personal Responsibility and Work Opportunity Reconciliation Act of 1996.

Some provisions were changed in 1997. For example, Title IV, which restricts welfare and public benefits for aliens, was modified so that noncitizens who were living in the United States on August 22, 1996, the day the bill became law, were restored to eligibility for benefits under the 1997 Balanced Budget Act. Under the Title VIII food stamp provisions, the law originally barred food stamp assistance to able-bodied adults who had no dependent children after three months every three years if they were not employed or in a work or training program.

This summary shows the details that go into social welfare policy and the extent of the changes that were made in almost every element of the federal public assistance and social service programs. The complexity also shows the importance of executive implementation of statutes and the wide latitude that may be exercised in dealing with the day-to-day meaning of complicated legal and programmatic changes.

Comparison of Prior Law and the Personal Responsibility and Work Opportunity Reconciliation Act of 1996

(P.L. 104–193)

Provision	Prior Law	P.L. 104–193

Title I: Block Grants for Temporary Assistance for Needy Families

AFDC, EA, and JOBS

Aid to Families with Dependent Children (AFDC) provided income support to families with children deprived of parental support. JOBS was an employment and training program for AFDC recipients. Emergency Assistance (EA) provided short-term emergency services and benefits to needy families. The federal government established eligibility criteria for AFDC and EA benefits and guidelines for the JOBS program. States determined benefit levels, which were required to be applied uniformly to all families in similar circumstances.

The law block grants AFDC, EA, and JOBS into a single capped entitlement to states—Temporary Assistance to Needy Families (TANF).

States are required to implement their block grants program by July 1, 1997. States have the option to submit plans immediately subsequent to the President's signing of the bill (August 22, 1996). The Department of Health and Human Services (HHS) reviews the plan for completeness.

Funding

Open-ended funding was on a matching basis for AFDC benefits and administration and EA. JOBS was an entitlement requiring state match and was capped at $1 billion in FY 1996.

The total cash assistance block grant is estimated to be $16.4 billion for each year from FY 1996 to FY 2003. Each state receives a fixed amount—based on historical expenditures for AFDC benefits and administration, EA, and JOBS—equal to the greater of: (1) the average of federal payments for these programs in FYs 1992–1994; (2) federal payments in FY 1994, plus additional EA funding for some states; or (3) estimated federal payments in FY 1995. States can carry over unused grant funds to subsequent fiscal years.

AFDC Entitlement	AFDC was an entitlement to states. Recipients of SSI and Foster Care payments were not eligible for AFDC. Eligible individuals were guaranteed aid at state-established benefit levels. Certain individuals also received guaranteed child care benefits. States received federal matching dollars for expenditures, without a cap. Benefits were guaranteed to eligible individuals even in recessions and fiscal downturns.	No individual guarantee of benefits, but the state plan must have "objective criteria for delivery of benefits and determining eligibility" and provide an "explanation of how the state will provide opportunities for recipients who have been adversely affected to be heard in an appeal process."
Time Limits for Cash Assistance	Recipients remained eligible for benefits as long as they met program eligibility rules.	Families who have received federally funded assistance for 5 cumulative years (or less at state option) would be ineligible for federally funded cash aid. States are permitted to exempt up to 20% of the caseload from this time limit. Months spent living on Indian reservations with populations of at least 1,000 and unemployment rates of at least 50% do not count against the time limit. Block grant money transferred to Title XX can be used to provide noncash assistance to families after the federal time limit. State funds that are used to count toward the maintenance of effort requirements may be used to provide assistance to families beyond the federal time limit.
Work Requirements	For FY 1994, 15% of nonexempt caseloads was required to participate in JOBS activities for at least 20 hours per week. This increased to 20% in FY 1995. (There were no statutory single-parent standards after FY 1995). For FY 1994, 40% of two-parent families were required to participate in work activities for at least 16 hours per week. This was scheduled to increase to 75% by FY 1997. Matching rate on JOBS	**General Requirements:** As part of their state plan, states must demonstrate that they will require families to work after two years on assistance. **Work Rates:** A state's required work participation rate for al families is set at 25% in FY 1997, rising to 50% by FY 2002 (states will be penalized for not meeting these rates). The rate for two-parent families increases

Provision	Prior Law	P.L. 104–193
Work Requirements (*continued*)	dollars could have been reduced for failing to meet general or AFDC-UP participation rates. Individuals were exempt from JOBS if they were will, incapacitated, or aged; had a child under age 3 (or 1 at state option); were under age 16 or in school full-time; were in 2d or 3d trimester of pregnancy; were needed in the home to care for an ill or incapacitated family member; were employed 30 hours or more per week; resided in an area where the program was not available; or were providing care to a child under 6 and child care would not be guaranteed.	from 75% to 90% by FY 1999. The law provides pro rate reduction in the participation rate for reductions in caseload levels below FY 1995 that are not due to eligibility or federal law changes. **Work Hours:** Single-parent recipients are required to participate 20 hours per week upon implementation of the law, increasing to at least 30 hours per week by FY 2000. Single parents with a child under age 6 are deemed to be meeting the work requirements if they work 20 hours per week. Two-parent families must work 35 hours per week. **Exemptions:** Single parents of children under age 6 who cannot find child care cannot be penalized for failure to meet work requirements. States can exempt from the work requirement single parents with children under age 1 and disregard these individuals in the calculation of participation rates for up to 12 months. **Other:** For two-parent families, the second spouse is required to participate 20 hours per week in work activities if they receive federally funded child care (and are not disabled or caring for a disabled child). Individuals who receive assistance for 2 months and are not working or exempt from the work require-ments are required to participate in community

service, with the hours and tasks to be determined by the state (states can opt out of this provision).

To count toward the work requirement, single-parent families are required to participate at least 20 hours per week and two-parent families 30 hours per week in unsubsidized or subsidized employment, on-the-job training, work experience, community service, up to 12 months of vocational training, or provide child care services to individuals who are participating in community service. Up to 6 weeks of job search (no more than 4 consecutive weeks) counts toward the requirement, except that states with unemployment rates at least 50% above the national average may count up to 12 weeks of job search. Beyond 20 hours per week for single-parent families (or 30 hours per week for two-parent families), participation may also include job skills training related to employment, education directly related to employment (for someone without high school or Graduate Equivalency Degree [GED]), and secondary school or GED (for someone without high school or GED). Teen heads of household (up to age 19) in secondary school also count toward work requirement. However, no more than 20% of the caseload can count vocational training toward meeting the work requirement (including teen parent sin secondary school). Individuals who had been sanctioned (for not more than 3 of 12 months) are not included in the denominator of the rate.

Work Activities

States were required to provide basic and secondary education, ESL, job skills training, job development and placement and job readiness. States were required to offer two of the following work activities: job search, on-the-job-training, work supplementation, or the community work experience program. Postsecondary education was optional. Two-parent families were required to participate in work activities.

Supplemental Funds

Establishes a $2 billion contingency fund. For eligible states, state TANF spending in excess of FY 1994 levels

For AFDC and EA, open-ended funds were available as needed. No provision for JOBS.

Provision	Prior Law

Supplemental Funds
(*continued*)

of AFDC-related spending is matched to draw down contingency fund dollars. If a state draws down matching child care funds (for which it must exceed its FY 1994 level of child care spending), its child care spending under TANF would not be eligible for a contingency fund match, and AFDC-related child care would be subtracted from the FY 1994 base. States can meet one of two triggers to access the contingency fund: (1) an unemployment rate for a 3-month period that was at least 6.5% and equal to 110% of the rate for the corresponding period in either of the two preceding calendar years; or (2) a trigger based on food stamps. Under the second trigger, a state is eligible for the contingency fund if its food stamp caseload increased by 10% over the FY 1994 or 1995 level (adjusted for the impact of the law's immigrant and food stamp provisions on the food stamp caseload). Payments from the fund for any fiscal year are limited to 20% of the state's base grant for that year. A state can be drawn down no more than one-twelfth of its maximum annual contingency fund amount in a given month. The match rate for the contingency fund is the state's Medicaid match rate, times the number of months the state received contingency funds in a fiscal year, divided by 12. The law also includes: (1) an $800 million grant fund for states with exceptionally high population growth, benefits lower than 35% of the national average, or above-average growth and below-average AFDC benefits (no state match); and (2) a $1.7 billion load fund.

Maintenance of Effort (MOE)	States were required to match the federal dollars provided for AFDC, EA, and JOBS. There was no maintenance of effort requirement in AFDC and EA. For JOBS, states were required to spend no less than total state and local expenditures for FY 1986 for training, employment, and education programs whose purpose was preventing welfare dependency.	Each state is required to maintain 80% of FY 1994 state spending on AFDC and related programs, including JOBS, EA, and child care. For states who meet the work participation requirements, the maintenance of effort provision may be reduced to 75%. States must maintain 100% maintenance of effort (MOE) for access to the contingency fund.
Transfers	No provision.	A state is permitted to transfer up to 30% of the cash assistance block grant to the child care block grant and/or the Title XX block grant. No more than one-third of transferred amounts can be transferred to Title XX, and all such funds transferred must be spent on children and their families whose income is less than 200% of the poverty line.
Persons Convicted of Drug-Related Crimes	No provision.	Individuals who after the date of enactment are convicted of drug-related felonies are prohibited for life from receiving benefits under the TANF and food stamp programs. States may opt out of this provision or limit the length of the sanction. Federal benefits specifically exempted: emergency medical services: short-term, noncash disaster; public health for immunizations and communicable diseases; prenatal care; job training programs; and drug treatment programs.

Appendix (*continued*)

Provision	Prior Law	P.L. 104–193
Penalties	Penalties could have been imposed for JOBS and AFDC.	The following penalties can be imposed on states: (1) for failure to meet the work participation rate, a penalty of 5% of the state's block grant in the first year increasing by 2 percentage points per year for each consecutive failure (with a cap of 21%); (2) a 4% reduction for failure to submit required reports;
	If a state failed to achieve general and two-parent participation rates, the federal matching rate for JOBS spending (which generally ranged from 60% to 79% among states) was to be reduced to 50%. In addition, states faced a reduced federal match unless 55% of JOBS funds was spent on long-term recipients, those under age 24 with no high school diploma, or those who were within two years of becoming ineligible for aid because of the age of their child.	(3) up to a 2% reduction for failure to participate in the Income and Eligibility Verification System; (4) for the misuse of funds, the amount of funds misused (if the secretary of HHS was able to prove that the misuse was intentional, an additional penalty equal to 5% of the block grant will be imposed); (5) up to a 5% penalty for failure, by the agency administering the cash assistance program, to impose penalties required by the child support enforcement agency; (6) escalating penalties of 1% to 5% of block grant payments for poor performance with respect to child support enforcement; (7) a 5% penalty for failing to comply with the 5-year limit on federally funded assistance; (8) a 5% penalty for failing to maintain assistance to a parent who cannot obtain child care for a child under age 6; and (9) penalties for failure to meet conditions for loan and contingency funds received. States that are penalized must expend additional state funds to replace federal grant penalty reductions.
	A state could also have been penalized if its AFDC payment error rate (based on quality control) exceeded national standards.	
Individual Responsibility Plans	An employability plan was required in JOBS.	States are required to make an initial assessment of recipients' skills. At state option, Individual Responsibility Plans can be required.

Teen Parents Provisions

AFDC benefits were available to each eligible dependent child and parent, regardless of whether the mother was under age 18. States were given the option to require minor parents t reside in their parents' household, with a legal guardian, or in another supervised living arrangement, with certain exceptions. Teens over 16 who were not in school were required to participate in educational activities.

Unmarried minor parents are required to live with an adult or in an adult-supervised setting and participate in educational and training activities in order to receive federal assistance.

No provision to locate adult-supervised homes.

States are responsible for locating or assisting in locating adult-supervised settings for teens.

The Secretary of HHS is required to establish and implement a strategy to: (1) prevent nonmarital teen pregnancies; and (2) assure that at least 25% of communities have teen pregnancy prevention programs. The department will report to Congress annually on progress in these areas. No later than January 1, 1997, the attorney general shall establish and implement a program that provides research, education, and training on the prevention and prosecution of statutory rape.

Performance Bonus to Reward Work

No provision.

The secretary of HHS, in consultation with the National Governor's Association and the American Public Welfare Association, is required to develop a formula measuring state performance relative to block grant goals. States will receive a bonus based on their score on the measure(s) in the previous year, but the bonus cannot exceed 5% of the family assistance grant. $200 million per year is available for performance bonuses (in addition to the block

Provision	Prior Law	P.L. 104–193
Performance Bonus to Reward Work (*continued*)		grant), for a total of $1 billion between FYs 1999 and 2003.
Family Cap	Families on welfare received additional AFDC benefits whenever they had another child.	No provision, no state option.
Illegitimacy Bonus	No provision for Illegitimacy Bonus; however, states were required to provide family planning services (to prevent/reduce the incidence of births out of wedlock) to any AFDC recipient who requested the services. The law required a reduction of 1% in AFDC matching funds if a state failed to offer and provide family planning.	The law establishes a bonus for states who demonstrate that the number of out-of-wedlock births and abortions that occurred in the state in the most recent two-year period decreased compared to the number of such births in the previous period. The top five states will receive a bonus of up to $20 million each. If fewer than five states qualify, the grant will be up to $25 million each. Bonuses are authorized in FYs 1999 through 2002.
Waivers	The secretary of HHS had the authority under Section 1115 of the Social Security Act to waive specified provisions of the act in the case of demonstration projects that were likely to promote the objectives of the act. Such demonstration projects were required to be cost-neutral to the federal government and rigorously evaluated.	Under the new law, states which receive approval for welfare reform waivers before 7/1/97 have the option to operate their cash assistance program and under some or all of these waivers. For states electing this option, provisions of the new law which are inconsistent with the waivers will not take effect until the expiration of the applicable waivers in the geographical areas covered by the waivers.
Medicaid Guarantee	*These policies remain in effect in P.L. 104–193.*	Regardless of a state's TANF eligibility requirements, for purposes of Medicaid eligibility the new law

Federal Medicaid law mandates that state Medicaid programs cover specified categories of individuals, including members of families receiving AFDC; other low-income families, children and pregnant women; low-income Medicare beneficiaries; and, in general, recipients of SSI. FederChildren with disabilities who did not meet or equal the Listing of Medical Impairments were determined to be disabled (thereby eligible for cash benefits if all other criteria were satisfied) if they suffered from any medically determinable physical or mental impairment of comparable severity to an adult. Comparable severity was found if the child was not functioning at an age-appropriate level as measured by the Individual Functional Assessment (IFA) and evaluated by the Social Security Administration (SSA).

requires states to provide medical assistance to individuals based on AFDC income and resource eligibility requirements they had in place on July 16, 1996; however, states may terminate Medicaid eligibility for adults who are terminated from TANF for failure to work. (The new law does not change other Medicaid eligibility categories.)

States have the option of using more liberal income and resource standards or methodologies for Medicaid eligibility. States are not permitted to reduce income standards below those in place on May 1, 1988. States are not permitted to increase the income standard above that of July 16, 1996 by more than the percentage increase in the consumer price index for all urban consumers over the same period.

Transitional Medicaid

These policies remain in effect in P.L. 104–193.

AFDC recipients are entitled to one year of transitional Medicaid when they lose welfare due to increased earnings from work. This provision sunsets September 30, 1998. Families who lose welfare due to collection of child or spousal support are entitled to 4 months of transitional Medicaid.

Families losing Medicaid benefits due to increased earnings from work, child support, or spousal support will receive transitional Medicaid benefits as under prior law.

The sunset has been extended to September 30, 1001.

Reductions in Federal Government

No provision.

The secretary of HHS is required to reduce the number of positions at HHS related to the conversion of AFDC, JOBS, and EA into the TANF block grant by 75% or by 245 full-time equivalent program positions and 60 managerial positions.

Provision

Prior Law

Title II: Supplemental Security Income

SSI for Children

Children with disabilities who did not meet or equal the Listing of Medical Impairments were determined to be disabled (thereby eligible for cash benefits if all other criteria were satisfied) if they suffered from any medically determinable physical or mental impairment of comparable severity to an adult. Comparable severity was found if the child was not functioning at an age-appropriate level as measured by the Individual Functional Assessment (IFA) and evaluated by the Social Security Administration (SSA).

Provides a new definition of disability for children. Under this new definition, a child will be considered to be disabled if he or she has a medically determinable physical or mental impairment which results in marked and severe functional limitations, which can be expected to result in death, or which has lasted or can be expected to last for at least 12 months. In addition, this law instructs SSA to remove references to maladaptive behavior as a medical criteria in its listing of impairments used for evaluating mental disabilities in children. All of these provisions will apply to new claims filed on or after enactment and to all claims that have not been finally adjudicated (including cases pending in the courts) prior to enactment SSA is also required to redetermine the cases of children currently receiving SSI to determine whether they meet the new definition of disability.

Redeterminations of current recipients must be completed during the year following the enactment. The earliest that a child currently receiving SSI can lose benefits is July 1, 1997. If the redetermination is made after that date, then benefits will end the months following the month in which the redetermination is made. SSA is required to notify all children potentially affected by the change in the definition by January 1,

1997. An additional $150 million for FY 1997 and $100 million for FY 1998 are authorized for continuing disability reviews and redeterminations.

For privately insured, institutionalized children, cash benefits will be limited to $30 per month. The law requires that large retroactive SSI payments due to child recipients be deposited into dedicated savings accounts, to be used only for certain specified needs appropriate to the child's condition.

The law provides that large retroactive benefit amounts will be paid in installments (applies to children and adults).

Requires CDRs once every 3 years for recipients under age 18 with nonpermanent impairments and not later than 12 months after birth for low-birth-weight babies.

Requires that the representative payee of a recipient with continuing eligibility is being reviewed to present evidence, at the time of the review, that the recipient is receiving medical treatment, unless the commissioner of SSA determines that such treatment would be inappropriate or unnecessary. The commissioner may change the payee if he or she refuses to cooperate. Applies to benefits for months beginning on or after enactment.

SSI Continuing Disability Reviews (CDRs)

Required the SSA to conduct a specified number of CDRs on SSI cases (including both adults and children) in each of FYs 1996 to 1998.

SSI Redetermination upon Attainment of Age 18

Required redeterminations, using adult initial eligibility criteria, of the eligibility of one-third of the

Provision	Prior Law	P.L. 104–193
SSI for Children (*continued*)	recipients who attain age 18 in or after May 1995 in each of the FYs 1996 through 1998.	
	Required SSA to submit a report regarding these reviews to Congress not later than October 1, 1998.	
Title III: Child Support		
Child Support	The state was required to establish paternity and establish and enforce child support orders for AFDC, Medicaid, IV-E recipients, and all others upon request.	States must operate a child support enforcement program meeting federal requirements in order to be eligible for the Family Assistance Program. Recipients must assign rights to child support and cooperate with paternity establishment efforts. Distribution rules are changed so that families no longer on assistance have priority in receipt of child support arrears. With the current law, $50 pass-through is not required.
	States were required to disregard the first $50 a month in child support payments collected by the state and pass that amount through to the family.	Individuals who fail to cooperate with paternity establishment will have their monthly cash assistance reduced by at least 25%.
		Streamlines the process for establishing paternity and expands the in-hospital voluntary paternity establishment program.
		The law requires states to establish central registries of child support orders and centralized collection and disbursement units. Requires states to have expedited procedures or child support enforcement. Establishes

a Federal Case Registry and National Direction of New Hires to track delinquent parents across state lines. Requires that employers report all new hires to state agencies and new hire information to be transmitted to the National Directory of New Hires. Expands and streamlines procedures for direct withholding of child support from wages.

Provides for uniform rules, procedures, and forms for interstate cases.

Requires states to have numerous new enforcement techniques, including the revoking of driver's and professional licenses for delinquent obligors, expanding wage garnishment, and allowing states to seize assets.

Provides grants to states for access and visitation programs.

Most legal immigrants (both current and future, and including current recipients) will be ineligible for SSI until citizenship. Exemptions are made for refugees for first 5 years in country; asylees and persons whose deportation has been withheld under section 243(h) of the Immigration and Naturalization Act until 5 years after granting of status; Active Armed Forces personnel, veterans, and their spouses and unmarried dependent children; and legal permanent residents

Title IV: Restricting Welfare and Public Benefits for Aliens

Immigrants

Aliens permanently residing under color of law (PRUCOL) were eligible for SSI benefits (subject to deeming); aliens who were not PRUCOL were not eligible.

Aliens who were PRUCOL were eligible for AFDC, Medicaid, food stamp, and Social Services benefits (subject to deeming in AFDC and food stamps); aliens who were not PRUCOL were not eligible, except for emergency Medicaid services. The Social

Appendix (*continued*)

Provision	Prior Law	P.L. 104–193
Immigrants (*continued*)	Services Block Grant did not take immigration status into account.	with 40 qualifying quarters of work. Eliminates eligibility of legal immigrants for SSI and food stamps immediately at the time of recertification (no later than one year after enactment).
	A portion of a sponsor's income and resources was "deemed" available to a sponsored immigrant for 3 years after the individual's entry into the United States under AFDC, food stamps, and SSI (although deeming was temporarily extended from 3 to 5 years in SSI (from January, 1 1994 to October, 1 1996).	Medicaid, TANF block grants, Title SS Social Services, state-funded assistance: States have the option to make most current legal immigrants already in the United States ineligible for Medicaid, TANF, Title XX of Social Services, and state-funded assistance until citizenship (with same refugee/asylee and other exemptions as described above). Current recipients are eligible to continue receiving benefits until January 1, 1997.
	Some immigrants were required to satisfy State Department or Immigration and Naturalization Service that they were not likely to become a public charge by obtaining an affidavit of support from a sponsor. Courts ruled affidavits of support (which were used by AFDC, SSI, and food stamps to determine when sponsor deeming was applied) to be morally, rather than legally, binding.	Qualified aliens entering on or after enactment will be ineligible for 5 years for certain federal means-tested programs, including Medicaid (except emergency Medicaid), with most of the dame refugee/asylee and other exemptions as described above.
		Applicants for federal public benefit programs would be subject to new verification requirements (with certain exceptions) to determine if they are qualified and eligible for benefits. Not later than 18 months after enactment, the attorney general, in consultation with the secretary of HHS, shall issue regulations

requiring verification for certain federal public benefit programs. States that administer a program that provides a federal public benefit have 24 months after such regulations are issued to implement a verification system that complies with the regulations. Nonprofit charitable organizations are exempt from verification requirements.

Future sponsors/immigrants will be required to sign new, legally binding affidavits of support (which will be available sometime mid-1997). For immigrants who have executed these new legally binding affidavits of support, the law extends deeming to citizenship or 40 qualifying work quarters; 100% of a sponsor's and the sponsor's spouse's income and resources are deemed; deeming is required for federal means-tested public benefit programs, including Medicaid (except emergency Medicaid). Certain battered and indigent immigrants are exempt from these new deeming rules.

States were generally determined to be constitutionally prohibited from denying benefits to legal immigrants due primarily to the equal protection clauses of the 14th Amendment to the Constitution.

Aliens who were not permanently residing under color of law were ineligible for major means-tested entitlement benefits (except emergency Medicaid). Immigration status was required to be verified. Eligibility criteria for many discretionary-funded programs (e.g., Head Start, public health clinics) did not take immigration status into consideration.

Health and welfare workers were generally prohibited from reporting illegal immigrants to law enforcement agencies.

Title V: Child Protection

Child Protection and Adoption

States received entitlement funds under several programs for a variety of purposes. Most funds were reimbursements to states for a portion of their costs incurred in maintaining eligible children in foster care or assisted adoptions, as well as related adminis-

Provisions include: (1) authority for states to make foster care maintenance payments using IV-E funds on behalf of children in for-profit child care institutions; (2) extension of the enhanced federal match for statewide automated child welfare information

Appendix (*continued*)

Provision

Prior Law

P.L. 104–193

Child Protection and Adoption
(*continued*)

trative and child placement services. States also received funds from formula grants for the provision of child welfare services, family preservation and support services, independent living services, and child abuse prevention and treatment services. Some of these programs were capped entitlements while others were appropriated funds. Several demonstration authorities were aimed at providing funds for innovative programs through which new knowledge may be developed.

The states were required to have in place approved plans with regard to funds provided under IV-B (Child Welfare Services and Family Preservation and Support Services) and IV-E (Foster Care and Adoption Assistance). Eligibility for CAPTA state grant program was tied principally to the existence of laws and procedures regarding child abuse and neglect reports and investigations.

States were required to comply with a series of protections designed to assure children were not removed from their parents unnecessarily and that efforts were made to assure that children in the state's care were quickly placed in a permanent home through either reunification or adoption. Every child was required to have a case plan, the child's status was to be reviewed periodically, and reasonable efforts must have been made to reunify the family.

systems through 1997; (3) appropriation of $6 million per year in each of FYs 1996 through 2002 for a national random sample study of abused and neglected children or children at risk of abuse and neglect; and (4) a requirement that states consider giving preference for kinship placements, provided that the relative meets state standards for child protection.

Title VI: Child Care

Child Care

There are two child care funding types:
(1) Title IV-A welfare-related child care entitlement—AFDC/JOBs, Transitional (TCC), and At-Risk Child Care.

(2) Discretionary Child Care and Development Block Grant (CCDBG).

Open-ended entitlement funding for AFDC and TCC in FY 1995 equaled approximately $893 million. At-Risk was capped at $300 million per year. $935 million was authorized in FY 1995 for CCDBG.

Child care was guaranteed for working AFDC recipients, those participating in JOBS or state-approved training or education programs, as well as for up to one year during transition off welfare due to employment. Provided good-cause exception from participation in JOBS to parents who did not have child care.

There is a separate allocation specifically for child care. The law authorizes $13.9 billion in mandatory funding for FYs 1997–2002. States receive approximately $1.2 billion of the mandatory funds each year. The remainder is available subject to state match (at the 1995 Medicaid rate). Also, states must maintain 100% of FY 1994 or FY1995 child care expenditures (whichever is greater) to draw down the matching funds. Also authorizes $7 billion in discretionary funding for FYs 1996–2002.

The law provides no child care guarantee, but single parents with children under 6 who cannot find child care may not e penalized for failure to engage in work activities.

Child Care—
Health and Safety/
Quality and Supply

Child Care providers receiving federal child care subsidy were required to meet health and safety standards set by the states. Under CCDBG, states were required to protect health and safety of children in child care by setting standards in three areas: (1) building and physical premises safety; (2) control of infectious disease; (3) health and safety training for providers. Required states to use 25% of CCDBG funds to improve the quality of child care and to increase the

Extends current law requirement that all states establish health and safety standards for prevention and control of infectious diseases, including immunizations, building and physical premises safety, and minimum health and safety training. Extends health and safety protections to all federally funded child care (including mandatory funding).

Requires states to use not less than 4% of total federal (mandatory and discretionary) child care funds to provide consumer education to parents and the public, to increase parental choice, and to improve the quality and availability of child care (such as resource and referral services).

Provision	Prior Law	P.L. 104–193

Health and Safety/
Quality and Supply (*continued*)

availability of early childhood development and before- and after-school programs. Appropriate quality expenses included (1) resource and referral; (2) grants or loans to assist in meeting state standards; (3) monitoring of compliance with licensing and regulatory requirements; (4) training; and (5) compensation.

Title VII: Child Nutrition Programs

Child Nutrition

Eligibility criteria did not take into account immigration/citizenship status.

The law makes individuals who are eligible for free public education benefits under state or local law not ineligible for school meal benefits under the National School Lunch Act and the Child Nutrition Act of 1966, regardless of citizenship or immigrant status. States have the option to determine whether to provide WIC and other child nutrition benefits to illegal aliens and certain other noncitizens.

Prior law rates were $2.235 for each lunch/support, $1.245 for each breakfast, and $.5875 for each snack. Rates were rounded to the nearest quarter-cent.

Effective for the summer of 1997, reduces maximum reimbursement rates for institutions participating in the Summer Food Service Program to $1.97 for each lunch/supper, $1.13 for each breakfast, and 46 cents for each snack/supplement. Rates are adjusted each January and rounded to the nearest lower cent.

All meals served in family or group day care homes received the same reimbursement rates of $1.625 for

Restructures reimbursements for family or group day care homes under the Child Care Food Program to

each lunch/supper, $.8875 for each breakfast, and $.485 for each snack.	better target benefits to homes serving low-income children and reduces reimbursement rates for higher income children to 95 cents for lunches/suppers, 27 cents for breakfasts, and 13 cents for supplements.
Reimbursement rates for full-price meals rounded down to the nearest quarter-cent.	Rounds down to the nearest cent when indexed to the reimbursement rates for full-price meals in the school breakfast and school lunch programs and in child care centers.
	Eliminates School Breakfast start-up and expansion grants. Makes funding for the Nutrition Education and Training (NET) Program discretionary.

Title VIII: Food Stamps and Commodity Distribution

Food Stamps	
Six categories of legal aliens were allowed to receive food stamp benefits if they met eligibility criteria.	Most legal immigrants (both current and future, and including current recipients) will be ineligible for food stamps until citizenship (exemptions for refugees/asylees, but only for the first five years in the United States; veterans; and people with 40 qualifying quarters of work). Eliminates eligibility of legal immigrants at the time of redetermination. (Implementation of this provision was delayed until April 1, 1997, by the subsequently passed immigration provisions in the 1997 appropriations law.) Redeterminations must take place by August 1, 1997. Future immigrants entering after enactment will be ineligible for five years (same exemptions as noted earlier).
The income and resources of an alien's sponsor and the sponsor's spouse, less a prorated share for the sponsor and spouse, were attributed to aliens for 3 years.	For sponsors/immigrants signing new legally binding affidavits of support: extends deeming until citizenship and changes deeming to count 100% of sponsor's income and resources.

Appendix (*continued*)

Provision	Prior Law	P.L. 104–193
Food Stamps (*continued*)	Maximum benefit levels were based on 103% of the cost of the Thrifty Food Plan and were indexed annually.	Reduces maximum benefit levels to the cost of the Thrifty Food Plan and maintains indexing.
	The shelter deduction cap was $247; it would have increased October1, 1996, and each October 1 thereafter. The standard deduction was $134; it would have increased October1, 1996, and each October 1 thereafter. All governmental energy assistance was excluded as income. Earnings of elementary and high school students under 22 were excluded as income. Individuals under 22 who lived with their parents could be certified as separate households if they also lived with their spouse and/or children.	Retains the cap on the excess shelter deduction and sets it at $247 through December 31, 1996; $250 from January 1, 1997, through September 30, 1998; $275 for FYs 1999 and 2000; and $300 from FY 2001 and thereafter. Freezes the standard deduction at the FY 1995 level of $134 for 48 states and DC, and makes similar reductions for other areas. Includes as income for the food stamp program energy assistance provided by state and local government entities. Lowers the age for excluding from income the earnings of elementary and secondary students to those who are 17 and under.
	Able-bodied adults between 16 and 60 were expected to register for and accept jobs or participate in the Employment and Training Program unless they were already working, subject to the requirements of other work programs, students, or responsible for dependents under age 6 or incapacitated people.	Establishes a new work requirement under which nonexempt 18 to 50-year-olds without dependent children or not responsible for dependent children will be ineligible to continue to receive food stamps after the first 3 months of 36 unless they are working or participating in a workfare, work, or employment and training program. Individuals may qualify for three additional months in the same 36-month period if they have worked or participated in a work or workfare program for 30 days and lose that placement. Permits states with waiver requests denied by August 1, 1996, to lower the age at which a child exempts a

parent/caregiver from food stamp work rules for 6 years to 1 to 3-year-old.

Program integrity and Additional Retailer Management Controls: Doubles recipient penalties for fraud violations to 1 year for first offense and 2 years for second offense; permanently disqualifies individuals convicted of trafficking in food stamp benefits of $500 or more; disqualifies for 10 years those convicted of fraudulently receiving multiple benefits; mandates that states collect claims by various means including the Federal Tax Refund Offset Program (FTROP); allows retention of 35% of collections for fraud claims and 20% for other client error claims; and allows allotment reductions for claims arising from state agency errors.

The law also requires a waiting period for retailers denied approval; permits disqualification of retailers disqualified under the Women, Infants, and Children (WIC) Program; expands criminal forfeiture; disqualifies up to permanently retailers who intentionally submit falsified applications; and improves USDA's ability to monitor authorized stores.

Simplifies program administration by expanding states' flexibility. Allows states to submit standard cost allowances to use in calculating self-employment income; deletes detailed federal requirements over application form; deletes detailed federal customer service requirements over areas such as toll-free

Disqualified recipients for 6 months for first intentional violations; 1 year for second violations or first drug violations, second drug violations, or first violations involving firearms. States were required to collect claims resulting from overissuances to households but could not require households whose claims were due to state errors to repay claims through allotment reductions; states could retain 50% of amounts recovered from fraud claims and 25% of nonfraud recoveries.

USDA had limited tools for insuring that only qualified stores were authorized to accept and redeem food stamps, monitoring their participation, and deterring violations.

The Food Stamp Act contained many prescriptive requirements related to states' administration of the FSP, particularly in the areas of client services, but also related to verification methods and training of states' employees. Demonstration project waiver authority prohibited approving projects that would

Provision	Prior Law	P.L. 104–193
Food Stamps (*continued*)	lower or further restrict FSP income or resource standards or benefits levels. A few demonstration projects cashed out food stamp benefits to specific populations (SSI, elderly) to provide benefits in the form of wages or provided cash benefits as part of welfare reform.	telephone numbers; extends expedited service processing period to 7 days and eliminates requirement to provide expedited service to homeless persons; makes use of the income and eligibility verification system (IEVS) and the immigration status verification system (SAVE), option; permits states to determine their own training needs; and authorizes the Simplified food stamp program, through which states can employ a single set of rules for their state cash assistance programs and the food stamp program. Expands food stamp waiver authority to permit projects that reduce, within set parameters, benefits to families. New demonstration projects testing cash-out of benefits are prohibited under the new waiver authority.
	The Fair Market Value of most licensed vehicles was counted toward household's resource limit to the extent that the value exceeded $4,600. This amount would have increased to $5,000 10/1/96 and was indexed thereafter.	
	USDA has been moving expeditiously to implement electronic benefit issuance.	Requires EBT implementation by all states by October 1, 2002, unless waived by USDA. Exempts Food Stamp EBT from the requirements of Regulation E.
		Consolidates the Emergency Food Assistance Program and the Soup Kitchen/Food Bank Program; provides

Title IX: Miscellaneous

Title XX: Social Services Block Grant

Title XX Social Services Block Grant (SSBG) program provided assistance to states to enable them to furnish services directed at (1) achieving or maintaining economic self-support to prevent, reduce, or eliminate dependency; (2) achieving or maintaining self-sufficiency, including reduction or prevention of dependency; (3) preventing or remedying neglect, abuse, or exploitation of children and adults unable to protect their own interests, or preserving, rehabilitating, or reuniting families; (4) preventing or reducing inappropriate institutional care by providing for community-based care, home-based care, or other forms of less intensive care; and (5) securing referral or admission for institutional care when other forms of care were not appropriate, or providing services to individuals in institutions, Funding for the SSBG was capped at $2.8 billion a year. Funds were allocated among states according to the state's share of its total population.

Annual funding for SSBG is $2.38 billion in FYs 1996 through 2002 and $2.8 billion in FY2003 and each succeeding fiscal year. (The omnibus spending bill changed the FY1997 spending level for the SSBG and appropriated $2.5 billion for that year.) Noncash vouchers for families that become ineligible for cash assistance under family caps or Title IV-A time limits are authorized as an allowable use of Title XX funds.

Drug Testing

No provision.

Nothing in federal law prohibits states from performing drug tests on recipients or from sanctioning recipients who test positive for controlled substances.

Abstinence Education

No provision.

Starting in FY1998, $50 million a year in mandatory funds will be added to the appropriations of the

Appendix (*continued*)

Provision

Prior Law

P.L. 104–193

Abstinence Education
(*continued*)

Maternal and Child Health (MCH) Block Gant.
The funds will be allocated to states using the same
formula used for Title V MCH Block Grant funds.
Funds will enable states to provide abstinence
education with the option of targeting the funds to
high risk groups (i.e., groups most likely to bear children out of wedlock). Education activities are explicitly defined.

INDEX